SERMON STUDIES ON THE GOSPELS

SERMON STUDIES ON THE GOSPELS

(ILCW Series A)

Richard D. Balge
General Editor

Roland Cap Ehlke
Manuscript Editor

NORTHWESTERN PUBLISHING HOUSE
Milwaukee, Wisconsin

Library of Congress Card 89-60651
Northwestern Publishing House
1250 N. 113th St., P.O. Box 26975, Milwaukee, WI 53226-0975

Published 1989
Printed in the United States of America
ISBN 0-8100-0312-0

CONTENTS

PREFACE

Northwestern Publishing House has published four earlier volumes of sermon studies on the ILCW series of texts. In 1982 Professor Ernst H. Wendland edited the Series C Gospels for publication in the United States, after they had been published for use in WELS sister churches around the world

Favorable response and widespread use encouraged the publication of studies on Series B Old Testament in 1984, Series A Epistles in 1986, and Series B Gospels in 1987. All of these were edited by Professor Wendland.

Because of his involvement in other important work, Professor Wendland declined to edit a fifth volume. Northwestern's Editor-in-chief Mentor E. Kujath then asked the homiletics department of Wisconsin Lutheran Seminary to participate in the publication of a volume on the Series A Gospels.

Partly because the earlier books were being used by pastors in Lutheran churches not of our fellowship, the department honored Pastor Kujath's request. A time-honored reluctance to offer "canned" materials for use by pastors has been offset by a desire to share our approach to Scripture and to sermonizing with other preachers in other church bodies.

The contributors to this volume have served in the public ministry of the Wisconsin Evangelical Lutheran Synod for at least seven years. They represent all twelve districts of the synod. Most are parish pastors; a few teach in Lutheran high schools or synodical academies. Their work was a labor of love, done with a high degree of cooperation and without remuneration. Listed alphabetically, these are the contributors to this book: Michael J. Albrecht, Paul W. Alliet, Kenneth R. Arndt, Richard D. Balge, James A. Bare, David J. Beckmann, Dennis W. Belter, John M. Brenner, Charles L. Cortright, Richard R. Durow, Marc P. Frey, Beck H. Goldbeck, Tim H. Gumm, Keith R. Haag, Gerald C. Hintz, Stephen C. Hintz, Philip J. Hoyer, James R. Huebner, Paul E. Huebner, Roger W. Huffman, David A. Kehl, Daniel W. Kelm, Alan R. Klessig, Roger Kovaciny, David A. Kriehn, Roger L. Kuerth, Thomas C. Kutz, Wayne A. Laitinen, James L. Langebartels, Gregory P. Lenz, Allen L. Lindke, Mark P. Lindner, Joel T. Luetke, Philip W. Merten, James W. Naumann, Peter J. Naumann, Mark A. Neitzel, James H. Oldfield, Timothy T. Petersen, James F. Pope, Nathan R. Pope, David M. Putz, James E. Rath, Robert Y. Rhyne, Jonathan E. Rimmert, William J. Schaefer

II, Douglas R. Scherschel, John C. Schneidervin, Thomas H. Schnick, Marc D. Schroeder, Mark G. Schroeder, John D. Schuetze, Anthony E. Schultz, Jonathan E. Schultz, Thomas A. Schulz, Raymond W. Schumacher, Robert J. Schumann, Norman F. Seeger, Stephen A. Smith, Steven P. Steiner, George P. Swanson, Dwight E. Vilhauer, Roger D. Wahl, Lynn E. Wiedmann, James G. Witt III, Michael A. Woldt, John W. Zarling.

The volume on Series A Epistles included comments on all three Scripture readings for each Sunday and holiday. There the authors pointed out the relationships that exist among the three readings. Users of this book are referred to that volume for the insights recorded there.

May the Lord of the church bless the use of this book by those who preach and for those who hear.

Richard D. Balge

THE GOSPEL OF MATTHEW

Most of the Gospel selections in the ILCW-Series A pericopes are from Matthew. There are eight narrative sections and five discourse sections in Matthew, and all of these are represented in the series. Except for certain Advent, Lenten and Easter selections the church year follows the chapters of the Gospel in order. Several Lenten texts, those for Holy Week and most of the Easter cycle selections are drawn from the Gospel according to John. So is the Gospel for Pentecost.

The place of Matthew in the canon has never been seriously questioned. As in the case of the other Gospels, its authorship was not challenged until the early nineteenth century. Second century writers quoted from it more frequently than from any of the other three Gospels. Tatian included it in his *Diatessaron*, a harmony of the four Gospels, around 170.

Among the four evangelists, Matthew most frequently quotes or alludes to the Old Testament. He cites twenty-nine prophecies, ten of which are peculiar to him. Sometimes he quotes the Septuagint, sometimes he translates the Hebrew. His general outlook is Jewish. There is no reason to doubt that the author is that Jew, named Matthew, whom Jesus called from tax-collecting to discipleship: "Follow Me" (Mt 9:9-13). Mark 2:14-17 and Luke 5:27-32 identify the tax collector as Levi, but we know that several of Jesus' disciples were known by more than one name.

The frequent reference to the Old Testament and the general Jewish outlook of the Gospel suggest that it was written to convince Jews that Jesus is the Messiah, especially to strengthen Jewish Christians in that conviction. It was the view of Papias, writing in the late first or early second century, that Matthew wrote the "sayings" (*logia*) of Jesus in Aramaic for the Jews of Jerusalem and Judea. Other ancient fathers assumed that Papias must be referring to Matthew's Gospel. However, none of them had ever seen such an Aramaic Gospel according to Matthew. Their text was in Greek. Scholars say that the Greek of this Gospel does not bear the earmarks of translation, that it is the kind of Greek which a civil servant living in Palestine could have written. It is, of course, possible that Matthew did write an Aramaic version either before or after writing his Gospel in Greek.

Although he was a Jew writing for Jews, Matthew ends his Gospel with the Great Commission, the command to make disciples of all nations (Mt 28:18-20). His Gospel also includes two Gentile women in the genealogy of Jesus (1:5). It reports the visit of the wise men (2:1-12). It also records the saying about the many coming from east and west (8:11,12) and the quotation concerning the Gentiles' hope in the Messiah (12:18,21). Matthew makes it clear that the good news which came first to Israel is also intended for the nations.

Most, if not all, ancient listings of the four Gospels placed Matthew first. The assumption seems to have been that it was written first because it was written especially for Jews, to whom the gospel was first preached. The view that it must be dependent on, and therefore later than, Mark because it is longer, it not as popular as it once was among modern scholars. Some date the writing as early as 50; more place it around 60. Many of those who date it later than 70, the date of Jerusalem's destruction, do so because they do not believe that Jesus predicted that event.

The approach of the sermon studies in this book is that all of Matthew's words are inspired by God and that therefore his account of Jesus' life and ministry, his death and resurrection, is trustworthy. The authors are confident that Matthew is reliable and so they take the narratives and discourses at face value, treating them accordingly. For them preaching is proclamation, not speculation. They report and apply God's word; they do not sit in judgment on it.

FIRST SUNDAY IN ADVENT

The Scriptures

Old Testament — *Isaiah 2:1-5*
Epistle — *Romans 13:11-14*
Gospel — *Matthew 24:37-44*

The Text — Matthew 24:37-44

Jesus' words are a part of his long answer to the disciples' question, asked in private: "When will this happen, and what will be the sign of your coming and of the end of the age" (24:3)? The question was prompted by the Lord's prediction that the temple buildings would be utterly destroyed (24:2). Whether they realized it or not, the disciples were really asking two questions and that is how Jesus answered them. He spoke of the signs of his coming at the end of the age in 24:4-14,23-31. He spoke of the destruction of the temple and the city in 24:15-22. The latter would serve, did serve, as a reminder and warning of the former.

Then, with the illustration of the fig tree (24:32-35), he encouraged them (and us) to read the signs of his coming. In 24:36 he stated that no human being, no angel, not even the Son of Man could know the day or hour of his second coming. In the words of our text he stresses the unexpected and sudden nature of that great event, warning his own to watch and be ready.

The importance of the Lord's teaching regarding the Last Day is evidenced by the fact that his answer to their question continues through the remainder of chapter 24 and all of chapter 25.

> vv. 37-39 — *"As it was in the day of Noah, so will it be at the coming of the Son of Man. For in the days before the flood, people were eating and drinking, marrying and giving in marriage, up to the day Noah entered the ark; and they knew nothing about what would happen until the flood came and took them all away. That is how it will be at the coming of the Son of Man."*

In the days of Noah there was so much corruption and violence that God determined to destroy the earth and its inhabitants. He warned Noah of this impending judgment. He instructed him to build the ark, providing space and food for the people and creatures that would be spared (Gn 6:11-21). Righteous Noah did as God commanded (Gn 6:9,22). He became a "preacher of righteousness" (2 Pe 2:5).

How did the people react? They continued their preoccupation with the workaday world. Jesus does not mention their violence and corruption. Rather, he speaks of their utter involvement with the secular. Note the present participles: τρώγοντες καὶ πίνοντες, γαμοῦντες καὶ γαμίζοντες. This was their characteristic activity, not sinful in itself but symptomatic of their unconcern. Compare T. S. Eliot's "decent godless race."

NIV's "they knew nothing about what would happen" (v. 39) is a somewhat weak rendering for καὶ οὐκ ἔγνωσαν. The verb implies more than a lack of knowledge. They did not acknowledge or pay attention even when Noah entered the ark (v. 38). Luther: " . . . Sie achteten es nicht," with reference to Noah's entry into the ark. *Living Bible*: "People wouldn't believe what was going to happen." Lenski: "They never 'realized.' " It was not an innocent ignorance.

Twice in these three verses Jesus says that at the time of his return it will be the same way: οὕτως. Before his coming the majority of people will act as though there were nothing more important than following their earthbound activities. Up to the very moment of his coming they will not acknowledge or realize that he who came in grace to save them will return in glory to judge them. "They will say, 'Where is this "coming" he promised? Ever since our fathers died, everything goes on as it has since the beginning of creation' " (2 Pe 3:4). And, as it was for the people at the time of the flood, it will be too late when he does come.

vv. 40,41 — *"Two men will be in the field; one will be taken and the other left. Two women will be grinding with a hand mill; one will be taken and the other left."*

There are always only two classes of people in God's judgment. In the day of Christ's coming they will be decisively, eternally and manifestly separated. On this earth, in time, the two may be associated in their work. They may even be members of the same household.

εἷς παραλαμβάνεται καὶ εἷς ἀφίεται.

The present tenses express the future idea; they also stress the urgency of the situation. The passives have either the angels (Bauer) or the Son of Man as agent.

To be "taken" is understood in the sense of taken to be with the Lord, accepted by him for eternal joy in his presence. To be "left" is the opposite, to be abandoned to eternal desolation. The two groups, of course, are believers and unbelievers.

v. 42 — *"Therefore keep watch, because you do not know on what day your Lord will come."*

Γρηγορεῖτε, the present imperative, is taken in a durative sense: "Keep on watching; constantly watch." Οὖν introduces a conclusion, based on what has been said before. No one knows the day or the hour (v. 36). There will be a deceptive normalcy before them (vv. 37-39). There will be a final and eternally fateful judgment on that day. *Therefore* keep watch.

"You do not know" personalizes the "no one knows" of verse 36. It warns the believer not to presume or be careless. Your gracious Savior is also your sovereign Judge. His imperative is "always keep watching." Don't be lulled into complacency, as the masses were in the days of Noah. Don't gamble on the time of his coming as the householder did (v. 43). Jesus' words are not an academic discourse on what will happen to unbelievers. They are full of urgent instruction and warning for believers.

v. 43 — *"But understand this: If the owner of the house had known at what time of night the thief was coming, he would have kept watch and would not have let his house be broken into."*

A second imperative, "understand," follows the "keep watch" of the previous verse. We are to understand why the owner failed to keep watch: he did not know when the thief was coming. We are to understand what he should have done: kept watch at *all* times. We are to understand the consequences of not keeping watch, not expecting the unexpected: a disastrous loss. We are to understand that the Lord's coming will be a disaster for those who do not keep watch.

The glorified Christ repeated this warning to the church at Sardis: "Remember, therefore, what you have received and heard; obey it, and repent. But if you do not wake up, I will come like a thief, and you will not know at what time I will come to you" (Re 3:3). The apostles Paul and Peter also used the picture of the thief to emphasize the suddenness and unexpectedness of the second coming (1 Th 5:2,3; 2 Pe 3:10).

The illustration of the thief coming at night does not, of course, mean that our Lord's coming will take place at night. It simply serves to warn against laxity in spiritual things. It will, of course, be night over half the earth when he returns.

v. 44 — *"So you also must be ready, because the Son of Man will come at an hour when you do not expect him."*

Γίνεσθε ἕτοιμοι is a third imperative, to go with the γρηγορεῖτε (v. 42) and γινώσκετε (v. 43). "Be ready" is not really saying something different from "keep watch" and "understand." The three together simply express the need for alert and intelligent preparedness.

Verse 44 restates the truth which Jesus expressed in verse 36: "No one knows about that day or hour." The question, "When?"is unanswerable. An attempt on our part to predict would be presumptuous. Speculation would amount to disbelieving what Jesus says here. Ignoring his words on the subject would be disastrous. There is only one thing to do: "Be ready."

Even his own will be surprised by his coming: " . . . when you do not expect him." How can we be ready? See the ILCW Epistle for the day, especially Romans 13:13,14. See also 1 John 2:28, 2 Peter 3:14; James 5:8,9; 1 Thessalonians 5:6.

Homiletical Suggestions

The historic Gospel for the First Sunday in Advent deals with our Lord's first coming, in humility and with grace (Mt 21:1-9). The historic propers also point to his coming to us in time, in Word and sacrament, in response to the church's prayer. It is the historic Epistle, Romans 13:11-14, which speaks of his second coming. ILCW-A has chosen that same Epistle. The second coming is the subject of the ILCW-A Gospel, today's text, and so the emphasis for the day is on the second advent.

Jesus' words in response to the disciples' curious question (24:3) are informative. No one knows when he will return (v. 36). However, in the time before his return an earthbound spirit of materialism and indifference will prevail (vv. 37-39). Examples abound in the world around us, even invading the lives of Christians. When he comes a fateful and final division will take place: "One will be taken and the other left" (vv. 40,41). The time of his coming will be unexpected, surprising even those who know he is coming (v. 43). The illustration of the householder's neglect contains the implication of great loss resulting from a failure to watch at all times.

This pericope also contains instruction for action. Jesus' words tell us what to do instead of speculating on the day and hour of his coming. There are three imperatives: "Keep watch," "understand this," and "be ready." They are not of equal weight and may be difficult to differentiate. Thus, it would not be practical to use the three imperatives as the basis for a three-fold division. One of them, however, could be used in the theme.

Those who were unprepared for the flood, in spite of Noah's warning, were indifferent. Those who will be left on the day of the Son of Man's coming are unbelievers. The man who did not keep watch was careless. These three negative examples, with Jesus' imperative to "keep watch," suggest:

Keep Watch for the Lord's Coming

1. Watch against indifference (vv. 37-39)
2. Watch against unbelief (vv. 40,41)
3. Watch against carelessness (vv. 42-44)

A similar treatment, keying on the imperative "Be ready," would be:

Be Ready When Jesus Comes

1. Not preoccupied with the affairs of this life (vv. 37-39)
2. Conscious of the eternal significance of his coming (vv. 40,41)
3. Always expecting his return (vv. 42-44)

Although only God knows when the day will come, it will surely come. We might borrow the theme from the hymnwriter:

The Day Is Surely Drawing Near

1. A day to take seriously (vv. 37-39)
2. A day of judgment (vv. 40,41)
3. A day to prepare for (vv. 42-44)

It may be difficult to distinguish between Parts 1 and 3 of the above outlines in the application of the text. A possible two-part division would be:

The Day Is Surely Drawing Near

1. A day of judgment (vv. 39-41,43)
2. A day to be ready for (vv. 37,38,42,44)

SECOND SUNDAY IN ADVENT

The Scriptures

Old Testament — *Isaiah 11:1-10*
Epistle — *Romans 15:4-13*
Gospel — *Matthew 3:1-12*

The Text — Matthew 3:1-12

There is no account of the birth of John the Baptist in Matthew. This is found only in Luke. Matthew introduces John here and gives us a summary of his ministry and message.

vv. 1,2 — *In those days John the Baptist came, preaching in the Desert of Judea and saying, "Repent for the kingdom of heaven is near."*

These few words present the message of John. He appeared rather abruptly in the desert areas of Judea. It was as if he appeared out of nowhere. He was not trained by the accepted religious teachers. He had no credentials. He simply appeared and began preaching. The present participle κηρύσσων connotes the characteristic activity of the herald who goes before a prominent person and prepares the people to receive him. The word has come to be used mainly of preaching the gospel. Such preaching introduces the Lord Jesus to people and prepares their hearts to receive him.

The Lord sent John out into the desert. He did not appear in the synagogue or in the temple where the other religious teachers were to be found. He was to carry out his ministry in a place apart. The present system was corrupt. The Lord wanted his people to take a fresh look at their relationship with him. The wilderness was to become a fruitful field (Is 32:15).

The heart of the message was "repent." The verb μετανοεῖν means to perceive or see differently, or, to change one's mind. It involves a change of heart and mind, a complete change of direction in a person's life. Since we cannot bring about such a change ourselves, it must be worked by the Lord. Repentance is always a miracle. Sometimes the word refers to contrition alone (Mk 1:15; Lk 24:47). Sometimes it refers to contrition and faith (Lk 15:7). Here it is used in the wider sense.

What does the γάρ indicate? It seems natural to understand it as providing motivation. There was reason to repent because the kingdom of heaven was at hand. God is the founder of this kingdom and its benevolent ruler. Heaven is its goal. Matthew uses the expression "kingdom of heaven" more than thirty times. The other gospels frequently refer to it as the kingdom of God. The kingdom of heaven was near because the Lord of heaven was soon to be revealed among his people.

v. 3 — *This is he who was spoken of through the prophet Isaiah: "A voice of one calling in the desert, 'Prepare the way for the Lord, make straight paths for him.' "*

The quotation is from Isaiah chapter 40. Matthew wanted to show how the Old Testament prophecies were fulfilled in Jesus. This prophecy spoke of one who was to be sent to prepare the way for his coming. The words are almost identical to those found in the Septuagint. The chapter opens with an assurance of comfort from the Lord. He offers a double measure of grace when a double measure of punishment is deserved. The one who was to bring comfort was to be preceded by a man who was to prepare the hearts of his people to receive him. See also Malachi 3:1.

John viewed himself as the fulfillment of this prophecy (Jn 1:23). Jesus declared that this was so (Mt 11:10). When the people found John out in the desert preaching, they were to know that he was sent to prepare the way for the coming of the Savior. Isaiah's words contained a promise that God was to become a man. John was to prepare the way for the coming of one greater than he. This preparation is compared to straightening out crooked paths in the desert. Nothing is more difficult to enter than the human heart. It cannot be accomplished by the working of men. God must do it. The Spirit would work through the message that John spoke to accomplish God's gracious purpose in the hearts of his people.

v. 4 — *John's clothes were made of camel's hair, and he had a leather belt around his waist. His food was locusts and wild honey.*

John's clothing was very plain. It was the normal dress of a prophet (Zch 13:4). Elijah had dressed in this way (2 Kgs 1:8). He had made his last appearance in this same desert. While the clothing was to identify John as the one sent by God, it was also to remind the people that the message was more important than the man. They were to pay close attention to what he said.

John's diet was also very plain. Locusts were permitted as food (Lv 11:22). Wild honey was commonly eaten (1 Sm 14:27). Again, the stress was to be on the message.

John's ministry was to stand in contrast to that of Jesus. He was to live like a hermit (Lk 1:80). Jesus was to mingle with the people (Mt

11:19). Many of the people refused to respond, whether the call was to mourn or to dance (Mt 11:17). They did not respond to the ministry of John or that of Jesus. We need to pray about our own response.

vv. 5,6 — *People went out to him from Jerusalem and all Judea and the whole region of the Jordan. Confessing their sins, they were baptized by him in the Jordan River.*

People went out from much of Judea to hear John. The verb ἐξεπορεύετο is a descriptive imperfect. The people kept going out to him. No doubt the crowds were small at the beginning, but they kept growing. People came from Jerusalem as well as the smaller towns and villages. What would draw them out into the wilds? It must have been the power of his message. It was a powerful message of law and gospel.

John called the people to repent and invited them to be baptized so that their guilt might be washed away. Many responded to the call. They confessed that they were sinners and received baptism. Many of the baptisms were performed in the Jordan River. This does not compel us to conclude, however, that they were carried out by immersion. The method is not mentioned. We must conclude that it is not important.

The people who came to be baptized confessed their sins as they received the sacrament. There is no mention of children here, but we cannot say that John did not baptize any of them. We know that Jesus later called his disciples to "go and make disciples of all nations, baptizing them in the name of the Father and of the Son and of the Holy Spirit" (Mt 28:19). The baptism of children has been part of the church's mission ever since that time. The baptism of John foreshadowed that of Jesus, even as it foreshadowed his ministry. We are called to baptize both children and adults (Ac 2:39).

The baptism of John was essentially the same as that of Jesus. He baptized in anticipation of Jesus' saving work. We baptize on the basis of his completed saving work.

The Jewish people were used to washings (Lv 14:7; Nu 19:8). Thus the act which John performed was not especially unusual for them. Yet they were not expecting a washing which was filled with God's power as baptism is.

vv. 7,8 — *But when he saw many of the Pharisees and Sadducees coming to where he was baptizing, he said to them: "You brood of vipers! Who warned you to flee from the coming wrath? Produce fruit in keeping with repentance."*

Many of the leaders went out to hear John and to be baptized by him. They felt that they had a responsibility to review what he was teaching. They also believed that they were entitled to receive the rite of baptism. This surprises us. We would think that they would feel compelled to condemn John for instituting a new practice. They apparently wanted to assure the people that they were still in charge without condemning them for receiving John's baptism.

Both the Pharisees and Sadducees were strict teachers of the law. The Pharisees put great stress on outward observance of the law. The Sadducees rejected much of the rabbinical tradition. They were freethinkers and skeptics. Both groups believed that they were right with God because of who they were and what they did. It did not occur to them that their teachings might be in error. They were confident of themselves. We are reminded that self-confidence is not a virtue unless it is preceded by complete dependence on the Lord.

John did not begin by exchanging pleasantries. He asked a very penetrating question: Who had given these men a warning to escape the wrath of God? John knew the hearts of these men. They were not sincere in their desire for baptism. They were not seeking it because they sought forgiveness. There was no repentance.

How could John know this? We can only assume the Holy Spirit made a special revelation to him. He could speak with certainty.

John describes them as a brood of vipers. The word γεννήματα refers to the offspring of any living creature. The snake has been a symbol of deception ever since the garden of Eden. To be a descendant of the serpent is to be a deceiver. It means to be an unbeliever who parades as a believer.

The question of John served to remind these men that they were under the wrath of God because of their unbelief. This was another call to repent and look to the Messiah. We are to speak about the wrath of God without hesitation. It is mentioned more than 300 times in Scripture.

Repentance always bears fruit. One of the first fruits is an honest confession of sin. Ποιήσατε simply means to "make." They were to bear fruit which would reveal their repentance as sincere. They were to depend on the grace of the Lord. There was no evidence of that here. There was no confession of sin and no confession of faith. These men took an open stand against the Lord and his plan of salvation. They sought to earn heaven by their own efforts.

v. 9 — *"And do not think you can say to yourselves, 'We have Abraham as our father.' I tell you that of these stones God can raise up children for Abraham."*

Δόξητε is an aorist subjunctive. The stress is on the action. These men were not even to begin thinking that they could rely on their ancestry to justify themselves. They were fond of doing this. They claimed to have a special place in God's eyes because they were descendants of Abraham. However, they needed to share the faith of Abraham before they were his true children. "Abram believed the Lord, and he credited it to him as righteousness" (Gn 15:6).

The Lord could turn stones into children if he wanted to. Was this a reference to the condition of their hearts? It might well have been. These men were no more responsive than stones at the moment. There was no real love of God in their hearts, no real love for his Word. God seeks children who love him and trust in him. He seeks those who are his children in spirit and truth. Many look upon these words as a prophecy concerning the conversion of the Gentiles. See Romans 11:12.

v. 10 — *"The ax is already at the root of the trees, and every tree that does not produce good fruit will be cut down and thrown into the fire."*

John spoke about punishment. He believed that it was ready to begin. The ax was laid at the root of the trees. When the ax is raised the fate of the tree is sealed. The blows will continue until the tree is felled. He who was to come would strike at the very root of the problem. He would judge sin and unbelief. These men were at the root of the problem. They were called to lead the people in the way of righteousness. Instead they were leading men down a path of self-righteousness which could only lead to destruction.

The ποιήσατε from verse eight is repeated. When there is a tree that does not bear fruit, the keeper of the orchard takes immediate action. He will not tolerate trees that do not produce. They are cut down and burned. Those who do not bear fruit for the Lord will be judged. They will be cut off from God and cast into eternal fire. Only that which we do as a fruit of our faith is acceptable to the Lord. May the Lord keep us in the faith which will enable us to escape the fire and find eternal glory!

v. 11 — *"I baptize you with water for repentance. But after me will come one who is more powerful than I, whose sandals I am not fit to carry. He will baptize you with the Holy Spirit and with fire."*

John's baptism was a means of grace. It was a means whereby people were led to repent of their sins and receive forgiveness. The εἰς indicates that repentance is the intended result of baptism. The Holy Spirit moves the hearts of people to confess their sins and find forgiveness in baptism. The outward act is that of applying water. The inward act is that which is wrought through the power of the gospel. The guilt of sin is washed away and the person is led in a new direction in life. With his reference to "one who is more powerful," John was not taking anything away from his baptism. He was rather pointing to the source of its power. That was to be found in the Lord Jesus.

John teaches us how to witness. We are to direct others to the Lord Jesus. He spent his whole life doing this. For him Jesus was the "coming one" (Mt 11:3). For us he is the one who has come. John's witness was always clear. See John 1:26,27.

John spoke of a baptism with the Holy Spirit and with fire. This is a baptism or outpouring which Jesus carries out as the water is applied and the word is spoken. He pours out his Spirit on all who are baptized. They receive forgiveness and the gift of salvation (1 Pe 3:21). Baptism is a sacred act because of the working of the Spirit through the power of the word.

Jesus kindles the fire of faith in the heart. Some refer this to the fire of judgment since this had been referred to in the verse before. Scripture also speaks of a refining fire (Ml 3:2,3; 1 Pe 1:7). It is more natural to think of that here. Some view this as a promise of the outpouring of the Spirit on the day of Pentecost. That was certainly one fulfillment, but this kind of baptism takes place whenever a person is brought to faith, whether it is through word or sacrament.

v. 12 — *"His winnowing fork is in his hand, and he will clear his threshing floor, gathering his wheat into the barn and burning up the chaff with unquenchable fire."*

John was given a complete vision of the Savior's work. He is also to serve as the judge of all mankind. When he comes again he will separate the believers from the unbelievers as the farmer separates the grain from the chaff. The believers are the grain that is gathered and treasured (Mk 4:29; Mt 13:30). The unbelievers will be burned like the chaff (Ps 1:4). We are reminded that life is not a game. It is serious business. He who seeks to kindle the fire of faith in our hearts will also control the fire of judgment in the end (Lk 12:49; Mt 25:41). Either we will be gathered to Jesus forever or we will face the unquenchable fire.

There are many who are reluctant to speak about judgment today. They can only speak of love and peace. We need to remember that our flesh still needs to hear the warning of the law, the warning of judgment. We need to ponder what Jesus has saved us from if we are to have a true appreciation for what He gained for us on the cross. He has saved us from the eternal fire of hell. He has saved us for the eternal joys of heaven. "You have made known to me the path of life; you will fill me with joy in your presence, with eternal pleasures at your right hand" (Ps 16:11).

Homiletical Suggestions

The Old Testament selection for the Second Sunday in Advent points us to the Lord Jesus as the Branch of Jesse. He is described as one upon whom the Spirit would rest in special measure. He would come to judge as well as to serve. He would be a man of righteousness. He would bring peace to his people, rest to weary souls. The Epistle lesson also points us to Christ. He is the one whose coming was foretold. What was written about him in the past was written for our blessing. We are called to glorify the Savior in our lives. We are to encourage one another in his name. A portion of Isaiah 11 is quoted. Jesus is held before us as one who gathers the peoples to himself.

In the Gospel lesson who find John the Baptist directing people to Jesus and urging them to repent. He urges us to repent in order to prepare our hearts anew to receive the Savior. We have an overview of the life and ministry of John. We have a summary of his message: repentance and faith. Several expressions in the text provide material for a theme: "Repent for the kingdom of heaven is near" (v. 2); "A voice of one calling in the desert" (v. 3); "Prepare the way for the Lord" (v. 3). It would be good to make use of some of this thematic material, especially if you have not preached on this text in some time. Since Advent is thought of as a special time for repentance we might suggest:

Repent, For the Kingdom of Heaven Is Near

1. Repentance prepares us for the present coming of the kingdom. (vv. 1-6)
2. Repentance prepares us for the coming of the future kingdom. (vv. 7-12)

A three part treatment which includes reference to the season:

Heed John's Advent Message

1. A message of repentance (vv. 1-4)
2. A message which must not be ignored (vv. 5-9)
3. A message by which we will be judged (vv. 10-12)

Another theme which keys on the season of Advent:

Why Is Advent a Season for Repentance?

1. There is no other way to prepare our hearts for Christ's coming (vv. 1-6)
2. There is no other way to escape the judgment to come (vv. 7-12)

THIRD SUNDAY IN ADVENT

The Scriptures

Old Testament — *Isaiah 35:1-10*
Epistle — *James 5:7-10*
Gospel — *Matthew 11:2-11*

The Text — Matthew 11:2-11

Since the Evangelist Matthew wrote to Jews, his main goal was to show that Jesus Christ is the Messiah who fulfills the Old Testament prophecies. His readers were familiar with God's word and could be expected to understand references to the Messiah and to recognize Old Testament quotes. The readers would also understand how important it was that Jesus measure up to all the requirements of the prophets.

This text must have been particularly interesting to Matthew because it shows how the fulfillment of prophecy answered the questions of some deeply concerned Jews and perhaps even the questions of the greatest prophet of all.

vv. 2,3 — *When Jesus heard in prison what Christ was doing, he sent his disciples to ask him, "Are you the one who was to come, or should we expect someone else?"*

We meet immediately one of the questions that have made this text rather difficult. For whose benefit were the disciples asking this question of Jesus? Were the disciples themselves wondering or could it be that their master, John, was wondering?

We are tempted to rule out doubting on John's part because he had identified Jesus as the Savior (Jn 1:29-34). He even based his identification on a sign from the Holy Spirit given at the baptism of Jesus. If John were superhuman we could expect perfect consistency of him, so that having said, "Behold the Lamb of God," he could never doubt thereafter. But Jesus reminds us that John too was one of "those born of women" (v. 11), a human being, subject to doubts and depression. Since he sent his disciples while he was in prison (Lk 3:20) it is not unlikely that John was downhearted and perhaps doubting.

But why should he have doubted Jesus? The text says he sent the disciples when he heard "what Christ was doing." So it was the activities of Jesus that raised the question. The things Jesus did were far different from the thing John did. Both were orthodox preachers but there is no denying that the stress of John's message was the law and the stress of Jesus' was the gospel of forgiveness. When John quoted Scripture he spoke of "the ax at the root of the trees" and of "burning up the chaff with unquenchable fire" (Mt 3:10,12). At least in the beginning of his ministry Jesus stressed, as he did in the following verses, "the good news" (v. 5) of forgiveness.

Might John have been a little impatient with the Messiah? Moses had been impatient with God (Nu 11:11ff). Elijah had tired of the burden God gave him (1 Ki 19:10ff). Perhaps John wanted Jesus to get on with it, to wield the ax and burn the chaff. He would not be the first or last of those born of women to propose a better way to God.

If John did doubt that Jesus was the Messiah or question the Savior's schedule, his struggles may be the source of comfort to one struggling with his own frailties. Not even so great a man as John could be saved by his own merit or worthiness but only through the forgiveness of Christ.

If John did not doubt he may have sent his disciples to put their own doubts to rest. It could not be easy for these loyal friends to watch Jesus increase while their teacher, John, decreased. Even though John had told them, their hearts would have had difficulty shifting loyalties from the Baptist to the Messiah. These men had already come to Jesus and asked, "How is it that we and the Pharisees fast, but your disciples do not fast?" (Mt 9:14) Apparently they too had problems with the different emphases in the preaching of John and Jesus. Were the people flocking to Jesus and away from their master because he seemed to dispense his forgiveness so easily? They may have concluded so and therefore resented Jesus' popularity.

Regardless of whether the question was theirs or John's they asked Jesus, "Are you the one who was to come?' They had heard John say, "After me will come one who is more powerful than I" (Mt 4:11), and they wanted Jesus to react to John's statement.

vv. 4-6 — *Jesus replied, "Go back and report to John what you hear and see: The blind receive sight, the lame walk, those who have leprosy are cured, the deaf hear, the dead are raised, and the good news is preached to the poor. Blessed is the man who does not fall away on account of me."*

To the question of his identity, Jesus replied with Scripture. Obviously referring to Isaiah 35:5,6 he listed his miracles of healing, the raising of the youth of Nain and the gospel of forgiveness he preached.

As prophecies, these were actions the prophet had predicted of the Messiah. They must be fulfilled as well as those that John and the disciples were concerned about.

But these acts of healing, raising from the dead and forgiving also served to show the effect of the Savior's ministry of reconciliation. All these actions served to reunite people with the community of worshiping believers. The blind, the lame, the leprous, the deaf and certainly the dead could not participate in the temple cultus (Lv 21:18ff). That had been forbidden under the law. But Jesus came to establish a new covenant that would restore people to the proper relationship with God (Jr 31:31ff).

Those mired in the past might easily stumble over these "innovations." The one who did not would be blessed. On that note Jesus sent the disciples away and spoke about the expectations people had of John.

> vv. 7,8 — *As John's disciples were leaving, Jesus began to speak to the crowd about John: "What did you go out into the desert to see? A man dressed in fine clothes? No, those who wear fine clothes are in kings' palaces."*

If the people's expectations of John had been in error, they were in danger of stumbling just as John's disciples had risked stumbling because they expected the wrong things of Jesus. It seems that Jesus sensed the concern of John's disciples. There may well have been many who had been repulsed by the stern message of the Baptist. These would have been only too happy to hear Jesus' words which seemed to them to justify their rejection of John. So Jesus directed the people back to John.

"What had they gone out to see?" Jesus asked. "See" is a strange word to use in reference to a prophet. A prophet is a speaker. His message is the important thing, not his appearance. But Jesus asked them what they went to see, implying that many of these people had gone for the spectacle of the Baptist with his robe of camel hair, his leather belt and his locusts and wild honey.

When they saw him, if they had expected a weak message that turned with every shift in the wind of popular opinion, they would have been disappointed in John. If they had expected to see a darling of the media, one who would make good copy for the major dailies they would also have been disappointed. John preached repentance and he lived the part. One could easily be offended by him but unjustly so.

> vv. 9,10 — *"Then what did you go out to see? A prophet? Yes, I tell you, and more than a prophet. This is the one about whom it is written:*
>
> *'I will send my messenger ahead of you,*
> *who will prepare your way before you.' "*

John may not have been what they expected but he was the real item. Quoting Malachi 3:1 Jesus identified John as the forerunner and himself as the Messiah. John was the greatest of the prophets for two reasons. He was the only one who had himself been prophesied in the Old Testament. And he was the one who immediately preceded and prepared the way for the Messiah. Any who were disappointed in so great a person as John had to have the wrong expectations. Vilify John? Jesus wouldn't think of it. He supported John and urged the people to respect and listen to him as well.

v. 11 — *"I tell you the truth: Among those born of women there has not risen anyone greater than John the Baptist; yet he who is least in the kingdom of heaven is greater than he."*

The last verse presents yet another difficult question. Who is the least in the kingdom of heaven? Jesus had just called John the greatest of those born of women. Then he said the one who is least in the kingdom of heaven is greater than he.

He may be alerting the people to the great blessings that will accompany the establishment of the kingdom. During the thousand years — that is, the New Testament era — ushered in by the Savior's conquest of the devil the spiritual blessings available to the people of the kingdom of heaven will be so great that even the greatest prophet from the Old Testament will be less blessed than the least citizen of the kingdom of heaven. John indeed had announced the kingdom of heaven — Jesus said it was close at hand — but John did not live to see the kingdom or the great blessings it would bring to its people, such as the conversion of 3000 people on a single day (Ac 2:41). That would mean that you and I are greater than John by virtue of the fact that we are living in the kingdom of God with the devil bound and the gospel given free course to be preached unhindered and used with blessing by the poured-out Holy Spirit.

Another explanation identifies Jesus as the least in the kingdom of heaven. He came among us as one who serves. He made himself nothing (Php 2:7). Yet John rightly said of him, "After me will come one who is more powerful than I" (Matt. 3:11). If this last interpretation is accepted Jesus is giving another identification of himself as the Messiah and another warning that people not be offended by his humility and meekness.

Homiletical Suggestions

Advent is the season of expectation. But it is a season fraught with many temptations to have the wrong expectations both of John and of Jesus. Those who expect the Christmas gospel without the Advent call to repentance sounded by John will find themselves surprised by John and unprepared for Jesus. Like the people of the text there is the danger that we reject the law personified by John. Like John's disciples there is the danger that we reject the gospel personified by Jesus. Blessed are the people whose pastor leads them to be offended at neither of these.

These two concerns suggest the following division:

What Do You Expect to See?

1. In Jesus (vv. 2-6,11b)
2. In John the Baptist (vv. 7-11a)

Applying the idea of expectations the preacher might warn that Christians can easily have expectations of each other and of potential believers that unnecessarily hinder the working of the gospel within the church or its spread to those not yet in the church. The text can be divided into three parts as follows:

Expectations That Can Cause Us to Stumble

1. Expecting Christ's actions to fit our agenda (vv. 2-6)
2. Expecting easy treatment from the law of God (vv. 7-10)
3. Expecting to be impressed by the humble servant, Jesus (v. 11)

FOURTH SUNDAY IN ADVENT

The Scriptures

Old Testament — *Isaiah 7:10-14(15-17)*
Epistle — *Romans 1:1-7*
Gospel — *Matthew 1:18-25*

The Text — Matthew 1:18-25

It is probably safe to say that most Christians are more familiar with Luke's account of Jesus' birth than with Matthew's account. Luke 2 is usually what people hear recited by children in Christmas Eve services; very often it is also read on Christmas Day. All too often Matthew's account of Jesus' birth is bypassed. A comparison of the two accounts of course shows that the Evangelist Matthew's record of the birth of God's Son is much briefer than Luke's. Matthew does not mention many of the details we have come to associate with Christ's birth. Matthew's God-given task was simply to relate the facts of the miraculous birth of Jesus Christ.

On the other hand, Matthew tells us details about the birth of Christ which are not recorded in Luke 2. Both Matthew and Luke allow us to view things which the prophets, "who spoke of the grace that was to come to you, searched intently and with the greatest care, trying to find out the time and circumstances to which the Spirit of Christ in them was pointing" (1 Pe 1:10,11).

As we look at Matthew's inspired words, we do well to heed the advice of Matthew Henry, "The mystery of Christ's incarnation is to be adored, not pried into." We won't be able to comprehend the incarnation completely, nor will we be able to expound it so that our hearers will understand it perfectly. Rather, a sermon on the incarnation of Christ should deepen our own appreciation for God's love and move our hearers to marvel at God's love for them in choosing the manner of birth he did.

v. 18 — *This is how the birth of Jesus Christ came about: His mother Mary was pledged to be married to Joseph, but before they came together, she was found to be with child through the Holy Spirit.*

The preacher will need to explain to his peole how betrothal in biblical times differed from modern-day engagement practices. Joseph and Mary had promised their lives to each other as husband and wife and in God's eyes that was the beginning of their marriage.

According to custom, though, they would not live together as husband and wife until a certain time period had elapsed. That is the time Matthew zeroes in on.

Joseph learned that Mary had become pregnant. The phrase ἐν γαστρὶ ἔχειν is the idiom for "becoming pregnant." The ἐκ before πνεύματος ἁγίου denotes origin and cause. Christ "was conceived by the Holy Spirit," as we say in the Apostles' Creed. This is certainly "the mystery of Christ's incarnation" of which Matthew Henry wrote. Human reason cannot fathom how Mary could become pregnant through the working of the Holy Spirit.

God-given faith, though, accepts that explanation and marvels at God's power.

v. 19 — *Because Joseph her husband was a righteous man and did not want to expose her to public disgrace, he had in mind to divorce her quietly.*

It is apparent from this verse exactly what betrothal meant in biblical days. Joseph is called Mary's *husband.* In addition, Joseph had thoughts of *divorcing* Mary when he found out about her pregnancy. Ἀπολύω, to divorce, is the same word used elsewhere in Matthew's Gospel for the human termination of a marriage (Cf. Mt 5:31; 19:3-9). Joseph and Mary were husband and wife in the eyes of God.

It was Joseph's intention to dissolve his marriage with Mary because of her pregnancy. If Joseph had wanted, he could have "exposed her [Mary] to public disgrace." He could have brought their situation before the proper authorities and demanded that the law take its course. According to Deuteronomy 22 the life of Mary (and ultimately Jesus) could have been in jeopardy if Joseph had wanted to press the issue. Yet Joseph showed a deep concern for Mary. Matthew shows us a side of Joseph which Luke does not.

Matthew describes Joseph as a righteous man. δίκαιος. This meant that Joseph was one who observed divine and human laws. Like everyone else, Joseph was far from perfect, but as a child of God he had used the law of God as a rule by which to live his life, to express his thankfulness for God's blessings. Joseph knew what the law of God said about unfaithfulness on the part of a wife, but at the same time he was concerned about the welfare of Mary.

v. 20 — *But after he had considered this, an angel of the Lord appeared to him in a dream and said, "Joseph son of David, do not be afraid to take Mary home as your wife, because what is conceived in her is from the Holy Spirit."*

Angels made important appearances throughout the life of Christ. Here we see how an angel served the Lord while he was still in Mary's womb. The angel redirected Joseph's intended course of action. The angel reminded Joseph that he was a son of David. It was implied in those words that if the Savior were to come from David's line as promised, Mary and he needed to remain together as husband and wife. Joseph was prevented from jumping to any more false conclusions about Mary by being informed about the miraculous working of the Holy Spirit within her.

v. 21 — *"She will give birth to a son, and you are to give him the name Jesus, because he will save his people from their sins."*

The precise wording of the angel's message made it clear to Joseph that the child born to Mary would not be his biological son. Nowhere in this account do we find Jesus being described as "Joseph's son." The angel did not tell Joseph, "Mary will give birth to *your son.*" The angel said, "She will give birth to *a son.*" Joseph understood his role as the foster father of Christ.

Luke 1:26ff relates how Mary was instructed regarding the name to give her child. Similarly, Joseph is told here what name to give to Mary's child. The personal name would be Jesus. Jesus is the New Testament counterpart of Joshua, "the Lord saves." Just as Joshua led God's Old Testament people into the promised land of Canaan, so Jesus came into the world to lead his followers to the heavenly Canaan. Jesus lived up to his name by saving people from their sins.

Jesus came into the world not merely to save one particular people or race. Λαός, as Trench explains, means "the crowd, the whole crowd, all the people, people as a nation." The preacher using this text will certainly emphasize this verse as being the heart and soul of Christmas.

vv. 22,23 — *All this took place to fulfill what the Lord had said through the prophet: "The virgin will be with child and will give birth to a son, and they will call him Immanuel" — which means, "God with us."*

Throughout the Gospels we hear that Jesus spoke and acted at various times to "fulfill the scripture." Jesus' concern in life was to do all that was prophesied of him as the Messiah. We see this concern even in the manner of his birth. The strange events that were taking place in the lives of Joseph and Mary were happening for a reason —"to fulfill what the Lord had said through the prophet."

In the eighth century B.C. the prophet Isaiah had foretold that the Messiah would enter the world in a miraculous way — he would be born of a virgin. The prophecy of the virgin birth itself was given in a very unusual setting. Isaiah 7 provides the details, while 2 Chronicles 28 sheds some light on the principal character involved.

The prophecy of the virgin birth was given during the reign of Ahaz, king of Judah. At that time the land of Judah was being threatened by surrounding nations. The Lord assured his people that they had no reason to fear their enemies at that time. (That promise of safety is remarkable when we keep in mind Ahaz's faulty leadership and personal godlessness.) The Lord instructed Ahaz to ask for a sign to be doubly sure of the people's safety from their enemies. Ahaz offered the outwardly pious answer that he didn't wish to tempt the Lord. The Bible reveals that the real reason he refused that offer from the Lord was because he had already made plans to get help from the Assyrians to defend his nation. Even though Ahaz did not want a sign of the Lord's promise of safekeeping, Isaiah said he would receive one anyway. The prophet then revealed that the Messiah would be born of a virgin.

עַלְמָה, the word Isaiah used, was rendered as παρθένος in the Septuagint. Παρθένος is the word Matthew uses here to describe the woman who would bring the Son of God into the world.

Παρθένος describes a woman who has not had sexual relations with a man. Such a woman was Mary. Such a conception made it possible for Jesus to become man without the normal spot of inherited sin.

The quotation from Isaiah also gives us one of the many names given to Jesus which describe the nature and character of his person. The name Immanuel, "God with us," reminds us that God, in the person of his Son, did become one of us to solve the problem of sin. The preacher will be able to provide comfort for God's people by reminding them that Jesus is still Immanuel. Jesus still promises to be with his followers. Matthew 28:20 contains the Lord's beautiful promise of being Immanuel "to the very end of the age." The twenty-third Psalm assures Christians that Jesus is Immanuel, God with us, even in the hour of death.

vv. 24,25 — *When Joseph woke up, he did what the angel of the Lord had commanded him and took Mary home as his wife. But he had no union with her until she gave birth to a son. And he gave him the name Jesus.*

Joseph's supernatural dream had an effect on him. He did what God wanted him to do, so that Jesus would be born as a Son of David and so that the Scripture would be fulfilled. All too often Joseph is the forgotten man in the Christmas account. Here Matthew gives him credit (humanly speaking) for seeing to it that the birth of Christ took place as planned. Because Joseph had no sexual relations with Mary during her pregnancy, there would be nothing to intimate that Jesus was the offspring of Joseph and Mary.

As both mother and "father" were instructed, the child was given the name Jesus, "the name that is above every name" (Php 2:10). It's a name that truly is "sweet in a believer's ear," in the words of John Newton. It's a name that we cherish and seek to share with others.

Homiletical Suggestions

It should not be too difficult for the preacher to share with his people how the Old Testament lesson and Epistle lesson complement this text. The Old Testament lesson provides the historical setting for the prophecy of Jesus' virgin birth. The Epistle lesson relates how grace and peace come through Christ, the God-man, a descendant of David according to his human nature.

The challenge that this text provides for the preacher is using it on the Fourth Sunday in Advent. Knowing that one or possibly two messages later in the week he will most certainly center on the birth of Christ, the preacher working on this text might be fearful of stealing his thunder for a Christmas Eve or Christmas Day address. If the preacher concentrates on the details of Christ's birth which are unique to Matthew's account, there should be no fear of repetition. On the other hand, repetition in speaking about the Lord's incarnation need not be feared. How can one possibly say too much about a miracle of love like that?

Since this text contains one of the three places in the Bible where Jesus is called Immanuel, a theme containing that word would have textual color. One suggestion is:

Immanuel Has Come

1. Miraculously (vv. 18-20, 24,25)
2. Purposefully (v. 21)
3. Prophetically (vv. 22,23)

A variation of the above theme and parts, adapting phrases from Luther's hymn, would be:

From Heaven Above to Earth He Comes

1. Of Mary, chosen virgin mild (vv. 18-20, 24,25)
2. From all your sins to set you free (vv. 21-23)

The text also provides the opportunity to look in depth at Joseph, someone who is all too often forgotten in the Christmas story. Using the text to look more closely at Joseph does not mean overlooking the birth of Christ. Rather, it can provide encouragement for the hearers to have Christian concern year-round. This would seem especially meaningfrul since the Christmas season is the only time of the year when many in the world make an effort to be concerned about others. With that in mind, we can see in Joseph and his life,

A Christmas Encouragement for Christian Concern

1. A concern for other people (vv. 18,19)
2. A concern for God's Word (vv. 20-25)

THE GOSPEL OF JOHN

Sixteen selections in the ILCW-Series A Gospels are taken from the Gospel according to John. All of these, with the exception of the Reformation text, occur in the festival half of the church year.

More than the synoptists do, the author stresses the deity of Jesus Christ. He does not repeat what they recorded about the Savior's genealogy, birth, baptism and temptation. His Prologue (1:1-14) boldly affirms the eternal Godhood of the Word who became Flesh. He records the many "I am" sayings, with their implication that Jesus is to be identified with Yahweh, the LORD of the Old Testament.

This Gospel says more about Jesus' promises concerning the Holy Spirit and his activity than do the others. There is proportionately more discourse and less action narrative than in the synoptic Gospels. All of these characteristics are represented in the texts of ILCW-A.

This Gospel was cited and alluded to in the writings of the second-century fathers. Irenaeus, writing about 180, spoke of its long and almost universal use in the church. Only the Alogoi, the sect who rejected all the Johannine writings, challenged its authorship and authority.

The writer was a Jew who translated Old Testament quotations from the Hebrew original. He applied Old Testament prophecies to Jesus, especially in the Passion narrative. He was well acquainted with Jewish feasts and customs, and evidenced familiarity with the geography of Palestine. He writes from the viewpoint of a contemporary of Jesus, presents himself as an eyewitness to the events of Christ's ministry from beginning to end, and reports incidents which only Peter, James and John witnessed personally. The first two of these three apostles were martyred long before the time when this Gospel was probably written.

The Gospel of John was almost always listed fourth in the ancient church's lists of the four, presumably because it was thought to be last written. Although some recent speculative scholarship has suggested a much earlier date for the writing, there remains a consensus that John wrote it from Ephesus in about 95. By that time it was natural for a Jewish Christian to refer to those who opposed Jesus and did not recognize him as the Messiah as, simply, "Jews." The distinction between Sadducees and Pharisees was no longer relevant and the final break between Judaism and the church had occurred.

Thus, the references to Jesus' antagonists as "the Jews" is not evidence that the writer was an anti-Semite who did not distinguish between believing and unbeliving Jews. Nor is it evidence that he was a non-Palestinian, perhaps a Gentile, who was not aware of the diverse parties and trends in the Judaism of the early first century. There is no compelling reason to refer to this work as "The Fourth Gospel" as though its authorship were uncertain.

John's stated purpose in writing this Gospel is the purpose for which the text studies and homiletical suggestions in this volume are published: "These are written that you may believe that Jesus is the Christ, the Son of God, and that by believing you may have life in his name" (Jn 20:31).

CHRISTMAS DAY — NATIVITY OF OUR LORD

The Scriptures

Old Testament — *Isaiah 52:7-10*
Epistle — *Hebrews 1:1-9*
Gospel — *John 1:1-14*

The Text — John 1:1-14

As the serious Bible student studies the first two and a half chapters of Luke, he will already be able to identify the tone, style, and general content of that gospel. Luke has an eye for the poor, the lowly, the humble, the helpless — a beleaguered priest, his barren wife, a tender-hearted virgin mother, her precious little child, poor shepherds, patient Simeon, an aged prophetess named Anna, the unique youngster among temple scholars, and the unusual Baptizer among desert crowds. After concentrating on just those opening paragraphs, the reader will begin to grasp Luke's theme, "The Son of Man came to seek and to save what was lost" (19:10). Then, as if to underline the fact that our Savior God came to save *all* the lost and that he took on real flesh and blood to do it, Luke closes these opening chapters with a list of Jesus' ancestors (3:23-28). This is the Savior's bloodline traced through his mother Mary back to Adam. Jesus, the Son of God, really is also the Son of Man; he really did take on human flesh like ours; and he really did come to seek and save all the lost, for all of Adam's descendants would have been lost in sin without him.

As the student of the Bible studies the opening chapters of Matthew, he again can detect the general tone and style of that book. The Gospel writer makes it clear from the outset that Jesus is the long-promised, long-awaited Messiah. Matthew begins by demonstrating the Savior's Jewish ancestry and royal line. Through Joseph Jesus can legally claim to be the seed of Abraham, the King of the Jews, great David's greater Son.

The opening paragraphs of John's gospel also offer us an opportunity to pick up on the writer's unique tone and style, as well as the general content of this gospel. But unlike Matthew and Luke, who introduce us to the Savior's humanity with family lists from his mother and earthly father, John introduces us to the Savior's divinity with a vivid link to his heavenly Father. While Matthew employs numerous Old Testament quotations to convince his readers of Jesus' fulfillment of all Messianic prophecies given through the Israelites and Luke's eyes for the lowly helps us appreciate the universal purpose of the Savior's mission, John weaves easy-to-understand vocables into a lofty and magnificent pattern so that we "*may believe that Jesus is the Christ, the Son of God, and that by believing* [*we*] *may have life in his name*" (20:31). This soaring, elegant style is clearly evident in the first fourteen verses of the gospel which serve as the basis for this Christmas Day text.

vv. 1,2 — *In the beginning was the Word, and the Word was with God, and the Word was God. He was with God in the beginning.*

The phrase "in the beginning" calls to mind the opening verse of the book of Genesis. Before time began, before God created the heavens and the earth, the pre-incarnate Word existed; he is eternal. He exists πρὸς τὸν θεόν, in an intimate relationship and inseparable communion with the Father. He is not greater or less than the Father, but one with the Father in essence and in all his attributes. In fact, "the Word was God." The article makes λόγος the subject, and the emphatic word order indicates that the anarthrous predicate θεὸς is also definite. The Word is divine. Let these clear statements regarding the Person of Christ ring out as the foundation for our confidence in him as our Savior. For only when we understand who he is will we really be able to appreciate what he did.

A comment is in order concerning that rare and unusual title for Jesus, "the Word." It is used only here and in verse 14, 1 John 1:1, and Revelation 19:13. Just as a person's words reveal what he is thinking and what he is like, so also God's words (the Scriptures) reveal what God is thinking and what he is like. Since Jesus Christ is the focal point for all the Scriptures, he is rightly called "the Word." He reveals what God is really like and how God feels about us. Without Jesus we could only assume that God is an angry Judge, a merciless Master. But since Jesus has covered all our sins with his blood, we know that our God is "compassionate and gracious, slow to anger, abounding in love and faithfulness" (Ex 34:6).

v. 3 — *Through him all things were made; without him nothing was made that has been made.*

All three Persons of the Trinity were active at Creation (Ps 33:6). But here our attention is on the second Person of the Trinity, the Son of God, and, in particular, on his power.

When πάντα appears with the article it refers to the universe. No article makes this term absolutely limitless. The Son of God created *all* things. All authority has been given to him in heaven and on earth. The apostle reinforces this truth, "By him all things were created: things in heaven and on earth, visible and invisible, whether thrones or powers or rulers or authorities; all things were created by him and for him" (Col 1:16). (See also Hebrews 1:2.) No one and nothing in all the universe can measure up to his greatness and supremacy.

Γέγονεν, the perfect active participle, also helps us see that his power has been active in the past, and its effect continues to the present.

vv. 4,5 — *In him was life, and that life was the light of men. The light shines in the darkness, but the darkness has not understood it.*

Having addressed the Person and power of the Son of God, John gives us a glimpse of his purpose. To do that the apostle interwines two forceful pictures — life and light. By nature all human beings were spiritually dead in their trespasses and sins. But Jesus is life and gives spiritual and eternal life. By nature all human beings were groping in the darkness of sin. But Jesus is the light of the world (8:12), and he shines and continues shining (φαίνει is a present active) over us with the light of his forgiving love.

But the darkness has not κατέλαβεν it. This verb can be understood in two ways. Both meanings fit the context. On the one hand, powers of darkness have not overcome or gotten the better of the Light of the world. For this we praise our Savior. On the other hand, we lament the fact that there are many who choose to remain in darkness and have not grasped this great Light by faith. *NIV*'s "has not understood it" adopts the latter meaning.

vv. 6-9 — *There came a man who was sent from God; his name was John. He came as a witness to testify concerning the light, so that through him all men might believe. He himself was not the light; he came only as a witness to the light. The true light that gives light to every man was coming into the world.*

These three verses may seem like an inappropriate interjection referring to John the Baptist when the prologue has so far been riveting our attention on Jesus. But upon more careful examination it is clear that the focus is still on "the Light" (the term is used five times in these four verses). Note also the connection with the previous verses. The Apostle John has presented the Person, power and purpose of the Word. Now he ties all of that to the Baptizer's proclamation of the Word, a testimony that had one main intent: that "all men might believe." John the Baptist was sent on a mission by God himself to deflect attention away from himself and reflect the true light that comes from Christ Jesus alone.

The testimony of the Baptizer reminds us that people become believers not by their own thinking or choosing. Rather, "Faith comes from hearing the message and the message is heard through the word of Christ" (Ro 10:17).

᾿Ερχόμενον εἰς τὸν κόσμον indicates that John the Baptist's emphasis was not on the pre-incarnate Word, but that he pointed to the Incarnate Word who was about to be introduced to the world.

vv. 10-13 — *He was in the world, and though the world was made through him, the world did not recognize him. He came to that which was his own, but his own did not receive him. Yet to all who received him, to those who believed in his name, he gave the right to become children of God — children born not of natural descent, nor of human decision or a husband's will, but born of God.*

The term κόσμος can refer to the ordered universe, the earth and everything in it and on it, the people of the world, or the sinful character of the people in the world. The second definition (the earth) seems to fit the first time the term is used in verse 10. The first definition (the ordered universe) fits the second use. The fourth definition (sinful people) fits the third time it is used.

What a foolish and senseless tragedy if spelunkers, lost in a deep dark cavern, smashed the flashlights of those who had come to their rescue. But that is exactly what the vast majority in Israel had done. They wanted a bread king, a war hero, an unrelenting rebel against Roman authority. Instead the Son of God appeared as a humble carpenter's Son from a backwoods rural village called Nazareth, with no formal training in the rabbinic schools of Jerusalem, no weapons, and no army. On top of that, he looked them straight in the eyes and announced, "You need me to remove your filthy sins, or else you will burn in hell forever."

While we rightly shake our heads in dismay and disappointment over the rejection suffered by Jesus, let's not forget that there are people today who need us to testify to the Light as John the Baptist did, because they are still befuddled by the mystery in the manger so marvelously revealed to us in verse 14.

Nor do we want to forget to praise God on Christmas Day (and every day) for the spiritual birth he has granted. Because of what the Christ-child did in life and death, we are now considered to be the children of God. The light of the Savior's forgiving love not only shines over us but also ignites the flame of faith burning in our hearts.

v. 14 — *The Word became flesh and made his dwelling among us. We have seen his glory, the glory of the One and Only, who came from the Father, full of grace and truth.*

The mystery unfolds before our eyes as John the Apostle, an eyewitness (ἐθεασάμεθα, not a casual glancing, but a careful viewing) to glory, reveals to us in his inimitable style a wondrous truth: in the Christmas manger we see a child who was born, yet he existed from all eternity; a child who was weak and dependent on his mother, yet the Creator of the world; a child who was humble and lowly, yet he was the King of kings and Lord of lords. Volumes could be written on each of the paragraphs of the prologue to John's Gospel and certainly on this verse. Suffice it to say, that we marvel anew each Christmas (and every day) that God's one and only Son, the totally unique God-man, tented for a while (ἐσκήνωσεν) among us and did everything necessary so that we might live in God's grace and the truth, the reality, of sins forgiven.

Homiletical Suggestions

These opening verses of John's Gospel provide a wealth of homiletical material for a sermon based on each paragraph, vv. 1-5, vv. 6-9, vv. 10-13, v. 14. For that reason the preacher may want to choose a briefer portion of the Prologue as a Christmas Day text. However, even though using all fourteen verses as the pericope suggests may pose special challenges in crafting the sermon, it will also afford special benefits for the preacher as well as for God's people who are being nourished by the word.

One approach might involve viewing the text as an intricate tapestry. A person can step back from a tapestry and drink in its splendor and beauty or step close and marvel at the beauty of each thread which is intricately and exquisitely woven into the pattern. So it is with John 1:1-14. The apostle has woven together four threads, four terms, into a beautiful verbal tapestry. The four terms are word, world, life, and light. We can step back and drink its beauty, or we can step close and marvel at the beauty of each thread intricately and exquisitely woven into the pattern.

But in order to appreciate this message and its significance at Christmas time, the preacher may want to invite his hearers to join him in grasping the thread labeled "light" and in tugging at it to unravel the meaning of this text. In doing so, the Person of the Savior, the purpose of his mission, and the effect he has on hearts seem to stand out. With that in mind, we offer this outline:

The Eternal Word Is Our Great Christmas Light

1. Matchless in all the universe (vv. 1-3,14)
2. Shining in all the world (vv. 4-5,9)
3. Burning in our hearts (vv. 6-8,10-13)

Another possibility:

What Child Is This?

1. The eternal Creator (vv. 1-3)
2. The life-giving Light (vv. 4-11)
3. The divine Savior (vv. 12-14)

FIRST SUNDAY AFTER CHRISTMAS

The Scriptures

Old Testament — *Isaiah 63:7-9*
Epistle — *Galatians 4:4-7*
Gospel — *Matthew 2:13-15,19-23*

The Text — Matthew 2:13-18

The church has traditionally marked the "Slaughter of the Innocents" on December 28. This sermon study shortens the Gospel to focus on that event and adds the full account presented in verses 16-18. After witnessing the spectacle of the world celebrating Christmas, the preacher may find it refreshing to remind the church that "though the world was made through him, the world did not recognize him," and "his own did not receive him" (Jn 1:10,11). After the world's platitudes about "peace on earth," here is an opportunity to remember that Christ did not come to bring earthly peace, but rather a sword. *The Lutheran Hymnal* provides for this observance Hymn 273, "Sweet Flowerets of the Martyr Band."

v. 13 — *When they had gone, an angel of the Lord appeared to Joseph in a dream. "Get up," he said, "take the child and his mother and escape to Egypt. Stay there until I tell you, for Herod is going to search for the child to kill him."*

With startling abruptness St. Matthew turns our attention from the Wise Men who came to worship Jesus to the mad man in Jerusalem who sent soldiers to murder him. We were given a hint of this development in 2:3, "When King Herod heard this he was disturbed, and all Jerusalem with him." Herod had heard from the Magi of "the one who has been born king of the Jews." King Herod was disturbed because the Jews, of course, *had* a king. But not one who was *born* king. Herod had usurped the throne of David, and was not even a Jew, but rather an Idumean (Edomite). The Magi revealed that God had now brought about the birth of the rightful heir to David's throne.

Long before this Herod had feared for his position, growing increasingly paranoid toward the end of his life. He put many people to death in order to secure his power. The Jewish historian Josephus provides examples in *Antiquities* XV.8.4. No wonder that when Herod was disturbed, all Jerusalem was disturbed with him.

In this instance, however, Herod's fear was senseless, for as the hymn says, "He takes no realms of earth away" (TLH 131). God was graciously establishing his own Son as king over a spiritual kingdom. Thus, while "the kings of the earth take their stand . . . against the Lord and against his Anointed One . . . the One enthroned in heaven laughs" (Psalm 2:2,4). He appears to Joseph in a dream to warn him of Herod's plot.

vv. 14,15 — *So he got up, took the child and his mother during the night and left for Egypt, where he stayed until the death of Herod. And so was fulfilled what the Lord had said through the prophet: "Out of Egypt I called my son."*

St. Matthew tells us that the flight to Egypt fulfills Hosea 11:1. This is a fulfillment not in the sense that Hosea was directly predicting Christ's flight into Egypt, but in the sense that Israel's sojourn in Egypt serves as a type of this event. Just as God preserved his Son in Egypt in the face of Herod's plot, so also he had preserved Israel in Egypt and kept his covenant with Abraham in spite of Pharaoh's opposition. God's plans cannot be cancelled by earthly kings. All is under the control of an all-gracious, all-powerful God.

v. 16 — *When Herod realized that he had been outwitted by the Magi, he was furious, and he gave orders to kill all the boys in Bethlehem and its vicinity who were two years old and under, in accordance with the time he had learned from the Magi.*

This does not necessarily mean that Jesus was supposed to be two years old by this time, but Herod allowed himself a generous margin for error. It is estimated that between fifteen and thirty boys of this age would have been found in Bethlehem and the vicinity.

From the slaughter of the innocents a parallel might be drawn to the practice of abortion. Both slaughters result from the clash of man's will with God's, from the desire of man to be master of his life rather than to obey and trust the Lord. When people usurp the lordship of Christ it brings about grief and weeping — even death.

vv. 17,18 — *Then what was said through the prophet Jeremiah was fulfilled: "A voice is heard in Ramah, weeping and great mourning, Rachel weeping for her children and refusing to be comforted, because they are no more."*

In Jeremiah 31:15 the prophet pictures Rachel, as the mother of the Israelites, weeping from her grave as her descendants gather in Ramah to be sent away into exile in Babylon. No longer would the Promised Land teem with her children. That was the result of the nation rejecting the lordship of Jehovah. Through Matthew God reveals that the tragedy in Bethlehem is a fulfillment of that typical event. The children "are no more" because of Herod's attempt to usurp the throne of Christ.

Homiletical Suggestions

This passage invites us to rejoice in God's ability to ensure the successful establishment of his King in Zion, and to carry his kingdom and its benefits to completion. It also invites us soberly to identify inside ourselves that nature — exhibited unchecked in Herod — which rejects Christ's lordship and seeks to retain mastery over our own lives. The king named Jesus — Savior — came to bring us forgiveness for that determination to be our own gods, which is the essence of sin. Christmas is not just a pleasant break in the gloom of winter; it is the celebration of the birth of a child who has come to take over our lives. Who is going to be king? Christ or Herod? Christ or I? Every day we make dozens of decisions which either acknowledge Christ's lordship or which assert our own. The star of the Magi reminds the Christian that he has a gracious king to whom he can, by the aid of the Holy Spirit, submit his will and live. By his word Christ desires to reign in our hearts through faith. Possible outlines:

Who Will Reign on David's Throne?

1. Not human usurpers (vv. 16-18)
2. But God's anointed Son (vv. 13-15)

The Man Who Would Stay King

1. Herod moves to retain his throne (vv. 16-18)
2. God moves to establish his Son (vv. 13-15)
3. Who is the king of *my* life? (application)

NEW YEAR'S DAY

The Scriptures

Old Testament — *Numbers 16:22-27*
Epistle — *Romans 1:1-7*
Gospel — *Luke 2:21*

The Text – Luke 2:21

The text is simple and straightforward enough to require no particular comment as to grammar, variant readings or similar matters. The preacher likewise will have little to do in explaining the events which took place. His responsibility will lie rather in clarifying for New Testament believers the meaning of the Old Testament practice of circumcision in general, and particularly its meaning in the case of our Savior. Then he must help his hearers to appropriate the significance of the name "Jesus."

v. 21 — *On the eighth day, when it was time to circumcise him, he was named Jesus, the name the angel had given him before he had been conceived.*

Circumcision was commanded by God in Genesis 17 when he directed Abraham to circumcise himself, his son Ishmael, all the males of his household and all males who would in the future be born in his house or acquired as slaves. This rite was specifically identified as the sign of the covenant of grace between the Lord and Abraham. As such it was a type of the sacrament of Holy Baptism (Ro 4:11; Col 2:11,12).

Although this particular choice of signs may strike us as unusual, it had deep significance. On the one hand it pointed to *sin* rather than *sins*, as Luther shows in his exposition of Genesis 17 and his sermons on this text. It was performed on the male organ of generation, pointing to original sin which is inherited from Adam by all his offspring born according to the course of nature (Ro 5:11,12; *Augsburg Confession*, Article II). By commanding that eight-day-old boys were to be circumcised God emphasized that his concern was not just with actual sins but with the sinful nature which is present even before it manifests itself in outward acts. Circumcision pointed out the need to put off the old self and put on a new, believing self (Dt 10:16; Jr 4:4; Eph 4:22-24; Ro 6:11-14).

On the other hand, because circumcision was connected with the promise of Isaac in Genesis 17, and therefore ultimately with the promise of Jesus Christ (Gn 17:21), circumcision was also a sign of the covenant of grace. From Abraham and his offspring would come the Redeemer who would truly put off our old sinful nature and make us alive through the forgiveness of sins (Col 2:11-13).

For Jesus, of course, circumcision was not necessary for forgiveness and rebirth. Conceived by the power of the Holy Spirit and born of the Virgin, he had no sin which needed to be removed (Lk 1:35). His circumcision was part of his substitutionary work, just as was his baptism (Mt 2:15). Not even Abraham, the friend of God and father of believers, had received circumcision in perfect faith. It was necessary for the incarnate Son of God, made like his brothers in every way (He 2:14-18), to receive circumcision in perfect faith in his heavenly Father and to fulfill all righteousness for us.

By circumcision Jesus not only identified himself with Abraham's descendants, but took upon himself the sin of Abraham's descendants, putting himself in the place of sinners to make atonement by his blood. He not only truly felt the pain of circumcision and here first shed his blood for us, but also he alone of all those who were circumcised received circumcision with a perfect confidence that in his humiliation the heavenly Father would carry out the redemption which was promised to Abraham (Ps 8:4-8; compare He 2:5-9).

To summarize: By his circumcision Jesus was physically marked as Abraham's offspring (Ro 9:5); he was shown to be the one who had come to bear the sin of the world — both the actual *sins* and the *sin* which underlies all sins; and by the shedding of his blood it was shown that he would carry out that salvation by humbling himself and shedding his blood.

The second historical fact of which St. Luke speaks is the giving of the name Jesus. In fact, the circumcision is mentioned in a subordinate clause, while the bestowal of the name is the main clause of the sentence. At the time that circumcision was commanded God changed Abram's name to Abraham (Gn 17:5). That new name was connected with the giving of the covenant of grace, and so it is most fitting that here the fulfiller of the covenant should be given his name at his circumcision.

As the evangelist points out, that name had significance. Jesus means "the Lord saves," and Jesus is the incarnate Lord who "will save his people from their sins" (Mt 1:21). Nor was this name chosen by Mary and Joseph, who as pious Israelites might have selected such a name as a confession of their own hope. That name had been given by the angel before his conception (Mt 1:21; Lk 1:31-33). From the moment of his conception Jesus was the incarnate Savior. As an infant he was carrying out his saving work for us, and was properly named the Lord who saves his people from their sins.

Both the fact of the Savior's name and the shedding of his blood already in infancy could be put to good use by the preacher in correcting the tendency to confine the Savior's work and especially his substitutionary suffering to the last days of his life. From his conception he was identified as the Savior; throughout the whole time of his humiliation he was always bearing the sin of the world.

Homiletical Suggestions

What, then, are we to make of this material in preaching? Four emphases seem to stand out.

One is the faithfulness of God. Some nineteen centuries had elapsed between the time when circumcision was given to Abraham as a sign of the promise and the fulfillment in Jesus Christ. Yet through all the vicissitudes of the centuries God did not forget his word. Especially on New Year's Day such a reminder is an assurance of God's continuing faithfulness.

Second is the fact that our Lord Jesus became true man, entering our human life, bearing our sins, shedding his blood for our redemption.

Third we, like Abraham, have inherited sin from Adam. Born in the course of nature, we also were under God's wrath and punishment. But in our baptism we were circumcised by Christ and regenerated (Col 2:11,12).

Fourth, just as our Savior was named at his circumcision as the Savior, in baptism we were given a new name as his saved people. He is Christ, and we are Christians. We have a new name given by the Lord (Is 62:2; Re 2:17) and are called and are the sons of God (1 Jn 3:1; Nu 6:27).

If the preacher desires to emphasize the New Year's aspect in the sermon, an outline of the following sort might be considered:

Jesus' Circumcision and Name Give Us Assurance for the New Year

1. His circumcision assures us of God's faithfulness to his word.
2. His name gives us assurance that he has reconciled us to God

Such an emphasis upon the New Year is certainly legitimate, but might run a certain risk of imposing the New Year's Day thought upon the text to the detriment of strict exposition of the text. For those who accept Luther's dictum that "The Gospel demands that our sermon be about the circumcision and the name Jesus, and we are going to observe this," the following outline may be more appealing:

Jesus Was Circumcised and Named for us

1. He became true man for us
2. He fulfilled God's promise for us
3. He took the burden of sin on himself for us
4. He obtained a new name for us

SECOND SUNDAY AFTER CHRISTMAS

The Scriptures

Old Testament — *Isaiah 61:10-62:3*
Epistle — *Ephesians 1:3-6,15-18*
Gospel — *John 1:1-18*

The Text — John 1:14-18

The central purpose for which John wrote his Gospel is stated by John himself near the end of the book (John 20:31): "But these are written that you may believe that Jesus is the Christ, the Son of God, and that by believing you may have life in his name."

Chapter 1:1-18 constitutes the Prologue of John's Gospel. In these introductory verses he lays out summary statements concerning the person and incarnation of Christ. Serving as God's mouthpiece, the apostle presents a series of theses that are simple and clear in grammar and fact, which go beyond the limits of the finite human mind in the complexity of the truths that are set forth. The remainder of his Gospel contains the proofs from Jesus' ministry —his life, suffering, death and resurrection — that substantiate the claims he is making. For this sermon study, we will limit ourselves to the last five verses (1:14-18) of the Prologue, which many view as the high point of the day's Gospel reading.

In the opening verses, the Word was described as the eternal God, active in the creation, and the source of eternal life. In the concluding verses of the Prologue he is described as the Word who became man.

v. 14 — *The Word became flesh and made his dwelling among us. We have seen his glory, the glory of the One and Only, who came from the Father, full of grace and truth.*

John states that by his birth, the Logos became flesh, σὰρξ ἐγένετο.

In Catechism class we stress that mankind needed a Savior, one who was both true God and true man. John makes that point here in simple and matter-of-fact language. In the term "flesh," σὰρξ, we understand that which constitutes the whole of man — body and soul (though without sin). The Logos couldn't have been the light of men if in the fullness of time he had not become flesh. The aorist tense of the verb ἐγένετο points to a momentary act through which the Logos became flesh. No transformation took place. The Word didn't cease to be what he had been. Rather, in addition to what he always was, he became something he hadn't previously been. The mystery of how the creator could assume our created nature will forever elude the finite human mind. But the fact is plainly spelled out in the Scriptures.

We approach this incomprehensible fact with faith as the Apostle Paul did. "Beyond all question, the mystery of godliness is great: He appeared in a body, . . . " (1 Tm 3:16). Thankfully, our commission is not to render these mysteries understandable to the human mind. It is simply to proclaim God's word for the assurance of salvation to our hearers.

By translating "and set up his tent among us" (καὶ ἐσκήνωσεν ἐν ἡμῖν,) instead of "and made his dwelling among us," we might be reminded more readily of the presence of God in the tabernacle as the Children of Israel made their way through the wilderness. The tabernacle, though, was simply a shadow of the heavenly tabernacle. The reality of human flesh filled with the presence of God is even more amazing and wonderful. The word "tent" itself insinuates that this "dwelling" was temporary. We all look forward to taking our place in the heavenly tabernacle which will be God's permanent dwelling with men.

Those among whom the God-man has set up his tent had seen the proof that this was no ordinary man. John summarized the manifestations of the divine attributes which they had witnessed as δόξαν, "glory".

The grammatical construction in the last part of verse 14 has been variously translated. Several translators, like Goodspeed in his translation of the New Testament, make the unfortunate mistake of assuming that in the absence of the definite article, "one and only Son" and "Father" are indefinite terms referring to any "only" son of any "father." Such translations ignore the fact that nouns in the predicate often lack the article, or that nouns which designate beings of which there is only one of a kind can lack the article, or that anarthrous nouns direct our attention to the bare thought conveyed in the noun. Thus they diminish the effect of the very point that John was using to substantiate his claim that the eternal Word had become flesh in Christ.

What the witnesses saw was a revelation of God's "grace," his undeserved love for sinners, and "truth," the reality of God's purpose and plan of salvation. For many others, the form of a servant concealed the divine majesty and his glory.

v. 15 — *John testifies concerning him. He cries out, saying, "This was he of whom I said, 'He who comes after me has surpassed me because he was before me.' "*

The Apostle John calls upon the witness of John the Baptist to further emphasize the truth of this mystery. The Baptist's statement seemed to present a riddle. How could the one who came after have existed before him? But Jesus surpassed John in "glory" (and power) because he is the eternal Son of God.

v. 16 — *From the fullness of his grace we have all received one blessing after another.*

After quoting from John the Baptist to support the statement that he had made, the Apostle John takes up and expands the thought which he had begun in verse 14. Not only were they able to see the reflection of his divine majesty through the curtain of the flesh as they witnessed his omnipotence and divine love, they also were able to share in the blessings of his grace. Although in verse 14 he was speaking in particular of those who were eyewitnesses, here all who look to him in faith can be included among those who share these blessings of grace. We have "received," ἐλάβομεν, but that is not an achievement on our part. In our relation to Christ, God's call always comes first. The call to faith is itself a part of God's grace. We receive his grace as a floundering swimmer takes a life jacket thrown at him or a blind beggar takes a coin that is thrown to him. The apostle pictures the supply of grace as one that overflows from its fullness. Luther, in discussing this verse, compared the fullness of this grace to the light of the sun. Just as the light of the sun is not used up even though the whole world enjoys and benefits from its light, so the whole world could draw from the wells of God's grace and yet the well would still always run over because of the abundance.

The expression κὰι χάριν ἀντὶ χάριτος is rendered well in the NIV: "one blessing after another." ᾿Αντὶ denotes an exchange. It presents a picture of the bountiful stores of God's grace. Each day comes with a new supply of grace to take the place of that which had already been given, like one wave that follows another on the seashore. It is this grace that makes us rich even though outwardly there may be poverty. It gives consolation even when there is sadness. It gives strength when we are weak. It gives us the fullness of life. This grace is God's undeserved love toward sinful men which offers to everyone the salvation obtained by Christ.

v. 17 — *For the law was given through Moses; grace and truth came through Jesus Christ.*

John now gives the reason we can say that we have grace from the fullness of Jesus. We didn't receive it from Moses. What Moses gave stood as proof of the condemnation against us. Though the law was not bad in itself, it was not the fullness from which one could receive grace. The law was full of types of deliverance and thus was only preparatory. The grace which is ours in forgiveness came only through Jesus Christ. As the living Word, Jesus is the complete revelation of God's plan of salvation. That is the "truth" which came through Jesus Christ.

v. 18 — *No one has ever seen God, but God the only Son, who is at the Father's side, has made him known.*

Verse 18 advances the thought of verse 16, which spoke of the gifts we receive, to the source of those gifts. The only way this grace and truth could be conveyed to us was through the only Son, who is at the Father's side. He alone could bring us the ultimate revelation of the greatest of blessings which we receive.

John's goal in writing of the significance of the incarnation of Christ was to help those who stumble in spiritual darkness so they might turn to that light which reveals God's grace to them.

Homiletical Suggestions

It is certainly fitting on the Second Sunday after Christmas, after we have contemplated the lowly birth of Jesus and his presentation in the temple, that the Gospel for the Sunday leads us to contemplate the profound truth that this lowly servant is in fact the one promised from of old — the very Son of God. In many churches today, special Epiphany services are no longer observed on January 6, except when that day falls on Sunday. Those who use the Sunday before January 6 to introduce the theme of the Epiphany season will find that this text serves well for such an introduction.

John was writing to a young church that stood face to face with temptation and conflict. The message of the cross was a stumbling block that stirred the Jews to hatred and opposition. It was a message of foolishness to the Greeks. The waves of opposition and hatred which the Apostle Paul encountered were also felt by others who stood in defense of the gospel. That opposition and the spread of various heresies were some of the tools that Satan would use to turn people from the hope found in Christ as the Savior. John wrote his Gospel to the Christians to strengthen their faith in Jesus as the Christ. That purpose of showing Jesus to be the Christ is evident from the very first verse of the first chapter. And the message is perhaps nowhere more forcefully stated than in the five verses of this sermon text.

Satan's handiwork is just as evident today as in John's day, even though generally in a less violent way. The heresy of today that has given Christmas the general meaning of peace and goodwill among men is one example. The heresy that paints the portrait of the child born in Bethlehem as a great preacher of social justice — therefore worthy of remembering on his birthday — is another example. So it is very fitting and necessary that before we leave the Christmas season, we sink our teeth into the meat of the gospel and be reminded why there is cause for such a grand celebration at Christmas time. It is because God "tented" with us in order to become our source of life.

As we pass through this season, it seems impossible to avoid the thought of gifts which are so closely associated with Christmas. Certainly the gifts that most people have in mind are of inferior quality. As we bring the season to a close, how appropriate it is that we are reminded of the true gift that we have received in God's Son. Because he condescended to come to live with us, we now receive gifts of God's grace on a daily basis — one after another. The words of Lamentations 3:22,23 express that great fact. "His compassions never fail. They are new every morning; great is your faithfulness."

The apostles had already seen the Messiah's glory shine forth as he had cared for the needs of the people with his miracles of feeding and healing. But when they would later be filled with the Holy Spirit, the glory of grace would dazzle them as they would ponder the meaning of Christ's death on the cross. Certainly it was undeserved love that would lead him to lay down his life willingly for sinful wretched people, suffering the full brunt of God's wrath. They would recognize that as an act of love with which he would open the door of heaven to them, though they little deserved it.

It was in this, through Christ, that God revealed himself to all mankind. Psychologists tell us that knowledge comes through the five senses. Since God is a spirit, he is beyond the grasp of our limited senses. It is only through Christ that we can begin to learn of God. It was on the hill called Calvary especially that the disciples caught a glimpse of God. There they learned what God is like, as John would later describe him in characteristic simplicity. "God is love" (1 Jn 4:16).

Because our sins have also built a wall that separates us from God, God's grace in Christ is of utmost importance to us as well. Through the words of the apostle we too have caught a glimpse of the glory and grace of God as we again contemplate his incarnation. How sad if the message of the Christmas season didn't give us that glimpse of God! How blessed we are if it does!

Recognize the Gift God Gave to Sinful Man

1. Jesus is the inexhaustible fountain of saving grace (vv. 14-17)
2. Jesus is the true interpreter of God (v. 18)

Behold the Only Son of God

1. A glimpse of glory shows who he is (vv. 14,16,17)
2. John the Baptist testifies of his greatness (v. 15)
3. In him we see the Father (v. 18)

EPIPHANY OF OUR LORD

The Scriptures

Old Testament — *Isaiah 60:1-6*
Epistle — *Ephesians 3:2-12*
Gospel — *Matthew 2:1-12*

The Text — Matthew 2:1-12

The three-year ILCW pericope series use this text each year for Epiphany day. Therefore, it was treated in the two previous volumes of *Sermon Studies on the Gospels.* The preacher will want to check out the useful commentaries and helpful homiletical suggestions in the volumes on Series B and Series C.

This account of the bright eastern star and the visit of the Gentile strangers illustrates the truths found in the Old Testament reading and the Epistle reading for this day. Isaiah declares, "Your light has come" (60:1). The sin of our human race has left a heavy and lethal shroud of darkness over all the earth. God banishes this darkness by sending us his light. His light is, of course, the light found in Jesus Christ. Isaiah tells the people of Zion, "the Lord rises upon you and his glory appears over you. Nations will come to your light" (60:2,3). Likewise, the Apostle Paul in his letter to the Ephesians assures us that this good news of light is for foreign strangers as well as for the people of Israel. "Through the gospel the Gentiles are heirs together with Israel," he writes, "members together of one body and sharers together in the promise of Christ Jesus" (3:6). But when the Gentile Magi came to Jerusalem to learn about the star, they found the city in the dark. Yet light from the star led them to the light found in God's word (vv. 5,6) And God's word pierced through the darkness and showed them the Light of the World (v. 11).

> vv. 1,2 — *After Jesus was born in Bethlehem in Judea, during the time of King Herod, Magi from the east came to Jerusalem and asked, "Where is the one who has been born king of the Jews? We saw his star in the east and have come to worship him."*

When did this happen? Who were these mysterious Magi? Where did they come from? What was that special star? Questions like these fill our minds, and the minds of our members, when we preach on this familiar text. Traditions and legends have tried to answer these questions. But as some have pointed out, the beginning of the familiar carol, "We Three Kings of Orient Are," may have already in its title given us three misleading impressions. We don't know the number of wisemen. Tradition has made them kings. And it is unlikely they came from the Far East which we customarily think of as the Orient. We will want to be careful not to say more than Scripture says. While such information in the body of the sermon may be distracting, it may be well to speak briefly of these misconceptions in the introduction.

Since only Matthew records this incident for us in Scripture, what we read here is what we know. This happened "after Jesus was born in Bethlehem." It was "during the time of King Herod." How long this was after the nativity is uncertain. Jesus was no longer "lying in a manger" (Luke 2:12), but was in "the house." Herod the Great ruled from 37 B.C. to A.D. 4. Later he saw fit to kill all the boys in Bethlehem who were two years old and younger. However, he probably overcompensated in setting the age limit for his heinous command, not wanting the new born king to be missed.

The Magi from the east are usually thought of as astrologers from Babylonia (Dn 2:2; 5:7). This is quite possible. Their caste could have learned of the messianic prophecies during Judah's exile from people like Daniel. They were Gentiles, not the people of God. This is important. For as our Old Testament reading for the day foretells to Zion, "Nations will come to your light, and kings to the brightness of your dawn" (Is 60:3). And the Epistle reading tells us, "through the gospel the Gentiles are heirs together with Israel" (Eph 3:6).

Much has been written to explain the Christmas star. Astronomers reconstruct the constellations of that time either "to disprove" or "to prove" the star's mystical appearance. Whether Jupiter and Venus came together in their orbits is interesting but not all that important. We simply notice what the Magi point out. They "saw *his* star in the east." The star belonged to the new king. It was owned by him through whom "all things were made" (John 1:3). How he made the star appear and whatever its appearance was, it served the purpose for which he made it. It led the Magi to him.

Notice the ἰδοὺ (v. 1) which is found sixty-two times in Matthew's Gospel. This is Matthew's *nota bene*. With it he seeks to draw our attention to something important. What is important is that the Magi, Gentiles from the east, came to Jerusalem.

vv. 3-6 — *When King Herod heard this he was disturbed, and all Jerusalem with him. When he had called together all the people's chief priests and teachers of the law, he asked them where the Christ was to be born. "In Bethlehem in Judea," they replied, "for this is what the prophet has written: 'But you, Bethlehem, in the land of Judah, are by no means least among the rulers of Judah; for out of you will come a ruler who will be the shepherd of my people Israel.' "*

To say Herod was paranoid at the news of a new king would be an understatement. He was, according to various translations, "disturbed" (NIV), "troubled" (KJV), or "alarmed" (AT). The Greek word (ταράσσω) is the same word used to describe the stirred up waters at the pool of Bethesda (Jn 5:4). It is used figuratively to tell how "the crowd and city officials were thrown into turmoil" (Ac 17:8), when Paul and Silas told the Thessalonians the same news which Herod now heard: "There is another king, one called Jesus" (Acts 17:7). Herod's adrenaline was flowing. His stomach was churning. And when King Herod was disturbed, so was "all Jerusalem with him" (v. 3). Pictures of rebellion and bloodshed came to everyone's mind. Everyone knew all too well what could happen when Herod felt threatened.

What amazes us, and must have amazed the Magi too, is how King Herod and all Jerusalem are in the dark about the Messiah's birth. They weren't watching and waiting for the Messiah to come and they missed him. There was no room in the inn for the Christchild and there wasn't any room in Jerusalem either. But are things really any different today? Notice, for example, especially in our mission congregations how people will travel over an hour to worship the King, but people in the neighborhood won't go seven miles from Jerusalem to Bethlehem. Today too the Gentiles come to worship him, while the Jews ignore him. And how many folks without a Christian Church, like the Magi, have seen his light and follow him, while some who have grown up in the church have left him to return to the darkness? We still live in a world that ignores this momentous happening in history which affects us all — the birthday of our King.

King Herod wastes no time, albeit for the wrong and wicked reasons, to *begin* inquiring and to *keep on* searching until he finds out about the Messiah who has come (ἐπυνθάνετο, imperfect tense). His own wisemen, the chief priest and teachers of the law, look to the Scriptures. But for the Magi the word they are shown turns out to be "a lamp for their feet and a light for their path." Micah's words written long ago guides them to Bethlehem in Judah. (There was also a city of Bethlehem in the land possessed by the tribe of Zebulun. (Cf. Josh 19:15.)

vv. 7,8 — *Then Herod called the Magi secretly and found out from them the exact time the star had appeared. He sent them to Bethlehem and said, "Go and make a careful search for the child. As soon as you find him, report to me, so that I too may go and worship him."*

King Herod sent the Magi on his great commission. "Go and make a careful search for the child." His professed purpose was that he might "worship him." But his subsequent horrendous actions (2:16) reveal his hypocrisy.

Herod held the meeting secretly. Jerusalem knew their king. Aware of this, Herod knew that only the Magi strangers could be hoodwinked into believing he actually wanted to worship the new King.

vv. 9,10 — *After they had heard the king, they went on their way, and the star they had seen in the east went ahead of them until it stopped over the place where the Child was. When they saw the star, they were overjoyed.*

Notice (ἰδοὺ) the star appears again. It was the same star the Magi saw back home when they decided to travel to Jerusalem. They couldn't conceal their emotions. They were overjoyed (ἐχάρησαν χαρὰν μεγάλην σφόδρα). The light which leads us to our Savior should always bring us great joy. However, just as the stars shine brightest against the black sky of the new moon, so it seems that the light of God's word shines brightest in our lives when things appear the darkest. How often hasn't a sinner who has long ago wandered off into this world of darkness been brought to tears of joy upon hearing the good news of forgiveness in Christ Jesus? How often hasn't a patient in the hospital found his only joy in the precious light of God's word when everything else in life seems dismal and dreary? Remember Luther's words of ecstasy when he discovered the gospel after living through the years which were also the Dark Ages in the people's spiritual lives. He wrote, "I felt as though I had been reborn and had been ushered through the doors into paradise." When we recognize the darkness of our sin, the light found in Christ will bring us the joy experienced by the Magi and do away with yawns of indifference in our worship.

vv. 11,12 — *On coming to the house, they saw the child with his mother Mary, and they bowed down and worshiped him. Then they opened their treasures and presented him with gifts of gold and of incense and of myrrh. And having been warned in a dream not to go back to Herod, they returned to their country by another route.*

Unlike Herod, the Gentile Magi truly intended to worship the Messiah King. The gifts they brought show the sincerity of their worship. Such gifts were commonly given in biblical times by one luminary to another. See Genesis 43:11, 1 Kings 10:2. It has been said, "You can give without loving, but you cannot love without giving." Wherever people truly worship our Lord Jesus, gifts are cheerfully and freely given.

What a sight to see these adult men, truly wise men, bow down and worship this Child! What power the Holy Spirit has to convince human hearts this child born of Mary is not only a human being but Immanuel, God himself come to be with us! This is the Epiphany. We see Jesus as he truly is, an actual human being and the true God.

The heavenly Father protects his Son so Jesus might carry out the mission for which he sent him. He is to be our Savior (Lk 2:11). With a special dream the Lord warns the Magi of Herod's real intentions. "They returned to their country by another route (δι' ἄλλης ὁδοῦ)." Anyone who has been led to the Christ and whom God has made wise to see him as our only Redeemer will find himself on new roads in life. "From now on we regard no one from a worldly point of view. . . . The old has gone, the new has come!" (2 Cor 5:16,17)

Homiletical Suggestions

The light of the Epiphany season reveals the Christchild as the human child whom believers know and worship as the true God. Herod and the Magi are interesting personalities in this historical account, but one does well to keep the Christchild central, with the others pointing to him.

We Have Come to Worship Him

1. Not with the horrendous hypocrisy of Herod (vv. 1-8)
2. But with the joyful sincerity of the Magi (vv. 9-11)

Inasmuch as the Magi are exemplary in their desire to find the Christchild and to worship him, a sermon could be presented encouraging us to follow their example. The familiar hymn provides this outline.

As with Gladness Men of Old

1. May we evermore be led by thee (vv. 1-6)
2. May we ever seek thy mercy seat (vv. 10,11)
3. May we our costliest treasures bring (vv. 11)

Some congregations appropriately hold their mission festival during the Epiphany season. This text is well suited for such an occasion. A mission hymn based on the Old Testament reading (TLH 498:6) suggests this theme:

Savior, Shine on Nations Near and Far

1. Guide them (vv. 1,2)
2. Enlighten them (vv. 3-6)
3. Inspire them (vv. 9-11)
4. Protect them (vv. 7,8,12)

Direct quotations from the text sometimes make appropriate themes.

Where Is the One Who Has Been Born King of the Jews?

1. Still the word leads us to him (vv. 4-6)
2. Still many in the world do not know him (v. 3)
3. Still many in the world would do away with him (vv. 7,8,12)
4. Still some in the world worship him (vv. 9-11)

Make a Careful Search for the Child

1. Not with Herod's madness (vv. 3-8,12)
2. But with the Magi's gladness (vv. 1,2,9-11)

FIRST SUNDAY AFTER EPIPHANY

The Scriptures

Old Testament — *Isaiah 42:1-7*
Epistle — *Acts 10:34-38*
Gospel — *Matthew 3:13-17*

The Text — Matthew 3:13-17

Approximately thirty years have passed since Jesus last appeared in Matthew's Gospel. He was but a toddler then. With little fanfare Jesus suddenly bursts upon the scene in this text. He is grown to manhood and seeks a baptism from John in order to "fulfill all righteousness." This is a great epiphany.

This baptism signals the start of something big for Jesus. Accordingly many have portrayed this epiphany as an inauguration, ordination or installation. But the question is, into what did Jesus enter by means of John's baptism? To say that this event marks the start of Jesus' public ministry is true enough. However, this answer is vague. Some answer that this baptism is the start of Jesus' saving work. This explanation is an attempt to be precise, but it's only half right. The complete answer is the sermon itself!

The baptism of Jesus is a fascinating story of God's love for sinners and the love of a Father for his Son. It is a thrilling sequel to the visit of the Magi and the subsequent "years of silence." A sermon preached on this text should be positive in tone, extolling the mercy and love of God.

v. 13 — *Then Jesus came from Galilee to the Jordan to be baptized by John.*

An accident that Matthew begins this epiphany with the adverb τότε? No. The saint loves the word. He dots his Gospel copiously with it, a word most often translated as "then."

Because it correlates the timely connection between events, τότε immedidately presents the preacher with a thematic idea: time. Τότε says, "The time has arrived." For what? For Jesus to enter a preordained work which will lead the way to the cross and empty tomb. How does he enter this work? Through John's baptism.

Another theme of verse 13 is the willingness of our Lord to enter this preordained work. This willing spirit twinkles like a star in the purposeful force of the passive voice of βαπτισθῆναι. Jesus had journeyed from Galilee "to be baptized." Consider the irony in his arduous journey south to the Judean landscape. Some thirty years earlier his mother Mary had similarly journeyed with Joseph south to Judea, bearing our Lord in her womb, so that he might enter the world in a place called Bethlehem. Through both trips is woven the thread of willingness. God's Son wills to do his Father's bidding — to save mankind.

But how does undergoing John's baptism further this saving work? Why must the Son of God receive a baptism "with water for repentance" (v. 11)? The many pious souls, troubled by such questions, are in good company. John the Baptist was the first to protest that such a thing should happen.

v. 14 — *But John tried to deter him, saying, "I need to be baptized by you, and do you come to me?"*

The "Greater" should submit himself to the lesser's baptism? No way, thinks the Baptizer. John is understandably chagrined by this prospect. Hadn't he just warned both Pharisee and Sadducee that the One-to-come would be more powerful than he? That he would also baptize with the Holy Spirit and with fire? The Lord's request was an apparent contradiction of John's confession that he wasn't even fit to tie the Messiah's sandals. One must appreciate the irony of this. John could not have imagined a more shocking turn of events.

The imperfect action of διεκώλυεν is a masterpiece of understatement. John was "trying to deter" Jesus. This means an argument. The incompleted action of διεκώλυεν is a bevy of implied emotions and actions, all marshalled to convince Jesus not to be baptized. And the preacher needs only to use his own experience and imagination to illustrate how humans act while in conflict; i.e., how does a forerunner look and sound when telling a Messiah that he's dead wrong? John's argument is impassioned. To round it out the Spirit even preserves the key passage of John's protest: "I need to be baptized by you, and do you come to me?"

The theme of verse 14 is shock. This is a surprising epiphany of Jesus.

v. 15 — *Jesus replied, "Let it be so now; it is proper for us to do this to fulfill all righteousness." Then John consented.*

This verse is the heart and soul of the text. Jesus' answer is given matter-of-factly and in two parts.

First Jesus answers, "Let it be so now." Ἄφες ἄρτι is a verbal parry which deftly wards off the Baptizer's protests. This to-the-point response puts John in his place but curiously also reassures John that his earlier testament to Christ's person was not exaggerated. He was correct when he had said, "After me will come one who is more powerful than I." Ἄφες ἄρτι expresses this greater power. Notice how our Lord has structured this response to John. Like a commanding officer Jesus has issued an order first of all, and Ἄφες ἄρτι means to say, "Attention!" Upon this command Jesus then proceeds to grant John an explanation to his unusual request.

The theme of this tete-a-tete is authority. The Messiah, who asks for such a lowly baptism of John, is still in charge.

Secondly Jesus answers, "It is proper for us to do this to fulfill all righteousness." Things, in other words, are not what they seem. There is nothing improper about Jesus' request for John's baptism because it somehow involves "righteousness."

Δικαιοσύνην represents God's gracious policy towards sinners. His righteousness not only condemns and punishes, but it also delivers and saves. So the Psalmist says, "Rescue me and deliver me in your righteousness." So Luther also discovered.

Jesus says he wants to "fulfill *all* righteousness," which is to say he has already worked *some* righteousness. Πᾶσαν is the clue to this startling epiphany. For to see why Jesus tethers πᾶσαν to δικαιοσύνην is to understand how he was to complete his saving work and how this then dovetails with John's baptism.

What Jesus still needed to do was to make atonement for sins. Already being worked was the "active" half of his saving work. From the beginning of his life our Lord was actively living the kind of life, free from sin, which God demands of everyone. The "active" righteousness Jesus would continue to pursue as our great Substitute.

But now the time had come for Jesus to enter the "passive" half of his saving work. The theme of this verse is therefore one of transition. At Jordan's bank Jesus willfully entered that phase of his ministry, a public phase, in which he would "passively" allow his life to be taken as a sacrificial atonement. Hence John the Baptist's cry of prophecy when Jesus came to meet him at the Jordan, "Look, the Lamb of God, who takes away the sin of the world!" Here was a prophetic finger which pointed the way to the cross.

Therefore those who dub the baptism of Jesus as the "beginning" of his ministry or of his saving work create the impression that Jesus had been doing nothing of consequence up to this point. Nothing could be more misleading. The expression πληρῶσαι πᾶσαν δικαιοσύνην denotes a ministry in transition. Jesus now embarks on a journey to make a sacrifice for sins, wedding the "passive" half of δικαιοσύνην to its "active" half, in order to "fulfill *all* righteousness."

What better way to signal, not just his willingness, but his actual entry into this second half of his ministry than to receive John's baptism? John preached a baptism expressly for the forgiveness of sins. Therefore Jesus wants to stand beside his "brothers" in the Jordan. To receive the baptism they are receiving will identify him clearly — this is God's sacrificial Lamb who bears the world's sin and who will win forgiveness for the world.

John consents to baptize his Lord. Matthew's characteristic τότε here reinforces the timely connection between the art of Jesus' persuasiveness and the change in John's attitude.

vv. 16,17 — *As soon as Jesus was baptized, he went up out of the water. At that moment heaven was opened, and he saw the Spirit of God descending like a dove and lighting on him. And a voice from heaven said, "This is my Son, whom I love; with him I am well pleased."*

Was Jesus immersed? Βαπτισθεὶς says that water was applied in a ceremonial way. Enough has been written elsewhere by confessional Lutherans to explain the mode and manner of this sacramental washing. Suffice it to say here that there is no textual evidence in ἀνέβη ἀπὸ τοῦ ὕδατος to warrant the conclusion that Jesus was immersed. What the Greek says is that Jesus went "up" or "away" from the water after his baptism.

Jesus was "anointed" with water — that is the first major point in this section. But this thought in turn is quickly eclipsed by another thought. This second theme is trumpeted by ἰδοὺ. Heaven is opened and the Holy Spirit lights on Jesus in the form of a dove. The theme is that of a divine anointing.

The nature of this anointing is quickly explained by the strategic use of another ἰδοὺ. The voice of God the Father adds commentary to this descent of the Spirit. The Father loves the Son, adding, "with him I am well pleased."

The anointing of the Spirit is the Father's way of identifying his Son. Also the Father dramatically approves what his Son is planning to do, to make atonement for sin. The audible and visible approval by the Father publicly authorizes Jesus. This authorization was fundamental for Jesus' ministry. It became the divine benchmark by which Jesus countered the unbelief of the Jews. Witness the challenges to Jesus by his opponents. "By what authority are you doing these things?" demanded the hostile clergy of Jesus during Holy Week. They added, "Who gave you this authority?" (Mt 21:23) Or they would criticize, "Here you are, appearing as your own witness; your testimony is not valid" (Jn 8:13).

Jesus always countered these arguments by saying his Father had approved and authorized his person and plans, and that John was a reliable witness to this divine authorization. See how Jesus is quick to draw John's baptism to his defense when the clergy attack him (Mt 21:23-27). Or see how Jesus refers to the testimonies of his Father and of the Baptizer in John 5:31-38.

This epiphany is a true "shining forth." After a thirty years' silence the baptism of Jesus is heaven's way of validating the Son of Mary as the Son of God to the world. The world is to know that Jesus of Nazareth has divine authority to complete his saving work. As such this epiphany is a call to faith for all generations.

Homiletical Suggestions

The baptism of Jesus is an epiphany of epic dimensions. Many themes invite development. The following outline is suggested by the word of St. Paul in 2 Corinthians 2:2 (KJV) which is a combination of the thoughts of time and willingness:

Now Is the Accepted Time

1. The Son accepts the work of atonement (vv. 13-15)
2. The Father accepts the Worker of atonement (vv. 16,17)

The next outline is divided along the same verses as the previous one, except that the order is inverted. The prime thought behind this theme is surprise, evidenced by John's initial resistance to baptizing Jesus:

Jesus, Why Do You Seek a Sinner's Baptism?

1. To show who the sinner's Savior is (vv. 16,17)
   - A. Father and Spirit team to identify Jesus
   - B. Jesus and John appeal to this divine witness
2. To show how the sinner is saved (vv. 13-15)
   - A. By the active obedience of Jesus
   - B. By the passive obedience of Jesus

Conclusion: This epiphany is a pleasant surprise. Jesus' willingness to do his Father's bidding results in our salvation.

The following outline attempts to underscore the transitional nature of Christ's ministry at the time of his baptism. Jesus enters into the final phase of his work of salvation, leaving behind the many years of his anonymous mediation in behalf of sinners. His goal now is that final, short but critical public atonement for sins:

The Last Leg of the Journey

1. Jesus enters his public ministry (vv. 13,14)
2. Jesus states his intent to complete salvation (v. 15)
3. Jesus receives God's blessings on his plans (vv. 16,17)

SECOND SUNDAY AFTER EPIPHANY

The Scriptures

Old Testament — *Isaiah 49:1-6*
Epistle — *1 Corinthians 1:1-9*
Gospel — *John 1:29-41*

The Text — John 1:29-41

John the Baptist was fulfilling his call to prepare people for the coming of the Messiah. He testified concerning Jesus' preeminence and preexistence (1:15), his grace (1:16,17) and his deity (1:18). John was not the Christ, not Elijah nor the Prophet; he was "the voice" who called, "Make straight the way for the Lord" (1:19-23). He baptized and he defended his baptizing as preparatory work for One much greater than himself (1:24-27).

John drew attention with his appearance, his diet and his activity, but it was only in order to direct his hearers to Jesus.

v. 29 — *The next day John saw Jesus coming toward him and said, "Look, the Lamb of God, who takes away the sin of the world!"*

It was the day after the Pharisees had challenged John in regard to his baptizing. We are not told explicitly why Jesus was coming toward John. However, his purpose is clear when we see what John said. Jesus came toward John so that John could identify him for all present.

John's words here are really a summary of the gospel. For the Jews the religious connotations of "lamb" were sacrifice for sin, atonement and the Passover deliverance from death. The word evoked Isaiah's prophecy concerning the Suffering Servant: "He was led like a lamb to the slaughter" (Is 53:7).

Here was God's Lamb, sent by him (genitive of source in θεοῦ) to carry out his purpose. God's purpose was that this Lamb should "take away the sin of the world." Ὁ αἴρων, the present participle, characterizes Jesus as doing that even while John spoke.

The verb as used here can mean "to take up and carry" in the sense of a substitutionary act: "God made him who had no sin to be sin for us, so that in him we might become the righteousness of God" (2 Cor 5:21). It can also mean "to carry off" in the sense of removing the guilt and punishment of sin: "He is the atoning sacrifice for our sins, and not only for ours but also for the sins of the whole world" (1 Jn 2:2).

This Lamb was not to be sacrificed for Israel alone but for the world. He is for everyone. There are only two places where sin can be, said Luther: on the sinner or on Christ. The law placed it on you and me. The gospel, preached here by John, declares that Christ has graciously taken it on himself and taken it away.

v. 30 — *"This is the one I meant when I said, 'A man who comes after me has surpassed me because he was before me.' "*

This is the second appearance of this quotation from the mouth of the Baptist. See verse 15, where the words serve as a heading for this entire report of John's activity and testimony.

Jesus came after John in age and in the onset of his public ministry. That is the idea of ὀπίσω μου. 'Εμπροσθέν μου contains the idea of Jesus' preeminence in rank; hence NIV's "has surpassed me." John explains that preeminence: ὅτι πρῶτος μου ἦν. Πρῶτος is used comparatively here. The Man younger than John is the eternal Word of the Prologue (1:1-14).

v. 31 — *"I myself did not know him, but the reason that I came baptizing with water was that he might be revealed to Israel."*

John was, no doubt, personally acquainted with his kinsman. He had not, however, understood Jesus' full significance and importance.

The reason for his characteristic work, baptizing, was the Epiphany of Jesus (φανερωθῇ) to Israel. To characterize his baptism as being "with water," ἐν used instrumentally, was not to deprecate it. John's baptism was a means of grace, "for the forgiveness of sins" (Mk 1:4; Lk 3:3). This was in anticipation of the Lamb's sin-bearing work.

God must supply the lack in John's knowledge and God must reveal Jesus to Israel. That he did so is reported in the remainder of the text (vv. 32-41).

vv. 32,33 — *Then John gave this testimony: "I saw the Spirit come down from heaven as a dove and remain on him. I would not have known him, except that the one who sent me to baptize with water told me, 'The man on whom you see the Spirit come down and remain is he who will baptize with the Holy Spirit.' "*

The Baptist had said, "I myself did not know him" (v. 31). Now he gives testimony as to how he did get to know Jesus. John was a prophet and more than a prophet, and a prophet's certainty must come from God. God provided that certainty for John at Jesus' baptism.

John's first person testimony here presupposes his hearers' knowledge of what happened when Jesus was baptized (Mt 3:16,17;

Mk 1:10,11; Lk 3:22). The One who sent John to baptize was, of course, God. How he told the Baptist what the descent of the Spirit would mean we do not know. He did tell him and what he told him was that Jesus is the Messiah. Baptizing with the Spirit is one of the characteristic activities, one of the identifying marks, of the promised Christ (Joel 2:28-32 and Acts 2:17-21). The risen Christ recalled John's words on the day of his ascension (Acts 1:5) and the promise was fulfilled on the day of Pentecost.

The contrast between John's baptizing with water and Jesus' baptizing with the Spirit does not deprecate or devalue baptism with water. Rather, it highlights the greater importance of Jesus and his work.

Jesus did not *become* the Messiah and the Son of God when the Spirit came down and remained on him at his baptism. No, the presence of the Spirit and the testimony of the Father were an acknowledgment of Jesus' Person and his saving mission.

We note in passing that all three Persons of the Trinity were present at Jesus' baptism, as they are present at every baptism.

v. 34 — *"I have seen and I testify that this is the Son of God."*

John gave faithful testimony to the truth which the Father and the Spirit had revealed to him. His work was to point to Christ, not to talk about himself or enhance his own position.

On the importance of believing and confessing the truth "that this is the Son of God" see John 3:16,36; 6:40; 1 John 2:22,23; 4:15.

A case can be made for the variant reading ὁ ἐκλεκτός, but there is no essential difference in meaning and there is no good reason in trying to make the case from the pulpit.

vv. 35,36 — *The next day John was there again with two of his disciples. When he saw Jesus passing by, he said, "Look, the Lamb of God!"*

Implicit in John's announcement was the imperative to follow and learn from and trust the Lamb of God. The same imperative is implicit in every preaching of the gospel, every testimony to the Savior.

John was doing the highest service any person can perform for another: pointing these two disciples to Jesus. May we assume that the two disciples had heard John's testimony on the previous day and that they had not acted on it? John repeated the good news, as the faithful witness ought always to persist.

vv. 37,38 — *When the two disciples heard him say this, they followed Jesus. Turning around, Jesus saw them following and asked, "What do you want?"*

They said, "Rabbi" (which means Teacher), "where are you staying?"

The two disciples acted on the implied imperative in the Baptist's words and followed Jesus. The Lord greeted them with a searching question.

They answered with a question of their own. We need not think of their response as inept or evasive. They wanted to be in his company, to learn from this rabbi, to understand the full significance of what John has said.

v. 39 — *"Come," he replied, "and you will see." So they went and saw where he was staying, and spent that day with him. It was about the tenth hour.*

The King of kings demonstrated hospitality and gave generously of his time. John the Evangelist was one of those two disciples and many years later he remembered the time of day when he first met Jesus, about 4:00 P.M.

It is easier to gain an audience with Jesus than with anyone. He is always ready to listen, always ready to teach.

vv. 40,41 — *Andrew, Simon Peter's brother, was one of the two who heard what John had said and who had followed Jesus. The first thing Andrew did was to find his brother Simon and tell him, "We have found the Messiah" (that is, the Christ).*

John the Baptist's testimony and Jesus' words were effective to convince Andrew that Jesus is the Messiah. He heard the good news, he believed it and he wanted to share it. The gospel moved and equipped him to share it.

The Lamb of God, the Son of God, is the Messiah. The Lord's Anointed, appointed by God to do God's work in God's good time, came to do what no mere man can do. That is, he fulfilled all righteousness and he took away the sin of the world. This truth is not to be hoarded but shared, as Andrew shared it with his brother.

Homiletical Suggestions

The emphasis of the Epiphany Season is on Jesus' manifestation to the world as the world's divine Savior. Today's gospel, along with the other ILCW selections, is true to that emphasis.

Isaiah 49:1-6 portrays the Servant of the Lord as "a light for the Gentiles," who is to bring God's salvation to the ends of the earth. In 1 Corinthians 1:1-9 it is the apostle to the Gentiles who writes: "I always thank God for you, because of his grace given you in Christ Jesus."

In its portrayal of the Baptist's faithful testimony and Andrew's eager sharing, the ILCW gospel reminds us that Jesus is not only manifested *to* people. He is also manifested *through* people. All of the outlines which follow reflect this missions and evangelism thrust.

In citing Andrew's eager sharing do not overlook John's faithful testimony.

Look, the Lamb of God!

1. Learn about him (vv. 29-39)
2. Tell about him (vv. 29,32,36,40,41)

Look, the Lamb of God!

1. See what he has done (vv. 29-34)
2. Hear what he says (vv. 35-39)
3. Share what you have learned (vv. 29,32,36,40,41)

Be an Epiphany Christian

1. Appreciate Jesus' Mission (vv. 29-36)
2. Imitate Jesus' Love (vv. 37-41)

Look at Jesus

1. The Lamb to die for us (vv. 29-31)
2. The Son to send us his Spirit (vv. 32-34)
3. The Messiah to be shared by us (vv. 29,32,34-41)

THIRD SUNDAY AFTER EPIPHANY

The Scriptures

Old Testament — *Isaiah 9:1-4*
Epistle — *1 Corinthians 1:10-17*
Gospel — *Matthew 4:12-23*

The Text — Matthew 4:12-23

This account is from Jesus' early Galilean ministry. Parallel Gospel accounts which may offer additional information are Mark 1:14-20; Luke 4:14-15,31; 5:1-11.

vv. 12,13 — *When Jesus heard that John had been put in prison, he returned to Galilee. Leaving Nazareth, he went and lived in Capernaum, which was by the lake in the area of Zebulun and Naphtali*

It will be helpful for the preacher to understand the time frame into which this account fits. The Synoptic Gospels jump from the baptism and temptation of Jesus into his Galilean ministry, omitting an entire year. John 1:19 — 3:36 provides what information we have about this "lost" year. John 1:35ff reports that Simon Peter and his brother were not strangers to Jesus. They had become his followers before the incident in this text takes place.

The imprisonment of John the Baptist marks the beginning of Jesus' ministry in Galilee. John's mission of preparing the way was nearly at an end. When John was no longer able to proclaim his message publicly, Jesus himself took up the cry. The Baptist was to linger on in Herod's prison for yet another year.

Following his unpleasant reception in Nazareth (Lk 4:16-30) Jesus moved his center of activity to Capernaum. Located on the northwest shore of the Sea of Galilee, Capernaum was a thriving center of trade and commerce. It was situated on the trade route that ran from Damascus to the eastern Mediterranean coast. The city contained a synagogue (Lk 7:5), a customhouse (Mt 9:9; Lk 5:17) and a Roman garrison, among other things. Here, on Sabbath days, the Savior would preach in the synagogue of which the good centurion was the builder and Jairus the chief ruler. Here Matthew would be called to leave his custom booth and follow Jesus. Here, or at least in the vicinity, were the homes of many of the earliest disciples. The city would serve as a central point from which Jesus and his disciples would later travel to more remote regions of Galilee.

vv. 14-16 — *to fulfill what was said through the prophet Isaiah: "Land of Zebulun and land of Naphtali, the way to the sea, along the Jordan, Galilee of the Gentiles — the people living in darkness have seen a great light; on those living in the land of the shadow of death a light has dawned."*

Behind Matthew's description of "the lake in the area of Zebulun and Naphtali" was the Jewish contention that the Messiah would carry out his work in Judea and particularly in Jerusalem. Addressing his words originally to Jews, Matthew was keenly aware that this false notion was imbedded in Jewish thinking. Apparently, for many, this Jewish tradition had been accepted at face value without thought of searching the Scriptures for verification. Such will always be a dangerous, even soul-jeopardizing practice! To each new generation the command is the same: " . . . diligently study the Scriptures" (Jn 5:39). To dispel this falsehood Matthew refers these messianic words of Isaiah (Is 9:1f) to Jesus. In this region of Galilee that had at one time been allotted to the tribes of Zebulun and Naphtali, a glorious ministry was about to unfold. The Scriptures had prophesied it. Jesus was about to fulfill that prophecy.

Those living in the border areas of Galilee had over the years been especially susceptible to the attacks and influences of heathen nations to the north. In Jesus' time the people of Galilee were to a large extent a mixed race. The spiritual heritage of their father Abraham had also become polluted. Pious traditions had beclouded the light of the Scriptures. Jesus' countrymen were living in a scriptural darkness. However, as the rising sun chases the darkness of night, so Jesus would dispel spiritual darkness. Many would walk in his light, but many others would not (Jn 3:19-21).

v. 17 — *From that time on Jesus began to preach, "Repent, for the kingdom of heaven is near."*

It should be noted that Jesus had been preaching for over a year already, but not in this area of Galilee. His message sounds very much like that of John the Baptist (Mt 3:2). He called people to repentance, urging them to turn their lives away from sin toward righteousness. This change begins in the heart, but permeates one's entire life. Note the present tense of the imperative μετανοεῖτε. Repentance is not a one-time thing, but a continuous, ongoing process. Through her history Israel had been waiting for the Messiah, always looking to the future. Jesus now bids the people to stop looking into the future and behold the One who now stood before them. What they had waited for was now "near" to them.

The same word for "preaching" (κηρύσσειν) from κῆρυξ, a herald, is used for both Jesus and John. Both proclaimed the good news of the kingdom. Jesus is more often described as the Teacher (ὁ διδάσκαλος) who taught the people. He was both herald and teacher as every preacher should be.

vv. 18-20 — *As Jesus was walking beside the Sea of Galilee, he saw two brothers, Simon called Peter and his brother Andrew. They were casting a net into the lake, for they were fishermen. "Come, follow me," Jesus said, "and I will make you fishers of men." At once they left their nets and followed him.*

The Sea of Galilee is a relatively small body of water having an average length of 13 miles and an average width of about 7 miles. Its waters are clear and contain an abundance of fish. Many must have made their living by fishing these waters. Among these were Peter and Andrew, as well as James and John.

Matthew recounts the calling of these men as disciples with straightforward simplicity. Yet in this brief account he captures the essence of true discipleship. As noted at verses 12,13 these men had been followers of Jesus before this time. It appears that they accompanied him north to Galilee and were present at the wedding in Cana. They witnessed the miraculous transformation of water into wine. Following the wedding celebration they returned to their homes and vocations. The Savior now sought out these men and called them to fulltime discipleship.

It was the practice, even the sacred duty, of the rabbis to gather a circle of disciples. These disciples, and even those of John the Baptist, "followed" in order to learn. Jesus' disciples would certainly learn from their Master. However, this call was not just for these men to learn, but also to do. Telling Peter and Andrew that he would make them fishers of men, Jesus was indicating what their new vocation was to be. Instead of casting out a draw net, these men would cast out the net of the gospel. Instead of harvesting fish from the sea, they would harvest souls for the kingdom of heaven.

It does not appear that these men had any special outward qualifications for apostleship. In all likelihood they were not "college educated" as Paul was. It is doubtful that they had ever been trained in public speaking or philosophy. They were common, everyday, blue-collar laborers. But the Savior does not ask them to prepare themselves for their new calling. He rather promises to make them into workers for God's kingdom. He would teach them what they needed to know. They would see his miraculous power. They would witness the crucifixion and the empty tomb. The Holy Spirit would provide them with the gifts they needed to become fishers of men. These men had, however, met the first and foremost qualification for service to the Lord: they knew him as their personal Savior — the Lamb of God that takes away the sin of the world.

There are a number of parallels between Jesus' calling of these men and our own calling as followers of Christ. (1) These men did not seek out Jesus. He, rather, came and found them. So we did not go looking for him either. As Luther puts it: "I believe that I cannot by my own thinking or choosing believe in Jesus Christ, my Lord, or come to him. . . . " Our sinful nature makes it impossible for us to find our Savior on our own. Yet in love he came and found us. (2) As the disciples were not deserving of, or outwardly qualified for their apostleship, so we are not worthy of our status as redeemed children of God. We are what we are solely by the grace of God. (3) As Jesus trained and equipped the men whom he called, he still equips his followers of today. He strenghtens us through his word and sacrament. He shapes us through trials and adversity. (4) Finally, as the calling of these disciples was now to be full-time and unconditional, so our calling is similar. There are no part time Christians.

vv. 21,22 — *Going on from there, he saw two other brothers, James son of Zebedee and his brother John. They were in a boat with their father Zebedee, preparing their nets. Jesus called them, and immediately they left the boat and their father and followed him.*

The calling of James and John is very similar to the calling of Peter and Andrew. There are only small differences. Whereas Peter and Andrew appear to have been fishing, James and John were tending their nets together with their father. After fishing it was necessary to clean and, if necessary, mend the nets so they would be ready for the next day's work.

Notice the reaction to the Savior's call. *Immediately* all four of the men responded to the call positively. They left their work and families behind to follow Jesus. No one dare think that these men did not love their families because they responded as they did. Rather, this response shows how much more they loved their Savior (Mt 10:37). Oh, that each of us might be so quick to respond when the Lord asks us to do something for him!

v. 23 — *Jesus went throughout Galilee, teaching in their synagogues, preaching the good news of the kingdom, and healing every disease and sickness among the people.*

With this final verse Matthew sums up Jesus' activity in Galilee. There would be three such tours of Galilee. The first is summarized in this verse. Notice the balance that is struck between ministering to spiritual needs and ministering to physical needs. Matthew would seem to emphasize Jesus' teaching and preaching, yet this was not to the exclusion of healing the sick. It was characteristic of Jesus to first minister to the soul, but not ignore the needs of the body (Mt 8:5-13; 9:1-8; 15:21-28).

Homiletical Suggestions

This text, or portions thereof, finds its way into several pericopes. With but a single exception these words of Matthew are assigned to the Epiphany season, and with good reason. The keynote of Epiphany is the revelation of Jesus Christ as the Son of God. At Jesus' baptism (Epiphany 1) God the Father revealed his Son. Following that, John the Baptist proclaimed him to be "the Lamb of God who takes away the sin of the world." The gospel for Epiphany 2 not only records that revelation, but also Andrew and John's reaction to it. In this text Matthew makes a similar proclamation by showing Jesus to be the fulfillment of Isaiah's messianic prophecy. Again we have the reaction of men to Jesus, the Messiah. Four men reacted by following Jesus when he issued his call.

This text contains many important truths about discipleship for believers of all times. Applications can easily be made. But rather than seeing here a set of rules for being Jesus' follower, the preacher will do well to focus on the joyful privileges and comforting promises that accompany discipleship. This should be the underlying tone for the sermon. Basic outlines for this text might include the following:

"Come, Follow Me!"

1. A call extended by the Savior (vv. 12-19,23)
2. A call heeded by believers (vv. 20-22)

Noting that two grammatical imperatives are found in this text (vv. 17,19), the following outline suggests itself:

Imperatives for discipleship

1. Recognize your Savior (vv. 12-16)
2. Repent of your sins (v. 17)
3. Follow that Savior (vv. 18-23)

This text also lends itself well to "recruitment" preaching. The following outline is suggested for vv. 17-22:

Wanted: Fishermen for God's Kingdom

1. Filling a position he has established (vv. 18-22)
2. Using the equipment he has provided (v. 17)

To serve the mission emphasis of the Epiphany season the preacher can try:

A Pattern for Mission Work

1. The place (vv. 12-16)
2. The message (v. 17)
3. The messengers (vv. 18-23)

FOURTH SUNDAY AFTER EPIPHANY

The Scriptures

Old Testament — *Micah 6:1-8*
Epistle — *1 Corinthians 1:26-31*
Gospel — *Matthew 5:1-12*

The Text — Matthew 5:1-12

Before we hear our Lord addressing our Christian life in the Beatitudes, the Old Testament Scriptures remind us of Israel's failure to conform to the will of their Lord. Micah utters the Lord's accusations, then expresses the Lord's desire that his people "act justly, love mercy and walk humbly with your God." In the Epistle Paul reminds us that our election and also our current sanctification have all come because of Christ. If we boast, therefore, we are to "boast in the Lord." Our standing as Christians is obviously not because of who we are or what we have done, but our election in Christ will determine how we now think and what we now do. In our text, Jesus addresses our attitudes and actions as his disciples.

vv. 1,2 — *Now when he saw the crowds, he went up on a mountainside and sat down. His disciples came to him, and he began to teach them, saying:*

The Sermon on the Mount was certainly a highpoint in Jesus' ministry. It occurred at a time when his twelve apostles were already selected, at a time when crowds were coming to be healed, to be amazed by his miracles. Seeking solitude for prayer, Jesus' used a more remote place to offer instruction to his followers, to explain how his law was to guide their lives.

v. 3 — *"Blessed are the poor in spirit, for theirs is the kingdom of heaven."*

"Blessed . . . blessed . . . blessed." Over and over our Lord will emphasize the benefits of this life of faith which he is describing. Our world would disagree, but Jesus pronounces his favorable judgment on the people he will describe. Isn't an overriding theme of Epiphany Jesus' revelation that what the world thinks of him (and his followers) is not what he and we really are?

Would unbelievers want to be "poor," even if they realized that Jesus isn't speaking of their possessions but of their spirit? Pride and self-assertiveness are evident all around us, but Jesus pronounces the poor in spirit blessed. Look at the Pharisee and the tax collector (Lk 18:9-14). The Pharisee was confident of his spiritual status. The tax collector was "poor in spirit," acknowledging his helplessness, begging for God's mercy. Who was blessed? The *tax collector* "went home justified before God."

Who would be willing to listen as Jesus offered his forgiveness? Not the "healthy," the self-righteous; but the "sick, sinners" (Mt 9:12,13). Isaiah had prophesied: "The Lord says . . . : 'This is the one I esteem: he who is humble and contrite in spirit, and trembles at my word' " (Is 66:2). Isaiah prophesied (61:1) and Jesus applied the prophecy to himself (Mt 11:5), "The Lord has anointed me to preach the good news to the poor . . . to bind up the brokenhearted."

How are the "poor in spirit" blessed? "Theirs is the kingdom of heaven." While heaven is our eternal home, the Lord tells us these blessings of heaven are already ours today. Through the gift of faith, God already gives the poor in spirit his blessings of forgiveness, eternal life with Christ.

Once we are blessed with Christ, do we become proud, "rich in spirit," self-sufficient? Read Romans 7:18,19,24.

v. 4 — *"Blessed are those who mourn, for they will be comforted."*

Why would Jesus' disciples be sad, grieve, mourn? Our worldly troubles will cause grief, but such hardships are to be expected, as Paul pointed out to the beleaguered believers in Lystra, Iconium and Antioch: "We must go through many hardships to enter the kingdom of God" (Ac 14:22). The life of the believer will not be all roses and no thorns.

What causes us Christians to "mourn"? Separation from our Lord's blessings, the separation we see because of our sins. This mourning is closely tied to the attitude of being "poor in spirit." We grieve as we see our sins. But this is a blessing, for our sorrow and grief over our sins is removed by our Lord's forgiveness. Whoever "mourns" thus "will be comforted," the passive making clear that this comfort is brought to us by our Lord.

"Will be comforted" could turn our eyes ahead to heaven where God "will wipe every tear from their eyes," where "there will be no more death or mourning or crying or pain" (Re 21:4). But why wait so long? Christ's comforting forgiveness comes as soon as he says to us who sorrow over our sins: "Take heart, son; your sins are forgiven" (Mt 9:2). Why look only into eternity? See 2 Corinthians 1:3-5.

v. 5 — *"Blessed are the meek, for they will inherit the earth."*

Quoting Psalm 37:11, our Lord urges meekness, the quality he exhibited so magnificently on the cross where, "when they hurled their insults at him, he did not retaliate; when he suffered, he made no threats. Instead, he entrusted himself to him who judges justly (1 Pe 2:23). In meekness, Jesus' disciples show patience and gentleness even toward people who are inflicting abuse. Rather than threatening revenge, they will offer forgiveness, allowing God to carry out his will on the wicked.

When they explain God's truths to a questioner, they will do so in a spirit of humility, "with gentleness and respect" (1 Pe 3:15), praying that their listener will also come to have Christ's sure hope of heaven, never looking down their noses as if they were somehow superior to this uninformed unbeliever. When they need to correct a sinning brother, they will "restore him gently" (Ga 6:1), realizing they too could fall into such a sin.

In their meekness they will be blessed with "the earth" as their inheritance. Some look ahead into eternity, pointing to the "new heaven and new earth" which God will give us as "the home of righteousness" (2 Pe 3:13). But why look only into eternity? The "new land" of Canaan which the Lord kept promising his peole was not only a picture of our final heavenly home but also a place where God provided his people's needs in this world. As the meekness of Christ is exhibited in our lives, isn't our Lord going to meet our earthly needs? And won't his provisions be gifts, not something we receive as wages but something we inherit as adopted sons of God? Later in Psalm 37 David declared: "I was young and now I am old, yet I have never seen the righteous forsaken or their children begging bread" (v. 25). Yes, our Lord will fill our needs, just as Jesus was providing for his disciples.

v. 6 — *"Blessed are those who hunger and thirst for righteousness, for they will be filled."*

As the body daily desires food and drink, so the Lord's disciples daily desire righteousness, the declared "righteousness from God" that "comes through faith in Jesus Christ to all who believe" (Ro 3:22).

But the Lord's disciple does more than just sit back satisfied that Christ has redeemed him from sin. The sanctified disciple now strives to offer his Lord loving obedience. Declared righteous through faith, we will desire to follow Christ in all our actions as well as our attitudes, not seeking some sort of work-righteous reward but trying to glorify God through our faithfulness to his will as it is expressed in his Word. The Lord will fill our desires, will answer our prayers for obedience. See Galatians 2:16,20; John 15:5,8; Ephesians 2:8-10.

v. 7 — *"Blessed are the merciful, for they will be shown mercy."*

Does anyone need assistance, spiritual or temporal? Our Lord's followers will show them mercy, putting a priority on assistance to fellow believers (Ga 6:10), but never excluding even their enemies. Jesus' example of the Good Samaritan pictures a man of mercy (Lk 10:30-37). John and James make it clear that our mercy is also to be translated from an attitude into action (1 Jn 3:17,18 and Ja 2:15,16).

And not only does the Lord display mercy through us. He promises to show mercy *to* us. Will our struggling with the effects of sin in our world ever go unnoticed? Will our Lord ever look the other way, refusing to help? Listen to his promise: "They will be shown mercy."

v. 8 — *"Blessed are the pure in heart, for they will see God."*

Hypocritical acts of civic righteousness may fool the world, but they will not fool God. Our Lord points to the purity, the single-mindedness, of the disciple's heart as it aspires only to glorify God by walking in his will. David defines "pure of heart" for us as he answers the question, "Who may ascend the hill of the Lord? Who may stand in his holy place? He who has clean hands and a pure heart, who does not lift up his soul to an idol or swear by what is false" (Ps 24:3,4). This purity of heart only God can bring about, as we ask him to do each Sunday: "Create in me a clean heart, O God."

When shall such devoted disciples see God? We may speak of seeing God through the eyes of faith or seeing God in his word today. The more singularly devoted we are to our Lord, the better we will understand him or "see" him. But John points us to a future face-to-face encounter: "Dear friends, now we are children of God, and what we will be has not yet been made known. But we know that when he appears, we shall be like him, for we shall see him as he appears, we shall be like him, for we shall see him as he is" (1 Jn 3:2).

v. 9 — *"Blessed are the peacemakers, for they will be called sons of God."*

If Jesus is the "Prince of Peace" (Is 9:6), his followers will also be peaceful people. Not only are they at peace with God, but they will "make every effort to keep the unity of the Spirit through the bond of peace" (Eph 4:3), and will also "make every effort to live in peace with all men" (He 12:14). Rather than the "eye for eye, tooth for tooth" attitude of our world, our Lord's disciples will promote peace by serving rather than demanding to be served, by seeking the welfare of their neighbor rather than acting only on their behalf. See Romans 12:16-18.

The Lord will acknowledge such disciples as his own children: "They will be called sons of God." His Son will say, "Come, you who are blessed by my Father; take your inheritance. . . . " (Mt 25:34).

Also, the similarities between father and son will be recognized as Jesus' disciples not only *are* but *are recognized* as sons of God. Our efforts to promote peace among all people with whom we are associated will cause others to realize we are being led by Christ. As our Epiphany Lord revealed himself by his words and actions, so we followers of the Lord will be revealing ourselves as Christians by our peacemaking attitudes and actions.

v. 10 — *"Blessed are those who are persecuted because of righteousness, for theirs is the kingdom of heaven."*

Notice that the Lord doesn't promise peace in this world for his disciples even as they strive to "make peace." Quite the opposite. Opposition, even persecution, may be anticipated from a sinful world whose sinfulness will be more strikingly evident when set side-by-side with a disciple's life of faithfulness. But as evil consciences react in angry opposition, Jesus' believers will be blessed.

Peter points out a key element in this verse as he write about the blessedness of being persecuted for Christian activity, as opposed to suffering for something outside our Lord's will (1 Pe 4:12-16).

The blessing "theirs is the kingdom of heaven," the same as in verse 3, neatly ties Jesus' description of his followers into one package. Pointing to persecution, Jesus might have asked what was the worst anyone could do to a Christian. They could crucify him, as they did Jesus; they could put him to death, as they did Stephen and James. What would happen then? As Paul beautifully spoke of impending death, then the believer would "be with Christ, which is better by far" (Php 1:23). For those faithful to the Lord, even death at the hand of the world would be a blessing.

v. 11,12 — *"Blessed are you when people insult you, persecute you and falsely say all kinds of evil against you because of me. Rejoice and be glad, because great is your reward in heaven, for in the same way they persecuted the prophets who were before you."*

From a general description of his followers' lives, Jesus appears to offer a more specific application to his apostles sitting at his feet. In advance, he advises them not to worry when worldly men insult them as they insulted Christ while he was hanging on the cross. Let the disciples learn to ignore the lies spoken against them by a wicked world which labeled Jesus a "devil" as he was exorcising a demon.

Persecution would become a reason for rejoicing. As they were with Christ in this world, they could look forward to being with Christ in the world to come. Wasn't this always a reason to rejoice?

Suffering, even death, because I'm a Christian today can't compare with the "reward" we Christians will receive in heaven. This "reward" is of course a reward of God's grace, not anything we have earned in any way. Like all the other blessings which Jesus has mentioned, it will be purely a gift of God. This "reward" is not the salvation Christ has won for us before we were brought to believe, but the reward of glory he has promised his faithful followers.

Could the Lord's apostles suffer persecution without falling from faith? Jesus points them to the prophets as examples of disciples who had endured even death because they were faithfully speaking the words of their Lord. It was possible. Now, we can also look at Peter and John who, when they were flogged by the Sanhedrin for proclaiming Jesus Christ, were "rejoicing because they had been counted worthy of suffering disgrace for the Name" of their Lord Jesus (Ac 5:41). Is it possible for us to endure persecution, insults, all types of evil because we are Christians? Our Lord will make us able to endure.

Homiletical Suggestions

A constant theme during Epiphany is Jesus revealing himself as more than mere man. Often he does this by means of his miracles, controlling nature as only God can. On other occasions he reveals his godliness by speaking words of wisdom man could never have imagined. Our text is an example of truths only God could speak. Man would see no blessing in mourning and meekness, in a peacemaker being persecuted. Only God could teach us why we can rejoice in the situations we will encounter because of our relationship with Christ. Only God could point us to the blessings which are assured to his suffering followers.

As we hear Jesus describing his followers' lives, we are also able to see how he will be revealed in the attitudes and actions of his followers. The unusual approach which disciples take to the problems of life may well prepare an observer to ask about their motivation, allowing an opportunity to testify for our Savior with words as well as works. Paul and Silas, for example, prepared the jailer at Philippi to question their source of joy when they were singing hymns of praise to the Lord in prison.

Or we may consider the way our Lord reveals himself to us again and again by bringing blessed results out of less than desirable situations. Our particular approach may well be determined by our hearers: Will we be speaking mainly to lifelong believers or will we be revealing the Lord Jesus to prospects who are not familiar with the sorrows and joys of discipleship?

Due to the length and depth of this text, it might be better to preach a series of eight sermons on the Beatitudes. When trying to tackle the whole package in twenty minutes, you will need to watch against being superficial.

It has been said that Jesus himself is the perfect exemplar of the persons describes in the Beatitudes. An analytical treatment of the text with that in mind would be:

Jesus' Disciples Imitate Him

1. In his attitude toward God (vv. 3-6)
2. In his actions toward people (vv. 7-9)
3. In his reactions toward opponents (vv. 10-12)

Keying on the word "blessed," one could use:

Happy Is the Person . . .

1. Who looks to Christ for salvation (vv. 3-6)
2. Whose life imitates Jesus (vv. 7-9)
3. Who suffers for the Savior's sake (vv. 10-12)

A synthetic outline, drawing on various thoughts of the text and incorporating some of the ideas in the other two outlines:

Jesus' Teaching on True Happiness

1. It contradicts the world's view of things
2. It is demonstrated in Jesus' ministry
3. It challenges us to live our faith

Another synthetic outline:

The Beatitudes Are . . .

1. Statements of fact
2. Promises of blessing
3. Invitations to joy

FIFTH SUNDAY AFTER EPIPHANY

The Scriptures

Old Testament — *Isaiah 58:5-9*
Epistle — *1 Corinthians 2:1-5*
Gospel — *Matthew 5:13-20*

The Text — Matthew 5:13-20

v. 13 — *"You are the salt of the earth. But if the salt loses its saltiness, how can it be made salty again? It is no longer good for anything, except to be thrown out and trampled by men."*

"You are the salt of the earth." The statement is very familiar and clear to the reader, but potentially confusing to the exegete. The question is, "How can salt not be salt?" Some have gone to great lengths to explain how salt can become "unsalty." It is pointed out that the salt of Jesus' day came in a very impure form; if it would become moist or wet the chemical compound NaCl could be washed out, leaving only a pile of sand. The remaining slag would be good for nothing but building roads. The interpretation will have to remain simple and go no further than the words and sense intend.

The statement about the salt will cause little trouble, however, if it is remembered that this is a conditional phrase. All we really have is a hypothetical question, "What if . . . ?" "Just supposing . . . ." In figurative writing the similarity between the likeness and the reality must never be pressed too far. The point of comparison is the value of salt. Salt is good for something as long as it is salt. If the substance in hand is not salt it cannot be used to flavor or preserve food. The similar truth is that Christians have a purpose in this world. That purpose is to preserve and season the people of this world by means of the gospel. If one does not do this he is not fulfilling his purpose and in fact is most likely not a Christian at all.

While two uses of salt can be presented, preservation and cleansing on the one hand and seasoning on the other, it would seem to be easier and more effective to stress the first. Salt was used to counteract decay. In his commentary on the Sermon on the Mount Luther has an excellent description of the action of believers as they carry out this function. By means of the law they are to convict the world of sin. This activity will sting and will not always be appreciated but it must be done. If this is not done it will not be possible to season with the gospel of salvation. Jesus promises his disciples elsewhere that the Holy Spirit will help them to carry out this ministry (Mt 10:19,20; Jn 16:8).

It is good to notice the present statement of fact that the Savior uses in comparing his followers with salt and with light. He does not say, "You will be (or may be, or ought to be) the salt/light of the world" but rather, "You *are* the salt/light." It is the very nature of the Christian to speak and live for his Savior. The apostles declared, "We cannot help speaking about what we have seen and heard" (Ac 4:20).

vv. 14-16 — *"You are the light of the world. A city on a hill cannot be hidden. Neither do people light a lamp and put it under a bowl. Instead they put it on its stand, and it gives light to everyone in the house. In the same way, let your light shine before men, that they may see your good deeds and praise your Father in heaven."*

What is said about salt applies also to the figure of a light. The purpose of light is to shine so that eyes may see. How ridiculous it would be to light a candle — or today, to throw on a light switch —and then immediately to cover it up with a bowl or, more true to the original Greek, a peck measure. Wisdom would dictate not lighting the candle if one did not want to see. The same common sense applies to a city on a hill. Even if the city has only one light in it, people for miles around will be able to see it. The Christian is told by the Savior "up front" that he will be noticed by the world, but he will not always be appreciated. His visibility will force him to carry crosses now and then (Mt 5:11,12; 16:24).

The life and work of the Christian are not totally dreary, however. His is actually the very rewarding work of bringing praise to God by his words and actions. What that activity is all about will have to be "imported" from elsewhere in the Bible since this is a "law" text. There are many, many passages in the Bible which use the idea of light. Psalm 119:105 comes to mind immediately, "Your word is a lamp to my feet and a light for my path." The word of God is light because it presents the Lord of life and light, Jesus Christ. Of him John says, "In him was life, and the life was the light of men" (Jn 1:4). Jesus says of himself, "I am the light of the world" (Jn 8:12). It is the great privilege of the believer to reflect the glorious, saving light of his Lord. God has actually placed his people on a pedestal, not only to honor and bless them but to have them display his glory to all people.

vv. 17,18 — *"Do not think that I have come to abolish the Law or the Prophets; I have not come to abolish them but to fulfill them. I tell you the truth, until heaven and earth disappear, not the smallest letter, not the least stroke of a pen, will by any means disappear from the Law until everything is accomplished."*

Having told his disciples to stand as witnesses before the world Jesus tells them next to display his righteousness. Jesus' holiness is from the true God, the God who has made himself and his will known in the Law and Prophets. The terms "Law and Prophets" or "Moses and the Prophets" are common references to the Old Testament of the Bible (Ac 13:15; Lk 16:29,31; Jn 1:45). Jesus states that he has no intention of setting aside God's commands in order to follow human rules and desires as the religious leaders of the day are in the habit of doing. He will follow the word of God to the letter. It wasn't so long ago that Jesus was being portrayed as the greatest rebel of all time. His statement here puts the lie to that claim. Jesus hadn't even come to change or ignore the Old Testament. He had come to observe it scrupulously.

Here a word needs to be said about a passage which apparently contradicts Jesus' statement. That passage is Romans 10:4, "Christ is the end of the law so that there may be righteousness for everyone who believes." These two passages are not at odds if we remember the distinction between law and gospel. The passage before us is a preachment of the law. Neither the Father nor the Son will set aside any command of God. Every single one must be kept. Jesus had to keep every law of God perfectly to become our holy and innocent Savior. The Romans passage is a statement of the gospel. It tells us the good news that the curse of the law hanging over us has been removed from us because Jesus has been righteous in our place.

Jesus' statement, "to fulfill them," is understood or pictured in various ways. One man likens all the Old Testament ceremonial and moral laws to jars waiting to be filled by the Messiah. He would do this by keeping each prediction about his ministry. This view has merit when we think of passages like John 5:39, "These are the Scriptures that testify about me." It also fits when we think of the many times we hear in the Gospels that what was said through a prophet was fulfilled (cf. Mt 2:17; 12:17; Jn 19:28).

Close to this interpretation is the one that Jesus would fulfill the demands of the Law in our place with his own righteousness. This view receives great support from such passages as Jeremiah 23:6, "The Lord Our Righteousness," and Matthew 3:15, "It is proper for us to do this to fulfill all righteousness."

A third idea understands the word "fulfill" as seconding or reaffirming the Law of God. Jesus will not treat God's Law in a haphazard way as the Pharisees do. His observance will not be pick-and-choose but absolute. Indeed, Jesus treats the Law absolutely in this Sermon on the Mount. By his teaching Jesus sets the Law of God in bold relief and shows how far its true meaning extends.

Jesus shows his seriousness for the Law and Prophets with the statement of verse 18. The *KJV*'s "jot or tittle" have become the more literal and more understandable "smallest letter" and "least stroke of a pen" in the *NIV*. The smallest Hebrew letter is the *yod* which is similar to our "y." One man counted 66,420 *yods* in the Old Testament. The smallest pen stroke is only a part of a letter like the hook which changes our capital O to a Q. Beck translates, "Not an 'i' or the dot of an 'i.' "

This statement must be understood as intended. Textual research shows that various letters have been added to and subtracted from the original manuscripts through the copying process. Literally speaking some *yods* may have disappeared. If God would have wanted every single original pen stroke kept he would have seen to it that there would be absolutely no variants. What Jesus says is that the demand of the Law that man lead a righteous life will never be revoked. Man speaks of "little white lies" and feels his life is "not that bad" because he has "tried" to please God. Scripture allows no exceptions to perfection. Just one infraction is all it takes to render a person a sinner (Ja 2:10). Former goodness is of no avail to the present sinner (Ez 3:20). God demands absolute perfection (Mt 5:48).

This is the demand or word or will of God which will never pass away (1 Pe 1:25). Everyone can count on this. Jesus says, "I tell you the truth." The original for this is a transliteration of the Hebrew word for asseveration. The English transliteration of the same word is our familiar "Amen". It is good to note that Jesus makes this oath-like promise on his own authority. The prophets say, "This is what the Lord says . . . , " and the apostles say, "It is written." But Jesus, as true God, has the right to say, "I tell you the truth."

v. 19 — *"Anyone who breaks one of the least of these commandments and teaches others to do the same will be called least in the kingdom of heaven, but whoever practices and teaches these commands will be called great in the kingdom of heaven."*

The threat to any and all who set aside or break any of God's Law is now given. It should be obvious from Jesus' preceding statement and many other passages of the Bible that he does not consider any commandment more or less important than others. But here Jesus is speaking according to man's understanding and valuation of the commandments. Related to this point is the fact that Jesus joins actions and convictions. He speaks of "breaking and teaching" and "practicing and teaching." Certainly every transgression is a sin but to claim that sin is not disobedience toward God or to lead others to such disobedience is certainly a compounding sin if not an even greater sin.

The bigger question of the verse is the phrase "in the kingdom of heaven." Believers whose sins have been washed away will certainly be in heaven, but will false teachers also be there? We would certainly say not. Then what does "in the kingdom of heaven" mean? The phrase could be understood according to 1 Corinthians 3:10-15. There we are told that the work of some teachers will not survive the fires of the judgments and they themselves will only survive by the seat of their pants. Is that the meaning of this verse? Or could the meaning be that those who are in heaven will look down upon these false teachers? For this interpretation the Greek ἐν could be interpreted instrumentally. We prefer this interpretation. Perhaps the term "kingdom of heaven" refers to the entire New Testament era in which unbelievers and false teachers are both to be found. Or finally, could the phrase include the broadest of the Savior's three kingdoms, his kingdom of power, in which he also rules over Satan and the forces of hell? These last two explanations would have to contend with the use of the same phrase in verse 20 which does not help them. It will again be helpful to remember that this is a conditional sentence. The main teaching is that there is no positive reward for unrepented sin, but that those who grasp the righteousness of Christ will be blessed for eternity.

v. 20 — *"For I tell you that unless your righteousness surpasses that of the Pharisees and the teachers of the law, you will certainly not enter the kingdom of heaven."*

Now Jesus gives the clincher. If anyone has misunderstood his teaching to this point he can't miss it any longer. Jesus says, "If you want to get to heaven by your own merit you will have to be more holy than the 'holy-holies'." This must have caused many hearts to sink. We should not forget that the Pharisees and teachers of the law were extremely holy people, in an outward way. They were, in fact, perhaps the best earthly models of righteousness to which Jesus could point. And even though theirs was an outward, hypocritical holiness, the people could not see this. Perhaps a similar statement now would be, "Unless you are more holy than saintly old Grandma So-and-so, or the Apostle Paul, or Martin Luther, you will not get to heaven."

The point of the verses is to show the people that they could not possibly keep God's law perfectly and so earn heaven. Jesus wants to shatter the *opinio legis* of his hearers, to make them despair of saving themselves, and to make them turn their attention to his saving righteousness.

Homiletical Suggestions

The first thing the preacher must realize is that this is a "law" text. This pericope from Jesus' Sermon on the Mount is his introduction to his commentary on the Ten Commandments, a listing of God's moral law. To find gospel in it would be to pervert it. This should not be a frightening prospect, however. There are many such sections in Scripture. The sweetness of the gospel can be easily brought in from the rest of God's word. The word is replete with statements regarding the righteousness which avails before God (Mt 11:28-30; Ro 1:17; Ga 2:20).

It would also be good to remember the proper place of parable, similes, and other figures of speech. As elsewhere, the figures used here are intended only to excite the reader or hearer's attention and thinking. When this has been done the presentation moves on to explanation and clear teaching. Accordingly, it would be good not to get too bogged down in discussion of the salt and light figures at the expense of the real message of the following verses.

Applications to the present world are many. The church of Luther's day was also ruled by pharisaic hypocrites. There are such people in the church today, and there always will be (Mt 7:15; Jn 10:1). The televangelist scandals of recent memory are a case in point. Beyond the church other pressures attack the will of God in an attempt to break down the moral fiber of the world and these attacks will also affect the church and the Christian. At the present time one of the leading forces of this kind is unbelieving psychology. Too many churches and individuals believe its lie that there is no eternal, divine standard of right and wrong. Perhaps an even more subtle trick of Satan to woo souls today is the lack of persecution in Christian lands. The dominant attitude is that everyone is entitled to his own opinions, no matter how strange others may believe them to be. But the greatest enemy of the soul remains the individual's sinful nature itself. Until this nature is broken the saving gospel can do it no good. The purpose of this law text is to bring the hardened soul to repentance.

An outline showing how the gospel may be brought in could be one such as this. The preacher would have to expand the second part from passages and truths elsewhere in the Bible. This would also add an evangelical touch to the third point.

Living a True Righteousness

1. Righteousness demanded (vv. 18-20)
2. Righteousness fulfilled (v. 17)
3. Righteousness to share (vv. 13-16)

A similar arrangement of the verses but stressing the Epiphany concept of light and missions could be this.

Saving Light for the World

1. The need for light (vv. 18-20)
2. The Light himself (v. 17)
3. The light bearers (vv. 13-16)

A straightforward presentation of the verses which again emphasizes the Epiphany season's call to do mission work for Christ could follow along these lines.

The Christian Called to Work

1. The need (vv. 18-20)
2. The message (v. 17)
3. The assignment (vv. 13-16)

SIXTH SUNDAY AFTER EPIPHANY

The Scriptures

Old Testament — *Deuteronomy 30:15-20*
Epistle — *1 Corinthians 2:6-13*
Gospel — *Matthew 5:20-37*

The Text — Matthew 5:20-37

This text is another portion of the Sermon on the Mount and it continues Jesus' address to his disciples before that large multitude of listeners. In it Jesus is attempting to bring home a tremendously important point to his followers both then and now. It is stated clearly in the words of the first verse of the text.

v. 20 — *"I tell you that unless your righteousness surpasses that of the Pharisees and the teachers of the law, you will certainly not enter the kingdom of heaven."*

In order fully to understand this text one needs to take verses 17—19 into consideration. See also the text study for the Fifth Sunday after Epiphany. In these verses the Lord Jesus is speaking in direct opposition to the accepted religious assumptions of his day. Almost everyone in Jesus' day was under the impression that the most "religious" and "righteous" people around were the teachers of the law and Pharisees. Most certainly the teachers of the law and the Pharisees held that assumption about themselves. Both groups believed that they were doing everything that was necessary for their salvation. They were fulfilling all that God demanded, wanted or asked of his people. This belief, of course, was totally false and the following words of Jesus' sermon intended to make that perfectly clear. Jesus' intention was to draw a crystal clear picture of the contrast between the false and purely outward righteousness of the teachers of the law and the Pharisees (which was not a righteousness at all) and the true righteousness with which God is pleased.

According to the context "righteousness," as used here, is a reference to the righteousness of life. Jesus' intention is to draw a sharp comparison between the "righteousness" of the teachers of the law and Pharisees and the true righteousness which pleases God. The "righteousness" of the scribes and Pharisees was merely one of show and pretense.

In the previous verses Jesus had spoken of the fulfilling of the law, the teaching and keeping of God's commands. Now he intends to show how the fulfilling of the law, the keeping of God's rules, must even exceed that of the Pharisees and the teachers of the Law if one wants to gain God's acceptance. The Scribes and Pharisees failed to realize that the righteousness which God wanted meant that one's heart was to be right with God, not just the outward actions. This righteousness is one that is God-given, not man-achieved. That was a lesson that all needed to learn and know and that is what Jesus was here to teach.

That this "righteousness of life" is the result of the "righteousness of faith" is understood. It is a righteousness which shows itself, which comes alive and acts, only as a result of the faith in one's heart. Such a righteousness means that the heart, not only the outward action, is right with God. After he has made his point, Jesus moves on with several examples which will prove it, which will show clearly that superficial understanding and mere outward observance are not enough.

vv. 21,22 — *"You have heard that it was said to the people long ago, 'Do not murder, and anyone who murders will be subject to judgment.' But I tell you that anyone who is angry with his brother will be subject to judgment. Again, anyone who says to his brother 'Raca', is answerable to the Sanhedrin. But anyone who says, 'You fool!' will be in danger of the fire of hell."*

Jesus begins this section of his sermon with a phrase that will be used for the rest of this chapter and into the next. Note carefully the parallel words: "You have heard . . . but I tell you." This special form is used again in verses 28,32,34,39 and 44. Jesus has an important purpose to accomplish with his carefully chosen words. He is pointing out that there is an assumption being made about God's law. It is an assumption held by the people, but certainly fully believed by the teachers of the law and the Pharisees. The assumption deals with the keeping of the law, the fulfilling of God's demands. This assumption was the one that the disciples had often heard from these very teachers and Pharisees. It was the accepted teaching of the time. But now, Jesus was going to fill them in on the truth, God's truth, which was far different from the accepted thought of the people and the scribes and Pharisees. In order to do this Jesus points out the contrasts in several commandments between the accepted teaching ("you have heard") and the truth ("but I tell you"). He first uses the Fifth Commandment.

Jesus reminds the people of the commonly accepted thought that only taking the physical life of another human being was sin. As long as one did not "murder" he had kept the commandment. This was the accepted idea because this is what the people had always heard from the teachers of the law and the Pharisees. But there was so much the people had not heard which Jesus was now going to say. This revealed truth from the Son of God himself would be far different from the commonly accepted thought of the time.

Jesus takes up the matter of sin in the heart. A feeling of hatred is, in God's eyes, just as evil and sinful as if the deed itself has taken place, as if the thought were really put into action, as if a murder actually has been committed See 1 Jn 3:15 for additional proof. Jesus includes not just the hateful thought but also the spiteful word and disdainful sneer. Three sins commonly committed, three sins normally not seen as murder, but three sins which deserve punishment equal to murder, according to God. And avoiding those sins was equally demanded by God for righteousness.

vv. 23,24 — *"Therefore, if you are offering your gift at the altar and there remember that your brother has something against you leave your gift there in front of the altar. First go and be reconciled to your brother; then come and offer your gift."*

Jesus turns from the general principle to a specific practical example of the truth. The word "therefore" indicates that these words now follow directly from what has just been said. Under no circumstances is it ever even permitted to harbor anger in one's heart. The heart must at all times be filled with love for one's brother, never with anger or hatred. A man is pictured coming to worship. His intention is to enter into close personal fellowship with his God. But as he approaches God's altar he remembers that there is one who has been offended, who has been wronged. The offense was something real. The sin was there on his part. While the man is still burdened with his guilt, he cannot worship in spirit and in truth. The sin must be repented of and be forgiven. The time for the reconciliation must always be right now, not later when it is more convenient or easy. *Now* is the time to settle matters, even before you worship. Tomorrow may be too late. You must go to your brother and ask for his pardon. Only after that, after you have become reconciled can you truly approach God in worship.

vv. 25,26 — *"Settle matters quickly with your adversary who is taking you to court. Do it while you are still with him on the way, or he may hand you over to the judge and the judge may hand you over to the officer, and you may be thrown into prison. I tell you the truth, you will not get out until you have paid the last penny."*

Jesus is still dealing with the matter of sins of the heart. Here the man has not gone to settle matters and be reconciled with his brother. He has not gone to confess and to receive pardon. The offended brother now intends to take the matter to court. The offense was sufficient to warrant a court case and the trial date has been set. Jesus' advice is to settle matters now as quickly as possible before it becomes too late to settle anything. He says, "Settle matters while you both still can settle, because there are severe consequences if things are *not* settled."

If a man refuses to apologize for some wrong that he has committed against one of his brothers and continues in that impenitence throughout his life, and then dies, he cannot expect salvation. He shall be lost and will "be thrown into [the] prison" of hell, where he "will not get out until [he has] paid the last penny." The punishment of hell is eternal. There is no possibility for the sinner ever to be able to pay his way out of hell, for Scripture knows of no such way.

We are to do all in our power to reconcile with any brother. If he refuses to accept our attempts, if he refuses to hear our apology and accept it, then the burden falls fully upon him.

vv. 27-30 — *"You have heard that it was said, 'Do not commit adultery.' But I tell you that anyone who looks at a woman lustfully has already committed adultery with her in his heart. If your right eye causes you to sin, gouge it out and throw it away. It is better for you to lose one part of your body than for your whole body to be thrown into hell. And if your right hand causes you to sin, cut it off and throw it away. It is better for you to lose one part of your body than for your whole body to go into hell."*

Jesus continues to teach about sins of the heart and turns from the Fifth Commandment to the Sixth. Note again, "You have heard . . . but I say to you." Again the accepted idea of the people was that the sin of adultery was limited only to the act itself. All agreed that this sexual sin is wrong. But Jesus wished to clearly point out that it is not just the outward act alone that is sinful. There is more to the sin of adultery than illegitimate sexual intercourse outside of marriage. Just as hatred in the heart or bitterness in one's words equals murder, so lust in the heart and eye is equal to adultery. Merely looking at a woman is not sinful, but looking at her with impure thought and sexual desire is equal to adultery. See 1 John 2: 15 and 2 Peter 2:14.

Jesus, using figurative language, drives home the point he is making. Nothing, even a hand or an eye, should ever be allowed to rob a person of eternity, if it becomes a cause for sin. Sins of the heart are to be avoided at all costs. If going so far as to pluck out one's eye or chop off one's hand would actually help one avoid a sin of the heart, it would be better to do that than to allow the sin to become rampant and cause a person to end up being lost in hell. With that strong language Jesus is trying to have us see the immensely powerful influences and consequences of the sins of the heart. They are destructive. They, all by themselves, could cost one his salvation even if they were never put into action. Jesus is urging people, believers, to see the destructive power of inner sins and do all to cast them out of the heart. See Colossians 3:5; Galatians 5:24; Matthew 18:7-9. A Christian will see every sin, whether one committed out in the open or one held secret in the heart, as a bringer of death. Avoid it as if your life depended on it, for it might.

vv. 31,32 — *"It has been said, 'Anyone who divorces his wife must give her a certificate of divorce.' But I tell you that anyone who divorces his wife, except for marital unfaithfulness, causes her to become an adulteress, and anyone who marries a woman so divorced commits adultery."*

Jesus gives some additional thoughts on the Sixth Commandment involving marriage itself. Again he uses the parallel, "It was said . . . but I say to you." The problem of his day was that the Pharisees and the teachers of the law had a very casual approach to marriage and divorce. Marriage was entered into easily and ended just as easily. It was the common practice merely to draw up a "certificate of divorce" and end the marriage. Oh, yes, the Pharisees had a word of Scripture to back them up. Moses had allowed this practice in the wilderness (Dt 24:1).

"But I tell you," Jesus says, "that anyone who divorces his wife, except for marital unfaithfulness, causes her to become an adultress, and anyone who marries a woman so divorced commits adultery."

Jesus here is listing one legitimate cause for divorce, fornication. Simply writing out a paper saying that one no longer wants his or her spouse does not end a marriage in God's eyes. But unfaithfulness does. If a wife or a husband has sexual intercourse with another outside of marriage, that act severs the bond of trust which made the marriage in the first place. In that case a divorce is allowed for the innocent party.

But if, on the other hand, a husband simply pushes his wife out of the marriage because she no longer pleases him he puts her in the position of one who has "suffered adultery" or "is put in the position of an adulteress." NIV's "become an adulteress"does not reflect the passive μοιχευθῆναι.

The husband is also sinning against any future husband the woman may have, by putting him in the position of an adulterer: "Anyone who marries a woman so divorced commits adultery," for in God's eyes the woman is still married to her first husband.

Jesus is calling upon the erring husband to repent of his sin and return to his wife. If he refuses, then the woman is free to marry and there is no adultery, either on her part or that of a second husband. See also Matthew 19:1-11; Mark 10:1-12; Luke 16:18.

vv. 33-37 — *"Again, you have heard that it was said to the people long ago, 'Do not break your oath, but keep the oaths you have made to the Lord.' But I tell you, Do not swear at all: either by heaven, for it is God's throne; or by the earth, for it is his footstool; or by Jerusalem, for it is the city of the Great King. And do not swear by your head, for you cannot make even one hair white or black. Simply let your 'Yes' be 'Yes,' and your 'No,' 'No'; anything beyond this comes from the evil one."*

Jesus continues his examples with the Second Commandment, dealing with swearing. Again he draws the sharp contrast between the accepted thought of the people and the truth of God's word: "Again, you have heard . . . but I tell you." He again quotes an Old Testament passage, Leviticus 12:12, which had been misunderstood by the people due to a misteaching by the Pharisees and teachers of the law. They felt that breaking an oath made in God's name was wrong, but if it were not made in God's name then breaking that oath was not as serious, and perhaps was not even wrong.

Jesus points out that all swearing is actually taking an oath in God's name (vv. 34-36). The distinction which the teachers of the law made, between genuine oaths and false oaths, was a false distinction, a device employed to justify dishonesty. Such people could deceive their fellowman; they could not evade the force of God's command: "Do not break your oath."

Why does God's law provide for oath-taking and regulate it? The reason lies in man's sinful heart. The sinner needs to be reminded that he is responsible to God for what comes out of his mouth.

"Do not swear at all." Jesus' word to his disciples is that in their dealings with others there are to be no oaths. They are to be so truthful that fellow Christians, and other people, can trust their every word. Then there is no need or place for calling on God to witness. The source of anything beyond the simple "Yes" and "No" is that evil one who is the father of all dishonesty.

Does Jesus forbid his disciples to make an oath in legal or civil matters? In a world full of dishonesty, where there are many people who do not acknowledge their accountability to God for what they say, oaths have a place. The Christian willingly submits to this procedure as did Jesus himself before the Sanhedrin (Mt 26:63,64).

In these verses, 33-37, Christ warns against false swearing, needless swearing and swearing in uncertain things. He calls for simple truthfulness in every thought, word and deed.

Homiletical Suggestions

This is a challenging text. It very easily could be broken up into no fewer than six sections, each of which could be developed into a full sermon by itself. There are excellent texts here for any preacher who might want to pick a smaller portion of the text and use it by itself. For example: (1) The clear rejection of work righteousness — (v. 20); (2) the teaching of Christ regarding the sins of the heart and their deadly equivalence to openly sinful deeds (vv. 22 and 28); (3) the question of murder and hateful thoughts and words, and their destructive nature (vv. 21,22); (4) the matter of sin between brothers and the urgent need for reconciliation (vv. 23-26); (5) the lessons on marriage in a modern day society which condones, even promotes easy divorce (vv. 27-32); (6) the seriousness of false, needless and uncertain swearing which is so often thought of as the most minor of transgressions (vv. 33-37).

Smaller texts abound in this larger text. Our goal is to make a unit of this portion of the Sermon on the Mount. As we look at the entire section we see that in verse 20 Jesus states a principle and then gives examples of it in each following section. This text will drive the work-righteous person to the brink of despair. If being as righteous as the Pharisees is not enough, how can anyone ever hope to save himself? But that is exactly the point Jesus wants people to get. *They* can never hope to save themselves with their own righteousness, no matter how great it is. *They* can not even begin to be good enough for God.

Look at all the potential ways of failing which have already become reality. Hatred has become murder, looking has become lust and adultery, boasting and colorful language has become swearing. It is all there in my own life. This text provides an excellent opportunity for the pastor to point out that all those little sins — so often ignored, so seemingly trivial — are in reality death-dealing and as totally destructive as any terrible open sin.

The gospel must be imported into the text. The message of grace through faith, the teaching of Christ's vicarious atonement, the truth of God's gracious forgiveness of my sins because of the doing and dying of the Lord Jesus is *not* to be found expressly written in these verses. But ample opportunity is there to express the precious words of salvation through the comparison of what God demands, what we are unable to do ourselves and what the Lord Jesus has therefore done for us.

The following outlines attempt to treat the entire text in one sermon.

Demands Beyond Our Abilities

1. God demands a perfect righteousness from each of us (v. 20)
2. It is one which is far beyond our ability to achieve (vv. 21-36)
3. In Christ, by faith, he gives us what we can't achieve

The Impossible Made Possible

1. The utter impossibility of our keeping the law of God (vv. 20-36)
   A. When hatred is equal to murder (vv. 21-26)
   B. When lustful looking is equal to adultery (vv. 27-30)
   C. When divorce is not as easy as some like to think (vv. 31,32)
   D. When false swearing is forbidden (vv. 33-36)
2. The blessing we have from God's Son, the Law-keeper for us
   A. He did all that we are unable to do (active obedience)
   B. He paid for all that we should never have done (passive obedience)
   C. He enables us to live in righteousness (sanctification)

SEVENTH SUNDAY AFTER EPIPHANY

The Scriptures

Old Testament — *Leviticus 19:1,2,17,18*
Epistle — *1 Corinthians 3:10,11,16-23*
Gospel — *Matthew 5:38-48*

The Text — Matthew 5:38-48

Beautiful for its clarity, remarkable for its depth, unsurpassed for its readability and study, Jesus' familiar and best-loved Sermon on the Mount (Mt 5-7) directs its hearers and readers to put their faith into action. The Savior's timeless message is concise and clear to all who take the time to hear what he has to say. And certainly, all his many exhortations point the Christian in this one direction — that the Christian life is a life of positive sanctification. That daily we practice what Jesus preaches, never out of fear, but out of love for him and gratitude for all that he has done and still does for us. Coupled with the two other readings for the Seventh Sunday after Epiphany, Jesus calls on us to show the world that "love is the Christian's ID card."

vv. 38,39 — *"You have heard that it was said, 'Eye for eye, and tooth for tooth.' But I tell you, Do not resist an evil person. If someone strikes you on the right cheek, turn to him the other also."*

Seeking revenge, getting back at the other guy, "What about my rights?" Today's cries for "justice" are so similar to those heard back in Jesus' day. But then, they've been a part of this sinful world ever since our first parents transgressed the express will of God. "I won't get mad, I'll just get even!" And although there is basis for such sentiments in the old Mosaic covenant (Ex 21:22-25), God's prescriptions were given to limit the desire for vengeance, to defuse the inclination toward retaliation. After all, vengeance belongs solely to the Lord (Rm 12:19).

The purpose of the Levitical ordinances was for the judges and civil courts to discourage the practice of seeking private revenge. Their judicial guideline was that fair compensation should be granted for injuries received. The Pharisees, however, appealed to these laws to justify personal retribution and revenge, to exact the proverbial "pound of flesh."

In sharp contrast to those Old Testament principles and to the Pharisaical misappropriations of the same, Jesus speaks out in favor of the law of love. There is no place for vengeance in the heart or the life of the Christian. Here he is condemning the spirit of lovelessness, hatred and a yearning for revenge. "Turn the other cheek!" In other words, accept the insults, whether physical or verbal, that people hurl in your direction. Show your adversary by attitude, word and deed that yours is a life of true Christian charity.

Nevertheless, this exhortation does not completely militate against the concept of self-defense. Certainly any law of retaliation must be made consistent with the higher law of love. That is why Kretzmann says, "A disciple of Christ has duties toward his family, his community, his country, which will sometimes compel him to protect and defend them against injustice and insult" (*Popular Commentary of the Bible*, New Testament, Volume 1, p. 30).

v. 40 — *"And if someone wants to sue you and take your tunic, let him have your cloak as well."*

No matter what the age, people have long been concerned about their rights, especially if certain legal rights are involved. Jesus refers to a case with underlying principles at stake. The tunic (χιτών) was the shirt-like inner garment, the cloak (ἱμάτιον) was the warmer outer garment. This cloak had long been considered so indispensable that, when it was taken for a pledge, it had to be returned by sundown (Ex 22:26), since the man would need it as his bed-covering for the night (Dt 24:12,13).

Jesus is saying that our primary concern is not to be directed inward, toward our rights and feelings, as much as it should be directed toward reconciliation with our brother or sister. Roehrs/Franzmann: "Jesus removes the impulse from his disciples' hearts and bids them live, as he himself lives, in a love that recklessly exposes itself to the lovelessness of the world and the need of men" (*Concordia Self-Study Commentary*, New Testament, p. 20). Come what may, we have *no* right to hate the person who tries to deprive us of our rightful possessions.

v. 41 — *"If someone forces you to go one mile, go with him two miles."*

A popular song of recent vintage encouraged the friend of the songwriter to "walk a mile in my shoes." Jesus says don't stop there — offer to go an *extra* mile if you can. Galilee was an occupied country. The Roman soldiers, based there to keep the peace, were permitted to compel the local citizens to carry their baggage or cargo one mile for them. It was only natural for the people to rebel against such servitude, to despise those Romans for "asking."

Jesus counsels us to go beyond mere necessity or just the basic requirements. Even under extreme conditions, he urges a willing spirit that gladly offers and then goes that "extra mile." There is no room for bitterness or annoyance toward the person who forces a burden upon another — take it with a smile. And if not a smile, then at least with an attitude of Christian concern that hopes to make the best of the situation.

v. 42 — *"Give to the one who asks you, and do not turn away from the one who wants to borrow from you."*

Greed and selfishness have no place in the life of a true child of God. Conversely, the Christian should use proper wisdom and common sense as he applies the tenets of brotherly love. Hendricksen advises: "Not only *show* kindness but *love* kindess!" (*New Testament Commentary*: Matthew, p. 311). Yes, when someone in distress or genuine need asks for assistance, be ready to respond. Don't turn a deaf ear and walk the other way. Give not grudgingly or gingerly but generously; lend not selfishly but liberally.

However, to be willing to do everything does not mean that God expects you to do everything. In such a spirit of willingness and generosity, we are not to give away all that we have so that we ourselves become a burden to others. Putting ourselves or our families at risk or in danger is not what Jesus has in mind. Yet, as we do look for ways to help others, we will not allow greed or selfishness to limit what we can do.

v. 43 — *"You have heard that it was said, 'Love your neighbor and hate your enemy.' "*

God's Law had long enjoined his people to love their neighbors (Lv 19:18). But nowhere in all the Old Testament or in any other code for living was there an injunction to "hate your enemy." The Greek ἀγαπάω betokens a filial/brotherly love, a real, honest affection for one another. Such a love seeks the neighbor's good. On the other hand, μισέω is just the opposite — a prejudicial hatred for the other person, an intense dislike and disaffection for him or her or them.

Now apparently, the scribes and Pharisees held to and espoused this love your neighbor/hate your enemy approach to daily life and conduct. We recall how legalism (the attempt to find favor with God and to stand in his judgment by way of works of the law) had raised the question, "*Who is my neighbor*?" (Lk 10:29) The prevailing attitude was that if I love my neighbor, well then, so who cares about everyone else — I've done all that I need to do.

vv. 44,45 — *"But I tell you: Love your enemies and pray for those who persecute you, that you may be sons of your Father in heaven. He causes his sun to rise on the evil and the good, and sends rain on the righteous and the unrighteous."*

'Αγαπᾶτε (present imperative) = "love constantly." Jesus here describes that the ultimate purpose of Christian charity is to free our enemy from his own hate, to rescue him from sin and thus to save his soul. There is only evil in hatred — there is no evil in love. Jesus is attempting to reverse the traditional teaching about enemies. Instead of cursing, bring forth blessing; instead of hatred, good; instead of abuse, prayer. Lenski: "Only the ἀγάπη which Jesus puts into our hearts as his disciples is able to produce such prayer." (*The Interpretation of St. Matthew's Gospel*, p. 248).

Besides, true children of the heavenly Father will want to show themselves to be his children by the way they live, by the way they treat *all* their neighbors, both believers and non-believers. Just as God is no respecter of persons (Ac 10:34; Rm 2:11), so his children will want to demonstrate the same impartiality towards all people. Jesus himself would later say in this same Sermon on the Mount, "Thus, by their fruit you will recognize them" (Mt 7:20). Good deeds reveal faith and sonship — evil deeds show up a lack of the same.

vv. 46,47 — *"If you love those who love you, what reward will you get? Are not even the tax collectors doing that? And if you greet only your brothers, what are you doing more than others? Do not even pagans do that?"*

Jesus continues the same thought of impartiality with regard to our Christian sonship. We cannot pick and choose those whom we will love, or resort to some sort of selective process to determine how to measure out our affections. All humans were made to run on love; they do not function too well on anything else.

For so long, however, the rabbinical teaching "to love only those who love you" had been too much a part of everyday life. Even the publicans did that, and nobody, but nobody could love them. That is nothing if not the essence of human morality (i.e. "I scratch your back, you scratch mine"). But can Christian disciples, the sons of the heavenly Father, be satisfied with this kind of behavior? Returning good for good is commendable; returning good for evil is Christlike. Christian courtesy is to extend beyond the circle of Christians.

v. 48 — *"Be perfect, therefore, as your heavenly Father is perfect."*

As used here, τέλειος connotes "perfection" in a moral sense, the state of being fully developed and having reached the highest level of maturity. Which, of course, is the ideal that God sets before the whole of his creation. However, in and of ourselves, by nature and by practice such perfection is *impossible* to achieve and attain (cf. Rm 3:23; 1 Jn 1:18). So at first glance, Jesus' command seems implausible, so far beyond our mere mortal reach.

Nonetheless, the goal is not too high. Although we sinners cannot attain (or even come close to) such a level of perfection in this life, with God's help and by his grace we will continue the struggle to heed the Lord's command. True followers of Jesus cannot be satisfied to do otherwise. The problem with the average Christian is that he *is* just an average Christian. Our Lord exhorts us never to stand still nor to rest easy, but to follow him more closely day by day. To cry out, "God, have mercy on me, a sinner" (Lk 18:13), and then to get back into the good fight of faith.

Homiletical Suggestions

This section of Jesus' Sermon on the Mount sounds like an extended "What Does This Mean?" to the Lord's *second* great commandment: "Love your neighbor as yourself" (Mk 12:31). As the true children of God our heavenly Father, we cannot be content to settle for anything less. Simply going through the motions or paying mere lip service to such a spirit of love is not consistent with our brotherhood in the family of faith.

It's been said that he who is no better than he has to be cannot be comfortable with God, who is loving and generous without limit. Inspired by our Savior, true Christian love bears and forbears, it gives and forgives. It will look for *every* opportunity to enable our neighbors to see just what such love can do:

Love Is the Christian's ID Card

1. It takes vengeance out of the picture (vv. 38-42)
2. It puts its focus on our neighbor (vv. 43-48)

The best way to destroy an enemy is to make him your friend. Of course, such a change of heart requires a genuine honest, ongoing affection for the other party. We might reflect this with:

Love Can Turn Things Around

1. The best way to influence our neighbor (vv. 38-42)
2. The only way to serve our heavenly Father (vv. 43-48)

As long as revenge would seem sweet, there is still some bitterness in our heart. Thus, with God's promised help and direction, we must get rid of such a spiteful spirit whenever we can:

Let Love Take You Back to Square One

1. Put an end to revenge (vv. 38-42)
2. Start all over with love (vv. 43-48)

Another treatment of this section would be to base our thoughts for Christian sanctification and living only on vv. 43-48:

A Divine Standard of Living

1. Love your enemies (vv. 44,45)
2. Be ye therefore perfect! (vv. 46-48)

The thought of "going the extra mile" has often intrigued people with its connotation of not being content with just getting by. The true child of God will always look for any way that he or she can to serve the Lord Jesus — as well as to further the cause of his gospel among all mankind. The natural thought progression would simply be a take-off from verse 41 in this section:

Going the Extra Mile!

1. What it meant for Jesus
2. What it means for us

EIGHTH SUNDAY AFTER EPIPHANY

The Scriptures

Old Testament — *Isaiah 49:13-18*
Epistle — *1 Corinthians 4:1-13*
Gospel — *Matthew 6:24-34*

The Text — Matthew 6:24-34

In this section of his Sermon on the Mount (6:1-7:12), Jesus further explains for his followers how to live the life of faith in his kingdom. He contrasts the pious life of God's children with the impious life of the Pharisees and hypocrites. A common error of Pharisees (ancient and modern) is their emphasis on material wealth as concrete evidence of God's favor. To dispel this heresy, Jesus reminds his followers that there is only one true treasure, the one he has laid aside for us in heaven (vv. 19-23). The first verse of our text is a transition between the thought about heavenly treasures and the topic of being anxious about material possessions:

v. 24 — *"No one can serve two masters. Either he will hate the one and love the other, or he will be devoted to the one and despise the other. You cannot serve both God and Money."*

These words fall as a judgment on the Pharisees and Jews who sought to worship God through sacrifices in his temple, and yet ended up selling the animals for sacrifice to weary pilgrims at their money-changing tables. In their greed, the Jews had attempted to serve God while living for the sake of material wealth. Jesus makes it clear that it is impossible to serve these two masters at the same time.

The emphasis here is on the word "serve." It is certainly not a sin in itself to acquire money or property, house or home. These material things are to serve the believer as genuine blessings from our Lord himself. But should money and possessions hold a place of devotion within the believer's heart, then they are no longer his servants but his masters. Then the believer has become enslaved to the things of this world.

It is impossible to serve these two masters, God and Money, Jesus says. They are diametrically opposed to each other. Either a person will bow down before one master, or he will bow down before the other. It is self-delusion for a person to think that he can bow down in two different directions at the same time.

The word "Money" or "Mammon" comes from the Aramaic language and culture of Palestine in those days. Mammon refers to more than money in the strict sense. It includes a person's possessions, everything that has value equivalent to money, and everything a person possesses apart from his body and life. In rabbinic writing, it often included negative connotations, such as hints of dishonest gain or even bribery. Jesus personifies Mammon in this verse, making it a monolithic master demanding a person's loyalty and service in opposition to the eternal God.

When it comes to serving these two masters, it is a question of priority in love and devotion. The Lord God calls us to love him with all our heart, mind and strength. Our heart will be found where our treasure is (6:21). That which a person loves becomes the object of his attention and desire. Augustine said, "Whatever I love, that is my God." God does not want our love to rest on our possessions, even if he abundantly blesses us with them (Ps 62:10). Our heart belongs to God alone.

vv. 25-27 — *"Therefore I tell you, do not worry about your life, what you will eat or drink; or about your body, what you will wear. Is not life more important than food, and the body more important than clothes? Look at the birds of the air; they do not sow or reap or store away in barns, and yet your heavenly Father feeds them. Are you not much more valuable than they? Who of you by worrying can add a single hour to his life?"*

Those who are poor in worldly things are hardly free from Mammon's idolatrous powers. He can make them his victims through their anxieties over their daily needs. Jesus reminds his followers that for God's children, such anxieties are faithless worries.

Jesus lists two cases in point as his sermon examples. First of all, Jesus says, since God provides life itself and its bodily needs, shall we not trust him to provide our less important daily needs just as well? Secondly, since God sustains even the birds who do not have the ability to plan and store for their future, how much more will he sustain us humans who have these added gifts of God as well?

The term πῆχυς can refer either to physical age or to physical height. Although the KJV translates, " . . . add one cubit unto his stature," the context implies that an anxiety over one's age and life span is the intended meaning. This meaning is also supported in other places throughout the Scriptures (cf. He 11:11; Jn 9:21,23; Ps 39:4-6).

vv. 28-30 — *"And why do you worry about clothes? See how the lilies of the field grow. They do not labor or spin. Yet I tell you that not even Solomon in all his splendor was dressed like one of these. If that is how God clothes the grass of the field, which is here today and tomorrow is thrown into the fire, will he not much more clothe you, O you of little faith?"*

Jesus points his audience to the flowering fields which surround them on the hillsides. Reminding the people that the beauty of the flowers is short-lived, Jesus now argues from the lesser to the greater. If God dresses the ephemeral flowers in the field with royal robes, how much more will he give ordinary clothing to his disciples who are going to live forever?

Jesus also uses the phrase, "O you of little faith," elsewhere in the Gospels (cf. Mt 8:26; 14:31; 16:8). The admonition is used in situations where the disciples fail to unequivocally place their confidence and trust in the promises and power of Christ. "Trust in the Lord with all your heart and lean not on your own understanding" (Pr 3:5).

vv. 31,32 — *"So do not worry, saying, 'What shall we eat?' or 'What shall we drink?' or 'What shall we wear?' For the pagans run after all these things, and your heavenly Father knows that you need them. But seek first his kingdom and his righteousness, and all these things will be given to you as well. Therefore do not worry about tomorrow, for tomorrow will worry about itself. Each day has enough trouble of its own."*

The Christian is not to worry at all. Worry is like the unbelief of the heathen world. Unbelievers think that they "earn their own way in this world," that they provide for their own needs. Trusting themselves, they seek after the mammon of unrighteousness.

But the child of God lives by a different creed because he resides in a different kingdom. His heart belongs in the kingdom of grace. Since he has a heavenly Father who knows exactly what he needs, then why worry at all? Only . . .

" . . . Seek first his kingdom and his righteousness." Every disciple is already a member of Christ's kingdom. Yet the follower of Christ is to go on seeking, to continue to desire nothing more highly than God's rule of grace in his heart. The righteousness of Christ to which the believer holds firmly in faith is always to continue to be the greatest treasure of his heart. And when his heart is found in Christ's loving hands, then such material items as food, drink and clothing will all flow from those same hands as well. "He who did not spare his own Son, but gave him up for us all — how will he not also, along with him, graciously give us all things" (Ro 8:32).

In verse 34, the word "tomorrow" is strikingly personified. Let tomorrow worry all by itself, Jesus says. Well it should. Tomorrow will have its own share of troubles in this sinful world, just like yesterday or today. No wonder the Lord God provided manna and quail for his children in the wilderness day by day. No wonder our Lord taught us to ask for our bodily needs "this day."

A primary focus within this text, then, is that the child of God is not to worry, not to be anxious for daily needs, or in anything. The reason is self-evident: we have a Father in heaven who cares for us and provides for us. Trusting in him for all our needs is the sure antidote for worry.

Homiletical Suggestions

The biggest temptation facing the preacher in this text is to drone on about the providential care of God at the expense of his mercy and grace. In considering possible themes, one needs to weigh the antithesis between God and Money in verse 24. This antithesis could become the seed for a two-part sermon, or it might make for an adequate theme, such as "No Man Can Serve Two Masters." Yet since it is a transition verse, it might best be left to the introduction.

Before the theme is chosen, the words of verses 33,34 also need to be weighed carefully, for they are a summary of the text. If the preacher fails to focus upon one or both of these two key sections, he will have missed his opportunity to proclaim a wonderful gospel word.

For what is the real reason why Jesus reminds us not to be anxious about tomorrow? Is it not faith in Jesus Christ, and faith alone, which frees the soul from its earthly cares? Jesus does not tell us what we ought to do but cannot; he tells us what God has given us and promises still to give. If we have Christ and his righteousness, what do we lack? If we belong to his kingdom, what cares can we have? (Ps 55:22; 1 Pe 5:7)

One possible way to express this idea would be as follows:

The Sure Antidote for Worry

1. People are prone to worry (vv. 25-28)
2. But God will provide (vv. 29-34)

Another emphasis could be:

Do Not Be Anxious

1. We worry a lot (vv. 25,26a, 27-29,31,32a,34)
2. God has satisfied all our needs (vv 26b,30,32b,33)

TRANSFIGURATION — LAST SUNDAY AFTER EPIPHANY

The Scriptures

Old Testament — *Exodus 24:12,15-18*
Epistle — *2 Peter 1:16-19*
Gospel — *Matthew 17:1-9*

The Text — Matthew 17:1-9

v. 1 — *After six days Jesus took with him Peter, James and John the brother of James, and led them up a high mountain by themselves.*

About two-thirds of the way through his public ministry (probably during the summer of A.D. 28), Jesus paused from his active routine of preaching and teaching, healing and counseling. He went away to a remote area of Palestine, accompanied by his three closest friends —Peter, James and John. Where exactly Jesus and his disciples went is unknown, however, the phrase εἰς ὄρος ὑψηλὸν suggests a rugged area where there would be solitude. Jesus journeyed to such a spot because he did not want his disciples to be distracted from what they were about to experience nor did he wish to have curious onlookers become befuddled by what would soon occur.

In this verse the Christian can certainly see the lesson for himself of from time to time withdrawing from the hubbub of this world to spend quiet time with his Lord. The surroundings, of course, are immaterial — whether they be the sanctuary of a church building, the privacy of one's home or a quiet area out in nature.

v. 2 — *There he was transfigured before them. His face shone like the sun, and his clothes became as white as the light.*

In this verse one finds the record of an awesome event which human language is inadequate to describe. Jesus' form was altered. The Greek μετεμορφώθη conveys what our use of metamorphosis in English expresses. What occurred to Jesus' appearance and form was as drastic a change as a caterpillar becoming a butterfly or a tadpole becoming a frog. Brilliance and majesty are connected with Jesus' appearance: his face as bright as the sun and his clothing as white as light. The other gospel writers offer still more similes conjuring up brightness: "His clothes became dazzling white, whiter than anyone in the world could bleach them" (Mk 9:3) and "his clothes became as bright as a flash of lightning" (Lk 9:29).

Jesus was allowing some of the splendor of his divine nature to show through. Indeed, Jesus had told his disciples repeatedly that he was God and he had demonstrated that fact through the performance of miracles. Yet, here he is making a very visible statement about his divinity. The answer to the question "Why?" is not hard to discern. Within about nine months Jesus would enter into the depths of his humiliation by being arrested, mocked, tortured, cruelly executed on a cross, and buried in a tomb. Above all this he would triumph, he had told his disciples, by rising from the dead. His transfiguration certainly authenticated that claim. Peter ties into this thought in his second epistle when he states: "We did not follow cleverly invented stories when we told you about the power and coming of our Lord Jesus Christ, but we were eyewitnesses of his majesty" (2 Pe 1:16).

v. 3 — *Just then there appeared before them Moses and Elijah, talking with Jesus.*

The verb ὤφθη is an aorist passive from ὁράω and means "to become visible" or "to appear." Jesus' disciples were not dreaming. They actually saw two individuals who had died centuries before this time. How Peter, James and John were able to correctly identify these two people as Moses and Elijah we are not told. But these disciples were experiencing a little glimpse of heaven and perhaps one finds here some support for the thought that in heaven all citizens will recognize one another without introduction.

Why Moses and Elijah were chosen to appear with Jesus is open for speculation. Perhaps it was because these two men did yeoman service for their Lord during critical points in Israel's history. Yet regardless of the reason, having two of God's faithful from the Old Testament times appear truly demonstrated the reality of life beyond the grave and the fact that Jesus is the Savior for all seasons. There was not one method of salvation in the Old Testament (i.e. keeping the law) and another program in the New (i.e. believing in Jesus). Jesus is the timeless Savior.

v. 4 — *Peter said to Jesus, "Lord, it is good for us to be here. If you wish, I will put up three shelters — one for you, one for Moses and one for Elijah."*

To glimpse Jesus in his splendor and to see in the flesh men long before dead was for Peter and the others a preview of heaven and a faith-strengthening experience. Peter wants to prolong this event so he offers to construct some dwellings for Jesus and the two Old Testament dignitaries. One's thoughts leap to a similar situation on the occasion of Jesus' ascension into heaven where Jesus' band of disciples stood still with their mouths gaping, wanting to keep basking in the event, until stirred into action by angelic ambassadors (Ac 1:11).

From time to time every Christian has mountaintop experiences (e.g. on the day of confirmation or during the funeral service for a loved one) and often there is the desire to freeze the moment. But heaven is not this side of the grave, our feelings will not always be in tune with our faith. Yet one need not despair, for there is the word of God "made more certain" (2 Pe 1:19) which states that the Lord is always with his people. Or, as the hymnist put it so beautifully, Jesus will "come with us to the plain."

v. 5 — *While he was still speaking, a bright cloud enveloped them, and a voice from the cloud said, "This is my Son, whom I love; with him I am well pleased. Listen to him!"*

Peter finds himself suddenly cut off by a cloud bedecking the mountain on which he and the others are situated. This cloud does not bring mist and murkiness, but is described as being φωτεινὴ, "bright" or "radiant." This is a theophany, a visible appearance of God to man. God the Father takes on a mode consistent with his essence — brightness or splendor. This manner of divine presence was well-known to the Jews, for God had led the Israelite nation through forty years of wilderness wandering by means of a pillar of cloud by day and a pillar of fire by night.

From this cloud, God the Father speaks lovingly about his Son Jesus. The occasion parallels perfectly what occurred at the time of Jesus' baptism (Mt 3:17). One sees God talking about God. This is a concept beyond the grasp of human reasoning. Yet it is factual, for God has revealed himself as three persons in one Being. The work of salvation performed by Jesus is approved here by God the Father in his use of the term εὐδόκησα, which could be translated as "I approve of" or "I take delight in."

The imperative ἀκούετε points out that Jesus is to be taken seriously. Sad to say, multitudes in the world have no time for Jesus or don't care about what he has to say. There is a general feeling that all religions teach the same and that there are many highways to heaven. Such people need to know that Jesus is the one and only Savior this world is ever going to have (Jn 14:6). What is more, there are many others who profess to be followers of Christ and belong to a church which is Christian, but do not desire to accept or follow portions of Jesus' words. For these individuals, finally, for all who bear the name of Christ, one must note the imperative, "Listen to him."

vv. 6-8 — *When the disciples heard this, they fell facedown to the ground, terrified. But Jesus came and touched them. "Get up," he said. "Don't be afraid." When they looked up, they saw no one except Jesus.*

Sinful human beings are afraid of the holy, almighty God. Even minor demonstrations of his power cause people to quake as is seen in the human reaction to the approach of a tornado or the eruption of a volcano. Here Peter, James and John, though believers in Jesus, react according to their sinful nature and are frightened σφόδρα —"exceedingly" or "out of their wits." They lose contact with what is occurring and collapse to the ground.

The theophany has ended. Jesus reassures his disciples with the comforting words, "Don't be afraid," while physically touching them to bring them back to their senses. There is no docetic nonsense here. What just happened was real. But the moment has passed. The cloud, Moses and Elijah are gone. Jesus is back in his natural earthly state, again cloaking his divinity.

v. 9 — *As they were coming down the mountain, Jesus instructed them, "Don't tell anyone what you have seen, until the Son of Man has been raised from the dead."*

As Jesus and the three disciples leave behind the remote mountain heights Jesus literally commands (ἐνετείλατο) the three not to divulge to anyone what they had just witnessed until after his resurrection from the dead. The reason for this was so as not to fuel any false "superman" ideas about him. Lenski states that this is the same reason why Jesus ordinarily did not use the title "Messiah" for himself, but chose instead the term "the Son of Man."

The concluding adverbial clause of this verse beautifully points out the underlying purpose for Jesus' allowing Peter, James and John to observe this mountaintop incident: Jesus shows himself to be God who is indeed capable of rising from the dead.

Homiletical Suggestions

This text is the historic Gospel reading for the Transfiguration of our Lord, which is also known as the last Sunday after Epiphany. The Old Testament lesson and the epistle very nicely tie into this text and the average parishioner can readily discern this.

As evidenced in the text study, there are many preaching values in this portion of God's word. Nonetheless, upon a first reading the items which leap out immediately are the supernatural occurrences (i.e. Jesus' transfiguration, Moses and Elijah's appearance, and the visible/audible presence of God the Father). These mysteries could be examined and then applied to the hearers. With this basic premise in mind, the following is suggested:

Jesus Discloses It All

1. His person (vv. 1,2)
2. His connections (vv. 5,6)
3. His mission (vv. 3,4,7-9)

Another approach to this text would be to place oneself and one's hearers on the mountaintop with the disciples. The thrust of such a visit could be to enumerate the benefits of being there. One could select hymn 135 from TLH as the sermon hymn and borrow its title for the sermon theme:

"Tis Good, Lord, to Be Here"

1. To witness your glory (vv. 1,2)
2. To hear your Father (vv. 5-8)
3. To preview your heaven (vv. 3,4,9)

Since the Transfiguration of our Lord (the last Sunday after Epiphany) traditionally serves as the lead into the Lenten season, the following theme would suggest itself:

Jesus Readies His Disciples for His Passion

1. By displaying his divinity (vv. 1,2)
2. By offering a glimpse of heaven (vv. 3,4)
3. By receiving the Father's stamp of approval (vv. 5-9)

ASH WEDNESDAY

The Scriptures

Old Testament — *Joel 2:12-19*
Epistle — *2 Corinthians 5:20b-6:2*
Gospel — *Matthew 6:1-6,16-21*

The Text — Matthew 6:1-6,16-21

In the first part of the Sermon on the Mount Jesus had denounced a twisted superficial interpretation of the law that ignored the heart of the law, which is love. Now he addresses a twisted superficial piety that lacked a heart directed toward and by God's love.

v. 1 — *"Be careful not to do your 'acts of righteousness' before men, to be seen by them. If you do, you will have no reward from your Father in heaven."*

After teaching about true Christian love (5:43-48) Jesus voices a warning. He speaks about τὴν δικαιοσύνην ὑμῶν, meaning "your righteous act." The reference here is to "good deeds" in general. They may be in agreement with God's will, at least on the surface, but Christianity is not a surface religion.

The veneer of piety cannot cover up sin. God reveals the truth about our righteousness. "There is no one righteous" (Ro 3:10; Ga 3:10). "All our righteous acts are like filthy rags" (Is 64:6). Being right before God is ours only through Christ (2 Cor 5:21,22) who lived a life of holiness for us and died as a full and complete sacrifice for our unrighteousness. And there are no true "deeds of righteousness" without faith in that Savior as the full atonement for our sins (Ro 3:21,22).

God doesn't tell us to deny good works or even downplay them in any way. He reminds us that we were created to do them (Eph 2:10). Yet all too often what is done has been done only for our own benefit — "to be seen by men." In that case, Jesus said, don't expect any reward before your Father in heaven, for there will be none.

God talks to us about rewards that follow living for him. Proper acts of service done in the name of Jesus Christ will not go unnoticed (He 6:10) or be unrewarded (1 Cor 3:14). Surely there is such an outpouring of blessing already here on this earth (Is 58:8-14), but most rewards may not occur in this lifetime. Jesus said "great is your reward in heaven" for enduring persecution (Mt 5:12), for helping the needy (Lk 14:14). The rewards are, of course, rewards of grace and not on account of any merit from our works.

v. 2 — *"So when you give to the needy, do not announce it with trumpets, as the hypocrites do in the synagogues and on the streets, to be honored by men. I tell you the truth, they have received their reward in full."*

Jesus begins his list of "acts of righteousness" with the "kind deed" or "charitable giving" (ἐλεημοσύνη). "When you give to the needy" already suggests that such good works should be done regularly.

"Hypocrites" describes pretenders or play-actors wearing masks that hide their true identity. There can be little doubt that Jesus was especially referring to the Pharisees' ways of doing things (cf. Mt 23). They gave their tithes, but neglected justice, mercy and faithfulness (Lk 10:25-37). Because of Jesus' condemnations of their ways, we immediately associate the word "Pharisee" with hypocritical, self-righteous living. Yet to the people of the time it must have been quite a bombshell to blast the Pharisees whose lifestyle signified holiness in the eyes of the people. It is no different today. It is not well received when the words of Scripture speak against the things the world sees as honorable and pure, as beneficial and pious.

The problem with the hypocrites' deeds was not so much the deeds themselves but the attitude or motive in which they were done — "to be noticed by others." They were not doing it for the glory of God or love of neighbor but only for their own benefit, their own glory and honor.

We find nothing that would say Pharisees literally used trumpets to announce the deeds, but the figurative language is easily understood. Pharisees did deeds in public places so that people might see them.

"They have received their reward in full" is repeated in verses 2,5,16. It describes the momentary pleasure of the praise they received with nothing more owed them, nothing future to receive. The momentary praise of men on earth would be all the glory they would receive.

vv. 3,4 — *"But when you give to the needy, do not let your left hand know what your right hand is doing, so that your giving may be in secret. Then your Father, who sees what is done in secret, will reward you."*

After telling us how not to do our good deeds, Jesus now tells how to proceed properly. It should be in such a way that the left hand should not "find out" or "notice" what the right hand is giving or doing. It reminds us of Matthew 25:37-40 where things done for others were such natural and unassuming responses of the believers' faith that they didn't even remember doing them. Yet, giving in this world so often is done with the idea of getting something in return. If we didn't receive any earthly recognition for our charitable actions, would we still do them?

Jesus says, let it be done in secret. This directive is not at variance with God's desire that good deeds be seen by all men to glorify the Father in heaven (5:16). It doesn't mean you have to do your deeds of kindness under the veil of darkness so that no one sees you, but refers to the attitude of the heart that gives without concern for others' recognition of the deed, doing for God and not for what others may think.

v. 5 — *"But when you pray, do not be like the hypocrites, for they love to pray standing in the synagogues and on the street corners to be seen by men. I tell you the truth, they have received their reward in full."*

Here also the ὅταν and the present subjunctive expect us to be praying regularly. The fact that these hypocrites "love" (φιλέω) their type of praying shows where their hearts are. They made sure they prayed on the corners of the busiest streets to "make their appearance" (φαίνω) before others.

They also had received their full reward in the praise and awe they drew out of the people around. The blessing of answered prayer, the joy of a childlike talk with our heavenly Father, the peace of laying our sins before God for the assurance of forgiveness would not be there for them.

v. 6 — *"But when you pray, go into your room, close the door and pray to your Father, who is unseen. Then your Father, who sees what is done in secret, will reward you."*

Although public prayer is important (in church, in family devotions, mealtime, etc.), prayer itself really is a private matter, a conversation with God. Jesus stresses again that our prayer ought not to be done "in order to be seen by men."

Our prayer should be a quiet conversation with our Father and not a show for the people around us. "In a closed room" is not only a beautiful way of describing such a private communication with God but also is in reality a good way to get away from the distractions and pour out heart and soul to our Father.

Our Father sees into the secret recesses of our hearts and responds to our motives and attitudes appropriately. He is the one who sends the Spirit to bring our request when it is so secret even we are grappling to figure out exactly what we are asking or don't know how to put it into words (Ro 8:26,27).

v. 16 — *"When you fast, do not look somber as the hypocrites do, for they disfigure their faces to show men they are fasting. I tell you the truth, they have received their reward in full."*

Old Testament law prescribed fasting only on the Day of Atonement (Lv 23:27). The Jews fasted on anniversaries of national calamities. For the most part, fasting was an outward expression of inner sorrow and repentance for sin. But as with other beneficial things, the Pharisees made it into a meritorious work. They had fasts above and beyond the common ones to show that they were higher and more spiritual.

The Lord supports a proper use of fasting. Fasting can be a useful means to discipline and control our own bodies as well as giving us special times and ways to praise and thank God. What Jesus condemns is self-righteous, glory-seeking motivation like that of the Pharisees. Anything that becomes a boast that you are more holy and spiritual than others puts you in the camp of the Pharisees. One might master outward disciplines, or overcome wicked ways, but may end up replacing them with a greater (although more socially acceptable) wickedness of pride and self-righteousness.

vv. 17,18 — *"But when you fast, put oil on your head and wash your face, so that it will not be obvious to men that you are fasting, but only to your Father, who is unseen; and your Father, who sees what is done in secret, will reward you."*

Since fasting is to be an inward thing of the heart and not some outward show, Jesus tells them to anoint their heads as the Pharisees would have done during times of celebration. In that way people will not realize you are fasting. Instead of boasting or moaning to draw attention to the things we are enduring before God, let it be hidden to others and done before God, who will reward you.

v. 19 — *"Do not store up for yourselves treasures on earth, where moth and rust destroy and where the thieves break in and steal."*

The various hypocritical actions of the Pharisees were only symptoms. The root of the problem lay in where their treasure was. The treasure on earth could be living for things, wealth or goals of this world as well as the previously mentioned warning against living for the praise of men.

One of the reasons for not storing up or living for the things of the earth is that they are very temporary. The primary meaning of βρῶσις is "eating." This can refer to any eating away of a substance for its demise, whether it be rust or corrosion, normal eating or expenses which make income disappear or perhaps sudden health bills or calamities which eat up what had been saved.

Earthly treasures are also subject to thieves who break in and in a few moments may take what took us years to store up. Things of this world are fleeting and will soon be gone, yet we spend time acquiring and storing them up, but for what? Where are our treasures? Do the moth holes in clothing, the rust on the car, the loss of our possessions and the depletion of our finances cause more concern and attention than a possible loss of eternal treasures?

v. 20 — *"But store up for yourself treasures in heaven, where moth and rust do not destroy, and where thieves do not break in and steal."*

What are the true treasures? They are (v. 33) the kingdom of God and his righteousness. How do you store them up? Through repentance and faith, by living not for the things of the world but growing in grace, forgiveness, love and the peace that all center in Christ (Eph 3:15-21). What is the payoff? It is "a new birth into . . . an inheritance that can never perish, spoil or fade — kept in heaven for you." It is "faith — of greater worth than gold. . . . " which "may result in praise, glory and honor when Jesus Christ is revealed" (1 Pe 1:3-7).

v. 21 — *"For where your treasure is, there your heart will be also."*

But where you store up your future, what you realize is your hope, what you have come to see as most important, your heart and emotions will follow. And what you've set your heart on, that you will pursue with all carefulness and energy as naturally as a plant stretching for the sunlight. It is foolishness to make our treasure something that can so easily be taken away from us. If our treasure is in the praise and approval of men, we will find it is quickly subject to the corrosion of slander and fickle human rejection. If we have our treasure in the Son of God, we have treasure eternally and our hearts will show in the motives and unselfish attitude of serving God in what we do for others.

Thanks be to God that through his Word he has pointed us to the glory of heaven that is ours in Christ so that we may truly reap the blessings (Col 3:1-4).

Homiletical Suggestions

Lent is a season of preparation, not just an outward one but an inner one. The ashes in medieval times tossed over one's head on this day remind us of the ashes of repentance mentioned in Scripture (sackcloth and ashes). But even those can be a show. Outward preparations and outward expressions of grief over sin may have a very beneficial place in this season. But the Old Testament reading in Joel points out that true repentance in the heart is most important and not just some empty outward ritual. "Rend your hearts and not your garments." He calls us to put forth every effort to return to the Lord with a repentant life in view of his abounding love and compassion. The Epistle reading from 2 Corinthians spells out the gospel message of grace in Jesus as he took our sin on himself so that in him we and our deeds might become righteous before God.

We need to be careful that we properly treat the text with the gospel lest we fall into moralizing. One also needs to be careful in the condemnation of others' pious rituals lest in so doing he exhibits another type of false piety.

Jesus' words regarding works, prayer, fasting and treasure can be treated in four separate parts and applied to Christian living. A theme which relates this teaching to the season is:

Lenten Christianity: More than Rituals

1. It is selfless concern for others (vv. 1-3)
2. It is private communication with God (vv. 4-6)
3. It is humble discipline of life (vv. 16-18)
4. It is pursuing the lasting treasure (vv. 19-21)

Invite the hearers to evaluate their acts of righteousness by means of two questions:

You Can't Judge a Work by Its Cover

1. For whom is it done? (vv. 1-6,16-18)
2. What is its lasting value? (vv. 19-21)

A synthetic treatment, drawing on all verses of the text to develop each part:

Set Your Heart on Lasting Treasure

1. Classify your treasures:
   Are they earthly or heavenly?
2. Compare their lasting value:
   Look at the earthly and live for the heavenly.

Another possibility:

Being Religious Doesn't Make You Christian

1. Check your motives (vv. 1-6,16-18)
2. Check your treasure (vv. 19-21)

FIRST SUNDAY IN LENT

The Scriptures

Old Testament — *Genesis 2:7-9,15-17;3:1-7*
Epistle — *Romans 5;12,17-19*
Gospel — *Matthew 4:1-11*

The Text — Matthew 4:11

Jesus began his public ministry with his baptism. The first assignment in his ministry was to overcome the devil in a face-to-face confrontation.

Adam had fallen into sin in Eden. Through his sin he had led mankind into sin, enslavement to Satan and eternal punishment. The Old Testament lesson reveals the devil's temptation and Adam's tragic fall from created innocence by eating the forbidden fruit.

Against the background of that Old Testament lesson this Gospel text presents Jesus facing the devil's temptations to undo the damage Adam had done. Jesus successfully resisted the devil's temptations as man's substitute to bring righteousness and salvation to all men. The Epistle lesson explains the meaning of Jesus' righteous obedience for all people in contrast to the tragic meaning of Adam's sin. The Epistle reveals that Jesus' righteous obedience has brought justification and eternal life to all people.

For forty days Jesus was tempted by the devil in the wilderness. Luke's Gospel relates that the temptations extended throughout that entire period of time (Lk 4:2). But out of all of those temptations the Lord has seen fit to preserve in the Scriptures only three of them. What is important is this: Jesus as the Savior of mankind sinlessly resisted all of the temptations to win man's salvation from sin, Satan and hell.

vv. 1,2 — *Then Jesus was led by the Spirit into the desert to be tempted by the devil. After fasting forty days and forty nights, he was hungry.*

The Holy Spirit led Jesus into the wilderness after he was baptized. Jesus had been anointed with the Holy Spirit at his baptism (3:16f) for the difficult redemptive work that lay before him. He did not foolishly or haphazardly enter into this confrontation with the devil. It was his Father's will that he should be tempted by the devil and overcome those temptations to redeem fallen mankind. To that end the Holy Spirit led him into the wilderness.

Although the passive verb ἀνήχθη states Jesus was led out to be tempted, it should not be understood that Jesus was reluctant or unwilling to go himself. Just the opposite was true. Scripture plainly teaches that he had come to do his Father's will by redeeming sinners. Jesus himself said, "My food is to do the will of him who sent me and to finish his work" (Jn 4:34). Jesus' willingness to do his Father's will is seen also in Philippians 2:8, where it is stated, "And being found in appearance as a man, he humbled himself and became obedient to death — even death on a cross!" Therefore since it was his Father's will that he should be tempted by the devil to redeem fallen mankind, Jesus himself willingly went out to fight that battle with the tempter.

But Jesus did not fight that battle by using his divine power, which he possessed according to the personal union of his divine and human natures. He fought the devil armed only with the full armor of God available to God's people, particularly with the sword of the Spirit, which is the word of God (Eph 6:17). The humanness with which Jesus entered into this struggle with the devil is brought out by the fact that he fasted and then became hungry as any human would after forty days.

The devil is called διάβολος in this verse. It means "slanderer." It is an appropriate name for him who does not hold to the truth and who is the father of lies (Jn 8:44). In this text the devil recognized Jesus to be God's Messiah, the One first promised to Adam and Eve. The devil had been victorious over Adam, now he sought to defeat this Second Adam who had come to crush his head and destroy his evil work. He sought to defeat him at the very outset of his redemptive work. By cunning trickery and temptations he attempted to prevent him from doing God's will. If he were to prevent Jesus from doing God's will just once, he would have the victory.

v. 3 — *The temper came to him and said, "If you are the Son of God, tell these stones to become bread."*

Satan is named in this verse by what he continues to do. The present active participle ὁ πειράθων indicates he is the one who continues to tempt. It is impossible to determine in what manner or form he approached Jesus. But the purpose of his coming to Jesus is clear: it was to tempt Jesus to avoid suffering and to cease trusting in his heavenly Father.

The devil began the temptation as he had done with Eve by questioning and seeking to raise certain suspicions. In this case he questioned Jesus' true divinity and suggested there actually was no reason for him to suffer physical hunger, if he was indeed the Son of

God. He did not have to wait for his heavenly Father to provide him with life-giving food. He himself could simply turn those stones into bread. For surely all things were possible for him, if he was in fact God's Son.

The devil posed an insidious temptation. For if Jesus were to answer the devil's challenge to use his divine power to satisfy his hunger, he would not be trusting in his Father's providential care. He would have to act contrary to his Father's will for himself.

v. 4 — *Jesus answered, "It is written: 'Man does not live on bread alone, but on every word that comes from the mouth of God.' "*

To counter this temptation Jesus used the sword of the Spirit (Eph 6:17).

Jesus' sword was Deuteronomy 8:3. The perfect passive γέγραπται indicates that what was written in that passage of God's word continues to be true and in force. God inspired Moses to record that he had caused the Israelites to go hungry and then had fed them miraculously with the manna to teach them that mankind does not live because of food, but because of the word God speaks. That divine truth which pertained to the Israelites in the exodus, Jesus held as also pertaining to himself centuries later, as it continues to do with respect to all people of all ages.

By quoting the passage Jesus demonstrated his complete trust in his Father to keep his body and life. There was no need for him to use his divine power at the devil's instigation to avoid suffering the hunger that was his Father's will for him at that time.

The future indicative ζήσεται is gnomic, expressing a general truth for all ages. It is then translated "does live" as the NIV has translated it, rather than "will live." The preposition ἐπί with the dative in the phrases "on bread alone" and "on every word" means "on the basis of." Man does live on the basis of the word which God speaks. Ῥήματι is a "word, saying or expression," which continues to proceed from God, as stated by the present participle ἐκπορευομένῳ.

The word or expression of God in this passage does not refer to the written word in Scripture, but to the unwritten creative and preserving word of God: "Let there be . . . and continue to be." The thrust of Jesus' answer was that not all the bread in the world would keep him alive if his Father did not want him to live. If his Father wanted him to live he would live, even if he was then going hungry after not eating for forty days.

vv. 5,6 — *Then the devil took him to the holy city and had him stand on the highest point of the temple. "If you are the Son of God," he said, "throw yourself down. For it is written:*

'He will command his angels concerning you,
and they will lift you up in their hands,
so that you will not strike your foot against a stone.' "

The devil took Jesus along to the temple in Jerusalem. In what manner he took Jesus to the temple is not certain.

The NIV has translated πτερύγιον τοῦ ἱεροῦ as the "highest point of the temple." Πτερύγιον is literally an "end, edge, summit or pinnacle." Edersheim located the place as the pinnacle of the temple tower at the southeastern angle of the temple, which fell away to the Kidron Valley four hundred and fifty feet below. Wherever the exact place may have been, it was at a lofty height.

From that lofty height the tempter told Jesus to throw himself down. Once again the devil's temptation began by trying to create doubt. If Jesus was indeed the true Son of God, certainly his Father loved him and would protect him.

The tempter's train of thought was: "You believe your Father will care for you and prolong your life. So throw yourself down," he commanded. "Prove it!" (The aorist imperative βάλε is a sharp command.) "And since you are in the habit of quoting Scripture, look at what your Father has said in Psalm 91:11,12! He will command his angels to protect you from harm and danger. So throw yourself down! For you have nothing to fear — if you do believe your Father will protect you."

v. 7 — *Jesus answered him, "It is also written: 'Do not put the Lord your God to the test.' "*

The devil had quoted Scripture to persuade Jesus there was scriptural warrant for recklessly throwing himself down. But Satan had misapplied the passage. He had torn it out of its context in order to incite Jesus to put his Father's promised protection to the test. However, our Lord correctly interpreted the misapplied passage with another passage. Swinging the sword of the Spirit from Deuteronomy 6:16 he said, "Do not put the Lord your God to the test."

The future tense of ἐκπειράσεις with the negative particle οὐκ expresses a prohibition — "do not put to the test." Here the word is ἐκπειράθω instead of πειράθω, which appeared previously in vv. 1,3. The prepositional prefix ἐκ intensifies the action of the verb πειράθω, so that the meaning according to Moulton suggests the daring of the act, or the effort to put to a decisive test.

With the sword of the Spirit Jesus parried Satan's temptation and misapplication of Scripture, pointing out that God had forbidden the Israelites to put him to the test. For the Israelites had brazenly put the Lord to such a decisive test in the wilderness. In Exodus 17:7

Moses recorded how the Israelites had demanded they be given water to drink and tempted God, saying, "Is the Lord among us or not?" Jesus would not repeat their sin.

It would be wise not to overemphasize the fact that the devil had omitted the phrase "in all your ways" from his quotation of Psalm 91:11,12. For emphasizing the omission of that phrase turns the devil's temptation into an intentional distortion of the passage. Satan was not tempting Jesus by twisting the meaning of the passage. If the temptation had been the distorting of Scripture, Jesus' proper response would have been to quote Deuteronomy 4:2: "Do not add to what I commanded you and do not subtract from it." Jesus' answer shows that the temptation was to tempt God, not distort Scripture.

vv. 8,9 — *Again, the devil took him to a very high mountain and showed him all the kingdoms of the world and their splendor. "All this I will give you," he said, "if you will bow down and worship me."*

Again Satan tempted Jesus. Again, it cannot be stated in what way Satan took him along. Nor can it be stated with certainty how he showed Jesus all the kingdoms of the world.

Verse 9 is a future more vivid condition with the future δώσω in the apodosis and the particle ἐάν and the aorist subjunctive προσκυνήσης in the protasis. This condition expresses what was a possibility from Satan's point of view. If Jesus were to worship him, he would give Jesus all those kingdoms with their splendor. Whether or not he would in fact give those kingdoms to Jesus depended upon what Jesus would do next.

This temptation may have been the most insidious and alluring temptation of all. For it held out to Jesus the promise of gaining all the kingdoms of the world which he had come to win, only without having to suffer the agony and shame of being crucified to gain them. This temptation presented a shortcut to his goal as the suffering Savior. He could skirt his Father's will and obtain the kingdoms of the world which he had come for. He could accomplish that goal in Satan's way without the suffering. All Jesus had to do was worship the devil that one time.

If all the kingdoms had been Satan's to give, had Jesus worshipped him he would have come under Satan's power. Then all the kingdoms would still have been the devil's. Instead of receiving the kingdoms as the devil had promised, Jesus would have become his slave. Satan's temptations offer much. But in the end they give nothing like what was promised — only sin, misery and death. Satan is the master of vain hope and empty promises.

Satan lied. He made a bold boast when he lied that all the kingdoms and their splendor were his to give away. But "the earth is the Lord's, and everything in it, the world, and all who live in it" (Ps 24:1). His promise to give Jesus all those kingdoms was a lie, which was fitting for him whose title is "liar and the father of lies" (Jn 8:44).

v. 10 — *Jesus said to him, "Away from me, Satan! For it is written: 'Worship the Lord your God, and serve him only.' "*

There is a variant reading which adds: ὀπίσω μοῦ. "Go behind me! Satan." The UBS text seems to be the preferred reading. It has early and geographically widespread manuscripts to support it. If the variant reading had been the original text, then there is no satisfactory explanation for its omission. But if it had not been the original reading, then copyists could have easily added the words in question to the text because they remembered the words Jesus spoke to Peter, "Get behind me, Satan!" (Mt 16:23.)

Jesus knew and obeyed the First Commandment which forbids the worship of false gods. Satan was indeed a false god — the chief, ultimate false god. For all the idols of the world are demons in actuality (1 Cor 10:19,20). And Satan is the chief of demons. Jesus would not commit such an idolatrous act.

With the sword of the Spirit recorded in Deuteronomy 6:13 Jesus deflected the temptation. He said, "For it is written: 'Worship the Lord your God, and serve him only.' " The two verbs in the future tense, προσκυνήσεις and λατρεύσεις, express a command like an imperative does. It was God's command that only he, the true God, be worshiped and served.

Once again Jesus demonstrated his faithfulness to his heavenly Father and his willingness to follow his Father's will. He would not try to skirt his Father's will to win mankind's salvation through suffering. The cross lay three years before him. But he would walk the straight path his Father had set before him which led to that cross. For he had come to do his Father's will.

v. 11 — *Then the devil left him, and angels came and attended him.*

Having to follow Jesus' command to go, the devil left him at that time. But he would return to tempt him again at another opportune time (Lk 4:13). The text closes with the revelation that his Father did indeed have his angels watching over him to keep him in all his ways.

Homiletical Suggestions

During the season of Lent the church directs its attention to Jesus' redemptive work as the humble suffering Servant. This text presents

Jesus in his state of humiliation as he began his ministry to redeem fallen mankind from Satan and sin. His faithful obedience to his Father in resisting Satan's temptations helped bring God's declaration of righteousness to fallen mankind. As sinners who have been justified by faith in Jesus we are also encouraged to turn from sin and to follow our Savior in doing what is right. We can learn from Jesus how to overcome the devil, temptations and sin.

This text may be expounded from several viewpoints. One exposition could be from the viewpoint of the type of temptations Jesus fought against. That treatment of this text suggests:

In our Place Jesus Overcame the Temptation

1. To stop trusting God (vv. 1-4)
2. To tempt God (vv. 5-7)
3. To worship a false god (vv. 8-11)

With Jesus Resist the Temptation To Sin Against God

1. By doubting God's providence (vv. 1-4)
2. By testing God's protection (vv. 5 -7)
3. By breaking God's first commandment (vv. 8-11)

Another viewpoint from which this text may be expounded is how Jesus defeated the devil's temptations. This treatment will unfold the devil's devices as well, and will provide ample material to apply to God's people. This suggests:

Jesus Defeated the Devil in the Wilderness

1. He saw through the devil's schemes
   A. To create doubts and suspicions (vv. 3,6)
   B. To give misguided directions (vv. 3,6,9)
   C. To misapply Scripture (v. 6)
   D. To short-cut God's will (vv. 3,9)
   E. To hold out empty promises (vv. 8,9)
2. He resisted the devil's schemes
   A. He continued to trust in his Father (v. 3)
   B. He did not heed the devil's directions (vv. 4,7,10)
   C. He interpreted Scripture with Scripture (v. 7)
   D. He accepted God's will for himself (vv. 4,10)

SECOND SUNDAY IN LENT

The Scriptures

Old Testament — *Genesis 12:1-8*
Epistle — *Romans 4:1-5,13-17*
Gospel — *John 4:5-26*

The Text — John 4:5-26

Jesus had revealed himself as the Lord by his first miracle in Cana. His disciples had put their faith in him after seeing his glory. But Christ had not come just to educate a select group of people in the truths of eternal life. He had come for all people. Although he spent a greater share of his ministry seeking the "lost sheep of the house of Israel," he never neglected an opportunity to share his word with the non-Jewish community.

Our text demonstrates Jesus' love for all people, a love which finally led him to Calvary. He had been in Jerusalem where he had cleared the temple (Jn 2:12-25). He had discussed the miracle of rebirth with Nicodemus (Jn 3:1-21). He then withdrew from Jerusalem, carrying on his work in Judea (Jn 3:22-36). When his enemies noticed the crowds of people listening to him, Jesus withdrew from Judea, the seat of hostility, and returned to Galilee.

"Now he had to go through Samaria," we hear (Jn 4:4). The most direct route lay through Samaria, but most Jews took the longer route through the Jordan Valley to avoid Samaria. The Samaritans were half-breeds, who accepted Genesis to Deuteronomy as their Scriptures, but also kept many of their heathen ideas. The Jews despised the Samaritans and avoided them at all costs. But Jesus "had to go through Samaria." The Savior went through this countryside on a search and rescue mission.

Christ in love singled out a Samaritan woman. Her past was tarnished. She had destroyed her life. Her guilt was overwhelming, but he approached her in love. He patiently led her to see in him more than a tired, thirsty Jew. She saw in him the Christ, the one who could cleanse her from her sin. She became a believer, for Jesus' powerful words drew her to faith. She became a witness, for everyone who trusts in Jesus becomes a missionary.

vv. 5-10 — *So he came to a town in Samaria called Sychar, near the plot of ground Jacob had given to his son Joseph. Jacob's well was there, and Jesus, tired as he was from the journey, sat down by the well. It was about the sixth hour. When a Samaritan woman came to draw water, Jesus said to her, "Will you give me a drink?" (His disciples had gone into the town to buy food.) The Samaritan woman said to him, "You are a Jew and I am a Samaritan woman. How can you ask me for a drink?" (For Jews do not associate with Samaritans.) Jesus answered her, "If you knew the gift of God and who it is that asks you for a drink, you would have asked him and he would have given you living water."*

John emphasizes the true human nature of Jesus with the perfect participle, κεκοπιακὼς, "having been wearied." He draws our attention to Jesus' tired condition, for the Son of God truly shares our humanity and understands our needs. When the Samaritan woman first encountered him, she would have had no reason to suspect he was anyone but a footsore traveler.

The hour was the sixth, noon by Jewish reckoning. The Samaritan woman came upon Jesus in this lonely hour at the well. She came alone, for she was a social outcast due to her broken marriages and her current extra-marital relationship.

She would not have spoken to this Jew, but Jesus in his compassion and love drew her to hear his words of life. He began a marvelous conversation that ended with her receiving eternal life. He began it so simply. "Will you give me a drink?"

Undoubtedly the woman recognized that Jesus was a Jew by his speech. His request surprised her, for it was totally out of character for a Jew to associate with a Samaritan. She knew the Jews' racism and discrimination against the Samaritans. Συγχράομαι means associating with someone on friendly terms. The relationship between Jew and Samaritan was anything but friendly.

Jesus used the woman's objection to turn the conversation to the spiritual: "If you knew . . . you would have asked and he would have given." She was ignorant of the gift of God. In the context the gift is the same as the living water. "Living water" was literally running water. Jacob's well was filled by water from the rains percolating through the soil. People might prefer spring water to water which has been standing in a well. Jesus was referring symbolically to the eternal life he alone could grant this woman. He had spoken to Nicodemus of the gift of God, John 3:16. Since this woman was unaware that Jesus was the source of this spiritually life-giving water, she had not asked him for it, at least not yet. Jesus was, however, arousing her curiosity.

vv. 11-15 — *"Sir," the woman said, "you have nothing to draw with and the well is deep. Where can you get this living water?*

Are you greater than our father Jacob, who gave us the well and drank from it himself, as did also his sons and his flocks and herds?" Jesus answered, "Everyone who drinks this water will be thirsty again, but whoever drinks the water I give him will never thirst. Indeed, the water I give him will become in him a spring of water welling up to eternal life." The woman said to him, "Sir, give me this water so that I won't get thirsty and have to keep coming here to draw water."

The woman calls Jesus κύριε, "sir." She had not yet come to know him as her Lord. She concluded that Jesus was speaking of something greater than physical water. She hadn't yet grasped the full import of his promise of "living water." She surmised, however, that since Chrst had nothing with which to draw water, he was offering her something extraordinary.

Jacob, from whom the Samaritans claimed descent through Ephraim and Manasseh, the sons of Joseph, had been satisfied with the water of this well. This Jew was not. What kind of water could he possibly have to offer? Jesus' tactic had worked. Her curiosity compelled her to remain and interrogate this strange traveler.

Jesus' answer (vv. 13,14) helped the woman understand the nature of the water and the nature of this man who offered it to her. The water was spiritual. Drinking it would quench permanently the heart's thirst for life everlasting. "Will never thirst" expresses the double negative, οὐ μή, plus the future indicative. This combination is the strongest possible negative. Just as the water is eternal life, so drinking the water is faith in Jesus as the Savior from sin. By trusting in him alone, the human's thirst for everlasting life is quenched. The water Jesus gives becomes a spring welling up to eternal life. By faith in Jesus we are spiritually alive, and we are living forever.

How did Jesus emphasize who he was? The pronoun ἐγώ emphasized his person. He alone can give this water of life everlasting. He is the source of eternal life since he is true God. Compare Jeremiah 16:13. Jehovah is the spring of living water. Jesus offers this water. Jesus himself is the true Lord.

Jesus had aroused the woman's curiosity. He had led her to see he was more than human. Still she missed the point. She wanted what Jesus offered, but she was puzzled and confused about the gift he could give her. She still supposed he was speaking of physical water. If he could give her water that would prevent any future thirst, she wouldn't have to bear her water jars in the heat of the day. Relief from physical thirst was enough for her at the moment.

vv. 16-18 — *He told her, "Go, call your husband and come back." "I have no husband," she replied. Jesus said to her, "You are right when you say you have no husband. The fact is, you have had five husbands, and the man you now have is not your husband. What you have just said is quite true."*

Jesus now used a thrust of the holy law to bring this woman to her senses. Only when she acknowledged her sin, guilt and need of everlasting life would she understand Jesus' offer. Christ commanded her to do something she could not do. "Go, call your husband," is the same as, "Be perfect, therefore, as your heavenly Father is perfect" (Mt 5:48). No one can keep God's law perfectly. This woman could not call her husband for, as she willingly confessed, she had none.

Jeus displayed his omniscience, for he knew she had been married to five men. The man she was presently living with was not her legal husband. Her thirst for lasting happiness, for real life, had led her to a dead-end of sexual impurity. She readily admitted her sin. Jesus commented, "You are right when you say you have no husband." Καλῶς εἶπες, literally "well said," was Jesus' approval of her confession. We consider how denying our sin is foolish self-deception. By confessing our sin, however, we are acknowledging our need of God's unconditional pardon. See 1 John 1:8,9 — a fitting commentary on Jesus' "well said."

vv. 19-26 — *"Sir," the woman said, "I can see that you are a prophet. Our fathers worshiped on this mountain, but you Jews claim that the place where we must worship is in Jerusalem." Jesus declared, "Believe me, woman, a time is coming when you will worship the Father neither on this mountain nor in Jerusalem. You Samaritans worship what you do not know; we worship what we do know, for salvation is from the Jews. Yet a time is coming and has now come when the true worshipers will worship the Father in spirit and truth, for they are the kind of worshipers the Father seeks. God is spirit, and his worshipers must worship in spirit and in truth." The woman said, "I know that Messiah" (called Christ) "is coming. When he comes, he will explain everything to us." Then Jesus declared, "I who speak to you am he."*

Christ's knowledge of this woman's personal life led her to the unmistakable conclusion, "You are a prophet." She had confessed her sin. She stood before a prophet. In sincere desire for forgiveness, she now raised an important issue. Where should she worship God? Where should she go to seek his mercy? The Samaritans had their worship center on Mt. Gerizim just south of Sychar. The Jews insisted that all sin offerings must be brought to Jerusalem. She hoped this prophet would help her seek God correctly.

Jesus did help her. He invited and commanded her to keep on believing him as he revealed the acceptable worship. Πίστευέ μοι, present active imperative means, "Keep on believing me." Jesus instructed her to express her belief, not by worshiping in a specific place, but by worshiping in a specific way. He turned her to the truth. Salvation is from the Jews. The Savior would be born of the tribe of Judah, not of Samaritan blood. With the comforting gospel revelation, that we worship God as our Father through faith in Christ, Jesus instructed her to worship the Father in spirit and in truth.

God is spirit. His nature is spiritual. He dwells not in buildings and temples made with human hands. We worship him properly when he moves our spirit. We worship him properly when we worship in truth, according to the true revelation he has given of himself in his Word. The δεῖ, "it is necessary," in verse 24 brings us face to face with this reality. Any worship that is mere ritual and form is in vain. Any worship that seeks God apart from or contrary to his truth is blasphemy.

The woman looked for the Messiah (v. 25). The Samaritans hoped for that prophet to whom all must listen (Dt 18:15). She turned to Jesus as the possible fulfillment of this hope. Jesus did not disappoint her. In plain language he now declared to her that he was the Messiah, the Savior, the One who had power to give her the living waters of life eternal, the One who could direct her to a blessed relationship with God as her heavenly Father.

Homiletical Suggestions

The Scripture lessons for this Sunday emphasize these truths: The Lord saved the human race from its sins through a Savior, through one Savior. The Son of God was born into the human race to cleanse us from our sins by his holy life and by his sacrificial death. He came from Abraham's descent, according to his human nature. But he is Savior of all. No one can merit the kingdom of heaven. Rather, those who are of the faith of Abraham receive God's promise of life everlasting.

The lessons for Lent prepare us to properly celebrate Good Friday and Easter. This Sunday we rejoice to remember that the Savior came for all. The Gospel, our sermon text, presents Jesus in all his compassion and love seeking a lost sinner of the Samaritan race. We see the Son of God's power in action, a power that works through his

Word to create spiritual life. We see that Jesus alone can quench our thirst for life with God.

By observing the Samaritan woman, we see a mirror reflection of ourselves. We have no right to claim we are God's chosen people due to our race, background or human effort. Like the woman, we would rush headlong into a lifetime of sin, trying to gratify that inner craving, that unquenchable thirst for real life, eternal life. Are not the epidemic of drug and alcohol abuse, the pursuit of sinful pleasure and the mad craze for earthly wealth symptoms of this thirst?

Jesus comes to us. He offers us the living water of eternal life. By believing in him we are drinking of that water freely, fully. Our consciences rest. Our haunting doubts dissolve. Our vain pursuit for real life, empty and hopeless without Jesus, is over. Jesus satisfies our thirst. By the gospel in word and sacrament the Holy Spirit has called us to faith in Jesus. The gifts of forgiveness of sins, peace with God, the confidence to call God our Father and fellowship with God now and forever in heaven quench our thirst for eternal life.

Religion has become popular again in America. Students on college campuses don't hide their quest for the spiritual. You no longer are considered odd if you speak openly of your religion. But the religion that is popular is false. Many profess to worship in spirit. Their emotional exuberance, their introspective meditation, or their "supernatural" experiences convince them that they have found true worship. The truth of Christ crucified and salvation through him alone, however, is still unpopular. Natural man rebels in pride against the necessity of a Savior from sin.

Jesus taught the woman of her need. He has taught us of our need through his holy law. He has taught us of forgiveness through his death and of justification through his resurrection. Thank God that he has given you the gift of faith. Worship him then in spirit and in truth. Lead your hearers to appreciate anew our worship service. Warn them about insincerity and mere formalism in worship. Encourage them by giving them the truth, the teachings of God's holy Word.

While religion is popular today, confusion reigns. People are searching the stars for guidance. They consult the gurus of Eastern cults. They seek to find hope in New Age pantheistic ideas. They look for the god within themselves. Their thirst rages on. The woman knew that the Messiah could answer her questions. How she must have thrilled to hear Jesus say, "I am he!" Take heart in knowing that the same Jesus, the holy Son of God, is our Savior. He answers our questions about the true God and how to have life with him. The news, "I am he," will bring peace to our troubled, often doubting and confused hearts.

What can we learn from Jesus about personal witness? Jesus was weary. Yet he used the opportunity to bring his word to the woman. She seemed beyond reach. She seemed not worth Jesus' while. But he cared. He cured. We too will grow weary. But we must remember Jesus is the only Savior, the Savior of all. Christ's love for us will move us to care for others who still don't have the living water. It will lead us to set aside prejudices of race, sex or social class. It will lead us to initiate conversations of a spiritual nature and to turn mundane talk to matters eternal. We too can be aware that those who are the most unlikely prospects due to their wanton sins may be the most likely to realize their need for rescue.

Jesus aroused the woman's curiosity. How shall we arouse in others a curious desire to learn more about Jesus? Perhaps Peter said it best when he wrote by inspiration, "Always be prepared to give an answer to everyone who asks you to give the reason for the hope that you have" (1 Pe 3:15).

The symbolism of thirst and living water suggests the following outline:

Quench Your Thirst with the Living Water!

1. Our sins give us an unquenchable thirst (vv. 5-18)
2. Our Savior offers us living water to quench our thirst (vv. 10-14,19-26)

The restless heart of man, which will not rest until it rests in the true God, suggests the following outline regarding true worship:

Who Says You Don't Need to Go to Church?

1. Jesus says you need more than going to church (vv. 19-21)
2. Jesus says you need to come to him (vv. 5-17)
3. Jesus says you need to worship the true God properly (vv. 22-26)

Part one explodes the myth that the proper building makes proper worship. It also reminds us that churchgoing doesn't make us Christians. Part two develops the Law/Gospel message of life through Christ alone. Part three stresses true worship, in spirit and in truth. The conclusion leads the hearer to understand how going to church, hearing God's Word and worshiping God with our fellow believers is God's unchanging will.

The mission emphasis of this text and the truth that Christ is Savior of all, as the Scripture lessons so clearly portray, lead to this development of theme and parts:

Learn to Witness at the Well of Salvation

1. See the spiritual needs of those who draw only natural water (vv. 15-17)
2. Offer them the living water of eternal life (vv. 5-11)
3. Lead them to see that Jesus alone is their Savior (vv. 19-26)

THIRD SUNDAY IN LENT

The Scriptures

Old Testament — *Isaiah 42:14-21*
Epistle — *Ephesians 5:8-14*
Gospel — *John 9:13-17,34-39*

The Text — John 9:13-17,34-39

The entire ninth chapter of John's Gospel treats Jesus' miracle of healing a man blind from birth, the investigation and unbelief of the Pharisees and Jesus' application. Since this chapter is a unit we shall briefly summarize the remaining verses which are not part of the text.

vv. 1-5 — One day as Jesus and his disciples were walking through Jerusalem they came upon a man afflicted with congenital blindness. Holding to a popular opinion of the day, that sin caused suffering, Jesus' disciples asked whose sin caused this handicap. Jesus answered that no one sinned in this case. Some suffering is caused by sin, but we should see suffering as an opportunity to see God's divine works and purpose. Here, in the man born blind, we have a case of this kind. Jesus instructs his disciples that they too will have works of God to do during their alloted time on earth. Jesus identifies himself as the Light of the world (Jn 1:9; 8:12).

vv. 6,7 — John describes the miracle. For this blind man to follow Jesus' instructions required some faith, which Jesus intended to awaken and strengthen in what followed.

vv. 8-12 — This miracle caused great excitement throughout the city. Like reporters at a presidential press conference, the neighbors and others ply the beggar with questions. His answer is unadorned and unembellished, dressed only in the truth. His answer reveals the name of his benefactor, but apparently he does not realize this miracle-worker is the world's Savior.

vv. 13,14 — *They brought to the Pharisees the man who had been blind. Now the day on which Jesus had made the mud and opened the man's eyes was a Sabbath.*

The Sabbath day had no doubt elapsed when this man was led to the Pharisees by his neighbors, townspeople and possibly some Pharisees. The question commentators struggle with is, Who are the Pharisees? Are they an informal gathering of men who are bent on making their influence felt? Or are they an organized court with the power and authority to excommunicate? The latter seems to have stronger support (vv. 22,34). Before this group Jesus is charged with breaking the rabbinical rules of the Sabbath (also v. 16). This can be seen as another effort on the part of the Pharisees to discredit Jesus.

v. 15 — *Therefore the Pharisees also asked him how he had received his sight. "He put mud on my eyes," the man replied, "and I washed, and now I see."*

Πάλιν, "again," indicates this was not the first time the blind man was asked this question. His friends and neighbors asked it. Now the Pharisees asked it. He had been bombarded with it. The man's answer is again very brief and a simple statement of the truth.

v. 16 — *Some of the Pharisees said, "This man is not from God, for he does not keep the Sabbath." But others asked, "How can a sinner do such miraculous signs?" So they were divided.*

As is often the case, Jesus' words and works produce different effects on different people. The Pharisees were divided into two opposing views regarding this miracle. One group mistakenly equated the Sabbath regulations set up by the Pharisees with those given by God. They believed Jesus could not be from God because he did not keep the Sabbath. They thus denied Jesus the possibility of doing this miracle. Something must be phony about this case.

The other group accepted the reality of the miracle in spite of the alleged Sabbath violations. They recognized Jesus' power. This statement from the Pharisees is proof of the effect Jesus produced upon the people. It stands in close association with the words of Nicodemus in 3:2, "Rabbi, we know you are a teacher who has come from God. For no one could perform the miraculous signs you are doing if God were not with him."

Unable to agree among themselves, the Pharisees turn again to the man who had been cured of his blindness.

v. 17 — *Finally they turned again to the blind man, "What have you to say about him? It was your eyes he opened." The man replied, "He is a prophet."*

There was the chance that this beggar might have given a vague answer or one which would have minimized the miracle of Jesus. Courageously he testified before his accusers. He recognized that his healing was a divine act. Therefore he concluded that the one who healed him was a prophet. How often a simple unlettered believer sees what learned doctors, teachers and theologians cannot see!

vv. 18-23 — The blind Jews, still contending that no miracle had been performed, continue their investigation with the man's parents. Intimidated by their cross-examination and afraid of being excommunicated, the parents plead ignorance.

vv. 24-33 — Still wanting to close the case the Pharisees call back the man who had been blind a third time. The Pharisees continued their derogatory attack on Jesus and they also sarcastically discredited the beggar. The Pharisees' foolish accusations help the beggar to draw his own simple, straightforward, truthful conclusions. The man grows in courage. Finally the beggar boldly concludes, "If this man were not from God, he could do nothing."

v. 34 — *To this they replied, "You were steeped in sin at birth; how dare you lecture to us!" And they threw him out.*

Having lost the argument the Pharisees resort to arrogant abuse. What the disciples of Jesus thought possible, and what Jesus denied (vv. 2,3) the Jews use for their shameful revenge. They state that this man's blindness proved his wickedness then and now. They call it an outrage that such a man should pretend to teach them. In their blindness the Pharisees still refused to recognize the miracle or Jesus' deity.

"And they threw him out." Out of the building and out of the religious fellowship of Israel. From what was stated before in verse 22, we see that this was a form of excommunication.

v. 35 — *Jesus heard that they had thrown him out, and when he found him he said, "Do you believe in the Son of Man?"*

Although the Pharisees had cast the man out, the Lord, the Good Shepherd, sought him out to finish the work he had begun in him. Jesus here seeks to go beyond the granting of physical sight to lead this man to true spiritual sight.

Since faith is a personal matter and is imperative for a relationship with the Savior (3:16,18) Jesus asks this man the all important question, "Do you believe in the Son of Man?" Jesus uses this expression on numerous occasions throughout the Gospels to refer to his deity (Mt 16:13; 17:9; Mk 2:10; 9:12; Lk 6:5; 19:10; Jn 3:13,14; 6:27). A variant reads, "the Son of God."

vv. 36-38 — *"Who is he, sir?" the man asked. "Tell me so that I may believe in him." Jesus said, "You have now seen him; in fact, he is the one speaking with you." Then the man said, "Lord, I believe," and he worshiped him.*

Like the woman at Jacob's well (4:5-26) this man had faith, but he lacked a full knowledge. The man requests that full knowledge with his questions. Jesus does not disappoint him. Jesus leads this man away from the idea that he is merely a prophet (v. 17) or a godly man (v. 31) to the fact that he is the true Messiah, the Son of Man, the Savior.

Now his spiritual eyes were opened to believe that the one who addressed him was the one who had healed him, namely Jesus, the Savior. In response the man worshiped Jesus. Thus the "work of God" (v. 3) was displayed in this man. His physical blindness had resulted in spiritual sight. God was glorified in this work.

v. 39 — *Jesus said, "For judgment I have come into this world, so that the blind will see and those who see will become blind."*

With this verse Jesus makes the application for the entire chapter in the form of a paradox. He speaks to the man who was blind, as well as the disciples and the Pharisees. He speaks about spiritual blindness and spiritual sight. Jesus states that his coming into the world has two diametrically opposed effects. Some, who are made to realize that they are indeed blind, receive him with joy and are blessed with a spiritual sight that remains. Others, who do not realize they are blind, boast that they see. They reject him and their blindness remains. This is the verdict of judgment (κρίμα) for which Jesus has come (3:17-21).

vv. 40,41 — Some Pharisees standing near Jesus resent what they felt was a reference to themselves. Jesus' reply is not meant to be a crushing final condemnation to hopelessness, but to lead them, who are still in sin, to the true spiritual light.

Homiletical Suggestions

This text provides an excellent opportunity to preach about spiritual sight and spiritual blindness. All people by nature are spiritually blind from birth. The Holy Spirit works faith and gives spiritual sight through God's word and sacraments. By God's grace many see and believe in Jesus as their Savior and are saved. Through their own fault others reject Jesus and are condemned. Many of the Jews, including the Pharisees of Jesus' day, saw Jesus the Light of the World, yet remained in spiritual darkness.

This text lends itself well to the Lenten season by contrasting the dreadful consequences of unbelief, which necessitated the Savior's suffering and death, with the glorious results of his redemptive work for us.

Jesus Christ, the Light of the World

1. Gives physical sight (vv. 13-17)
2. Gives spiritual sight (vv. 35-39)

Part one would show that by healing this man Jesus is the all-powerful God. Part two shows Jesus' power to save.

Natural eyes need help to see things that cannot be seen with the naked eye (e.g. magnifying glass, telescope, microscope, x-ray). As Christians we also need the eyes of Jesus to help us properly view life. This suggests:

What Can We See with the Eyes of Jesus?

1. Our natural condition of blindness (vv. 1-3)
2. Jesus' concern for us (v. 35)
3. The divine nature of Jesus (vv. 35-38)

Romans 8:28 tells us that "in all things God works for the good of those who love him." Using the thought of verse 3 that God's might and works were displayed in this man's blindness, a possible treatment would be:

God Worked Through This Blindness

1. To show this man mercy (vv. 13-17)
2. To lead him to Jesus (vv. 35-38)
3. To work spiritual life in him (v. 38)

Focusing on the thought in verse 39 that Jesus' coming produces a double effect or judgment among the people of the world, the preacher could try:

The Effects of Jesus' Coming

1. Enlightenment for those who accept him
2. Continued blindness for those who reject him

FOURTH SUNDAY IN LENT

The Scriptures

Old Testament — *Hosea 5:15-6:2*
Epistle — *Romans 8:1-10*
Gospel — *Matthew 20:17-28*

The Text — Matthew 20:17-28

The text divides itself neatly into two parts. The NIV heading for verses 17-19 is "Jesus Again Predicts His Death." For verses 20-28 the heading reads, "A Mother's Request."

The headings might just as correctly have read, "Jesus Predicts His *Life*" and "Jesus Predicts His Disciples' Lives." Verses 17-19 do not end with Jesus' prediction of his death. They end emphatically with a prediction of his rising to life. The succeeding verses involve a discussion regarding life in the world to come. Jesus himself is God's way of predicting that life for his people. Jesus is also God's way of prefiguring that life and the relationships of which it is constituted. Jesus takes some pains to make this clear to his followers.

vv. 17-19 — *Now as Jesus was going up to Jerusalem, he took the twelve disciples aside and said to them, "We are going up to Jerusalem, and the Son of Man will be betrayed to the chief priests and the teachers of the law. They will condemn him to death and will turn him over to the Gentiles to be mocked and flogged and crucified. On the third day he will be raised to life!"*

Jesus discusses the events which will take place in the coming days. He doesn't ask the disciples to make suggestions, consider options or provide for alternatives just in case things don't work out as he plans. He says he is going to be killed and be raised to life.

In his predictions, Jesus makes a point of calling himself the Son of Man. In him God became the offspring of the human race. Acting as the representative of the race, he submitted to the demands of the law and fulfilled them. Without sin himself, he endured the wrath of God against sin and the sinful race. Dying in the place of all, he was vindicated in his substitutionary work by his Father, who raised him from the dead.

He predicts that his death will come at the hands of both Jewish and Gentile leaders, at the hands of both God's people and godless peoples. Their action will typify and embody the innate hatred of all human beings for the Lord and his Anointed. Gentle, rightly behaved, church-going individuals carry in themselves the same inborn loathing for the true God as do persons of a dissolute and civilly unacceptable behavior.

To some extent, it is only in discovering how much we hate God by nature that we can truly begin to know in what way and to what degree God loves us.

vv. 20,21 — *Then the mother of Zebedee's sons came to Jesus with her sons and, kneeling down, asked a favor of him. "What is it you want?" he asked. She said, "Grant that one of these two sons of mine may sit at your right and the other at your left in your kingdom."*

The depth of the natural selfishness, even of those who follow Jesus, is demonstrated in this mother's question. Jesus had spoken of the price he would pay. Her thoughts, expressed in her request, were on the privilege and profit her sons could derive from his payment.

Jesus asks, "What do you want?" This will be the telling question when all is said and done. It is, after all, true that only those who want only what God wants them to want will have all their desires fulfilled.

vv. 22,23 — *"You don't know what you are asking," Jesus said to them. "Can you drink the cup I am going to drink?" "We can," they answered. Jesus said to them, "You will indeed drink from my cup, but to sit at my right or left is not for me to grant. These places belong to those for whom they have been prepared by my Father."*

It is obvious that the mother of the two fishermen didn't fathom the depth of the conversation in which she was involved. Jesus discerned this, as evidenced by his comment: "You don't know what you are asking." The rebuke is appreciated by every believer who has outgrown earlier simplistic ideas of what heaven is all about, who has left behind past foggy perceptions of just what it is that sinners truly need in order to become happy again.

Jesus asks a question about a *cup* and then makes a comment about that same cup. The question and comment appear to run contrary to each other. The question, "Can you drink?" seems to seek a negative answer. But when an affirmative is suppled Jesus responds with a prediction that coincides with the answer, as though in some way the affirmative is something he can put to good use.

The *cup* to which Jesus refers is apparently the swallowing of sufferings we have deserved which he will accomplish in his dying. In this sense, we obviously cannot swallow what he swallows. We cannot through our behavior establish our right to go uncondemned; that is precisely what he will do with his behavior.

On the other hand, we can swallow profitably the truth Jesus establishes in his sufferings. In this sense we drink from his cup, the same cup from which he drinks in suffering. We drink from the same cup; yet the results of our respective drinkings are different. Through his drinking he establishes the sinner's right to stand uncondemned. In swallowing his truth we gain the ability to establish that right for ourselves by learning to base our pleas on his behavior instead of on our own.

The cup is always an instrument of satisfaction. With his cup Jesus satisfied the demands of God's laws. Those who swallow that truth become unable to find satisfaction in doing anything other than fulfilling the laws of God and those who continue to swallow this truth until the very end come at last to the satisfaction of doing that very thing, i.e., fulfilling the laws of God themselves. This is the idea upon which Jesus proceeds to enlarge.

vv. 24-28 — *When the ten heard about this, they were indignant with the two brothers. Jesus called them together and said, "You know that the rulers of the Gentiles lord it over them, and their high officials exercise authority over them. Not so with you. Instead, whoever wants to be first must be your slave —just as the Son of Man did not come to be served, but to serve, and to give his life as a ransom for many."*

Apparently the other disciples were perturbed at the idea of God's kingdom being a place where someone else's wishes would be the basis for their activities. Jesus does not reprimand them for their outrage. On the other hand, he makes it very clear that there is a partial correctness in the interests which James and John express.

"You know that the rulers of the Gentiles lord it over them and their high officials exercise authority over them." Κατακυριεύω and κατεξουσιάζω both contain the idea of force, of external constraint, of the desires of one party being foisted upon a second party, of subjects being compelled to act in one way while wishing they could get away with behavior of a different sort. This is the way worldly kingdoms often operate. This is not the way God's kingdom operates.

God's kingdom is a place where individuals don't do anything except the things they want to do. To this extent, God's kingdom is different from those we are familiar with. Likewise, to this extent, the brothers' request was a poor one. It was based on some misconceptions concerning the dominion of God.

On the other hand, God's kingdom does in fact have a great deal to do with the desires of one party becoming the basis for the activities of certain other parties. We can correctly say that heaven is a place where individuals don't do anything they don't want to do. It is just as important to point out that heaven is full of individuals who don't want to do anything except the things the King of heaven wants them to do. Those who dwell there have been gifted with desires which reflect precisely in size and shape those which are constantly conceived in the heart of God.

The kingdom of God differs from the kingdoms of men not in the nature of the relationships of which it is comprised but in the thoroughness of the domination practiced there. Worldly dominion rarely develops an undivided allegiance of the heart. Heavenly dominion never fails to do so. Both our readings for today take this fact into consideration. Hosea 5:15 says, "He will restore us that we may live in his presence." How could we call it "living" to dwell in the presence of One whose desires we were constantly required to carry out unless our desires were a perfect duplicate of his own? Romans 8:4 says, "He condemned sin in sinful man that the righteous requirements of the [God's] law might be fully met in us." Jesus didn't only declare us righteous. He came that at last we ourselves should be made righteous, carrying out God's wishes with the same wholehearted devotion we saw in him, finding in that activity the same satisfaction he knew, tasting at last "the food to eat that you know nothing about"(Jn 4:32-38).

In God's kingdom, greatness consists in being rendered undividedly subject to the desires of another. It will be great to be that way (v. 26). Those who want to share in that greatness must adopt our desires as their own (v. 27) which is to say they must adopt God's desires as their own. This adoption commences only when we accept the fact that the Son of Man himself paid a price we could not afford to pay (v. 28) and got us out of a predicament from which we could not begin to extricate ourselves.

Homiletical Suggestions

The text lends itself well to this season of the church year. We are about to turn the corner from Lent/Easter into Pentecost/Trinity. Lent/Easter recalls the historical facts which introduce those who accept them to a situation in which no variety of sinning can ever be described as "living." The text reviews the facts. It describes in detail the saintly freedom from sinning which is desired by all who are unable to describe sinning as "living" and who yet find themselves incessantly involved in that sinning.

The text will not suit us if we prefer to talk about heaven as a place where sinners are freed from the externally oppressive results of sin. Sickness, pain and physical death are not at issue here. The freedom discussed here is specifically the freedom from evil, freedom from all propensity toward violation of God's standards.

If the preacher should prefer not to discuss this variety of freedom, he might want to base his message on verses 17-19 alone. Simple review of the history presented here and faithful mention of that history's significance will awaken in the hearts of hearers a hope for this variety of freedom without putting the preacher through the development of propositions based on concepts better experienced than described. Holiness is difficult for sinners to grasp with words. We tend to be much better at awaiting it than talking about it.

There is both magnanimity and magnitude in our text. What Jesus did for us is great. What he promises us is great. These facts would lead us to conclude that:

Life Is Great

1. His life on our behalf (vv. 17-19,28)
2. Our life in his kingdom (vv. 20-27)

It is extraordinary for someone to find the idea of constant service an appealing sort of thing. Most people who make a living in performing services don't describe serving as living. On the other hand there is one exclusive service in which all those fully involved can't imagine describing any other activity as "living." Therefore we might talk about:

Life in the Service

1. His life was used in serving us (vv. 17-19,28)
2. Our life consists in serving him (vv. 20-27)

Living a good life is not ordinarily the kind of behavior the world regards as perfectly enjoyable. However, the good life Jesus lived eventually leads believers to regard leading a good life as the only activity they find pleasurable. An interesting contrast therefore might involve considering:

Living the Good Life

1. Is what Jesus did from birth to death (vv. 17-19,28)
2. Is the only proper response to his death and resurrection (vv. 20-27)

FIFTH SUNDAY IN LENT

The Scriptures

Old Testament — *Ezekiel 37:1-3,(4-10),11-14*
Epistle — *Romans 8:11-19*
Gospel — *John 11:47-53*

Since the fall of man into sin it has always been our loving Father's plan to bring life from death. In this Sunday's Old Testament lesson, God pictures that plan through the striking vision of the dry bones being brought to life. In the Epistle the person made alive by the Spirit anticipates sharing in the glory of Christ in the life to come. The Gospel shows the life-giving promise near its fulfillment as the Sanhedrin forges the plot "that one man die for the people."

The Text — John 11:47-53

The incident in our text takes place during "the last months" in response to the raising of Lazarus from the dead. We note especially the dual response to the great miracle in verses 45 and 46: some believed, but some went right back to Jesus' enemies the Pharisees and reported to them what had happened. All of Jesus' enemies are now in the mood to "do something" before the whole matter gets out of hand.

Immediately after the text John reports that Jesus knew of the plot and therefore removed himself from the immediate area. Some commentators believe that Jesus then engaged in what is called his "Perean ministry" (Lk 13:10ff).

The choice of this text for Lent 5 emphasizes that things are now set for the death of Christ to take place. There's no turning back. The week of Jesus' passion is right around the corner. As our text begins, the plotting begins.

vv. 47,48 — *Then the chief priests and the Pharisees called a meeting of the Sanhedrin.*

"What are we accomplishing?" they asked. "Here is this man performing many miraculous signs. If we let him go on like this, everyone will believe in him, and then the Romans will come and take away both our place and our nation."

A meeting of the Sanhedrin was called in response to the report of those who had seen Lazarus raised. The "chief priests and Pharisees" mentioned here are a representative group of the Sanhedrin that called the entire assembly together for official action. The

Sanhedrin was the council of 70 headed by the high priest and composed of certain members of the high priest's family, elders (respected leaders) and Bible scholars (teachers of the Law). Any of these members could belong to either of the two prominent spiritual sects, the Pharisees and Sadducees. These two sects, which usually opposed one another, found unity in purpose at this meeting as they both sought to get rid of Jesus of Nazareth.

The question this group asks itself indicates that, in their opinion, things were going from bad to worse in regard to Jesus. All their previous attempts to trap him in his words and discredit him publicly have been fruitless. Jesus' signs (σημεῖα) completely counteracted their attempts to nullify his effectiveness as a spiritual leader.

It's ironic that earlier they had demanded "signs" of Jesus so that he might prove himself (Mt 12:38,39). They had wanted visible proof that what he said was true and that he really did come from God. They had demanded a σημεῖον, which was a deed that would "authenticate the ministry of Jesus and refute all doubts concerning him" (*The Theological Dictionary of the New Testament, Abridged*, p. 1019). Now they simple state the fact that Jesus' deeds are true and substantial enough for people to take him as coming from God. Yet in their stubborn unbelief they refuse to accept the obvious facts and are intent upon doing something to get ride of the one who performs the signs.

The Sanhedrin feels compelled to do something to stop these signs, especially in view of the effect of this latest and greatest miracle performed by Jesus. The raising of Lazarus had caused such a sensation, it seemed to them that everyone would soon believe in him — everyone, that is, except those who were on their side, the side of adamant unbelief in spite of the clear evidence. Jesus would say to his unsure disciples on the night before his death, "Believe me when I say that I am in the Father and the Father is in me; or at least believe on the evidence of the miracles themselves" (Jn 14:11). The purpose of the miracles or "signs" of Jesus was to convince those who were receptive to his words that he really was the true Son of God. Though they did not accept the evidence themselves, the Sanhedrin was perceptive enough to realize what a tremendous effect the unchecked miracles of Jesus would continue to have. More and more people were believing in Jesus. Something had to be done that was far more drastic than their previous challenges, or more serious trouble lay ahead.

The Sanhedrin's conclusion concerning what the unchecked popularity of Jesus would bring was totally inaccurate. They drew a false conclusion on the basis of their unbelief, their misconception of the Messiah's purpose and their concern for their own position. They thought that with all these people hailing Jesus as the Messiah, he would succumb to the same sinful weaknesses they had and elevate himself as a worldly revolutionary ruler, thus inviting the Romans to squash the rebellion in a forceful way. That would be a threat to them, for whatever authority they still possessed under Roman rule would then be taken away altogether. How ironic that they, in their unbelief, are worried about losing their "place" and "nation" when the true work of the Christ was to bring an everlasting spiritual kingdom that would transcend any place or any nation.

The word of God still straightens out people's misconceptions in regard to the importance of "place" and "nation." In regard to the "place" of worship, Jesus had to straighten out both a Samaritan woman (Jn 4:22) and his own apostles (Mt 24:2). As Jesus battled the false notion that membership in the right "nation" made people acceptable to God, he held up as an example of faith a soldier who was outside the chosen nation. Faith in Christ views "place" and "nation" in the proper perspective as the people of God see themselves as the Savior's dwelling place.

vv. 49,50 — *Then one of them, named Caiaphas, who was high priest that year, spoke up, "You know nothing at all! You do not realize that it is better for you that one man die for the people than that the whole nation perish."*

Caiaphas's words imply that the members of the Sanhedrin were lacking in factual knowledge. He's telling them they didn't have a handle on the situation because they hadn't properly analyzed the facts. John's reference to Caiaphas being high priest "that year" does not imply that this was the only year that he was high priest but that during this most significant year Caiaphas happened to be the high priest.

Caiaphas takes charge of this dignified body and states his opinion in an abrasive and insulting manner. His stubborn pride resulted in his impatience and rudeness. It also resulted in something far more serious than that. Stubborn pride caused Caiaphas's heart to remain cold and hard, even when confronted with the prophetic words of the One who would someday judge him. He would hear Jesus say, "In the future you will see the Son of Man sitting at the right hand of the Mighty One and coming on the clouds of heaven" (Mt 26:64). Stubborn pride still causes impatience, rudeness and unbelief, even when confronted with God's saving truth.

In stating "you do not realize," Caiaphas uses the Greek word λογίζεσθε, meaning to calculate, take into account or consider. According to Caiaphas's cold calculations, there is only one possible solution to this serious problem. Jesus must die. Either Jesus dies, he says, or we all die at the hands of the Romans. Let Jesus die so that we do not have to. In order to manipulate the body into seeing the situation his way, he presents only two extreme alternatives, as though there was no other possible course of action. To Caiaphas it was such a logical choice. It apparently had not even occurred to the rest. This shows the true wickedness of his heart.

This course of action would require either an assassination or a mock trial at which the guilty verdict and death sentence were predetermined. John does not indicate that anyone objected to the plot, although Scripture states that Nicodemus objected earlier (Jn 7:50) and Joseph of Arimathea did not give his consent to the death of Jesus (Lk 23:51).

The wording Caiaphas uses in stating that "one man die for the people" (ὑπέρ plus the genitive) indicates a substitution. It could be translated "one man die in place of the people." In his heart it was a wicked plot to get rid of one undesirable so that he and his people would not have to die. In the heart of God it was a loving plan through which he would embrace a world of undesirables so that they would not have to die the kind of death required of his son.

vv. 51,52 — *He did not say this on his own, but as high priest that year he prophesied that Jesus would die for the Jewish nation, and not only for that nation but also for the scattered children of God, to bring them together and make them one.*

"Not on his own" did Caiaphas speak the words of his carefully worded plan, but God chose to move the high priest to express his wicked plot in just this way. God controls events and people to make evil work together for good (Ex 50:20; Ro 8:28). In the case of Caiaphas, God even controls the words he speaks. God chose the high priest to utter a prophetic statement that would benefit not only the people of Israel but also all people in general. The high priest was not a prophet, and God was no longer revealing his will through the high priest by means of Urim and Thummin. The text does not imply that God had the custom of giving revelations through the high priest annually. Yet at this significant point in history God chose to use the high priest's words to offer a divine comment on what was about to happen.

The fact that Caiaphas states so clearly and in just the right way what God wanted him to say gives us an example of verbal inspiration. God chose the very thoughts and words that he wanted the high priest to express, even though the high priest did not even understand the real meaning behind his statement, and even though the high priest thought only in terms of evil for Jesus and not good for all people. 1 Peter 1:10,11 implies that the inspired prophets themselves studied what God had moved them to write without a total understanding of the words which the Spirit had chosen. God's Spirit, through the miracle of Holy Scripture, has revealed a clear and saving message in spite of the wickedness of sinners who rebel and fight against it.

Caiaphas had used the term "people" (λαοῦ), a term used for the Jews as God's covenant people. This was God's intention, that his Son die in the place of people who would benefit from his gospel covenant. This was first of all the Jews through whom the promise would be realized. But it was also the entire human race. As John comments on this promise he switches to the word "nation" (ἔθνος), emphasizing that the Jewish people had for the most part forsaken God's covenant. They were now merely the nation through whom God had made the promise and were not the "people of God" by faith. John then immediately adds that this promise was not merely for the Jewish nation, but for all people of all nations for all time. From all the nations of the world the children of God would be gathered into the one holy Christian church by Spirit-worked faith in the Savior who gave his life to earn forgiveness for all people.

John also switches from using the Greek ὑπέρ ("for," "in place of") to a ἵνα purpose clause. It was God's purpose in Christ to gather all people together into the body of believers, for Christ provided forgiveness for all with his universal, vicarious atonement (Jn 1:29; 2 Cor 5:19). God's purpose will be accomplished as people, who are not only scatterd throughout the world but are straying away from God in unbelief (Is 53:6), are brought together by faith into the one church of Jesus Christ (Jn 17:11,22; Eph 4:4-6). The gathering of scattered sinners into the church of Jesus Christ is the ultimate fulfillment of restoration prophecies such as Zephaniah 3:9,10,19,20. The death and resurrection of Jesus provided the powerful, saving message which the Spirit uses to do the gathering.

v. 53 — *So from that day on they plotted to take his life.*

We can almost see the 70 heads of the Sanhedrin nodding in enthusiastic agreement to Caiaphas's wicked suggestion. It appears to be so logical. Yet with all their power and influence they are unable to carry out their plan without the direct assistance of the Lord himself. He would allow the betrayer to assist them and fulfill Old Testament prophecy in doing so, and their plot would materialize only as Jesus himself would submit to their arrest and lay down his life in humble submission. For he clearly stated concerning his life, "No one takes it from me" (Jn 10:18). A gracious God was in control, making sure that "one man die for the people."

Homiletical Suggestions

Obviously the central truth emphasized in this text is the substitutionary death of Christ. No better theme could be emphasized as God's people make their final preparations for Holy Week. God's providence and the doctrine of inspiration also play a supporting role in presenting that truth. The Lord guides Caiaphas to capture prophetically the central theme.

One Man Dies for the People

1. The plot of a wicked court (vv. 47-50,53)
2. The plan of a perfect Judge (vv. 51,52)

These same thoughts could be emphasized from a slightly different perspective.

Look What a Gathering This Is

1. Evil leaders gather to plot death (vv. 47-50,53)
2. Scattered people will be gathered and given life (vv. 51,52)

The desperate question of the Sanhedrin suggests a three-part outline emphasizing the redemptive work of the Savior and applying the truths directly to our Christian lives.

Look at What the One Man Is Accomplishing

1. He invites us to believe the signs (vv. 47,48)
2. He dies in our place (vv. 49,50)
3. He gathers us into his family (vv. 51,52)

PALM SUNDAY

The Scriptures

Old Testament — *Isaiah 50:4-9b*
Epistle — *Philippians 2:5-11*
Gospel — *Matthew 27:11-54*

The Text — Matthew 27:27-44

The text is a shorter portion of the Gospel reading. It is hoped that a shorter text will allow the preacher to focus the sermon more sharply.

The traditional emphasis of Palm Sunday has been on Jesus as king. When he entered Jerusalem on the first Palm Sunday, the people acclaimed him as king. Nowhere else in Scripture does Jesus have all the symbols (crown of thorns, scepter, purple garment, obeisance) of royalty as in this text.

The text focuses on the climactic event in God's saving activity in rescuing the human race from the consequences and the power of sin. There are two important facts to keep in mind. One is the willingness of Jesus to go through all of this. The other is that it was planned.

We can see the willingness of Jesus in several ways. He could have called on twelve legions of angels (Mt 26:53) to avoid arrest. He identified himself to those who had come to arrest him. He prayed: "Father, if you are willing, take this cup from me; yet not my will, but yours be done!"

God had been planning and revealing details about Jesus' death and its impact for a long time. The Old Testament selection for this Sunday (Is 50:6) reads, "I offered my back to those who pulled out my beard; I did not hide my face from mocking and spitting." Isaiah 53 also gives us many details about what God was planning to do.

It was not an accident that Jesus ended up on the cross. God planned it and then executed his plan for the sake of world's salvation. Jesus was suffering all this for you and me.

v. 27 — *Then the governor's soldiers took Jesus into the Praetorium and gathered the whole company of soldiers around him.*

The soldiers were Roman, stationed in Jerusalem to keep the peace. The group of soldiers was a σπεῖρα, that is a cohort or company. A cohort was one-tenth of a legion, so a sizable number of soldiers (between 600 and 1000) took part in the mistreatment of the prisoner.

vv. 28-30 — *They stripped him and put a scarlet robe on him, and then twisted together a crown of thorns and set it on his head. They put a staff in his right hand and knelt in front of him and mocked him. "Hail, King of the Jews!" they said. They spit on him, and took the staff and struck him on the head again and again.*

Here we see Jesus with every symbol of royalty. These symbols signified the power and position of a king. The soldiers intended to mock and make fun of him. Without realizing the aptness of what they were doing, they were making a true statement about him.

They grabbed a faded scarlet robe and put it on him. This was in place of the royal purple. They made a crown for him as well. In this case, it was made of ἄκανθα — a thorn plant. They put a staff in his right hand to serve as a scepter, a symbol of royal power. In every way they were trying to make him look ridiculous.

Oriental kings demanded that their subjects bow before them. So the soldiers bowed before Jesus, but with the mocking words, "Hail, King of the Jews!" They spit on him. With his "scepter" they repeatedly struck him (the imperfect ἔτυπτον).

This scene was in fulfillment of prophecy. The Old Testament reading comes from Isaiah 50. Verse 6 describes some of the torture, the mocking and spitting that the Messiah would endure.

v. 31 — *After they had mocked him, they took off the robe and put his own clothes on him. Then they led him away to crucify him.*

Finally the soldiers finished their "fun." They returned Jesus' own clothes to him. It was time to move on to the crucifixion, the most shameful and excruciating execution available under Roman law.

v. 32 — *As they were going out, they met a man from Cyrene, named Simon, and they forced him to carry the cross.*

The Roman practice was to make the victim carry the cross to the site of execution. This was always outside the city. A procession was formed. Often it went through various parts of the city so that people would know what was going on. The place of execution would be near the town, at a crossroads or on a well-traveled highway. Many people would see it and be reminded of the consequences of crime.

It was impossible for Jesus to carry the cross all the way. We can understand why when we consider all that he had already endured. The soldiers drafted Simon.

v. 33 — *They came to a place called Golgotha (which means The Place of the Skull).*

Γολγοθᾶ received its name either because it had features similar to that of a skull or because it was a place of execution. We must not think, however, of unburied skulls lying around this place of execution. The Jews would never have tolerated that.

vv. 34-36 — *There they offered Jesus wine to drink, mixed with gall; but after tasting it, he refused to drink it. When they had crucified him, they divided up his clothes by casting lots. And sitting down, they kept watch over him there.*

Often executioners offered their victims a drink such as gall to deaden the pain somewhat. Jesus did not want anything to do with that. He was willing to suffer the punishment for the world's sins without any relief or palliative of any sort.

As the soldiers waited for the victim to die, they amused themselves by gambling. The winner got a portion of Jesus' garments. God had predicted this would happen in Psalm 22:18.

vv. 37-39 — *Above his head they placed the written charge against him: THIS IS JESUS, THE KING OF THE JEWS. Two robbers were crucified with him, one on his right and one on his left. Those who passed by hurled insults at him, shaking their heads.*

Here again is testimony that Jesus is a king. The Romans put the offense of which the criminal was guilty on a placard and placed it where everyone could see and read it. John 19:20 tells us that it was written in Aramaic, Latin and Greek.

The charge placed on Jesus' cross testified to Pilate's desire to insult the Jews whose bidding he was doing. He was as much as saying, "You surely have a fine king who dies such a death." But the placard also testified to the truth.

Pilate decided to execute two other men as well. They were both robbers. One of the robbers later admitted (Lk 23:4) that they both were getting what they deserved. Jesus was to die in the company of criminals. This fulfilled the prophecy of Isaiah 53:12, which reads: "[He] was numbered with the transgressors."

As people passed by the site, they mocked and insulted Jesus. Our text uses ἐβλασφήμουν, the imperfect, telling us that this kept on; many people joined in the mockery. God had also predicted in writing that Jesus would suffer such mockery (Ps 22:7; 109:25; Lm 2:15).

v. 40 — *and saying, "You who are going to destroy the temple and build it in three days, save yourself! Come down from the cross, if you are the Son of God!"*

As they insulted Jesus the Jews even quoted him. John 2:19 tells us how Jesus had instructed the people with the words which the scoffers quote here. "But the temple he had spoken of was his body. After he was raised from the dead, his disciples recalled what he had said. Then they believed the Scriptures and the words Jesus had spoken" (Jn 2:21,22).

The mockers at Golgotha did not realize the truth of what they were saying. Were some of these same people part of the crowd that had honored and hailed Jesus just five days previously when he entered Jerusalem on Palm Sunday? We cannot say.

vv. 41-44 — *In the same way the chief priests, the teachers of the law and the elders mocked him. "He saved others," they said, "but he can't save himself! He's the king of Israel! Let him come down from the cross, and we will believe in him. He trusts in God. Let God rescue him now if he wants him, for he said, "I am the Son of God." In the same way the robbers who were crucified with him also heaped insults on him.*

The members of the Sanhedrin lowered themselves to join the crowd's mockery. Note the present participle, ἐμπαίζοντες: They kept at it and came up with quite a few insults.

They spoke of Jesus saving others. Undoubtedly they were thinking of some of his healing miracles. Now they mistook his restraint for weakness. Jesus had the power to come down from the cross. But he *wanted* to be there because he knew it was the only way to pay for the sins of the world. In one very real sense he could not come down — if he wanted the sins of the world to be paid for.

Not only were they taunting Jesus. They were also demanding certain signs before they would believe. Even these insults fulfilled prophecy. Compare Psalm 22:8 with verse 43. They were identifying Jesus as Messiah, even though they did not realize it.

Even the robbers joined in. The imperfect ὠνείδιζον tells us that this was an ongoing action. The robbers kept at it.

So we see Jesus in the depth of humiliation. He suffers a degrading execution. His friends had abandoned him and his enemies were insulting him. All of this and more Jesus sufferd on our behalf.

Homiletical Suggestions

The historic Gospel for Palm Sunday describes Jesus' triumphant entry into Jerusalem. The Epistle, Philippians 2:5-11, treats of his humiliation. It shows that Jesus is God, but that he made himself nothing in his humiliation. So the emphasis for the day is on Jesus as the King who comes in great humility in order to save.

Your King Comes to You

1. Humbly
2. Willingly
3. To Save

God was bringing his plan of salvation to fruition. None of this happened by accident. God was guiding and controlling events so that the end result was the substitutionary death of his Son. The many fulfillments of prophecy show clearly that God had planned this.

This Is Jesus, King of the Jews

1. That was the mockers' taunt.
2. That was the Scriptures' prophecy.
3. That is our confession.

Those who mocked Jesus and insulted him were making true statements about him. Even "he saved others"was an unintended acknowledgment of Jesus' purpose and achievement. Even they, with their sneers, correctly answered the question:

Who Is That Man on the Cross?

1. The King of the Jews
2. The Son of God
3. The Savior of the World

MAUNDY THURSDAY

The Scriptures

Old Testament — *Exodus 12:1-14*
Epistle — *1 Corinthians 11:23-26*
Gospel — *John 13:1-17,34*

The Text — John 13:1-17,34

Those who learn about the origin of the word Maundy are often surprised. The word comes from the Latin word *mandatum*, meaning command. When we speak of Maundy Thursday, we mean *commandment Thursday*. Additional surprise comes in finding out that Thursday of Holy Week was not named for Jesus' words, "Do this in remembrance of me," but for his beautiful words of John 13:34, "A new command I give you: Love one another. As I have loved you, so you must love one another."

In John 13:1-17,34 we have a summary of Jesus' entire passion (verse 1), Jesus' object lesson of love (verses 2-17), and Jesus' command from which Maundy Thursday derived its name (verse 34).

v. 1 — *It was just before the Passover Feast. Jesus knew that the time had come for him to leave this world and go to the Father. Having loved his own who were in the world, he now showed them the full extent of his love.*

The Passover Feast referred to in verse 1 is the third one during Jesus' ministry. John's Gospel records the others in 2:13 and 6:4. This third Passover is first mentioned in John 11:55.

Jesus knew the events that would occur within the next 24 hours because of his omniscience (Jn 21:17), and he had even predicted them at least twice (Mt 16:21; 20:18). The word ὥρα is translated either "hour" or "time" in the NIV. The context determines whether a specific hour of the day is meant, or an indefinite period of time. The translation "time" is a good choice, here, since John refers to the whole period of Jesus' Passion.

The ἵνα clause with the aorist subjunctive expresses purpose, and has the force of an infinitive. "To go to the Father" shows us the victory Christ already has in mind. "To leave this world" sums up the battle and the victory. This all would culminate in Jesus' expression of love, his suffering and death. "Showed the full extent of his love" expresses this idea and is later restated in Jesus' words of John 15:13, "Greater love has no one than this, that he lay down his life for his friends."

Thus John introduces us to Jesus' Passion, using the brief verse to highlight Jesus *agape* love for the world. It was this love that also moved him to take on the humble task of washing the disciples' feet.

vv. 2-5 — *The evening meal was being served, and the devil had already prompted Judas Iscariot, son of Simon, to betray Jesus. Jesus knew that the Father had put all things under his power, and that he had come from God and was returning to God; so he got up from the meal, took off his outer clothing, and wrapped a towel around his waist. After that, he poured water into a basin and began to wash his disciples' feet, drying them with the towel that was wrapped around him.*

The supper the group was about to eat was the Passover meal. Jesus' own disciples had prepared it in advance according to the Lord's instructions (Mt 26:18,19).

The devil prompted Judas. The perfect participle indicates that the devilish influence had begun in the past and continued to the present.

Verse 3 brings out the truth that Jesus had power over the events taking place. He was in firm control. Further, the references to Father and God remind us of the beautiful relationship we enjoy with the Creator: He is *our* Father and *our* God. See John 20:17.

Verses 4 and 5 remind us that the disciples were more interested in being the greatest than in volunteering for the most menial task of servants, washing feet. The Lord, who came to serve and not to be served, took up the task to the shame of them all. Peter's later reaction reveals the guilt in all their hearts. The verb forms of verses 4 and 5 are set in John's simple, straightforward style and require no deeper examination. John has related the facts as the Spirit gave them, and as he experienced them on that Holy Thursday. John's account in verses 2-5 reviews the important lesson Jesus wanted to teach.

vv. 6-11 — *He came to Simon Peter, who said to him, "Lord, are you going to wash my feet?" Jesus replied, "You do not realize now what I am doing, but later you will understand." "No", said Peter, "you shall never wash my feet." Jesus answered, "Unless I wash you, you have no part with me." "Then, Lord," Simon Peter replied, "not just my feet but my hands and my head as well!" Jesus answered, "A person who has had a bath needs only to wash his feet; his whole body is clean. And you are clean, though not every one of you." For he knew who was going to betray him, and that was why he said not every one was clean.*

The Apostle Peter was never at a loss for words. Here, too, he expresses himself. His question reveals the guilt that all of them felt. Peter sought to stop this humiliation. But Jesus answered him with words that helped answer Peter's wondering question. In the context of his coming sacrifice, this menial service is further evidence of his great love. It is also an example of loving service which instructs and inspires all his disciples.

Verses 6-8 are simple sentences with indicatives used in most verbs. The aorist subjunctive of verse 8, νίψῃς, expresses a strong future negation. Robertson describes the double negative usage with the subjunctive at 365, 2. He calls it "vulgar koine." Jesus' answer also uses the aorist subjunctive in a present general condition. The use relates Jesus' thoughts to Peter. "This is the way it has to be," seems to be the sense of it. Jesus is trying to teach Peter a lesson in humility, and so Peter must receive the washing from Jesus.

Verse 9 shows the quick change of Peter's attitude. First, he wouldn't allow Jesus to wash his feet, then he switched and wanted his hands and head done also. His great desire to have part in Jesus' cause is commendable. The next verse shows that such extremes are not necessary for Peter to be clean and have a part with Jesus.

In verse 10, Jesus continues the illustration about cleansing. The sense is double, as Jesus speaks of spiritual and physical cleanliness. The persons are all clean, have bathed, but they are not all morally clean. Judas is the exception. Lenski brings up the idea of baptism, but that is pushing the illustration too far.

In verse 11, John reminds his readers that Jesus knew what Judas had planned. In the midst of his example on humility, Jesus was aware of Judas' unclean heart. One wonders what went through Judas's heart as Jesus washed his feet.

Peter's objections have been answered, and the menial task is completed. Jesus sought to bring home the whole point of this in his following words in verses 12-17 and 34.

> vv. 12-17,34 — *When he had finished washing their feet, he put on his clothes and returned to his place. "Do you understand what I have done for you?" he asked them. "You call me 'Teacher' and 'Lord,' and rightly so, for that is what I am. Now that I, your Lord and Teacher have washed your feet, you also should wash one another's feet. I have set you an example that you should do as I have done for you. I tell you the truth, no servant is greater than his master, nor is a messenger greater than the one who sent him. Now that you know these things, you will be blessed if you do them. . . . A new command I give*

you: Love one another. As I have loved you, so you must love one another."

Jesus' question of verse 12 is intended to drive home the whole point of his object lesson. Of course they have seen what he did, and they know what he did. But do they understand it? That is the force of the verb, γινώσκω to perceive, to understand, to recognize. They were to understand his example of humility and love. He as their Teacher and Lord had done this for them. Their pride was too great if they believed they couldn't do the same for one another. That was part of the lesson involved. To love as Jesus does means laying pride aside. It means to be willing to serve. If the Lord and Teacher had done it, his followers ought to also.

Verses 15 and 16 record Jesus' idea that this has been his example, his object lesson. He did it so that they might follow it. With the solemn pronouncement of verse 16, he tells them that they are not greater than their Lord, as no servant is greater than his master. The example has shown this. They have felt the guilt involved; their consciences have been pricked.

Verse 17 gives the motivation to follow his love, and the promise their hurting consciences need. They will be blessed. The present subjunctive of the conditional clause indicates the blessing will be an ongoing thing.

Verse 34 is the crown verse of this text. Jesus has shown them the example and given them motivation to follow it: his blessing. Now he gives them his new commandment. It is not characterized by threats and demands, but rests on his love: "As I have loved you." The commandment is not new in the sense that it had never been given before. The essence of all God's law is "Love." What is new is the motivation and example of Jesus' sacrificial love: "*As I* have loved you, *so you* must love one another."

So the great new command is given and demonstrated on this Thursday of Holy Week. One almost wishes the day had been named for the love shown by Christ. God's people, who hear this beautiful account presented, will also come to know the day as "Loving Thursday."

Homiletical Suggestions

The Scripture lessons for Maundy Thursday beautifully weave together the many thoughts of this memorable night. The Exodus 12 account gives Moses' instructions for the Passover meal and celebration. The First Corinthians 11 reading is Paul's account of the institution of the Lord's Supper. The Epistle lesson is the conclusion to the Old Testament Scripture, for the Passover finds its completion in Christ and the Lord's Supper. The Gospel treated in this study is the sanctification message. The Old Testament and Epistle readings are tied together in the Passover and Lord's Supper, with the Gospel lesson in the middle giving us the fulfillment and practical application. The key is, "Love one another. As I have loved you, so you must love one another." His love for his people was seen in the Passover events, in the Lord's Supper, and at Calvary. His parting thought, beautifully demonstrated in word and act, is "Love one another."

The sermon for this text will center on Jesus' love and humility, and the corresponding example in washing the feet. The following outlines are offered.

Jesus Took on the Form of a Servant

1. To show the love of the Servant of the Lord (vv. 1-10)
2. To show the Lord's servants how to love (vv. 11-17,34)

Jesus Was Serious About His Love

1. He demonstrated his love to his disciples (vv. 1-10)
2. He encouraged his disciples to love (vv. 11-17,34)

GOOD FRIDAY

The Scriptures

Old Testament — *Isaiah 52:13-53:12*
Epistle — *Hebrews 4:14-16;5:7-9*
Gospel — *John 19:17-30*

The Text — John 19:17-30

The groundwork has been laid in the previous chapters of John's Gospel. Now the Evangelist records for us how the events of Maundy Thursday and Good Friday reached their inevitable climax. After several attempts to release Jesus, Pilate reluctantly delivered him over to be crucified.

vv. 17,18 — *Carrying his own cross, he went out to the place of the Skull (which in Aramaic is called Golgotha). Here they crucified him, and with him two others — one on each side and Jesus in the middle.*

The words of these verses are clear and concise. John does not go into detail concerning Jesus' walk to Golgotha. See Luke 23:26-32 for additional information.

The manner of our Savior's death (crucifixion) had been predetermined, not by Pilate's edict or the shouts of the angry mob, but by the will of God (Jn 3:14). Jesus willingly took on himself the burden of the cross and all that it implied: shame, suffering, death. The crucifixion was to take place outside the city walls at a location called "the place of the Skull." Speculation abounds concerning this designation. Some of the more plausible explanations for the name seem to favor the skull-like shape of the hill (although the Bible does not specifically say it was a hill) or that this place was a known site of executions.

With two simple words (αὐτὸν ἐσταύρωσαν) John relates the most remarkable sacrifice in the history of the world. It is interesting to note that the subject of the verb is left indefinite. John does not write "the soldiers" crucified Jesus, even though it was a band of Roman soldiers to whom the task was assigned. John does not write "the Jews" crucified Jesus, even though it was the shouts of the mob which from a human standpoint led to his death. Every person who has been given the gift of life in this world shares the responsibility for nailing Jesus to the rough wood of the cross (cf. Is 53:5,6).

Jesus was not alone on Golgotha. With him were "two others." John gives us no more information about the pair. The other Evangelists inform us that these men were robbers (Mt 27:38) and criminals (Lk 23:32). The words of Isaiah's prophecy were indeed fulfilled, "He was numbered with the transgressors" (Is 53:12).

vv. 19-22 — *Pilate had a notice prepared and fastened to the cross. It read: JESUS OF NAZARETH, THE KING OF THE JEWS. Many of the Jews read this sign, for the place where Jesus was crucified was near the city, and the sign was written in Aramaic, Latin and Greek. The chief priests of the Jews protested to Pilate, "Do not write 'The King of the Jews,' but that this man claimed to be king of the Jews." Pilate answered, "What I have written, I have written."*

John uses the word τίτλον (title) to designate the notice placed on the cross of our Lord. Customarily such a superscription included the crime of the convicted. No such accusation is found on the cross of Christ, only the title "King of the Jews." (The absence of a condemning charge can rightly be taken as another attestation to Jesus' "innocent" suffering and death.) It is clear that Pilate intended this notice as a slap in the face for the leaders of the Jews. Note their reaction. In reality Pilate had written the truth. Jesus is the "King of the Jews" and also of the entire world in a spiritual sense. Less than two months from now, this same Jesus would ascend gloriously to heaven and claim his place ruling at the right hand of the Father (Eph 1:20-22).

The title was posted in the three common languages of the land for all to read, much to the embarrassment of the Jews who requested Jesus' death. They did not want to be identified with Jesus in any way at all. But their attempts to change the title to read like the ridiculous claims of a madman failed.

The discrepancies in the superscription as reported by the other Evangelists (Mt 27:37; Mk 15:26; Lk 23:38) have been attributed to variations in the notice as it was drawn up in the three languages or to the incomplete reporting of some of the Gospel writers.

vv. 23,24 — *When the soldiers crucified Jesus, they took his clothes, dividing them into four shares, one for each of them, with the undergarment remaining. This garment was seamless, woven in one piece from top to bottom. "Let's not tear it," they said to one another. "Let's decide by lot who will get it." This happened that the scripture might be fulfilled which said, "They divided my garments among them and cast lots for my clothing." So this is what the soldiers did.*

It seems that the clothing of the condemned man was one of the perquisites for Roman soldiers assigned the unenviable task of discharging execution orders. When the text reads ἐποίησαν τέσσαρα μέρη we should not think that each article of clothing was divided into four parts. It is assumed that Jesus would have been wearing the five parts of clothing in the usual Jewish attire: headdress, sandals, belt, outer robe (ἱμάτιον) and tunic (χιτὼν). Four of these articles were most likely of comparable value and thus easily divided. One garment, the undergarment or tunic, stood out. The soldiers realized that the value of the garment would be lost if torn, so they decided to cast lots. We see another fulfillment of prophecy (Ps 22:18).

The shame of public nakedness was part of the price Jesus had to pay for our redemption. As the last of his earthly possessions are stripped from his beaten body, we are reminded of the words of Paul in 2 Corinthians 8:9, "Though he was rich, yet for your sakes he became poor." The one whose command called the universe into being was left with nothing.

vv. 25-27 — *Near the cross of Jesus stood his mother, his mother's sister, Mary the wife of Clopas, and Mary Magdalene. When Jesus saw his mother there, and the disciple whom he loved standing nearby, he said to his mother, "Dear woman, here is your son," and to the disciple, "Here is your mother." From that time on, this disciple took her into his home.*

The women who played a supportive role during Jesus' public ministry (Mk 15:41) were now present at the time of his death. There is some question as to whether John mentions three or four women here in his list. Those who favor the number three take the sister of Jesus' mother to be Mary, the wife of Cleopas. Compare also the lists of women given by Matthew (27:56) and Mark (15:40). Various attempts at harmonization have proved interesting, but inconclusive.

Mary's presence at the foot of the cross leads one to recall the words of prophecy spoken by the aged Simeon, "And a sword will pierce your own soul too" (Lk 2:35). The suffering Savior now turns his attention to the woman who gave him birth. He saw "the disciple whom he loved" (i.e. John) standing next to her and committed Mary to John's care. Jesus' use of the word Γύναι to address Mary was a special reminder that her parental role had to yield to another, higher relationship with Jesus. Jesus was her Savior too. She must also look to him in faith for the forgiveness of her sins.

What love and concern our Lord shows during the last moments of his life! In spite of the agony of body and soul on the cross, he thinks of his mother's needs and sees to it that they are taken care of. It is assumed that Joseph, Mary's husband, had already died. The question as to whether Mary bore other children remains open for debate. However, Jesus finds a willing "son" in John, who immediately (ἀπ ἐκείνης τῆς ὥρας) took Mary in.

It is notable that from this time on, Jesus' mother recedes into the background. She is mentioned only once more in the sacred record (Ac 1:14). It was not her sorrow and suffering which worked our redemption. Jesus alone did all that was necessary to complete the work of our salvation as we shall soon see.

vv. 28,29 — *Later, knowing that all was now completed, and so that the Scripture would be fulfilled, Jesus said, "I am thirsty." A jar of wine vinegar was there, so they soaked a sponge on it, put the sponge on a stalk of the hyssop plant, and lifted it to Jesus' lips.*

The phrase μετὰ τοῦτο indicates that an interval of time has passed since Jesus' conversation with John and Mary — a time during which Jesus suffered the very torments of hell (cf. Mk 15:34). Now, sensing death to be moments away, Jesus was well aware (εἰδὼς) that his redemptive work on behalf of the world was complete (τετέλεσται, perfect passive). The editors of the NIV connect the phrase ἵνα τελειωθῇ, etc. with λέγει as the reason for Jesus speaking the words "I thirst." (Compare Ps 22:15 and Ps 69:21.) However, Lenski presents an appealing argument for tying the ἵνα clause with the preceding τετέλεσται. He points to the use of the verb τελειωθῇ rather than the usual πληρωθῇ as proof that John is here referring to more than the single prophecy regarding his thirst. Everything Jesus has done up to this time has led to this goal, i.e. the accomplishment of scriptural prophecies concerning the Messiah and his work of salvation.

Previously Jesus had refused a drink intended to numb or subdue the victim of crucifixion (Mt 27:34). Now he accepts the offered wine vinegar, perhaps to moisten his parched throat for the last, loud cry from the cross. Jesus' thirst reminds us of the reality of his human nature. His physical suffering was genuine.

v. 30 — *When he had received the drink, Jesus said, "It is finished." With that, he bowed his head and gave up his spirit.*

After moistening his lips, Jesus spoke aloud what he already knew in his heart. "It is finished" (τετέλεσται). The price had been paid in full. The one sacrifice for sin to which all others pointed would now stand as an accomplished fact (cf. He 7:27; 9:12,26; Ro 6:10). In love, God had sent his one and only Son to be the atoning sacrifice for our sins. In love Jesus lived the perfect life which God required of us (active obedience) and in love Jesus willingly gave up his spirit (παρέδωκεν) in death so his perfection might be credited to our account (passive obedience). All that now remained was God's stamp of approval on the work of Christ which would come before the first light of dawn early Easter morning.

Homiletical Suggestions

The message of Good Friday evokes a wide range of emotion within the believer's heart. It is hardly possible for the child of God to remain unmoved as he witnesses the pain and suffering of his Savior. The Christian's sorrow is intensified by the realization that he, as a sinner, is personally responsible for his Lord's torment. And yet there is great joy in knowing that Jesus willingly took our punishment upon himself to free us forever from the chains of death and hell.

The preacher of the Good Friday message might be tempted to dwell on the graphic details of death by crucifixion and its torturous strains on the human body, but John's account gives us no warrant for this activity. The advice E. Wendland gives concerning Lenten sermons is certainly in place: "The preacher will have to guard against maudlin sentimentality in speaking of what Jesus suffered. While sympathy is in place, gratitude for what the Savior accomplished for us is much more in place" (*Sermon Texts*, Milwaukee: Northwestern Publishing House, 1984, p. 80). The cross presents us with a clear picture of God's stern justice and the terrible consequences of sin (law). It also protrays the infinite love and compassion of our Lord for undeserving sinners (gospel). As always, both messages must be presented to the listener.

Taken as a whole, John's eyewitness account of the crucifixion might be divided as follows:

The Cross: Evidence of Our Savior's Complete Work

1. It fulfills every prophecy (vv. 17,18,23,24,28,29)
2. It testifies to his perfect life (vv. 19-22, 25-27)
3. It reminds us of his death (v. 30)

Part one in the above outline is self-evident. Part two might call attention to the lack of condemning accusation on the superscription as well as the concern Jesus showed for his mother as an example of his active obedience (Fourth Commandment). Part three would of course afford the opportunity to speak of the Savior's willingness to offer the supreme sacrifice for the sins of the world.

Many subdivisions could be (and have been) made of the text before us. The preacher might consider presenting vv. 17-22 in this fashion:

They Crucified a King!

1. A King who had done no wrong (vv. 18,19)
2. A King rejected by his people (vv. 20-22)
3. A King on a mission of love (v. 17)

Part one would again call attention to the fact that Pilate could find no legitimate charge against Jesus. Part two would address the fact that many rejected Jesus as the one sent by God. Part three would serve as a reminder that Jesus willingly walked the way of sorrows to suffer and die for all people, including those who rejected him as King. The application should include no finger pointing at any people or groups of people responsible for Jesus' death. Rather, let it be a reminder that we too are guilty of rejecting Jesus as our King every time we sin and that he walked the way of sorrows to Golgotha for us also.

An exposition of verses 23-30 might take advantage of the fact that John was an eyewitness of the events he reports on Calvary:

A Good Friday Witness Speaks to Us

1. With his eyes, he saw the shame of the cross (vv. 23-29)
2. With his ears, he heard words of great comfort (v. 30)

Part one would deal with the utter humiliation our Lord suffered in having even his garments taken away. The apparent helplessness of not being able personally to care for his mother any longer, not even being able to assuage his own thirst. The preacher would also remind the listener why this humiliation was suffered. Part two will bring us the comforting message that, with his death, Jesus has won the final victory over sin, death and the devil. What a comfort to the sin-burdened conscience to hear the words of Jesus, "It is finished!" Your eternal salvation has been won!

EASTER — RESURRECTION OF OUR LORD

The Scriptures

First Reading — *Acts 10:34-43*
Epistle — *Colossians 3:1-4*
Gospel — *John 20:1-9*

The Text — John 20:1-9

The wondrous news of the resurrection of Jesus Christ occurs in all four Gospels. John and the other evangelists have left us records of several incidents involving the empty tomb or contacts with the risen Savior. The many proofs demonstrate the authenticity of the bodily resurrection. Scripture leaves no doubt. Those who deny that Jesus physically, bodily rose from the dead oppose the gospel writers, the entire New Testament and numerous prophecies of the Old Testament.

vv. 1,2 — *Early on the first day of the week, while it was still dark, Mary Magdalene went to the tomb and saw that the stone had been removed from the entrance. So she came running to Simon Peter and the other disciple, the one Jesus loved, and said, "They have taken the Lord out of the tomb, and we don't know where they have put him!"*

The Apostle John wrote later than the other evangelists and assumes we are familiar with their accounts. Thus he made no explanation about the stone in his record of the burial in the preceding chapter. Nor did he mention the other women who headed for the tomb with Mary, although his account reflects their presence ("*we* don't know" in v. 2). He focused on the one who made contact with himself and Peter.

These events happened on "the first day of the week" or Sunday. The Jews didn't use names for the days of the week. The women began their trip to the garden early in the morning. They left home while it was still dark, so that they could arrive at dawn. Their eagerness to perform the task and their devotion to the Lord stood out. John's use of the present tense in these verses adds vividness to his description. We are observing the action firsthand.

The presence of the stone had been a concern of the women on the way out (Mk 16:3). By the time they neared the tomb Jesus had risen and departed, the angel had come and rolled the stone from the opening and the guards had left. Mary of Magdala and her companions could see the stone was gone. What could they assume but the worst? After all, they were coming for a dead Jesus, not a living Savior. The stone away from the tomb, out of its groove, suggested violence.

While the others went on, Mary turned back and ran for help, probably with speed, her adrenalin pumping. Where she found Peter and John was not identified. Typically, John did not mention his own name, but used the designation "the other disciple, the one Jesus loved." Here he used φιλέω, showing Jesus had the love of warm friendship for him as well as ἀγάπη, the purposeful, giving love.

Mary's breathless excitement showed in her words, "They have taken the Lord out of the tomb, and we don't know where they have put him!" The verbs ἦραν and ἔθηκαν are indefinite, lacking a subject. Certainly she was thinking of the Jews, for who else would bother the grave? Killing Jesus wasn't enough. Now they had to desecrate the body. They couldn't leave him in the nice tomb of Joseph. She expressed not only the observable facts, but her own conclusions. We see the danger of following your own surmisings. What unneeded trouble and heartache she caused herself! It is noteworthy that she spoke of Jesus as "the Lord" (τὸν κύριον), even though she thought him dead.

vv. 3,4 — *So Peter and the other disciple started for the tomb. Both were running, but the other disciple outran Peter and reached the tomb first.*

Action was immediate. The report called for investigation. On the way out the men probably met the other women returning (Lk 24:9ff). That really started them running (ἔτρεχον, inchoative). John speeded ahead and arrived first. It's generally assumed he was the younger.

vv. 5-7 — *He bent over and looked in at the strips of linen lying there but did not go in. Then Simon Peter, who was behind him, arrived and went into the tomb. He saw the strips of linen lying there, as well as the burial cloth that had been around Jesus' head. The cloth was folded up by itself, separate from the linen.*

The sight riveted John to the spot as he hesitated at the entrance and peered in. Peter didn't stop but went right inside and studied the scene intently. Θεωρέω involves perception based on what one sees and hears. What the men saw spoke volumes. The "strips of linen," the many layers of cloth in which Jesus' body has been wrapped, were lying there undisturbed. They had not been unwound or cut off but lay where they had been, except there was no body inside. In a hasty robbing of the tomb body and all would have been gone. A violent act by enemies would not have left such a neat scene. Even removal by friends would have caused some disruption. But these cloths were not folded neatly by the side. Only the face-cloth which had been on the head was folded. That article was similiar to a handkerchief. It was regularly used for wiping perspiration. It lay apart by itself. The neatness of this second item gave additional evidence of a peaceful exit. The materials were left behind because Christ no longer had need of them. This physical evidence corroborated the facts: Jesus had risen from the dead.

vv. 8,9 — *Finally the other disciple, who had reached the tomb first, also went inside. He saw and believed. (They still did not understand from Scripture that Jesus had to rise from the dead.)*

After a time John also entered the tomb and viewed the evidence from closeup. It led him to the conclusion that Jesus had risen. What about Peter? Luke 24:12 tells his reaction: "He went away, wondering to himself what had happend." He didn't yet grasp the message of the cloths.

John isn't patting himself on the back in this account. He had heard the later words of Jesus to Thomas, "Because you have seen me, you have believed" (v. 29). Furthermore, full conviction was lacking, it seems. He reports no sharing of his conclusions with wondering Peter on the way home. When Mary later told about actually seeing Jesus, the disciples did not believe her, Mark reported. Recall the fear and bewilderment which still existed when Jesus appeared to the disciples.

John also admits he hadn't come to the understanding that the resurrection was a necessary part of God's plan of salvation. The final verse shows that his faith came from seeing the facts before he realized Scripture taught the resurrection. He and the other disciples were not filled with an expectancy that caused them to wish for and imagine a resurrection, as some skeptics have claimed.

It's not that they couldn't have expected it. Jesus told them he would lay down his life and take it up again (Jn 10:17f). His foretelling of his passion in Luke 18 ended with the exact statement, "On the third day he will rise again" (v. 33).

The real basis of faith, however, is Scripture, and that's what John referred to, not even Jesus' own words. Later Jesus used the Bible's statements to convince the disciples, not just his appearances. What God had promised he was bound to fulfill. That's why Jesus "had to rise" (δεῖ . . . ἀναστῆναι). Passages like Psalm 16:10 come to mind: "You will not abandon me to the grave, nor will you let your Holy

One see decay." Portions of Psalms 2 and 110 show his lasting triumph. Isaiah 53:10 spoke of seeing his offspring and prolonging his days. When Jesus later drew upon the biblical message he included the "Law of Moses, the Prophets and the Psalms" (Luke 24:44). The entire Old Testament centered in him and his work of salvation. He fulfilled it to perfection. The resurrection was a fact of history. Through the testimony of God's word the Holy Spirit gives us lasting assurance.

Those Scriptures spell out the meaning of Christ's resurrection for us, as well as the event. It provided a forceful demonstration of Christ's deity (Ro 1:4). It announced our justification (Ro 4:25). We know that we shall follow Jesus in rising from the dead (1 Cor 15:22f). Our faith is sure since we have a living Savior (1 Cor 15:14,20).

Homiletical Suggestions

Christ's resurrection declared victory not only for himself but also for us. Without a doubt the Easter festival is the high point of the church year, reflected in the number of hearers the preacher will address this day. We may lament the attention that some give to only a couple of days in the church year. Let us rather rejoice in the opportunity to present the good news of Christ's resurrection clearly and forcefully. We Christians base our certainty of salvation on the miracle of Christ's resurrection. Let the Easter joy and victory ring forth.

The other readings, Acts 10:34-43 and Colossians 3:1-4, share the results of the day: the peace of forgiveness for all, the home in glory that is ours and its effect on our lives. The gospel brings the event itself and its certainly.

In this text we see the Easter event from different angles: the mistaken sadness of Mary, the uncertain awe of Peter and John and the closing reference to the full testimony of Scripture. All have something to tell us.

Hear Easter Testimony

1. From a grieving believer (vv. 1,2)
2. From wondering disciples (vv. 3-8)
3. From fulfilled Scriptures (v. 9)

Sometimes we have sadness rather than the joyful trust of knowing we are victorious rulers with Christ. That is because we look too low, just as Mary sought a dead Jesus. Our faith may be timid and unsure like that of John and Peter. We need the sure message of Scripture to know Easter's joyous victory completely. The text thus builds to a natural climax of that which is absolutely convincing.

We may find it sad that some people enter the church only on Easter. Yet we can build positively on their presence by drawing them into the Word for its joyous message.

Be Easter Christians

1. Serving the Savior (vv. 1,2)
2. Studying the evidence (vv. 3-8)
3. Believing the Scriptures (v. 9)

In this account we don't actually meet Jesus (although he definitely showed himself later). Some look at the Easter accounts and can't seem to find him either, so they deny that he actually rose. We need not let those gloomy doubters dampen our Easter joy. The proof in these verses is too great. We can note it under this format:

Where's Jesus?

1. Not among the dead (vv. 1-5)
2. Risen as Scripture said (vv. 6-9)

SECOND SUNDAY OF EASTER

The Scriptures

First Reading — *Acts 2:14a,22-32*
Epistle — *1 Peter 1:3-9*
Gospel — *John 20:19-31*

The Text — John 20:19-31

The two incidents of our text occur on Easter and the following Sunday. Thomas "stars" in this text, but it is necessary to know the attitudes of the other disciples that first Easter. Read Luke 24:11,17, 21,37,38; Mark 16:14; John 20:9,13. Sorrow, bewilderment, fear, cautious hope and even unbelief had infiltrated these most faithful followers of Christ. These two encounters with the risen Savior establish important truths for disciples then and now. Jesus lives. Jesus forgives. Jesus authorizes forgiving and retaining sins by his followers. People are to believe without seeing. God's word is sufficient.

vv. 19,20 — *On the evening of that first day of the week, when the disciples were together, with the doors locked for fear of the Jews, Jesus came and stood among them and said, "Peace be with you!" After he said this, he showed them his hands and side. The disciples were overjoyed when they saw the Lord.*

This appearance was on the first day of the week. It was that (ἐκείνῃ) day, meaning Easter as the context indicates. Why were the doors locked? They feared the Jews. Probably, the planted rumor of grave robbery on their part had reached them (Mt 28:13). Jesus stood or appeared (ἔστη) in their midst. He did not need to pass through a door or wall. In his glorified body he simply appeared. What comfort the word "peace" from the risen Lord conveyed. These were troublesome times. The wounds of the battle which produced peace confirm it's the Lord.

vv. 21-23 — *Again Jesus said, "Peace be with you! As the Father has sent me, I am sending you." And with that he breathed on them and said, "Receive the Holy Spirit. If you forgive anyone his sins, they are forgiven; if you do not forgive them, they are not forgiven."*

The Savior not only assures them of peace, but he also commissions them to announce peace to the world. Today many churches preach a peace of nuclear disarmament or cutting military aid to foreign countries. They ignore or compromise doctrine in the name of peace. Jesus leaves no room for misunderstanding. Peace comes from forgiveness (ἀφίημι = cancel, send away, let go) of sins. It is peace between God and men through the work of Christ. It is peace of conscience to the sinner. The authority to free the penitent from the guilt and consequences of sin and to bind the guilt and consequences of sins to the impenitent we call the Ministry of the Keys. The NIV weakens the binding key with the translation of "not forgive." Κρατέω means to hold fast or retain. Sin and its consequences adhere to the unrepentant. The keys are for all believers. All Christians are priests, 1 Peter 2:9.

vv. 24,25 — *Now Thomas (called Didymus), one of the Twelve, was not with the disciples when Jesus came. So the other disciples told him, "We have seen the Lord!" But he said to them, "Unless I see the nail marks in his hands and put my finger where the nails were, and put my hand into his side, I will not believe it."*

Why was Thomas not there? Some commentators have made a negative issue of his absence. Some sermons have developed it as a major point. The Bible does not tell us the reason Thomas was not with the others. Why speculate at length? We have so many clear points in this text. Jesus offered the others the chance to touch the wounds (Lk 24:39). Thomas demanded it. He refused to believe unless his terms were met. Jesus permits him to languish in uncertainty for a week. Thomas' degree of doubt surpasses the other ten. Let's be careful, however, not to paint Thomas as the only disciple with problems of faith. He is singled out for obstinacy and duration. Recall the other disciples' attitudes: sorrow, bewilderment, fear, even unbelief.

vv. 26,27 — *A week later his disciples were in the house again, and Thomas was with them. Though the doors were locked, Jesus came and stood among them and said, "Peace be with you!" Then he said to Thomas, "Put your finger here; see my hands. Reach out your hand and put it into my side. Stop doubting and believe."*

Once again the doors were locked. Boldness would come as faith grew. Jesus would fertilize the seed this day. The Savior gave Thomas what he demanded. Meeting the doubter's demands was an act of pure grace. Believe! This is what the Savior wants.

v. 28 — *Thomas said to him, "My Lord and my God!"*

Thomas says only seven simple words in Greek. But what a powerful confession. Jesus is κύριος, the one to whom we belong. We were bought with the price of his blood. He is θεός, fully God. He is *Thomas's* Lord and God (μου). Thomas did not bring himself to this conviction. God alone can work or increase faith.

v. 29 — *Then Jesus told him, "Because you have seen me, you have believed; blessed are those who have not seen and yet have believed."*

God made an exception in this case. Most people will need to believe sight unseen. Hebrews 11:1 defines faith as being "certain of what we do not see." We have not seen the events of the Bible times. We have not met the people. We have not seen our God or his heaven. Truly, we walk by faith, not by sight (2 Cor 5:7).

vv. 30,31 — *Jesus did many other miraculous signs in the presence of his disciples, which are not recorded in this book. But these are written that you may believe that Jesus is the Christ, the Son of God, and that by believing you may have life in his name.*

The faith we are to hold sight unseen rests upon the word of God. John summarizes the purpose of his entire Gospel. The aim is faith in the Savior, Jesus Christ. The outcome of such faith is eternal life. This is the supreme goal of the entire Scripture and all true preaching.

Homiletical Suggestions

Three times Jesus bids them peace. The preacher could expound on the peace of God. Part one would repeat Easter assurances. Part two would explain and show the sure comfort from the keys. Part three reminds us that Jesus addresses our doubts in the Bible.

Peace Be with You!

1. Jesus confirms his resurrection (vv. 19,20)
2. Jesus confers the keys (vv. 21-23)
3. Jesus convinces the doubting (vv. 24-31)

Some people hold strange views about faith. Jesus shows what it really is. The following sermon outline employs the words of Hebrews 11:1 Part one stresses the disciples hoped for a living Christ, forgiveness and continuation of his work. Part two calls us to trust the word of God for what we have not seen.

This Is Faith

1. Sure of what we hope for (vv. 19-23)
2. Certain of what we do not see (vv. 24-31)

Jesus lives. We have something to live for. We have purpose. We have a faith to aspire to, with God's help.

Living For the Living Lord

1. The work he requires (vv. 19-23)
2. The faith he desires (vv. 24-31)

People go places for a reason. They go to the store to shop. To the barbershop for a haircut. To the park for recreation. Jesus comes to the disciples for good reasons:

Why Did Jesus Appear to His Disciples?

1. To give a special authority (vv. 19-23)
2. To teach a lesson on faith (vv. 24-31)

THIRD SUNDAY OF EASTER

The Scriptures

First Reading — *Acts 2:14a,36-47*
Epistle — *1 Peter 1:17-21*
Gospel — *Luke 24:13-35*

The Text — Luke 24:13-35

Most earthly celebrations are very brief. But the festival of Easter inspires an "afterglow" that by God's grace burns ever brighter as each Sunday after Easter is truly celebrated!

Today's first lesson overlaps and continues Peter's special Pentecost sermon to the people God had gathered in Jerusalem. "Cut to the heart" we too stand condemned — guilty of crucifying the Lord Jesus. Peter calls us to repent daily and to believe the gospel. Devoted to the apostles' doctrine we will share in the precious fruits of faith and fellowship.

The Epistle readings from Easter 2 through Easter 7 are from 1 Peter. Remember the exceedingly high price Jesus paid to redeem us — holy, innocent blood. Remember the Father chose us before creation to be his own.

The Gospel lesson is one more of many accounts of the risen Lord appearing to his students and followers. The famous painting by Zund pictures Jesus and the two disciples walking down the wooded path. The familiar "heartwarming" account is filled with comfort and encouragement to grow.

The first 12 verses of Luke 24 are the historical account of Mary Magdalene, Joanna, Mary the mother of James and others going to Jesus' tomb early Easter morning. They hear the Easter gospel from two angels. Hearts seized with fright, excitement and wonder they report back to the Eleven. Though their words seemed "like nonsense" (Lk 24:11) still Peter ran and saw the empty tomb for himself.

vv. 13-17 — *Now that same day two of them were going to a village called Emmaus, about seven miles from Jerusalem. They were talking with each other about everything that had happened. As they talked and discussed these things with each other, Jesus himself came up and walked along with them; but they were kept from recognizing him. He asked them, "What are you discussing together as you walk along?"*

The exact location of ancient Emmaus is not known. Our current inability to locate it in no way reflects poorly on the completeness or accuracy of Luke's account. It is sufficient for us to know it was about a seven-mile hike home for the disciples. Συζητεῖν is to look at something together. It includes the ideas of discussion, of dispute —of questioning each other. In verse 17 the word for "discussing" ἀντιβάλλετε literally means to throw in turn. It is easy to draw a mental picture of their walking while talking. Because they felt so strongly about it, all their talk must have been animated — using colorful words with broad excited gestures. They in turn asked each other hard, even unanswerable questions. Like those children's toy cars that bump and roll, they hit one roadblock after another. There was a very real sense of urgency as they tried to solve the mystery, fill in the blank and solve the puzzle. In frustration they failed to find the answer.

Just as traffic smoothly merges on the freeway the Lord Jesus quietly meets, walks beside, then joins them. Never ever rude or obnoxious, Jesus waits for a natural opening before asking them what they are discussing. They stop. Their faces are σκυθρωποί. Here is a word rich in texture and — alas! — familiarity. We know the feeling. We can detect it. The eyes are downcast — the twinkle and sparkle gone. The mouth is bent downward — the forehead deeply wrinkled. The head hangs down — the shoulders slump. There is a sort of bitter weariness that colors every word and action.

> vv. 18-24 — *One of them, name Cleopas, asked him, "Are you only a visitor to Jerusalem and do not know the things that have happened there in these days?" "What things?" he asked. "About Jesus of Nazareth," they replied. "He was a prophet, powerful in word and deed before God and all the people. The chief priests and our rulers handed him over to be sentenced to death, and they crucified him; but we had hoped that he was the one who was going to redeem Israel. And what is more, it is the third day since all this took place. In addition, some of our women amazed us. They went to the tomb early this morning but didn't find his body. They came and told us that they had seen a vision of angels, who said he was alive. Then some of our companions went to the tomb and found it just as the women had said, but him they did not see."*

One of the disciples was named Cleopas. Though we might be curious about the name of the other our Father in his wisdom has not seen fit to tell us. Guesses and speculation about his identity are just that. It is perhaps part of sinful human perversity that we so often fail to give a straightforward answer to a simple question. Cleopas answers a question with a question of his own. Jesus, the ever patient teacher asks again. Cleopas answers that Jesus was δυνατὸς, dynamite — powerful and effective in preaching, teaching, counseling and healing. Jesus' words and actions were always in the light of the Scriptures. Thus Jesus operated with an obvious, almost palpable, authority that the people longed for — that the Pharisees and teachers of the law painfully lacked. Cleopas gives a fine summary of Jesus' ministry.

There are few sadder phrases than δὲ ἠλπίζομεν, "but we had hoped." They had watched. They had waited. Peter himself had gone to investigate. They had lingered in Jerusalem. But now it was time to go back to Emmaus. How they had hoped Jesus would λυτροῦσθαι (redeem, buy back, rescue with a ransom) Israel from all her sins.

vv. 25-27 — *He said to them, "How foolish you are, and how slow of heart to believe all that the prophets have spoken! Did not the Christ have to suffer these things and then enter his glory?" And beginning with Moses and all the Prophets, he explained to them what was said in all the Scriptures concerning himself.*

When do we scold our children the most severely? Isn't it when they should know better? These disciples should have known better! Jesus who knows all things — who alone can look into hearts and minds — must have shaken his head. They were guilty of being slow in mind and heart. Had they not read the Scriptures? Wasn't the passion an essential part of God's plan to save them? Wasn't it all mapped out in the Scriptures? Again, we might wish Luke had recorded which passages Jesus quoted from Moses and from the Prophets. With what word did he make vivid applications? Again, our Father in his perfect wisdom doesn't tell us. It is for each of us to wrest these blessings from God's word as the Spirit blesses our prayerful meditation.

vv. 28-32 — *As they approached the village to which they were going, Jesus acted as if he were going farther. But they urged him strongly, "Stay with us, for it is nearly evening; the day is almost over. So he went in to stay with them. When he was at the table with them, he took bread, gave thanks, broke it and began to give it to them. Then their eyes were opened and they recognized him, and he disappeared from their sight. They asked each other, "Were not our hearts burning within us while he talked with us on the road and opened the Scriptures to us?"*

Some are troubled by the verb προσεποιήσατο, "acted as if." Jesus is not guilty of some sort of lie, deception or subterfuge. Jesus was never pushy, rude, presumptuous, thoughtless or arrogant in any way. He who washed his disciples' feet would not have presumed to invite himself into the disciples' home — to invite himself to supper or to sleep over. If he had not been asked to stay he most certainly would have left. They παρεβιάσαντο, they "urged him strongly." They really wanted him to stay. And Jesus really wanted to stay, too!

Jesus — their teacher for the afternoon — was their host at the table. In the excitement of their conversation the Lord didn't forget to have the table prayers. As was his custom he gave thanks to his Father for the food. As was the custom of the time and place, the bread was broken and distributed rather than sliced and passed on a plate. Jesus was not celebrating Holy Communion. He wouldn't be there long enough to offer the cup! No, Jesus was simply serving the supper.

Now was the right time. Jesus opened their eyes. The same one who had kept his identity a secret now made it as plain as day who he really was. Some have speculated that when Jesus handed the disciples the bread they saw the nail marks in his hands and recognized him. However the Lord made himself known, he remained only a moment then he was ἄφαντος, was made invisible, disappeared, vanished. Jesus did not linger for their foolish questions or embarassed excuses for failing to recognize him. Here was a precious demonstration of his divine power and wisdom.

Now it all made sense. Weren't their hearts on fire as Jesus opened up the Scriptures to them? Sharper than any two-edged sword, God's word cut to the very heart of their lives, their guilt over sin, their hopes and dreams.

vv. 33-35 — *They got up and returned at once to Jerusalem. There they found the Eleven and those with them, assembled together and saying, "It is true! The Lord has risen and has appeared to Simon." Then the two told what had happened on the way, and how Jesus was recognized by them when he broke the bread.*

When the angel told the shepherds of the birth of the Christchild they hurried to Bethlehem to see him. When these disciples realized they had seen the risen Lord they "got up and returned at once" to Jerusalem. They didn't stop to eat their supper. They didn't make excuses about having just walked seven miles from Jerusalem. They didn't talk about going back "first thing in the morning"! This was news that just had to be shared. Feet that had been weary just minutes ago now barely touch the ground as they race back to Jerusalem with news too good to be true. We have seen the risen Christ!

Homiletical Suggestions

The joy and happiness of Easter are too great to be confined to just one Sunday morning. Because of that first Easter we can be supremely confident that the icy fingers of the grave will not hold us forever. How the devil must smile if by the second or third Sunday of Easter we stand in the pulpit or sit in the pews with scarcely a smile on our face. Certainly there is no place for shallow emotionalism or phony showy enthusiasm. But the certain confidence that heaven is ours by grace alone for Jesus' sake is reason indeed for a contagious joy deep inside. When we remember the precious blessings that are ours because of Maundy Thursday, Good Friday and Easter — the warm afterglow is sure to linger through the means of grace.

The following themes and parts will by the Spirit's power alone convey the excitement, warmth, confidence and comfort too great to be confined to the Easter season alone.

An introduction might discuss some of the great and fiery orators that could stir the hearts of men with their brilliant oratory or the old tent revival preachers who used to whip up the people into an emotional frenzy. In sharp contrast to these flashy speakers is the quietly effective Lord Jesus on the road to Emmaus.

Jesus Sets Our Hearts on Fire

1. The gospel fire warms my own heart (vv. 13-32)
2. The gospel fire is for me to spread (vv. 33-35)

An introduction might begin with a recent newspaper account of someone who overcame some terrible handicap or surmounted some tremendous obstacle or was rescued from almost certain disaster. They never lost hope. Our trust is not in any indomitable human spirit. We trust in Christ and because of him alone —

We Have Hope

1. The risen Lord overcomes our disappointment (vv. 13-24)
2. The risen Lord overcomes our confusion (vv. 25-27)
3. The risen Lord overcomes our grief (vv. 28-35)

An introduction that would most certainly appeal to the little children and the big "children" is the recitation of a well-known or better yet relatively obscure "fairy tale." The point can be easily drawn that while it might seem happy endings only come true in fairy tales and sentimental movies, it is part of the gospel truth that —

We Will Live Happily Ever After . . .

1. Because Jesus gives us hope (vv. 13-24)
2. Because Jesus gives us understanding (vv. 25-27)
3. Because Jesus gives us comfort (vv. 28-35)

An introduction could be based on any day's front page news. Mass murder, child abuse, domestic violence and disasters around the world are the stuff of heart-breaking stories. We find good news in the gospel —

The Heart-Warming Story From Emmaus

1. Jesus brought hope to hearts that were disappointed (vv. 13-24)
2. He brought clarity to hearts that were confused (vv. 25-27)
3. He brought joy to hearts that had been grieving (vv. 28-35)

FOURTH SUNDAY OF EASTER

The Scriptures

First Reading — *Acts 6:1-9;7:2a,51-60*
Epistle — *1 Peter 2:19-25*
Gospel — *John 10:1-10*

The Text — John 10:1-10

Jesus spoke the words of the text immediately following the events in the preceding chapter. At the beginning of chapter 9 Jesus had restored sight to a man born blind "so that the work of God might be displayed in his life" (9:3). By the end of that same chapter we see that the man's spiritual sight had also been restored. In response to Jesus' question, "Do you believe in the Son of Man?" the now-sighted man replied, "Lord, I believe" (9:35,38).

When the Pharisees had learned that Jesus was the one who had healed the man and that Jesus had performed the miracle on the Sabbath, they began their usual attacks against him saying, "This man is not from God, for he does not keep the Sabbath" (9:16). Finally, after arguing with the man whose sight had been restored, they threw him out of the synagogue, accusing him of spiritual blindness. It was then that they finally confronted Jesus himself only to be told by him that they were really the ones who were spiritually blind. Chapter 9 closes with Jesus' statement to the Pharisees, "If you were blind, you would not be guilty of sin; but now that you claim you can see, your guilt remains" (9:41).

The words of our text are addressed to his entire audience: his disciples, the formerly blind man, the Pharisees and the other Jews who happened to be there. The purpose of the entire parable was to point out to everyone the Pharisees' sin of leading people astray (so that the people would avoid them) and to try to lead those same Pharisees to repentance. The entire text forms a beautiful picture of Jesus' work for us as our Savior, being the one who truly gives us life in every sense of the word.

vv. 1,2 — *"I tell you the truth, the man who does not enter the sheep pen by the gate, but climbs in by some other way, is a thief and a robber. The man who enters by the gate is the shepherd of his sheep."*

Jesus begins with a parable (παροιμία, v. 6) with which we are all familiar. The picture of the sheep and the Good Shepherd is used repeatedly throughout Scripture. We would think immediately of the later verses of this chapter and the Psalm for the day, Psalm 23.

"I tell you the truth" (ἀμὴν ἀμὴν), Jesus begins. The double "amen" is Jesus' seal that what he is saying to us is the truth. It is dependable. It is to be believed. This is a statement which Jesus wants us to heed. He is about to say something very important.

He uses the picture of the sheep-pen, a walled enclosure designed to protect the sheep during the night. The walls were high enough to keep the sheep in and the wild animals out. There was also a gate which was guarded by a door-keeper during the night to make sure that no unwelcome guests could enter.

Notice the action of the two people mentioned by Jesus. One avoids the door and gets in some other way (ἀναβαίνων ἀλλαχόθεν, literally "climbs over and in by another way"). He is described as a thief (one who tries to steal something quietly) and a robber (one who steals things by force and violence). He does not own the sheep and does not really care about the sheep. The shepherd, however, uses the gate. Jesus explains the reason for these actions in the next verse.

v. 3 — *"The watchman opens the gate for him, and the sheep listen to his voice. He calls his own sheep by name and leads them out."*

The sheep-pen has a guard at the door. The guard would recognize the shepherd and would let only him in. It's no wonder the thief finds some other way in. The sheep also recognize (ἀκούει) their shepherd's voice. We see the special, close relationship the shepherd has with his sheep. Not only do they know him by voice, he also calls each one individually "by name" (κατ᾽ ὄνομα), one by one. The shepherd, having gathered his flock together, leads them out for the day.

vv. 4,5 — *"When he has brought out all his own, he goes on ahead of them, and his sheep follow him because they know his voice. But they will never follow a stranger; in fact, they will run away from him because they do not recognize a stranger's voice."*

Just as the shepherd knows each of his sheep, they also know him. Each day the shepherd comes into the sheep-pen and pushes his sheep out. Then he goes out in front of them to lead them to pasture. Because he is the shepherd, the sheep follow him obediently. They recognize him not only by his appearance but also by his voice.

How different a reaction the sheep give to the stranger (the "thief" and "robber"). They neither recognize him, nor his voice. They won't be fooled. Even though he approaches with reassuring words, dressed as a shepherd, they run away from him. They want to have nothing at all (οὐ μὴ) to do with him.

v. 6 — *Jesus used this figure of speech, but they did not understand what he was telling them.*

Jesus' words, meant primarily for the Pharisees, fell on deaf ears. They didn't understand a word he said, though in chapter 9 they had claimed to be the ones who saw everything. How sad, for they were the thieves and robbers who tried to steal and destroy the sheep. They tried to steal the people by fear and intimidation (7:13; 9:22,34). They robbed the people of the sure hope of forgiveness and life by means of their numerous, burdensome laws (Mt 23:3,4). They were the false shepherds condemned so vigorously in all of Scripture (e.g. Jr 23:1ff). It's no wonder Jesus again and again warned the people not to follow such "shepherds." It's no wonder Jesus used this figure of speech to call the Pharisees to repentance.

v. 7 — *Therefore Jesus said again, "I tell you the truth, I am the gate for the sheep."*

Jesus now speaks clearly so that there would be no misunderstanding of the point he was trying to make. He begins again with the words, "I tell you the truth" (ἀμὴν ἀμὴν), that remind us that he is going to say something vitally important to us.

"I am the gate for the sheep," Jesus says. Note the stress on the "I am" (ἐγώ εἰμι, at the beginning of the sentence). Jesus himself is the gate through which the shepherds must enter to get to their sheep. He is the one through whom the sheep must go to find their pasture. All who are truly shepherds (pastors, teachers) are those who believe in him as their Savior and guide the sheep only by means of his word.

v. 8 — *"All who ever came before me were thieves and robbers, but the sheep did not listen to them."*

Jesus goes on to explain who the "thieves" and "robbers" were. They were the Pharisees and other Jewish leaders. They had been around from the time before Jesus came (note the aorist ἦλθον) and were still around (note the present ἐισὶν). They were trying to gain an illegal and illegitimate entrance into the hearts of the people so that they could preserve their own position with the people. Truly, they were "thieves" and "robbers."

Certainly, there are still many of these false teachers around today. They still are trying to steal the sheep. And there are many who listen to them. But the sheep, Christ's real disciples, did not and still do not listen to them. They listen only to the voice of the true shepherd. How important it is that we, as preachers, make sure that *his* voice is the one our people hear! How important that they learn only to follow his voice and not those of a stranger!

v. 9 — *"I am the gate; whoever enters through me will be saved. He will come in and go out, and find pasture."*

Jesus repeats what he had to say in verse 7 with more emphasis (again note the emphatic position of ἐγώ εἰμι), "I am the gate." It is only through Jesus and his atoning work as our Good Shepherd that the "sheep" are saved. In both of these verses Jesus makes it plain that he is the only Savior, he is the only door to life and salvation. He is not just one of a series of many doors to God. In today's world we have religious pluralism: one religion is just as good as the next; they are all different paths to the same heaven. Jesus states just the opposite. The only door to salvation is through faith in Jesus Christ alone (cf. Jn 14:6; Ac 4:12). This is our entire basis for evangelism and mission work. Without Christ people are lost in sin and doomed to hell. With him there is heaven. We must share with them the good news of salvation through Christ.

v. 10 — *"The thief comes only to steal and kill and destroy; I have come that they may have life, and have it to the full."*

Jesus closes the picture with a stark contrast between the thief and himself. The thief is only out to steal the sheep, kill (θύσῃ, literally "slaughter") the sheep and thoroughly destroy them. The sheep are not safe from him. Certainly, this is the effect false teachers and leaders have upon people. They may speak the reassuring words of a shepherd. They may even come dressed as a real shepherd. But in the end they only destroy the precious souls of people by their false teachings.

In contrast Jesus comes to give life. That is why he laid down his life for the sheep (verse 11) by his perfect life and innocent suffering and death. That is what he guarantees to them through his triumphant resurrection. Through his work he gives real life which forgives sin, frees people from guilt, removes the fears and worries of everyday life and ultimately lasts for all eternity in heaven. As Jesus says, he came so people could have life "and have it to the full" (περισσὸν, "more than enough," "overflowing"). Jesus gives life that no one or nothing else can give. He gives us an abundance of grace (Jn 1:16; Ro 5:17), of joy (2 Cor 8:2) and of peace (Jn 14:27). He also gives us the ability to live for him, free from our slavery to sin and Satan. Jesus is the life-giver in every sense of the word.

Homiletical Suggestions

The theme for Easter 4 portrays Jesus as our Good Shepherd. He has laid down his life for his sheep. He has risen in glory and is soon to ascend to the Father on high. The text beautifully pictures the nature of our risen Lord. He is a shepherd who knows, cares, leads, protects and gives an abundance of enduring life to his sheep. By his death and resurrection he has rescued us from the wolves. His resurrection confirms his victory and he continues to live in glory as the shepherd of our souls.

The text contains a great deal of comfort which the preacher will want to make sure he passes on to his hearers. It gives him a golden opportunity to express what Christ's victory at the cross and empty grave means for us in our everyday lives. But at the same time the text also contains ample warning against the "thieves" so common and so prevalent in the religious world today. Jesus is the life-giver. Everyone else destroys life. Such an emphasis might suggest the following:

Watch Whom You Let into Your Life

1. There are dangerous intruders (vv. 1,5,8,10a)
2. Let in only the Good Shepherd (vv. 2-4,7,9,10b)

Another variation on the same idea with a bit more stress on the resurrection would be:

The Risen Lord Gives Us Victory

1. Over the thieves and robbers (vv. 1,5,8,10a)
2. So that we can have life (vv. 2-4,7,9,10b)

Because the text is also directed at the preacher himself, encouraging him to be faithful in his calling and reminding him that the only proper way into the people's hearts is through Christ alone, another approach would be:

Good Shepherds Imitate the Good Shepherd

1. There are those who destroy the sheep (vv. 8,10a)
2. Good shepherds point them to life in Christ (vv. 7,9,10b)

FIFTH SUNDAY OF EASTER

The Scriptures

First Reading — *Acts 17:1-15*
Epistle — *1 Peter 2:4-10*
Gospel — *John 14:1-12*

The Text — John 14:1-12

The ILCW Gospel readings for the last three Sundays of Easter are all taken from Jesus' farewell words to his disciples in John 14-17. It was Maundy Thursday evening, and Jesus had revealed to them that he would be betrayed by one of them. Peter had been warned that he would deny Jesus. The others had heard him say to them, "My little children, I will be with you only a little while longer" (John 13:33). As a result, the disciples were filled with dismay and sadness. John records the Savior's words of comfort and assurance given to them at this point:

vv. 1-4 — *"Do not let your hearts be troubled. Trust in God; trust also in me. In my Father's house are many rooms; if it were not so, I would have told you. I am going there to prepare a place for you. And if I go and prepare a place for you, I will come back and take you to be with me that you also may be where I am. You know the way to the place where I am going."*

How important to note that Jesus begins with words of comfort! This is the keynote of the entire section. How important also to note this fact against the backdrop of what is about to take place! Although Jesus faced betrayal, denial, abandonment, mockery, torture, crucifixion, the pains of hell, and death, he is filled with concern for his disciples. John began his reporting of the events of that night by saying: "Having loved his own who were in the world, he now showed them the full extent of his love" (Jn 13:1b). Throughout the evening Jesus underscored his love.

The text begins with the Lord's words of comfort, "Do not let your hearts be troubled." Jesus bids them to put away fear. Ταράσσω has the picture of water that is churning or seething, as in a rough surf. The news of their Lord's departure had filled the disciples with fear; their hearts were seething within them. As long as Jesus was with them they were strong. Peter felt he could even die with Jesus (13:37). But his departure would leave them in dismay.

Jesus uses several present imperatives. All of them are significant, especially as they look to action that had begun in the past concerning which the Lord either tells them to stop or continue. He says to them, "Stop letting your hearts be stirred up"; he also tells them, "Keep trusting in God; keep trusting in me." The NIV translation of πιστεύετε, "trust," helps us keep in focus what faith is all about: trust and confidence in God and his promises, not mere acknowledgment. And the Lord feeds the disciples' faith with his words of promise and hope as he tells them: "In my Father's house are many rooms; if it were not so, I would have told you."

Μοναί, "rooms," is most comforting. The word suggests permanence, being "at home," being settled, and contrasts with the shifting and changeability of earthly life. The lives of the men and women around Jesus were about to be drastically changed, first by his death, later by his resurrection; the familiar would be gone. Jesus is urging on them the comfort and assurance of what is the believer's by faith, a place that is lasting and certain "in my Father's house." Moreover, Jesus' departure was necessary to insure it.

The NIV editors opted to translate εἰ δὲ μή, εἶπον ἂν ὑμῖν, κτλ, as a statement; the UBS punctuates as a question ("If it were not so, would I have told you . . . ?") Either way, Jesus' point is to assure his disciples that they will not be abandoned (14:18), but that his departure is for their eternal good. And he combines this with the comfort of his second coming: "I will come back and take you to be with me that you also may be where I am." Writing long afterward, the Apostle Peter remembered and rejoiced in this comfort as he wrote about the certain hope believers have in their Lord, 1 Peter 1:3-9, especially vv. 4,5.

But Jesus did not bring only comfort, he also speaks words of instruction. The disciples are to move beyond their dismay to contemplate the meaning of suffering and death. Jesus told them: "You know the way to the place I am going." But the meaning of this was lost on them and Thomas is moved to ask:

v. 5 — *Thomas said to him, "Lord, we don't know where you are going, so how can we know the way?"*

"In a simple and carnal manner" (Luther) Thomas thinks Jesus is speaking of a literal road he plans to use! Time and again the disciples amaze us with their dullness in the face of Jesus' words. Their seeming inability to grasp the truth causes us to wonder. But honest reflection on our own failure to understand and, especially, to trust in Jesus' words ourselves should lead us to see that Thomas' reaction is not so surprising. In contrast, look how gracious Jesus' answer to Thomas is:

vv. 6,7 — *Jesus answered, "I am the way and the truth and the life. No one comes to the Father except through me. If you really knew me, you would know my Father as well. From now on, you do know him and have seen him."*

Jesus does not rebuke Thomas for his words. His response pursues his desire to assure and comfort. Far from not knowing, Thomas and the rest do know the way and the place to which Jesus is going. "I am the way . . . I am going to the Father." Throughout the section Jesus comforts his followers with what they had previously learned and experienced. Their lessons, knowledge and experiences of the past three years were now to be applied through trust in their Lord.

Jesus' "I am" statements are plainly of great significance. As the Lord declares himself "the way and the truth and the life," he reminds us that he is the world's one Lord and Savior. That makes him the most all-inclusive Lord and the most exclusive Lord. He is the Savior for all: "a light for revelation *to the Gentiles* and for glory to your people Israel" (Lk 2:32); his gospel is "the power of God for the salvation of everyone who believes: first for the Jew, then for the Gentile" (Ro 1:16). The Savior commands, "Repentance and forgiveness of sins will be preached in [my] name *to all nations*" (Lk 24:47). No one is excluded from his sacrifice for sin. But he *alone* is the Savior. Lenski quotes Julius Koegel in this regard: "He does not say, 'I *show* you the way,' like a second Moses; but, '*I am* the way.' Nor, '*I have* the truth,' like another Elijah; but '*I am* the truth.' Not only, '*I lead* into life,' as one of his apostles; but, '*I am* the life.' " The predicate nominatives declare Jesus not merely a way, a possessor of truth, etc., but to *be* all these things. Jesus is exclusively the way to the Father.

"If you really knew me. . . . " Is Jesus rebuking his disciples? The NIV opts to translate verse seven using ἐγνώκειτε, the pluperfect form which the UBS text lists as a variant. The perfect, ἐγνώκατε, appears in the UBS text. The pluperfect yields the NIV translation which makes Jesus' words into a rebuke. In contrast, the perfect tense yields the translation, "If you have known me," which, when combined with the apodosis — "you shall know my Father also" —makes Jesus' words to speak another message of comfort to the disciples. The perfect seems more in line with the tone of the section (cf. the translations of *Today's English Version* and the *Jerusalem Bible*). Also, as Lenski points out, the perfect (the better attested reading) also fits better with Jesus' additional comment: "From now on, you do know him and have seen him."

The disciples had known Jesus now for some time. They had witnessed his works and heard his words for three years. Jesus comforts them now with the mystery of what these things meant: his oneness with the Father. Having known him, they know the Father as well. Connection by faith with the Son means connection with the Father as well.

Jesus had sought to comfort his disciples earlier (vv. 1-4), but that had sparked Thomas' question of weakness and misunderstanding. In similar fashion, Philip responded to what Jesus had just said:

v. 8 — *Philip said, "Lord, show us the Father and that will be enough for us."*

Philip had not grasped what Jesus had said to Thomas. But instead of grappling with Jesus' words, Philip thinks if Jesus would just *show* them the Father, "that will be enough for us." A theophany would content Philip; if Jesus would be leaving them, such a vision of the Father would suffice to sustain them until his return. Philip was not remembering the privilege he had been given to walk with God himself for the past three years!

vv. 9-10a — *Jesus answered, "Don't you know me, Philip, even after I have been among you such a long time? Anyone who has seen me has seen the Father. How can you say, 'Show us the Father?' Don't you believe that I am in the Father, and that the Father is in me?"*

Jesus encourages Philip and the others to regain their perspective. Under the stress of that evening they were forgetting such scenes as the storm on the Sea of Galilee, the feeding of the 5000, and the raising of Lazarus. "We have seen his glory," John writes at the beginning of his gospel, "the glory of the one and only Son, who came from the Father, full of grace and truth" (Jn 1:14).

The full meaning of Jesus' words — "I am in the Father, and the Father is in me" — is shrouded in the mystery of the Godhead. His words are full of comfort for sinners in that the Father's love and compassion are made known through the Son's. Jesus' love is a declaration of the Father's love. But his words declare more than his oneness with the Father in terms of the love God has shown the world. Jesus and the Father are one God. "We worship one God in Trinity and Trinity in Unity," as the Athanasian Creed confesses. But comprehending this fully is beyond human reason.

Jesus continues:

vv. 10b-11 — *"The words I say to you are not just my own. Rather, it is the Father, living in me, who is doing his work. Believe me when I say I am in the Father and the Father is in me; or at least believe on the evidence of the miracles themselves."*

The Twelve had long called Jesus, "Rabbi," "My Teacher." Their association with him was that of student to teacher. And they had all (except Judas Iscariot) accepted his words as authoritative and true, as much as their human frailty allowed. Peter had confessed, "Lord, to whom shall we go? You have the words of eternal life" (Jn 6:68). Indeed, Jesus' words led Peter to continue: "We believe and know that you are the Holy One of God" (Jn 6:69). Jesus tells them that his words (ῥήματα) are "not just my own." They are also his Father's and proof of his oneness with the Father. In view of Jesus' words, how significant that the evangelist's name for the Son is "the Word"! (Jn 1:1,14)

So Jesus exhorts (again note the present imperative, πιστεύετε), "Keep on believing me when I say I am in the Father," etc. We note again the intent of the Savior to comfort and bolster the hearts of his disciples with what they had come to know and believe about him.

To this end, he also commends to them the evidence of the miracles he had done. The miracles, or "works" (τὰ ἔργα) of Jesus were meant to confirm his words. Indeed, all of the miracles of the Bible serve this purpose. Moses was given certain miraculous signs to perform before the elders of Israel as confirmation of his message to them (Ex 4). Jesus' miraculous healing of the paralyzed man whose friends had lowered him down through the roof served to confirm "that the Son of Man has authority on earth to forgive sins" (Lk 5:24). Nicodemus had recognized this about the miracles and said as much to Jesus during his secret visit: "Rabbi, we know you are a teacher who has come from God. For no one could perform the miraculous signs you are doing if God were not with him" (Jn 3:2). The Lord continues:

v. 12 — *"I tell you the truth, anyone who has faith in me will do what I have been doing. He will do even greater things than these, because I am going to the Father."*

Jesus follows his exhortation to faith with a promise to faith. The solemn assertion of truth, ἀμὴν ἀμὴν λέγω ὑμῖν, underscored to the disciples the importance and truth of Jesus' promise. The promise itself is staggering, comforting and exhilarating. With reference to the works which had left them awed, Jesus says that those who believe shall do even greater! Jesus is not promising an ability to perform "tricks" at a whim. He is referring to the force believers will exert in his name in the world after his departure. And this will accomplish "greater things than these" (i.e., "my miracles")! How? Franzmann comments: "Jesus' works were done in the shadow of the cross, and his activity was confined to Israel. The disciples' works will be done in the light of the resurrection, in the power of the Spirit sent by the exalted Christ (14:15-17,25,26), and will embrace the world of the Gentiles too." The despondency of the disciples because of Jesus' departure was to give way to joy and a sense of privilege because of what his departure would commission them to do. As their future co-worker Paul would one day write: "Therefore, since through God's mercy we have this ministry, we do not lose heart" (2 Cor 4:1). The events of the days ahead would not only see salvation won, but would also see these men sent forth with the joyful privilege of proclaiming their Savior!

Homiletical Suggestions

The richness of this text in preaching values is immense. Threads of comfort, eternal life and salvation, the mystery of Jesus' oneness with the Father, the *one* Savior, the message of the miracles, assurance, commission and promise are all woven together. Any of these would serve individually as a message for a Christian congregation. However, considering the placement of this text in the season of Easter leads us in a specific direction.

The Fifth Sunday of Easter (formerly *Cantate*) is a transition Sunday within the Easter cycle. While jubilation over the Resurrection still predominates, the themes of Ascension and Pentecost are being heard. The other readings for the day emphasize the priesthood of all believers (1 Pe 2) and mission work born of Resurrection joy (Ac 17). These are definitely Ascension themes. Verse 12 of the gospel text is an explicit tie-in. A preacher may wish to exploit this, especially if Ascension Day is not specially celebrated.

The text as a whole declares that Jesus' departure is not a source of dismay. It is a comfort as he has gone to prepare a place in the Father's house for his believers. This comfort rests on the assurance Christians have in the one who is "the way, the truth, and the life." Moreover, there is the promise of verse 12 of the text, a promise that bespeaks privilege and joy in serving our Lord through the spreading of the gospel.

As with most texts, but especially here in John, not every preaching value in the text will be able to receive full treatment. But placing Jesus' concern for the comfort and encouragement of his disciples foremost yields the following suggested outline:

The Departure That Brings Comfort

1. For eternity (vv. 1-4)
2. For certain (vv. 5-11)
3. For others (v. 12)

Approaching the matter from the standpoint of the disciples, especially Philip and his words, yields this suggestion:

Do You Know Him?

1. Do you know him and his comfort? (vv. 1-4)
2. Do you know him as your Lord and God? (vv. 5-11)
3. Do you know him as the one who empowers you for service? (v. 12)

Of course, the above may be changed from an interrogative to a declarative form:

You Know Him!

etc.

SIXTH SUNDAY OF EASTER

The Scriptures

First Reading — *Acts 17:22-31*
Epistle — *1 Peter 3:15-22*
Gospel — *John 14:15-21*

The Text — John 14:15-21

These are some of the last words Jesus spoke to his disciples before his death. This entire section (chapters 13-17) contains many comforting promises. Its climax is Jesus' High Priestly Prayer (chapter 17) where he prays for all believers in general and his disciples in particular.

Our text is part of an answer Jesus gave to Philip (Jn 14:8ff). The mystery of the Trinity is evident in these verses. We see how the Father, Son and Holy Spirit are all united in one main purpose: the creation and preservation of faith in Christ.

v. 15 — *"If you love me, you will obey what I command."*

Jesus is speaking these words to believers, specifically his disciples. He is assuming they love him; yet he is also testing their love. He wants each of them to reevaluate their love for him.

Note the word Jesus uses for love — ἀγάπη. This is not to be confused with φιλία which implies a mere liking or personal preference. *Agape* love describes God's love for us. It is a one-way love. It isn't based on the quality or value of the person loved. It is unearned and undeserved. God doesn't love us because we are so lovable. He loves us because he loves us. It's all his doing, not our being lovable and thus drawing affection to ourselves. This is the love Jesus had for his disciples. He was about to demonstrate this love for them and all people by dying on the cross.

Jesus also wants his disciples, then and now, to have an *agape* love for him.

The NIV translation "you will obey" (future indicative) is good. The variant reading is an aorist imperative. If we love Jesus, we will naturally keep his commandments. The thoughts are, of course, related.

Luther stresses that ἐντολάς are not admonitions but commissions to preach the word faithfully. This is Jesus' command to his believers.

vv. 16,17 — *"And I will ask the Father, and he will give you another Counselor to be with you forever — the Spirit of truth.*

The world cannot accept him, because it neither sees him nor knows him. But you know him, for he lives with you and will be in you."

Jesus has told the disciples he is leaving them (Jn 13:33). But he will not leave them without any help. He promises to send the Holy Spirit.

To be sure, the Holy Spirit had already entered their hearts and planted the seed of faith. Jesus promised to send the Holy Spirit again so their faith would grow and their loving obedience increase. This would take place with a special outpouring of the Spirit on Pentecost.

It is through the word of God that the Holy Spirit causes faith to grow. This shows the correlation between this verse and the preceding one. They were to keep his command to preach the word. As a result the Holy Spirit would work in their hearts and the hearts of others.

The verb δώσει stresses God's grace. He gives the Holy Spirit at Jesus' request.

The translation "Counselor" best conveys the sense of παράκλητον in this passage. Jesus is not referring to the Holy Spirit as an advocate who would plead our cause to God (1 Jn 2:1). He is speaking about a counselor who would reveal God's cause to man. A counselor comforts, guides and instructs. As the great Counselor, the Holy Spirit would comfort, guide and instruct the disciples with the word of God. The translation "Comforter" is weak, as it conveys only part of the picture.

There is a close connection between this "new" Counselor (Holy Spirit) and the "old" one (Jesus Christ). In a sense he will not replace Christ but will rather lead people to Christ (Jn 16:13,14).

The unbelieving world would not be able to accept this new Counselor even as it was not able to accept the old, Christ. Jesus is not speaking about natural man's inability to receive the Spirit. He is talking about willful resistance. In spite of clear evidence, the world would continue to reject the Spirit and remain blind to the truth.

The opposite was true for the disciples. They had a personal relationship with the Spirit. They knew him. The Spirit was with them. This relationship would be even deeper when Pentecost arrived. Then the Spirit would be in them. The NIV follows the reading ἔσται (future indicative). This seems to fit the context better as Jesus is looking ahead to the day of Pentecost.

vv. 18,19 — *"I will not leave you as orphans; I will come to you. Before long, the world will not see me anymore, but you will see me. Because I live, you also will live.*

Jesus stresses that the Holy Spirit would not replace him. He is going to return to them. The question is: What return is Jesus talking about? Jesus isn't talking about how he would appear to the disciples after his resurrection. Otherwise at his ascension they would again be left as orphans. Nor is he speaking about his final return on the last day. Jesus is speaking about how he would return through the Spirit and dwell in their hearts through faith.

῎Ετι μικρὸν reminds us that his death was now only a few hours away. The world would not see Jesus physically. More than that it would not see him with the eyes of faith. But through faith the disciples would see him. The Holy Spirit would bring Jesus and his teachings home to the disciples and would "teach you all things and will remind you of everything I have said to you" (Jn 14:26).

Through faith the disciples would also live with Christ. Even in the face of death Jesus exclaims, "I live." Death has no effect on him. In the same way his disciples would live. Jesus is referring to the spiritual lives of the disciples. He who is the Life (Jn 14:6) would also live in the disciples. This was the beginning of their eternal life, for "he who believes has everlasting life" (Jn 6:47).

v. 20 — *"On that day you will realize that I am in my Father and you are in me, and I am in you."*

᾿Εν ἐκείνῃ τῇ ἡμέρᾳ refers to Pentecost. At that time the disciples would understand more fully the mystery of the Trinity, that "I [Jesus] am in the Father." The unity and mystery of the Godhead is once again evident.

The disciples would realize that the Father and Son are one. Lenski: "All the love, grace, mercy, light, comfort, joy, hope and glory offered by the Father and the Son is one."

This union would be a pattern for the relationship between Christ and his followers. However the two would not be identical. The three ἐν are by no means parallel. The union between the Father and the Son is complete. Two distinct persons yet one God. The union between Christ and his believers is incomplete. It is in the process of growing but will never reach full maturity here on earth. Even in heaven this relationship will be different. We will never be one with God in the same sense that Jesus is one with the Father. We will always remain his creatures. He will always be our God. Hendriksen: "Nevertheless, in view of the fact that Christ by means of the Spirit actually lives in the hearts of believers, the former relationship is truly a pattern for the latter."

Revelation 3:21 uses similar words: "To him who overcomes, I will give the right to sit with me on my throne, just as I overcame and sat down with my Father on his throne."

v. 21 — *"Whoever has my commands and obeys them, he is the one who loves me. He who loves me will be loved by my Father, and I too will love him and show myself to him."*

All the promises Jesus mentioned before rest on the condition "if you love me." This doesn't mean they are no longer rewards of grace. Yet God's commands do have a promise attached to them. When we follow them the natural result is that we are blessed. This is especially true of Jesus' command to preach the gospel.

"He who loves me will be loved by my Father." This does not preclude God loving us first (1 Jn 4:10). Hendriksen: "God's love both precedes and follows our love."

Ἐμφανίσω does not refer to a special revelation. Jesus "shows" himself to us through his word (Jn 20:31).

Homiletical Suggestions

Traditionally the Sunday before Ascension was designated as Rogate, Prayer Sunday. However, the ILCW series directs our thoughts ahead to the day of Pentecost and concentrates on the blessings of the Holy Spirit. This is especially true of our text. Jesus is promising to send his disciples the Holy Spirit. It is true they had already received the Holy Spirit, for "no one can say 'Jesus is Lord' except by the Holy Spirit" (1 Cor 12:3). However Jesus is promising them a special outpouring of the Spirit. While Jesus has never promised us another Pentecost, his promises in this section do apply to us. He continues to send us the Holy Spirit to teach us all things and remind us of everything he said to us in his word (Jn 14:26).

Jesus comforts his disciples in this section. He promises he will not leave them but will continue to come to them through the Counselor and live in them through faith. A treatment which emphasizes the comfort Jesus gives would be:

Jesus Gives Us a Comforting Promise

1. He promises to care for us (vv. 15-17,21)
2. He promises to be with us (vv. 18-20)

This section also contains some application. These promises of Jesus are based on the condition that we love him. We need to stress that Jesus is speaking to believers who already love him and who love him only because he first loved them. We are in the area of sanctification here and not justification. A treatment of these thoughts would be:

Because We Love Jesus

1. We keep his commands (vv. 15,21)
2. We are blessed with the Spirit (vv. 16,17)
3. We are one with God (vv. 18-20)

In the first part one would bring out Jesus' command to preach the gospel. This would provide a natural transition to part two which deals with the promise of the Holy Spirit. Through the word the Holy Spirit strengthens our faith and creates faith in the hearts of others. Through the word the Holy Spirit also causes Christ to live in our hearts. This results in the spiritual unity suggested by part three.

ASCENSION OF OUR LORD

The Scriptures

First Reading — *Acts 1:1-11*
Epistle — *Ephesians 1:16-23*
Gospel — *Luke 24:44-53*

The Text — Luke 24:44-53

The verses immediately preceding the text relate Jesus' appearance on the evening of the first Easter (vv. 36-43). He appeared to the disciples who were behind locked door for fear of the Jews (Jn 20:19). They had been talking about the report of the Emmaus disciples. He urged them to touch him in order to establish that they were not seeing a ghost. He ate a piece of broiled fish in their presence to show that he was truly flesh and blood.

This appearance and those that followed during the forty days before his ascension confirmed the disciples in their conviction that he had truly risen. The forty days were also a time of instruction, as he informed them concerning his gracious rule, his kingdom.

vv. 44,45 — *He said to them, "This is what I told you while I was still with you: Everything must be fulfilled that is written about me in the Law of Moses, the Prophets and the Psalms." Then he opened their minds so they could understand the Scriptures.*

It is not certain that verses 44-49 were spoken in the Upper Room on Sunday evening of Resurrection Day. They may be a condensed account of Jesus' instruction during the forty days that followed. This uncertainty does not affect the content of Jesus' words and need not be discussed in the sermon.

While he was still with them, during his ministry and before his suffering and death, Jesus had told them about his coming death and resurrection. After their great confession concerning his identity as the Christ and the Son of God (Lk 9:22) and again while they were enroute to Jerusalem for the last time (Mt 18:17-19), he had foretold these events.

The things written in the Scriptures must be fulfilled because God had spoken. Note the divine δεῖ, God's "must." What God speaks is done. Even when it takes centuries and millennia to come to pass, it must occur.

"These are the Scriptures that testify about me," he had said (Jn 5:39). "If you believed Moses, you would believe me, for he wrote about me" (Jn 5:46). Not only "in the Law of Moses" (the Pentateuch), but also in "the Prophets and the Psalms," the holy men of God had been moved to write about him. "The Prophets" are the historical writings and the books of prophecy in the threefold Jewish division of the Scriptures. The Psalms begin the third portion. Moreover, the Psalms are particularly rich in messianic prophecies and references. Jesus is really saying here that all the Jewish Scriptures, what we call the Old Testament, were written concerning him.

In saying this he was teaching them and us how to understand the Bible. He provides the key to interpretation by showing us that he himself is the Key.

vv. 46,47 — *He told them, "This is what is written: The Christ will suffer and rise from the dead on the third day, and repentance and forgiveness of sins will be preached in his name to all nations, beginning at Jerusalem."*

Prevailing popular ideas concerning the Messiah could not allow that the Lord's Anointed should die. That he should die, especially in the manner in which Jesus died, was an offense to Jewish thinking. It had been a crushing blow to Jesus' own disciples when it happened. But, "This is what is written." Not only on the basis of what Jesus had been telling them, but also on the basis of the Scriptures, they ought to have known. Now, on the basis of the Scriptures and what they had witnessed they would know.

When he spoke of his coming death, Jesus had also stressed that he would rise again. In Genesis 3:15 the Law of Moses spoke of what Satan would do to the Woman's Seed *and* of the triumph of the Woman's Seed over Satan. An example of how the prophets taught both the death and resurrection of Messiah may be found in the comparison of Isaiah 53:4 with Isaiah 52:10. Psalm 22 is full of Christ's suffering and death; Psalm 16:9-11 teaches his resurrection. These, of course, are only small samplings.

In the name of this Christ, on the basis of (ἐπί) who he is and what he has done, "repentance and forgiveness of sins will be preached." He suffered the penalty for the sins of the world. God laid on him the sins of us all. For his sake sins are forgiven. That was the purpose and meaning of his suffering. God accepted his sacrifice, vindicated his Son and raised him from the dead. His resurrection is the guarantee that the sins of the world really are forgiven.

That message is to be preached to all nations. The apostles will not go out into the world telling people what steps to follow in order to get right with God. They will not, the church must not, propound a method for "getting saved." The subject of the preaching is "repentance and forgiveness of sins." It is not a conditional message but a truth to be heralded.

Μετάνοια is literally "change of mind." In Greek philosophy that change of mind meant renouncing a previously held, defective and inferior, point of view in order to embrace a new and superior philosophical tenet. The New Testament, however, uses the term to express the Old Testament concept of "turning" or "returning" —conversion. For example, from Isaiah 10:20f; 30:15; Jeremiah 3:22f; 25:5f; Hosea 14:1-4, we learn that it signifies a turning from all idols to absolute trust in the Lord. It is something God calls for and also effects (Ml 4:6).

There is a significant variant in verse 47. NIV adopts the reading καὶ ἄφεσιν: "and forgiveness." This καί may be simply conjunctive. Then preaching repentance is equivalent to preaching the law, preaching contrition, sorrow and terror over sin.

The καί may be epexegetical, "repentance, *that is*, the forgiveness of sins." Then repentance is faith in the forgiveness of sins.

The variant reads εἰς ἄφεσιν, "*for* the forgiveness." Then the message to be heralded is, "Turn from your sins to the Savior for the forgiveness of sins."

The choice between καί and εἰς, the understanding of καί as conjunctive or epexegetical, do not materially change the content of the message. There is a difference in expounding the text but there is no difference in the good news that in Christ all sins of all sinners of all time are forgiven.

This is to be preached to all nations because all need to repent and all are forgiven. Beginning at the heart of the Jewish nation, in Jerusalem, the believers are to carry out a mission. What begins in Jerusalem is to continue in ever-widening circles (cf. Ac 1:8, the first lesson). This mission remains as the church's unfinished business today. It will not be finished until the ascended Lord returns to judge the living and the dead (Ac 1:11).

v. 48 — *"You are witnesses of these things."*

What the disciples had seen and heard, what their hands had handled, they were to testify to. They were also to witness to what Jesus had taught them about the meaning of the Scriptures and the meaning of his work. We, who have not seen and heard in the way they saw and heard, are faithfully to transmit their testimony until the end of the age. In that sense we, too, are witnesses.

v. 49 — *"I am going to send you what my Father has promised; but stay in the city until you have been clothed with power from on high."*

What the Father had promised was the outpouring of the Holy Spirit (Jl 2:28f; Is 44:3; cp. Ac 1:5). The Spirit, when he had been bestowed, would empower them for the work of heralding and witnessing.

v. 50 — *When he had led them out to the vicinity of Bethany, he lifted up his hands and blessed them.*

On the Mount of Olives (Ac 1:12), near Bethany, less than a mile from Jerusalem, Jesus gathered his disciples one more time. There he lifted up his pierced hands, now glorified, and blessed his own. His blessing was more than a wish, more than a prayer. When he speaks his people are blessed.

v. 51 — *While he was blessing them, he left them and was taken up into heaven.*

During the forty days since his resurrection Jesus had come and gone, now seen and then unseen. There will be no more such appearances until he returns as Judge.

The reading, "and was taken up into heaven" is in dispute. NIV includes it and the preacher need not hesitate to include something that is attested elsewhere in Scripture. See the first lesson, Acts 1:9-11. See Ephesians 1:20 and 4:10.

The human nature which Jesus took on to redeem us shares in the divine glory which the Son of God had from eternity. The firstfruits of our flesh and blood are in heaven. The firstfruits of his Spirit are in our hearts as the pledge of the glory we will enjoy in heaven.

The Lord has not retired! See the Epistle, Ephesians 1:21-23, to learn that God's right hand is not merely a position of honor and not a circumscribed place where Jesus is confined. His activity is unlimited; he shares in the power of the Almighty Father; he rules all things in the interest of his church. He intercedes for us (Ro 8:34; He 7:24f).

vv. 52,53 — *Then they worshiped him and returned to Jerusalem with great joy. And they stayed continually at the temple, praising God.*

With their worship they acknowledged Jesus as God. Obediently they returned to the city as he had directed. They did not brood or despair over his absence. They rejoiced greatly, cheered by what the ascension means.

No longer did they hide behind doors. Publicly, in the temple precincts, they praised God for his wonderful works. This they did *before* the outpouring of the Spirit. They would do much more after Pentecost.

Homiletical Suggestions

If attendance is low on this festival which the world ignores and much of the church neglects, don't let that spoil the joy of the event or the cheering message of this text. Don't scold those who are present because others are absent. Don't give your hearers occasion to be puffed up because they are present. Herald repentance and forgiveness of sins. Witness to the mighty gracious deeds of God in Christ. Praise God that he has kept all his promises, including the promise of the Spirit.

Use the Epistle as a resource to speak of the significance of the ascension and of Jesus' continuing activity on our behalf. Resist the temptation to preach the whole dogmatics.

To stress our Lord's continuing activity, try this:

The Savior Still Blesses His Church

1. With the Word of truth (vv. 44-47)
2. With the Spirit of power (vv. 48,49)
3. With the joy of salvation (vv. 50-53)

To emphasize that he is still with us and still working:

Where Is He Now?

1. Still to be found in his word (vv. 44,45)
2. Still speaking through his church (vv. 46-49)
3. Still ruling over his world (vv. 50-53; Eph 1:21-23)

Key on the disciples' joy, which was not diminished but enhanced after his visible presence was removed:

Keep on Celebrating Our Lord's Ascension

1. Understanding his word (vv. 44-47)
2. Participating in his work (vv. 48,49)
3. Praising his name (vv. 50-53)

SEVENTH SUNDAY OF EASTER

The Scriptures

First Reading — *Acts 1:8-14*
Epistle — *1 Peter 4:12-17; 5:6-11*
Gospel — *John 17:1-11*

The Text — John 17:1-11

John 17 is the final chapter of Jesus' "Upper Room Discourse," John 13-17, addressed to his disciples on the night of his betrayal. The entire chapter is Jesus' high-priestly prayer offered to God the Father for the benefit of the disciples. As Jesus entered the final stages of his redeeming work (his arrest, trials, crucifixion, resurrection and ascension), he permitted his followers to hear him present his deepest, most heartfelt concerns to the heavenly Father. The prayer can be divided into three parts: a prayer concerning himself (vv. 1-5), a prayer for the disciples at his side (vv. 6-19), and a prayer for all future believers (vv. 20-26). The ILCW series makes use of John 17 for its three Gospel lessons on the Seventh Sunday of Easter. Series A uses verses 1-11. Series B uses verses 16-19. Series C uses verses 20-26.

In this series A text (vv. 1-11), Jesus prays first concerning his and the Father's glory (vv. 1-5) and then for the welfare of his disciples (vv. 6-11). As Jesus approaches the completion of his redeeming work, he asks his Father to glorify him. He longs to bring his mission to a successful conclusion so that he may bring glory to the Father and may also reassume his position of exalted glory as God the Son. Jesus then prays for his disciples. He would soon leave them and would not be able to protect them with his visible presence (v. 12). He asks that the Father would protect the disciples with his mighty power while they remain in the world.

> vv. 1-3 — *After Jesus said this, he looked toward heaven and prayed: "Father, the time has come. Glorify your Son, that your Son may glorify you. For you granted him authority over all people that he might give eternal ife to all those you have given him. Now this is eternal life: that they may know you, the only true God, and Jesus Christ, whom you have sent."*

Jesus had just completed his long discourse with the disciples, John 13-16. He now begins his exalted prayer to the Father, a prayer filled with majesty, authority, compassion and confidence. Jesus directs his prayer to the Father as the time comes for him to complete God's plan to save the world. The "hour" for Jesus' death, resurrection and ascension to the Father's right hand had come. By requesting that the Father glorify him so that he may glorify the Father, Jesus asks that the Father would invest his human nature with the full use of his divine attributes in the glory of heaven. In turn, Jesus would make the glorious attributes of the Father shine out in all the world through the work of the Holy Spirit in the gospel and in the church.

In verse 2 Jesus points out that this mutual glorifying is in perfect harmony with what God did when he gave Jesus authority over all people. The Father granted Jesus authority to give eternal life to all the Father gave him. The Father and the Son work together in perfect harmony on all aspects of Jesus' saving mission to the world. Note that God includes all people in his gracious plan of salvation. If people fail to enjoy the benefits of that salvation, it is only because they have excluded themselves through their unbelief.

In verse 3 Jesus reveals the essential relationship at the heart of eternal life, the relationship with God. To have eternal life is to have a true heart knowledge of the only true God and of Jesus, his Christ. To "know" God does not mean a mere intellectual understanding of facts about God, but a personal trusting, acquaintance with him.

vv. 4,5 — *"I have brought you glory on earth by completing the work you gave me to do. And now, Father, glorify me in your presence with the glory I had with you before the world began."*

Jesus continues his prayer concerning his and the Father's glory by stating that he had glorified the Father by completing the work of redemption the Father had given him. Even though Jesus had not yet been crucified or raised from the dead, he speaks of his work as an accomplished fact. So confident is he of the success of his work. The Father is glorified in the Son's redemption of the world. It is interesting to observe that Jesus regards his redemptive mission as a loving gift from the Father and not at all as an unwelcome burden.

When Jesus asks for glory in verse 5 he is not seeking personal reward. Rather, he is seeking the good of others. Jesus' glorification will bring added glory to the Father among people in future ages and it will bring eternal life to future believers. Jesus asks that the Father glorify him also according to his human nature with the glory that was eternally his as God the Son.

vv. 6-8 — *"I have revealed you to those whom you gave me out of the world. They were yours; you gave them to me and they have obeyed your word. Now they know that everything you have given me comes from you. For I gave them the words you gave me and they accepted them. They knew with certainty that I came from you, and they believed that you sent me."*

In verses 6-11 Jesus prays on behalf of his disciples. He makes specific requests in verse 11. In verses 6-10 he unfolds the reasons for his requests. In so doing Jesus voices his inmost thoughts of profound love for his disciples.

In verse 6 Jesus prays to the Father about those whom the Father gave him. By nature the disciples were part of the world estranged from God. But by God's grace working on their hearts, they became believers in Jesus, obedient to God's word. In verses 7,8 Jesus adds that they came to realize that everything about Jesus was from the Father who sent him. As Jesus gave them what the Father had given him, the disciples believed and knew with certainty that the Father had commissioned Jesus as the Christ.

vv. 9-11 — *"I pray for them. I am not praying for the world, but for those you have given me, for they are yours. All I have is yours, and all you have is mine. And glory has come to me through them. I will remain in the world no longer but they are still in the world, and I am coming to you. Holy Father, protect them by the power of your name — the name you gave me — so that they may be one as we are one."*

Jesus prays as One who is equal to the Father. He prays for the disciples who are jointly "owned" by him and the Father. Jesus says that he does not pray for the world. Jesus is not saying that he does not care about the unbelieving world. He does care deeply and he prays for unbelievers on other occasions. Here he especially prays for those who have become children of the Father through faith in him and heirs of God, privileged to enjoy his spiritual blessings. In verse 10 Jesus again expresses the mutual ownership which he and the Father have. He also mentions that he is glorified in the hearts of his disciples. This glory comes as they come to realize that Jesus came from the Father as his anointed One.

In verse 11 Jesus draws attention to the fact that he will soon leave his disciples and will no longer be visibly present with them to protect them as before. He prays that the Father will protect them against all evil by the power of his name. The disciples will need protection so they do not lose their believing connection with God's word. Jesus asks for this divine protection so that his disciples may reflect in their lives the unity which exists among the members of the Godhead.

Homiletical Suggestions

The Seventh Sunday of Easter comes three days after the Ascension and one week before Pentecost. It has an interesting place in the church year in this "bridge" position between these two great festivals. The ILCW-A "Old Testament" lesson is Acts 1:8-14. It covers both the Ascension and the pre-Pentecost preparations of the disciples. The preacher may want to stress either an Ascension theme (especially if the festival was not celebrated in a special service previously) or a preparation for Pentecost theme.

Some of the specific preaching values of the John 17:1-11 text are: (1) Jesus' final exaltation at the completion of his mission, (2) Jesus' continuing concern for his disciples, (3) Jesus' work as the high-priestly Intercessor for his believers, (4) eternal life as God's gracious gift in Christ, (5) the believers' need for protection in a spiritually hostile world and (6) glory for the Father and the Son as a result of Jesus' work.

Based on the Sunday of the church year and the preaching values of the text, here are some sermon themes:

A suggestion for using the entire text with its two major parts:

The Son Petitions His Father

1. Glorify your Son as he completes his mission (vv. 1-5)
2. Protect our people as they continue theirs (vv. 6-11)

A suggestion for using the first four verses with an Ascension theme:

Christ's Pre-Ascension Prayer for a Post-Ascension World

1. Let me give glory to you, Father (vv. 1,4)
2. Let me give life to men (vv. 2,3)

Using the last part of the text with an emphasis on Jesus' profound love for his disciples:

Do You Hear How Much He Loves Us?

1. He rejoices to his Father about us (vv. 6-8,10)
2. He intercedes with his Father for us (vv. 9,11)

Treating the theme of eternal life in vv. 2,3:

The Facts of Eternal Life

1. It lies in knowing the true God (v. 3)
2. It comes as this God's gracious gift (v. 2)

A suggestion for using only verse 11 and focusing on Jesus as the High Priest who prays for his believers:

Our Priest Prays for Things We Need

1. He prays for God's divine protection (vv. 11a)
2. He prays for our spiritual unity (vv. 11b)

PENTECOST

The Scriptures

Old Testament — *Joel 2:28,29*
Epistle — *Acts 2:1-21*
Gospel — *John 16:5-11*

The Text — John 16:5-11

This text has a history of differing interpretations and applications. Although assigned to the festival of Pentecost in this ILCW pericope, Jesus' words were spoken on a very different occasion. The text is part of the Maundy Thursday discourse which had a twofold purpose. The first was to comfort the sorrowing disciples during the immediate time after Jesus' imminent departure. The second was to prepare them to carry on his ministry without his visible presence. In this unique context, the words probably meant more to the disciples than they do to us today. But understanding this context will help us to clarify the problems of interpretation and appropriate for ourselves the rich meaning of Jesus' words.

vv. 5,6 — *"Now I am going to him who sent me, yet none of you asks me, 'Where are you going?' Because I have said these things, you are filled with grief."*

The disciples were so absorbed in the thought of Jesus' announced departure and their consequent bereavement that they had failed to ascertain clearly where he was going. Grief can so fill the bereaved that it may temporarily interrupt the rational thought process. Here Jesus wants to comfort his disciples and help them handle their grief.

v. 7 — *"But I tell you the truth: It is for your good that I am going away. Unless I go away, the Counselor will not come to you; but if I go, I will send him to you."*

As the one who can see the whole event in its proper perspective Jesus is eminently qualified to tell the disciples "the truth" that it is actually to their advantage and not their loss for him to go away. It is an incredible statement. Think of the advantages Jesus' bodily presence offered. Consider what it meant for the disciples. What could be better for the disciples, or anyone for that matter, than the physical presence of their God and Savior?

The bodily withdrawal of Jesus was an essential condition for his universal and abiding presence through the Holy Spirit. The presence and power of the Holy Spirit offer even more advantages to disciples than the physical presence of Jesus! Jesus sets the stage for describing these advantages when he calls the Holy Spirit "the Counselor" (ὁ παράκλητος).

In secular Greek literature of the New Testament era, the word παράκλητος was used to refer to a "person called in to help, summoned to give assistance." From that widest sense it came to refer to a "helper in court." A "paraclete" was often someone who gave legal assistance in court, perhaps even to the point of pleading the case.

Luther and others based their translation "Comforter" primarily on the etymological root παρακαλέω, which has a wide range of meanings, including "to comfort."

The word appears five times in the New Testament (Jn 14:16,26; 15:26; 16:7; 1 Jn 2:1). In his Gospel John uses the word four times to refer to the Holy Spirit. In his epistle he uses it to refer to Jesus. The meaning in each case must be determined primarily by the context.

vv. 8-11 — *When he comes, he will convict the world of guilt in regard to sin and righteousness and judgment: in regard to sin, because men do not believe in me; in regard to righteousness, because I am going to the Father, where you can see me no longer; and in regard to judgment, because the prince of this world now stands condemned."*

The NIV translation of ἐλέγξει as "to convict of guilt" can be defended linguistically and doctrinally, but it also has some problems.

First, there is a doctrinal and contextual weakness. The "convicting" work of the Holy Spirit is the "foreign work" of the gospel. When the gospel condemns sinners who reject Christ it is performing an *opus alienum*, and not the *opus proprium* (Formula of Concord, Epitome, V. 9,10; Triglotta p. 803) of salvation which God intends. What kind of comfort does the foreign and condemning work of the gospel offer to disciples who are filled with grief at the prospect of Jesus' leaving them?

Secondly, the sense of "convict of guilt" fits well with sin, but does not readily agree with the latter two objects, righteousness and judgment. How does the Holy Spirit "convict" people of righteousness and judgment?

The English word, "convict," has an archaic meaning that fits the context much better and corresponds exactly to another nuance of the Greek ἐλέγχω. The second edition of *Webster's New International Dictionary* defines this obsolete use as: "to demonstrate by proof or evidence; to prove." Webster then lists as a third archaic use: "to prove or show to be false or in the wrong; to refute; confute; *convince*" (emphasis mine).

Both "convict" and "convince" have the same etymological root, the Latin *convincere* which means "to conquer." Even more remarkable. Webster lists "convict of guilt" as an obsolete definition of "convince." As an example he cites John 8:46 in the KJV: "Which of you convinceth me of sin?"

These two nuances, "convict" and "convince," correspond exactly to two nuances of the Greek ἐλέγχω. Three major New Testament Greek lexicons (Bauer, Arndt, Gingrich; Thayer; Brown, *Dictionary of New Testament Theology*) all list both "convict" and "convince" as possible translations for ἐλέγχω.

Using the modern English word "convince" instead of "convict" solves all the problems and make the most sense. Jesus comforts the discipless with the promise of the Holy Spirit, the "Counselor" or "Helper," who will now work alongside of them. Through the gospel in word and sacrament, preached and administered by the apostles, the Holy Spirit will *convince* (savingly) the world of sinners (κόσμον). Without the visible presence of Jesus, the disciples have no evidence to prove their case. That's why the Holy Spirit will be such a blessing to them. He will help the disciples prove their case to an unbelieving world.

There can be no doubt now about the meaning of the significant words ἁμαρτίας, δικαιοσύνης and κρίσεως. Through the law/gospel witness of the apostles and all believers the Holy Spirit convinces unbelievers that their unbelief (οὐ πιστεύουσιν εἰς ἐμέ) is the one great sin (ἁμαρτία) which they must overcome. Through this same law/-gospel witness the Holy Spirit convinces unbelievers that Christ by his redemptive work has gained for all men a perfect righteousness (δικαιοσύνη) that avails before God ("because I am going to the Father"). Through this law/gospel witness the Holy Spirit convinces unbelievers that the victorious Christ is the one to be obeyed and worshiped, and not the devil who poses as the "prince of the world," but is now condemned (ὁ ἄρχων τοῦ κόσμου τούτου κέκριται).

Now it is possible to understand why the disciples can take comfort in Jesus' bodily departure. Through the Holy Spirit, who will reside in them and work in the message they preach, they will be empowered to make disciples of all nations. Their ministry is guaranteed success because of the presence of the Holy Spirit, their "helper" or "counselor." History records the truthfulness of Jesus' promise.

Homiletical Suggestions

Many Christians have failed to grasp a vivid concept of the Holy Spirit. This failure has led Christians to fall into two errors. On the one hand there are the Pentecostalists and charismatics who confuse the work of the Holy Spirit with mysticism, emotionalism and vague spiritual sentimentality. On the other hand there are the Christians who are apathetic about the practical influence of the Holy Spirit in their lives.

Jesus' words bridge the gap between his work of redemption and the work of the Holy Spirit.

The text offers ample opportunity to comfort Christians "who have not seen" the risen Christ "and yet have believed." It is the Holy Spirit who works faith, using the word of God preached by men. This comforting truth can be illustrated by the example of the father who leaves his family behind so he can come back with the daily bread that will keep them alive. Another illustration would be the soldier who volunteers to leave his comrades, besieged by an overwhelming enemy force in order to bring back help. He takes a tearful farewell of his comrades so that at the risk of his life he may penetrate enemy lines and return with rescuers. Jesus left his disciples so that he might send the Holy Spirit. The abiding presence of the Spirit is worth more than the visible presence of Jesus.

The text also offers opportunity to strengthen and encourage Christians in the ministry the Lord has placed into their hands. He has provided a powerful Helper.

A theme around which these thoughts could be built might be:

Jesus Sends the Paraclete (Counselor, Helper)

1. To comfort his disciples (vv. 5-7)
2. To convince the world (vv. 8-11)

Another outline which would also serve to connect the events of Ascension and Pentecost might be:

Ascension and Pentecost — The Christian's Loss and Gain

1. The Ascension loss (vv. 5,6)
2. The Pentecost gain (vv. 7-11)

One might also use the entire text for the sermon, but build the sermon parts chiefly on verses 8-11:

How the Holy Spirit Helps Us

1. He convinces people about sin (vv. 8,9)
2. He convinces people about righteousness (v. 10)
3. He convinces people about judgment (v. 11)

FIRST SUNDAY AFTER PENTECOST

The Scriptures

Old Testament — *Deuteronomy 4:32-34,39,40*
Epistle — *2 Corinthians 13:11-14*
Gospel — *Matthew 28:16-20*

The Text — Matthew 28:16-20

How do we describe the Holy Trinity? Do we picture three leaflets on a three-leaf clover? Do we speak of a cord of three strands? Do we point to the sides of a triangle or the three letters in the name G-O-D?

Do we line up Judaism, Mormonism and Jehovah's Witnesses as non-Christian denials of the Holy Trinity? Do we add Unitarians, secret societies and Eastern cults to the enemies of the triune God?

We know the Holy Trinity is far more than mental visualizations of an embattled idea. It is God — real and powerful, wanting all people to be saved, expecting you and me to proclaim repentance and the forgiveness of sins throughout the world — our constant companion and comfort.

vv. 16,17 — *Then the eleven disciples went to Galilee, to the mountain where Jesus had told them to go. When they saw him, they worshiped him; but some doubted.*

John the evangelist indicates that the disciples stayed in Jerusalem following the Passover for the seven day Feast of Unleaven Bread (Jn 20:26). He goes on to report Jesus' third appearance to the seven disciples fishing the Sea of Tiberias (Jn 21:1,2,14).

Our text marks at least the fourth time Jesus speaks with his disciples following his resurrection. This quiet time on the Galilean mountain may have extended nearly three weeks. It was a time for Jesus to open his disciples' minds so they could understand the Scriptures (Lk 24:45).

During his public ministry Jesus had used strategic retreats to avoid hostile Pharisees and Herodians (Mk 3:7) and to seek rest from the crowds of people (Lk 5:16). Withdrawing to lonely places to pray (Lk 22:41) was common for Jesus and his disciples. The Galilean mountain would provide the isolated setting Jesus desired (Mt 26:32; 28:7,10) for these last days with his own.

When the Eleven saw Jesus on the mountain they fell face down to worship him. Jesus was no longer just their rabbi and friend. He was Christ the exalted Son of God, their risen Lord and Savior. He had conquered their supernatural enemies. They were his humble subjects demonstrating what it means to confess, "All this he did that I should be his own, and live under him in his kingdom."

The setting of this post-resurrection appearance closes with the phrase οἱ δὲ ἐδίστασαν. The definite article is being used as a demonstrative pronoun. To whom does it point? Are all eleven disciples hesitantly bowing down in worship? In that case we would translate, "When they saw Jesus they worshiped him; but *these* doubted."

Traditional English translations suggest a group within the Eleven having doubts. However, the simple translation of οἱ δὲ yields, "When they saw Jesus they worship him, but *others* doubted." Compare Matthew 26:67,68 for the same construction. The Eleven who have all seen Jesus at least twice since he has risen are contrasted with others from the larger group of disciples. These others may well be seeing their risen Savior for the first time.

When and where did Jesus appear "to more than five hundred of the brothers at the same time" (1 Cor 15:6)? The Galilean retreat is the logical answer. What Matthew indicates Paul substantiates.

Actually it is not that important whether the doubters numbered a handful or hundreds. Now each readily declares, "Christ has indeed been raised from the dead, the firstfruits of those who have fallen asleep" (1 Cor 15:20).

v. 18 — *Then Jesus came to them and said, "All authority in heaven and on earth has been given to me."*

While Jesus approached this mixed group of worshiping and doubting disciples he spoke to them. He tells them of his authority. Authority (ἐξουσία) pictures a person's possessions. It is the right and ability to use what is at his disposal. Jesus was given the right and the ability to use all things in heaven and on earth.

Such authority reduced demons to beggars and caused fearful citizens to plead for Jesus' departure (Mt 8:31,34). The almighty power of God is real. For the sinner it is terrifying. Yet this power also demonstrated the Son's authority on earth to forgive sins (Mt 9:6).

Jesus tells of his authority in order to reassure his disciples. As the Scriptures foretold, the Christ did suffer, but the prince of this world had no hold on him (Jn 14:30). On the third day not even death itself could hold the One who is the resurrection and the life (Jn 11:25). Now the time has come to preach repentance and the forgiveness of sins to the nations (Lk 24:46,47).

vv. 19,20 — *"Therefore go and make disciples of all nations, baptizing them in the name of the Father and of the Son and of the Holy Spirit, and teaching them to obey everything I have commanded you. And surely I am with you always, to the very end of the age."*

The objective of the Galilean retreat is revealed (οὖν). All nations are to become followers of Christ. The aorist imperative μαθητεύσατε defines the disciples' mission. As his disciples traveled they would come into contact with all the ethnic groups of this world. The cure for sin was to be made known to each nation.

The means for accomplishing this mission of mercy is the gospel in word and sacraments (the present participles βαπτίζοντες and διδάσκοντες). Individuals baptized in the name of the Father and of the Son and of the Holy Spirit were also taught to obey the commands of Christ.

What does it mean to be baptized in the name of the Holy Trinity? In baptism God adopts a person into his family. The name Christian or Trinitarian properly identifies the adopted one. He inherits the Father's love, the Son's redemption and the Holy Spirit's gift of fruitful faith.

Why then is it necessary to include teaching as part of the disciple-making process? Each time the new family member stumbles, teaching points him to the forgiveness which belongs to God's children. This in turn motivates him to live in a manner worthy of his calling.

Jesus expects his followers to obey (τηρεῖν) all his commands. See John 15:10-12 where Jesus commands love. *Defend* all the commands of Christ despite the way "other-teaching" churches shred the Holy Scriptures. *Preserve* all the commands of Christ. Do not tread just shy of the line of transgression. Set up camp at a distance. *Fulfill* all the commands of Christ. Faith is to bear its fruit.

Finally Jesus assures his followers that he will be with them every single day until the completion of time. His disciple makers will never travel alone. With his full authority they will call for repentance and proclaim the forgiveness of sins.

Homiletical Suggestions

A clear presentation of the *authority* of Jesus is the key to any sermon on this text. God's holy authority brings every sinner trembling to his knees. The same authority provides pardon. The authority of Jesus institutes the great commission, the presentation of law and gospel.

Review Philippians 2:10, "At the name of Jesus every knee should bow, in heaven and on earth and under the earth." Legions of angels are put at his disposal (Mt 26:53). The sea becomes completely calm when he rebukes the winds and the waves (Mt 8:26). With a word he drives the spirits out of the demon-possessed (Mt 8:16).

John 17:1-5 completes the picture. "Father, the time has come. Glorify your Son, that your Son may glorify you. For you granted him authority over all people that he might give eternal life to all those you have given him. Now this is eternal life: that they may know you, the only true God, and Jesus Christ, whom you have sent. I have brought you glory on earth by completing the work you gave me to do. And now, Father, glorify me in your presence with the glory I had with you before the world began."

The preacher may wish to open the non-festival half of the church year with a strong mission theme.

Make Disciples of All Nations

1. The authoritative command (vv. 16-18)
2. The blessed means (vv. 19,20)

The law and gospel manifested in the authority of Christ dominates the first section. The gospel in word and sacrament gains the attention of the second.

A seasonal pivot between the festival and non-festival halves of the church year may be the pastor's desire.

Christ's Authority Is Present with Us

1. We ponder Christ's authority (vv. 16-18)
2. We proclaim Christ's authority (vv. 19,20)
3. We live under Christ's authority (v. 20)

The first section observes the contrasts of authority seen in the Epiphany, Lent and Easter seasons. The second sets forth God's means of grace. The third points to our life in the Savior's kingdom, the Pentecost season's message.

A sermon emphasizing the three Persons naturally flows from the Bible's best known reference to the Holy Trinity.

The Holy Trinity Is Revealed

1. In power (vv. 16-18)
2. In love (vv. 19,20)

The power of Father, Son and Holy Spirit is seen from Advent to Pentecost. The love of Father, Son and Holy Spirit is seen until the completion of the age.

SECOND SUNDAY AFTER PENTECOST

The Scriptures

Old Testament — *Deuteronomy 11:18-21,26-28*
Epistle — *Romans 3:21-25a,27,28*
Gospel — *Matthew 7:21-29*

The Text — Matthew 7:21-29

The Sermon on the Mount ends as it begins. It is an exposition of the law which shows believers their sin and gives them instruction for Christian living. It is of no use to unbelievers except to convince them of their hopelessly sinful condition or to help them develop some civic righteousness. Only by drawing on other sources in Scripture can a gospel sermon be developed from this text.

vv. 21,22 — *"Not everyone who says to me, 'Lord, Lord,' will enter the kingdom of heaven, but only he who does the will of my Father who is in heaven. Many will say to me on that day, 'Lord, Lord, did we not prophesy in your name, and in your name drive out demons and perform many miracles?' "*

Picture yourself on the day of judgment, following some "supersaints" up to the throne of God. You are quite aware that you haven't met the minimum requirements of God's law, and those ahead of you seem to have far exceeded them. You were commanded to hear God's word and have not always done that. They not only heard it, they preached it. You were commanded to resist the devil and haven't always succeeded. They not only resisted, they drove his demons out. You were commanded to do very ordinary things and have frequently fallen short. They have not only succeeded, they have done the extraordinary.

v. 23 — *"Then I will tell them plainly, 'I never knew you. Away from me, evildoers!' "*

Those "supersaints" are sternly condemned to hell. They are called "evildoers." It is implied that they haven't even *begun* to do God's will. So where does that leave *you*?

It is not God's purpose to terrorize and then leave us in fear and despair. This part of the text is a warning — a warning that the greatest works that anyone is likely to do will earn nothing but hell's fire. From elsewhere in the Bible we learn the reason: not that these works themselves are evil, but that by trusting in works for salvation they reject the cleansing blood of Christ which alone can remove their past sins. So they are still "evildoers."

Such warnings seem so hateful. But the purpose of a warning is not to make us suffer; it is to keep us from harm. The purpose of this warning is to drive us away from the idea which some gather from the Sermon on the Mount — that salvation comes to those who follow its moral precepts — and back to the other teachings of Christ, which explain that salvation comes by grace through faith.

Those who have heard verses 21-23 are driven in despair to the parable which follows, in which the way of salvation is implied. Two men, two methods of building, two outcomes are set forth.

vv. 24-27 — *"Therefore everyone who hears these words of mine and puts them into practice is like a wise man who built his house on the rock. But everyone who hears these words of mine and does not put them into practice is like a foolish man who built his house on sand. The rain came down, the streams rose, and the winds blew and beat against that house, and it fell with a great crash."*

Speaking to the multitudes, most of whom had dirt floors in their houses, the parable of Jesus is especially apt. A house that merely sat on the ground had nowhere near the strength of an equivalent dwelling whose builder had dug down to the bedrock before laying the first row of bricks. Πετρά, as distinct from πετρός, means a large mass of stone, such as bedrock — not a smaller, movable rock. After the second builder had brought the first floor back up to ground level with the dirt he'd dug out, the wall would be much stronger than otherwise. And if the first builder was foolish enough to build on erodable sand, instead of a firmer surface, the house was an accident waiting to happen.

Both houses would be perfectly serviceable in the dry season. But in the rainy season only one would survive. The other would collapse on its owner and kill him.

To the outward observer, the houses would look identical. It would only be during the final storm that one truth would shine forth: that the most important part of the house was invisible, buried underneath.

The application of this parable is obvious. The houses are our earthly lives. Most of the time, they appear equally serviceable. Most of the time it doesn't seem to matter what's under the superstructure. But in the ultimate storm of the judgment, one will survive and the other will suffer utter ruin. This is the difference between verse 25's προσπίπτω, to fall on without being able to penetrate, and verse 27's προςκόπτω, to cut into. Though both are in the same storm, one dwelling place will last forever while the other will fall in upon itself in fatal collapse.

The one who builds his life on bedrock is identified in verse 21 as "he who *does the will* of my Father who is in heaven." That scares us, doesn't it? What is "the will of God" that we are supposed to do?

One might assume that doing the will of God is following the precepts laid down in the Sermon on the Mount. This interpretation is ruled out by the judgment scene in verses 22,23, where people who seem to have met and even exceeded the law's requirements are called evildoers.

If we want to know what this elusive "will of God" is, we will not find it by speculating, by meditating on the text, or by searching the Sermon on the Mount. We will have to learn from the Scriptures what the "will of God" is.

In a closely related passage, John 6:28,29, the Jews ask Jesus what the will of God is, so that they can obtain everlasting life by doing it. "Then they asked him, 'What must we do to do the works God requires?' Jesus answered, 'The work of God is this: to believe in the one he has sent.' "

We have trouble with that because we naturally think the will of God is something we have to *do*. Jesus, however, says that God's will is that we trust the One he has sent. To nail down the point, he says it more explicitly in John 6:40, "For my Father's will is that everyone who looks to the Son and believes in him shall have eternal life, and I will raise him up at the last day." Let's condense that: "The Father's will is that everyone believe in the Son."

This believing is not an achievement of the human will, as those think who would take some credit for their salvation. Causing us to believe is a sovereign gracious act of divine monergism, "for it is God who works in you to will and to act according to his good purpose" (Php 2:13). Not only our redemption, but even the faith with which we receive it is a gift from God. With such a foundation we need not fear the storms of life, for our dwelling place will not crash down around us to ruin us, as will the unbeliever's at the day of his death.

vv. 28,29 — *When Jesus had finished saying these things, the crowds were amazed at his teaching, because he taught as one who had authority, and not as their teachers of the law.*

The result of the words of Jesus is that the people ἐξεπλήσσοντο —literally, they were "struck out of their senses." "They were beside themselves" would be an equivalent English idiom. Why were they thunderstruck? "Because he taught them as one who had authority, and not as their teachers of the law."

There is a twofold explanation of this. In the first place, Jesus taught with real authority rather than merely human opinion. Earlier in the Sermon on the Mount, he had repeatedly rejected popular beliefs. "You have heard it said by them of old time," Jesus said, "but I say unto you. . . . " The casual reader may think that Jesus is correcting excesses in the Old Testament. However, "Love your neighbor and hate your enemy" (Mt 5:43) is not a quotation from the Old Testament. It comes from the rabbis. Therefore we conclude that when Jesus uses this formula, he is not correcting the Bible. Rather, he is removing popular misinterpretations of it. When Jesus taught people, he was not like the rabbis of the day, endlessly quoting each other, endlessly arguing, never coming to ultimate truth. The teachings of Jesus were self-authenticating. They had the ring of truth in them, because they wakened the soul from its sleep and struck a chord that made the soul respond to God.

Homiletical Suggestions

Use the parable's imagery of building for the theme. Let Jesus' words and the reaction of the crowd to the Sermon on the Mount show how life is to be built on a solid foundation.

Build Your Life on a Firm Foundation

1. Do the Father's will, not yours (vv. 21-27; Jn 6:28,29,40)
2. Hear Jesus' words, not man's (vv. 24-29)

An outline which keys on "the will of God" in verse 21 is:

What Is the Will of God?

1. That no works of yours will save you (vv. 21-23,26,27)
2. That only God's work will save you (vv. 21,24,25,28,29, Jn 6:28,29,40; Php 2:12)

THIRD SUNDAY AFTER PENTECOST

The Scriptures

Old Testament — *Hosea 5:15—6:6*
Epistle — *Romans 4:18-25*
Gospel — *Matthew 9:9-13*

The Text — Matthew 9:9-13

The Holy Spirit directed Matthew to write this five-verse autobiography. With one word, our Lord Christ not only associated with an outcast, but called him into full-time work in the public ministry.

The power of such a gracious call was evident in Matthew's response. He got up and followed Jesus. Then, he threw a banquet where his friends could meet the Savior who had found him. Matthew's dinner also stimulated hostile responses from the Pharisees. This provided the forum where Jesus could reveal the merciful mission he was engaged in. The Savior came to save those who need saving.

This incident took place during Jesus' Galilean ministry. Jesus had healed a paralytic (Mt 9:1-8) and then went out beside the Sea of Galilee where he began to teach a large crowd (Mk 2:13). The location was Capernaum. This city was an important link in regional and international trade. It linked trading routes from Damascus and the East to the road which led to Egypt. Capernaum's location on the lake also made it an important source of fish for the region. It was an ideal location for a Roman toll booth.

Rome avoided running local tax booths directly. She would, instead, auction off a certain region for tax collection. Romans of the equestrian rank would form stock companies and bid for a region —usually on a five-year basis. They, in turn, would farm out each portion of that region to tax commissioners. Zacchaeus seemed to be such a tax commissioner in the district of Jericho. Finally, there were the tax gatherers or "publicans" as we know them in Scripture. Local tax collectors were able to speak the language of the empire and of the region. They had to be fairly well educated and knowledgeable about the people they worked with. As a rule, Jews were hired to tax Jews. Once Rome received the money it demanded from the region, the middlemen made a profit on the remainder. Anything beyond that was gravy for the tax collector. Nearly everything was taxed: durable goods, consumables, slaves and land. Publicans would often inflate the price of merchandise and tax it accordingly.

Legalized extortion was carried out for the Jews' bitter enemy, Rome, and it is understandable that rabbis put publicans out of the synagogue.

This had been the world in which Matthew lived.

News had reached Capernaum about the miracles Jesus had done in Judea. In fact, Jesus had spent some time in Capernaum before he called Matthew. It was very likely that Matthew had at least heard about the teaching of this rabbi. It is not impossible that Matthew may have been in the audience during one of Jesus' sermons. Whether Matthew had heard the word indirectly or seen the Word in person, it would be safe to assume that the Holy Spirit had been working in Matthew's heart before this call to discipleship.

v. 9 — *As Jesus went on from there, he saw a man named Matthew sitting at the tax collector's booth. "Follow me," he told him, and Matthew got up and followed him.*

"Matthew" (Μαθθαῖος), was the tax collector's name. There was a practice in Galilee to give a person two names: one was Jewish and the other Galilean. If this was true in his case, Levi was his Jewish name (Mk 2:14; Lk 5:27). The sacred writer omits this name. It would be ironic that a tax collector should be named "Matthew," which means, "Gift of God." This may also have been the name which Jesus gave Levi after his call to apostleship. The significance would be that he who had spent his earlier days extorting now offered an eternal inheritance to this world through the gospel of Christ. References to Matthew in other parts of Scripture are sparse. He is named in the catalog of the twelve apostles (Mt 10:3; Lk 6:15) and he was present in the upper room after Jesus' ascension (Ac 1:13).

Jesus' simple imperative, "Follow me," assumes that Matthew knows who Jesus is and has heard the gracious words of forgiveness Jesus had spoken to others in the area. Jesus called Philip with the same words (Jn 1:43). When Philip told Nathanael about Jesus, he offered Nathanael extensive information about the Savior: Jesus was Joseph's son, from Nazareth, who was the fulfillment of all the Old Testament prophecies.

We can imagine the great burden that Matthew carried under the rugged, businesslike veneer of a tax collector. He had been excluded from the synagogue. He was an outcast among his own people. His sins weighed heavily upon his conscience. Could he hope for a word of pardon from this teacher? Would this rabbi speak with him whose sin was as public as his office? "Follow Me" were words which guaranteed all of the eternal blessings of a lifelong association with the Savior. It was also a lifelong call into the service of the Lord's kingdom.

The cost of discipleship was weighed instantly in Matthew's mind. "Matthew got up and followed him." The aorist, ἠκολούθησεν, indicates that following Jesus began at that moment and continued uninterrupted into the future. Luke adds that "he left everything" to follow Jesus. After the miraculous catch of fish Simon and company left their boats, nets and everything else to catch men. In the same way, Matthew left his counting table and found in Jesus' command the promise that those who follow his call will never suffer need —here or in eternity.

vv. 10,11 — *While Jesus was having dinner at Matthew's house, many tax collectors and "sinners" came and ate with him and his disciples. When the Pharisees saw this, they asked his disciples, "Why does your teacher eat with tax collectors and 'sinners'?"*

Who can understand the depth of the riches of God's grace? He calls such a man as Matthew to eternal life! How much more amazing that Matthew is called into the public ministry! This grace of our Lord Jesus is explained in the final verses of the text.

Matthew's invitation to Jesus was not the well-intentioned service of Martha (Lk 10:40) whose ambition it was to wait on the Savior hand and foot. Matthew realized that the Son of Man came not to be served but to serve and to give his life as a ransom for many. What greater honor could be accorded Jesus than to introduce him to those he came to save? We are told that Matthew invited his coworkers. Sinners (ἁμαρτωλοὶ) are mentioned here, too. It is true that every human being has missed the mark as far as God's holy demands are concerned. However, here the word "sinner" has the connotation of a social reprobate. This could have ranged from prostitutes and thieves to those who were guilty by association with tax collectors and other excommunicates.

To this day people recognize that eating together is an expression of close association. It was detestable for Egyptians to eat with Hebrews (Gn 43:32). In the New Testament St. Paul gave the Christians in Corinth strict instructions not even to eat with one who claims to be a brother, but practices immorality (1 Cor 5:9-11). In doing this one gives unspoken encouragement to the sinner and shares in his wicked work (2 Jn 10,11). God intended shunning and excommunication to strike shame, remorse and a thirsting for forgiveness into the heart of the unrepentant. When this is accomplished it is necessary for complete pardon to be preached to the penitent. It goes without saying that there are times when it is necessary to associate with sinners to determine whether the gospel can be applied or not. The Pharisees, however, saw excommunication as an end in itself. As the name "Pharisee" indicated, they thought they were holy because they kept themselves separate from tax collectors, "sinners," and all that is considered unclean. The merciful purpose of the binding key had been forgotten. Therefore, Pharisees refused even to enter the house of a publican.

Little wonder that the Pharisees questioned Jesus' disciples about their Master's credentials. "Why does your teacher eat with tax collectors and 'sinners'?" The clear implication was that you can determine the credibility of a teacher by the company he keeps.

vv. 12,13 — *On hearing this, Jesus said, "It is not the healthy who need a doctor, but the sick. But go and learn what this means: 'I desire mercy, not sacrifice.' For I have not come to call the righteous, but sinners."*

In this brief paragraph, Jesus does two things: First, he explains the merciful purpose of his mission on earth. He came to call sinners like Matthew to eternal life. Then, he reaches out to the Pharisees who imagine they are righteous and uncovers their self-delusion. Perhaps they will become like Matthew and see their great need for the Great Physician.

Spiritually, the Pharisees considered themselves to be in sound health and strong (οἱ ἰσχύοντες). Physicians are for those who "have it bad" (οἱ κακῶς ἔχοντες), who are sick.

He plays their game for a moment: "You don't need me as this pathetic group does. They are sick and know it! But you . . . you are righteous!" Jesus laid the burden of proof before the bar of their consciences. All they had to do was flip through the catalog of their life's events to see if they qualified for a Savior's medical assistance. How had they treated their wives? Had they mercifully dealt with the widows in the community? Had they helped absolve others who were burdened with their sin? Or had they tied heavier restrictions onto their consciences? See Matthew 23 for a list of pharisaic sins which are common to mankind. If the Pharisees had fallen short in any area of holy living, they needed God's help.

Jesus drives the point home by citing the Pharisees' recent objection to his methods. Isn't it God's will that those he has blessed with health use their health by helping those who are sick? Indeed, that is a nobler sacrifice by far than avoiding the sick in order to celebrate one's wholeness. Jesus lets the inspired word do the talking: "I desire mercy, not sacrifice" (Ho 6:6).

Those who imagined themselves righteous before God had failed to worship God properly. They refused mercy to sinners. What is more, they were trying to hinder the Holy One from having mercy on sinners. Their deficiencies in holiness were evident for all to see.

On the other hand, the holiness of Jesus manifested itself not in separation from sinners, but by calling sinners to repentance. This is the obedience with which God is pleased.

Jesus excludes "the righteous" (δικαίους) from his call. Those who are righteous need no Savior. Although this was certainly not the case with the Pharisees, Jesus said this to show them how they were excluding themselves from his gracious forgiveness. Even the Apostle Paul hoped that by preaching to the Gentiles he might stir up the Jews to envy and save some of them (Ro 11:13,14).

Homiletical Suggestions

The Old Testament text for the third Sunday in Pentecost shows the response of God's people to his gracious promise. Even when God hides himself from them for a time they say, "Come, let us return to the LORD. He has torn us to pieces but he will heal us" (Ho 6:1).

The Epistle assures us that our faith, no less than Abraham's, is credited to us as righteousness.

Matthew was an example of a man from whom God had hidden his face. He was under the ban of God's people. Nevertheless, the Holy Spirit had worked faith in Matthew's heart through the message of Jesus. His faith was credited to him as righteousness and he was a true son of Abraham.

The sermon text portrays the undeserved love of Jesus. His grace is manifested in his purpose: He did "not come to call the righteous, but sinners" to repentance and eternal life. To do this, Jesus associates with sinners. He does not overlook their sin, but calls them away from sin to saving health. Nor does the Lord ignore attacks on his merciful mission to sinners. He lays the Pharisees' self-righteousness at the doorstep of their consciences in the hope that they, too, will see the folly of their ways and turn to him.

The call to forgiveness is also a call to service in the kingdom. Matthew was called to a specialized field of kingdom work — the apostolate. In Matthew's day disciples chose their masters. Matthew did not choose Jesus. Jesus chose Matthew. With the call to discipleship and apostleship came the implied promise that the One who called Matthew would provide for all of his needs (Lk 5:28b; Mt 6:33). Matthew began hiswork at home, in his own community, among his associates. We do not know for sure how widespread Matthew's mission was during his lifetime. This much we do know: Under God's direction this publican wrote the first gospel. The world knows it and has not been the same since! Only God knows how many "sinners" Jesus called to himself through the book of Matthew. Jesus made Matthew "God's gift" to a world full of sinners.

The thrust of this text is informational. It is information which excites the hearts of those who long for healing of the soul. The simplest outline sums it up the best:

Jesus Calls Sinners

1. He calls them to eternal life (vv. 11-13)
2. He calls them to work in his kingdom (vv. 9-12)

This text leans heavily toward sanctification. It lends itself well to the fruits of faith we call discipleship and evangelism. The basis of any legitimate sanctified living is justification. We will want to be sure that the everlasting benefits of discipleship which are implied in verses 12 and 13 are made explicit in the call to discipleship. Matthew practices what is today called "friendship evangelism" in verses 10 and 11. This could be treated under the invitation which Matthew extended to Jesus to come into his home.

Follow Me

1. Jesus' call: "Follow me — as my disciple" (vv. 9,12,13)
2. Matthew's response: "Follow me home" (vv. 10,11)

Matthew was called into full-time service of the church. A recruitment notice for full-time church workers can also be found here.

Ministers Wanted: Only Sinners Need Apply

1. Jesus came to call only sinners to salvation (vv. 11-13)
2. Jesus came to call only forgiven sinners to apostleship (vv. 9,10)

FOURTH SUNDAY AFTER PENTECOST

The Scriptures

Old Testament — *Exodus 19:2-8a*
Epistle — *Romans 5:6-11*
Gospel — *Matthew 9:35 — 10:8*

The Text — Matthew 9:35 — 10:8

The final section of Matthew 9 prepares us for what happens in chapter 10. As Jesus carried out his Galilean ministry he saw the people in great physical and spiritual need. His ministry served to meet these needs and he sent out more workers to help these lost sheep. Chapter 10 contains the instructions of Jesus to his called apostles who were sent to gather in the great harvest of souls.

vv. 35,36 — *Jesus went through all the towns and villages, teaching in their synagogues, preaching the good news of the kingdom and healing every disease and sickness. When he saw the crowds, he had compassion on them, because they were harassed and helpless, like sheep without a shepherd.*

The imperfect tense and the present participles indicate a continued action. The everyday ministry of Jesus never let up. He was both a teacher and a preacher. He often taught in the Jewish synagogues where the Jews met to read the Scriptures. His preaching and teaching were sometimes done outdoors. Jesus' ministry also involved healing those with physical needs. He had compassion on these people. With his healings he demonstrated that God was present among the people and that the blessings of the kingdom of God were being given to the people. Νόσος refers to the disease or sickness, while μαλακία refers to the weakness resulting in the body because of the disease or sickness.

When Jesus saw the crowds he recognized a greater need than the physical and he felt compassion for these people because they were lacking this greater need. Σπλαγχνίςομαι means "to have the heart, liver and lungs move." These organs were considered the seat of feelings. To have them move is to have the greatest pity for these people. The reason Jesus had such compassion for the people is found in the word σκύλλω. The verb has the root meaning of "flay" as in "flaying the skin." The picture is that of a sheep being cut up and bleeding after passing through a heavy patch of thorns. These people were harassed spiritually. Their religious leaders demanded much from them but offered no comfort. The people were also "helpless." The verb (ῥίπτω) indicates they were thrown off or possibly abandoned. These people were abandoned spiritually because their religious leaders did not lead them to God. They were like "sheep without a shepherd." They were harassed by sin and guilt and because they were never led to faith in Jesus their Savior, they were helpless and lost spiritually. How Jesus pitied them!

vv. 37,38 — *Then he said to his disciples, "The harvest is plentiful but the workers are few. Ask the Lord of the harvest, therefore, to send out workers into his harvest field."*

Jesus looked at these people and saw a large spiritual harvest (Jn 4:35,36). The "harvest" includes all people who will come to faith in Jesus through the Spirit's use of the means of grace. Just as the harvest cannot gather in itself, these people cannot come into God's kingdom by themselves (1 Cor 2:14; 12:3). Jesus recognized a great problem. The harvest of souls that must be reaped is great but the workers needed to do the work are few. How could Jesus and the Twelve even begin to penetrate the world with the gospel?

Jesus commanded his disciples to ask the Lord to send out workers into *his* harvest field. God the Father owns the harvest for he has produced it (Mk 4:26ff). Beg of him that he "send out workers." The Greek says, "throw out workers." There are people everywhere who need to be brought into God's kingdom. Jesus told the disciples to pray that God would call more workers from among the believers in Israel and throw them out into the world for the purpose (ὅπως) of gathering more souls into the harvest.

Jesus saw a harvest of souls even beyond Israel. In Acts we see God answering this prayer for more workers. When we pray as he tells us to pray, that prayer is answered when more workers are trained and called by the church to gather the harvest of souls.

vv. 1-4 — *He called his twelve disciples to him and gave them authority to drive our evil spirits and to heal every disease and sickness. These are the names of the twelve apostles: first, Simon (who is called Peter) and his brother Andrew; James son of Zebedee, and his brother John; Philip and Bartholomew; Thomas and Matthew the tax collector; James son of Alphaeus; Simon the Zealot and Judas Iscariot, who betrayed him.*

Jesus' prayer was followed by action. He called workers to reap the harvest. To help them in this work he gave them authority (ἐξουσία). This term includes both the power and the right to "drive out evil spirits" which hindered the work of harvesting souls and to "heal every disease and sickness." It cannot be established by this verse that evil spirits cause diseases and sicknesses. Jesus simply gave his disciples the authority to do both — drive out the evil spirits and heal the sick. When he gave his disciples this authority he revealed his deity.

The Twelve are called "apostles." These twelve were sent out as ambassadors speaking for Jesus. They received a special and immediate call from him.

Matthew lists the twelve original apostles. Peter is called Simon for the benefit of Jewish readers. His later ministry was among the Jews, at least as far as Babylon (1 Pe 5:13). Andrew is mentioned with Peter because they were brothers. He was originally a disciple of John the Baptist. Tradition says he later preached in Scythia, Greece and Asia Minor. James and John were the sons of Zebedee. James was beheaded by Herod about 44 A.D. and John lived to an old age, laboring among the churches of Asia Minor.

The other apostles are not as well known. Traditional accounts tell how these men traveled "into all the world" (Mt 16:15) with the gospel. The authority Jesus gave them was used to reap many souls for God's kingdom. The only exception was Judas. His role was to fulfill the Scripture as Jesus' betrayer (Jn 13:18; Ps 41:9; Ac 1:16). Acts 1:23-26 tells us that Matthias was chosen to replace Judas.

vv. 5-8 — *These twelve Jesus sent out with the following instructions: "Do not go among the Gentiles or enter any town of the Samaritans. Go rather to the lost sheep of Israel. As you go, preach this message: 'The kingdom of heaven is near.' Heal the sick, raise the dead, cleanse those who have leprosy, drive out demons. Freely you have received, freely give.' "*

The time for worldwide evangelism had not yet come. For the present Jesus wanted the destroyed (ἀπολωλότα) sheep of Israel to be found first. The Jews had the promise in previous generations but they lost it by their own unbelief. Now they are spiritually ruined, "lost sheep," who cannot find their way to God.

The lost soul is only found with the means of grace. The apostles were to keep proclaiming that gospel of Jesus Christ. They were not to be fooled into believing that some powerful work or sign would save even one soul. No! Only the gospel saves! Never stop proclaiming that powerful word of God!

These apostles did have power and authority to do great works. Jesus told them to use this authority as they went out among the people. By these miraculous acts the apostles could prove that their authority to preach was not from man but from God. Also, these miraculous acts showed compassion for the people. Yet these works were not used to bring the lost soul to faith. This was the work of the Spirit through the gospel alone.

The apostles were to preach and perform these miracles without charge to the people. Here is a lesson in God's grace. No one is ever to think he must pay God for anything! God gives to us freely without charging. Now we reflect that grace by giving to others freely as God gave to us.

Homiletical Suggestions

Even though Jesus' instructions to his apostles restricted them to carrying the gospel only to the nation of Israel, we realize that we live in the time after the great commission in Matthew 28. We have been given the responsibility to carry out a worldwide evangelistic effort in order to gather as many souls as possible into God's kingdom. Many people are still spiritually harassed because they have been ruined by humanism and false religion. Many have fallen away from the true gospel of Jesus and are sheep without a shepherd. The modern term to describe them would be "unchurched." Who is responsible for them? Jesus took on the responsibility for these lost souls. His ministry was a never-tiring activity to save many. We thus learn what our responsibilities are to the unchurched.

Our Responsibilities to the Unchurched

1. Have compassion on them (vv. 35,36)
2. Pray on their behalf (vv. 37,38)
3. Send out more workers to them (vv. 1-8)

The compassion of Jesus for these lost sheep suggests the theme:

Let Us Be Christlike in Compassion for Lost Souls

1. He continued to preach the gospel to them (vv. 35,36)
2. He told the church to pray for them (vv. 37,38)
3. He sent out more workers to save them (vv. 1-8)

The manner in which we are to do mission work is important. Jesus gives us some insight on this subject.

How Do We Reach Out to the Unchurched

1. We reach out with compassion (vv. 35,36)
2. We reach out with prayer (vv. 37,38)
3. We reach out with preaching (vv. 1-8)

Part one would deal with our attitude towards the unchurched. Do we really care about them? Jesus did. Part two reminds us that we must depend on God the Father when we do this work because this is his work. Part three leads into a discussion concerning the call to preach the gospel in order that many might hear it and be saved.

The preacher may chose to use only the first portion of the text. The theme of the spiritual harvest is prominent and a simple outline based on verse 37 could be effective.

God's Great Spiritual Harvest

1. The harvest is plentiful (vv. 35,36)
2. The workers are few (v. 38)

FIFTH SUNDAY AFTER PENTECOST

The Scriptures

Old Testament — *Jeremiah 20:7-13*
Epistle — *Romans 5:12-15*
Gospel — *Matthew 10:24-33*

The Text — Matthew 10:24-33

Jesus' words in this text are part of a long section which begins at 9:35 and in which Jesus commissions and sends his twelve apostles to preach the good news to Israel. Jesus' motive for doing this was his compassion on the people. He saw that they were "harassed and helpless, like sheep without a shepherd" (9:36). In the opening verses of chapter 10 the Lord commissions his twelve disciples (10:1). He tells them of the scope of their work — "the lost sheep of Israel" (10:6), instructs them concerning the content of their message — "the kingdom of heaven is near" (10:7), and teaches them about the confident spirit in which they will travel (10:9,10). The Lord also tells them about the outcome of their work (10:11-15).

In 10:16 a new thought begins. The twelve apostles, as Christ's spokesmen, will suffer and be rejected in much the same way as their Lord. Persecution, floggings, hatred and even death await them in their ministries. But these men need not fear. With a triple "Do not be afraid" (10:26,28,31), Jesus assures them that the enemies of the cross will not triumph. Instead, it is the apostles who will emerge victorious, triumphing even over death.

The closing verses of chapter 10 closely identify the apostles with Jesus. They are extensions of their Lord. They carry out his will. They preach his message. They do his work. If they are received, he is received. If they are rejected, the Lord is rejected.

vv. 24,25 — *"A student is not above his teacher, nor a servant above his master. It is enough for the student to be like his teacher, and the servant like his master. If the head of the house has been called Beelzebub, how much more the members of his household!"*

The apostles, no doubt, were somewhat disheartened by the words which are recorded in the preceding verses (16-23). Jesus had spoken in no uncertain terms about persecution and harassment. And lest the apostles think that they were not deserving of such treatment, or should be above such treatment, Jesus, without giving opportunity for objection, informs them that they should not expect to be treated any better than he was. This, of course, was only natural. They were only students and servants. He was their teacher and master. It would be foolishness to assume that they would be "above" him, that they would be treated better than he.

Rather, they would be treated "like" their teacher and master. This announcement, rather than demoralizing them, would give the apostles reason to feel honored. After all, what student wouldn't like to be treated the same as his teacher is treated? And what servant wouldn't thrill to be regarded as his master is regarded? The apostles then, and of course all of Jesus' followers of all time, should remember that when they are mistreated, when they meet with opposition and suffer persecution, they are being treated no differently than their Lord. What an honor! The apostles should find satisfaction and great contentment (ἀρκετὸν = "enough, sufficient, adequate") in this fact, and, of course, also in the fact that they are treated no worse than their Lord.

Jesus mentions one form of persecution which his apostles would suffer. He, as the "head of the house" (that is, the Christian household) had "been called," had been given the name "Beelzebub" (the Greek has βεελζεβοὺλ). On several occasions throughout his ministry the enemies of Christ had accused him of being in league with Satan (cf. Mt 9:34; 12:24), or of being demon-possessed (cf. Mk 3:30; Lk 7:20; 8:48). The apostles and all members of Christ's household can expect to suffer the same slanderous remarks and blasphemous statements.

vv. 26,27 — *"So do not be afraid of them. There is nothing concealed that will not be disclosed, or hidden that will not be made known. What I tell you in the dark, speak in the daylight; what is whispered in your ear, proclaim from the roofs."*

The aorist subjunctive is used in prohibitions to forbid a thing not yet done. Jesus' command (Μὴ οὖν φοβηθῆτε αὐτούς) might therefore be translated, "Don't ever begin to be afraid of them." Although fear of opposition might seem only natural, the ambassador of Christ must never feel that he is doomed to failure while his enemies are destined to succeed in their evil ways. The Lord is powerful enough to protect and guard those that are his, and on the Last Day, when everything is set in its proper light, he will render to each man his proper due.

Encouraged by this truth, every disciple must fearlessly confess Jesus Christ. The apostles are told to publicly proclaim from the roofs (a natural pulpit, by the way), in broad daylight, the things they have heard and learned while in the company of Jesus. The way of salvation must be preached to all!

Take note of the fact that in verse 26 the verb φοβέω is used in a prohibition for the first of three times in this text. The form is the aorist subjunctive. Verses 28 and 31 have the present imperative form.

v. 28 — *"Do not be afraid of those who kill the body but cannot kill the soul. Rather, be afraid of the One who can destroy both soul and body in hell."*

Here Jesus introduces a new reason why the apostles should not give way to fear as they carry out the Lord's work. The enemies of the cross have power to harm only the body, nothing more, and then only if the heavenly Father wills it. Each of the disciples (save Judas Iscariot) would in the future experience the truth of this statement firsthand. Most of these disciples would even taste death at the hands of their enemies. Their lives would be given for the sake of the gospel. But again, nothing more. Their enemies may "kill the body but cannot kill the soul."

Jesus, of course, is here battling the false notion which says, "If I've lost my life, I've lost everything." The view is worldly, materialistic. It focuses on the here and now, and loses sight of that which is of greatest importance, the hereafter. It causes an individual to hold back in his service to the Lord, to refrain from giving all for Christ, lest, having given all, there be nothing left.

Jesus would not have any of his disciples let such fear keep them from faithful service. Such fear is out of place. The disciple should rather fear God, "the one who can destroy both soul and body in hell." The enemies of the cross have no such power. Neither has Satan. Only the Lord has the power to judge and condemn both soul and body in everlasting destruction. He alone, therefore, deserves the awe and reverence of mankind.

vv. 29-31 — *"Are not two sparrows sold for a penny? Yet not one of them will fall to the ground apart from the will of your Father. And even the very hairs of your head are all numbered. So don't be afraid; you are worth more than many sparrows."*

God's special providence concerning his people is a third reason why the disciples should have no fear. Jesus uses an argument from the lesser to the greater. He reminds his disciples of the small value of the sparrow — two are sold for a penny. In fact, so little was the sparrow valued that it appears five were sold for the price of four (cf. Lk 12:6). And yet, Jesus says, not one of these seemingly insignificant creatures loses it life without the knowledge and consent of the heavenly Father.

Jesus then points to a second example of God's providential care —"even the very hairs of your head are all numbered." Again, something which might seem so insignificant to man is a concern to the Creator. Not only are the hairs of the head counted, but each is individually known and distinguished. If one falls to the ground, the Lord knows, and knows which one it is.

Certainly if God's providence extends itself over these *lesser* things in his creation, it will without question extend itself over the crown of his creation, man. The understatement, "You are worth more than many sparrows," makes this point clear. The disciples of Christ, who are God's precious children through faith in the Savior, can confidently expect that he who takes care of and protects the sparrows will also take care of and protect them. There is no reason to fear. The Lord will keep them safe from any real danger to their being.

vv. 32,33 — *"Whoever acknowledges me before men, I will also acknowledge him before my Father in heaven. But whoever disowns me before men, I will disown him before my Father in heaven."*

The text closes with a most glorious promise and encouragement. Whoever (ὅστις is indefinite, meaning "anyone" rather than "someone in particular") confesses Jesus publicly, before men, Jesus will also confess before the Father. We have the future active indicative of ὁμολογέω in both cases.

The Lord is again battling fear by stating the reward which comes to those who overcome fear. It has been stated that a bold confession of Christ will cost the confessor, maybe even his life. But to those who are willing to pay the price a promise is given: on the Last Day Jesus will acknowledge them as his own before the Father (cf. Re 3:5). Such a promise will, of course, move the disciples to be bold confessors. Who would exchange the approval of the Father for the approval of men? And who would let the abuse of men keep him from obtaining the glorious reward that comes to the faithful?

The encouragement in verse 32 is strengthened by the warning in verse 33. If any person is led by the opposition of the world to disown Jesus, Jesus will disown him before the Father. Such a person by his actions has proven himself to be lacking faith, and by his denial of the Savior has already cut himself off from the grace of God.

Every Christian has been called upon to be a witness for Jesus. To be a witness is a serious matter, for the Lord's attitude toward us will correspond exactly with our attitude toward him in the world. By a bold confession of Christ in word and action, and an open proclamation and defense of the gospel, we prove that we are truly the Lord's, and his forever. But the opposite is also true.

Homiletical Suggestions

By the grace of God forgiveness of sins and salvation is offered to all men. In and of himself the sinner cannot possibly hope to offer sufficient payment for his sins, or to bring about reconciliation with the Almighty. He is lost, facing an eternity of punishment in hell. But the heavenly Father sent his Son to redeem mankind, to pay the price demanded by God's justice, and to win for mankind an eternal home in heaven.

In the epistle for the day, Romans 5:12-15, St. Paul writes of the pitiful state in which the sin of Adam left mankind. As a result of the disobedience of that one man, all people ever since have been born in a sinful condition. This sinful condition leads to actual sins of word and deed, and the result is that all people are subject to death. But St. Paul also relates the best news this world will ever hear. The work of the one man, Jesus Christ, has more than canceled out the work of the one man, Adam. Jesus has taken away the guilt and punishment of the world's sins. Through him the world has been justified. There is a Savior.

Faith is the hand which makes the benefits of Christ's work one's own, and the Holy Spirit plants faith in a person's heart by means of the word. Both the Old Testament Scripture, Jeremiah 20:7-13, and the Gospel for the day emphasize the importance of preaching that word.

Jeremiah had been called to preach repentance to a backsliding Israel, but because of the hardening of the people, the preacher of repentance became the messenger of judgment. The message of judgment was, of course, unpopular, and Jeremiah's life was in danger as a result. Nonetheless, the prophet felt compelled to preach and was certain that the Lord would protect him.

The Gospel from Matthew focuses on the certainty which Jeremiah enjoyed, that certainty which every disciple can have. By virtue of his faith, the Christian is a messenger of Christ. Whether he is active in this capacity is another story. So often fear, as it did with the twelve disciples, will keep a Christian from proclaiming his Savior. We live in a world that is antagonistic toward Christ and his followers — if not outwardly, at least in a subtle manner. One who openly professes Jesus as Lord and Savior might very well meet with ridicule and slander. He may experience the loss of friends, of reputation, of employment, or he may be harassed in any of a number of ways because of his Christian confession.

Nevertheless, the same glorious promises spoken to the disciples of Jesus are spoken to Christians today. Without any fear whatsoever, Christians can boldly talk about the Savior. Our text suggests the following:

Confidently Proclaim the Christ

1. Without fear of those who oppose (vv. 24-28)
2. Without fear that the Lord has forgotten you (vv. 29-31)
3. Without fear on the day of judgment (vv. 32,33)

Another outline which emphasizes the confidence of the Christian herald might be:

Don't Allow Fear to Halt the Harvest

1. Those who oppose will not be victorious (vv. 24-28)
2. God's providential care extends over you (vv. 29-31)
3. The Lord promises you a glorious future (vv. 32,33)

SIXTH SUNDAY AFTER PENTECOST

The Scriptures

Old Testament — *Jeremiah 28:5-9*
Epistle — *Romans 6:1b-11*
Gospel — *Matthew 10:34-42*

The Text — Matthew 10:34-42

Our text contains the concluding paragraphs of the instruction Jesus gave about kingdom witnessing. He himself displayed a compassion for the lost and then urged his followers also to have such compassion.

This compassion will first of all put them on their knees, asking God to send out workers into the world (9:38). God often involves the petitioner when he answers prayer. Those who have a heart for mission work may become God's means for doing that work.

In this chapter we learn that Jesus gathered the Twelve and authorized them to go out in his name to proclaim the kingdom of God. As they had freely received grace, so they went out to freely dispense that grace.

But Jesus also wanted to prepare his dear disciples for discouragement and danger. Some to whom he sent them would not welcome their message about the kingdom of heaven. Disciples should be prepared for such rejection. Those who reject their words might arrest them or in some other way cause them to suffer. But the Holy Spirit will be with them to give them the words to speak.

In the text Jesus emphasizes that his disciples will meet up with persecution (σταυρός, v. 38). But they must be determined to be bold and continue to proclaim God's word. Even if it costs them their family, let Christ's followers boldly preach the Master's message.

vv. 34-36 — *"Do not suppose that I have come to bring peace to the earth. I did not come to bring peace, but a sword. For I have come to turn*
'a man against his father,
a daughter against her mother,
a daughter-in-law against her mother-in-law —
a man's enemies will be the members of his own household.' "

"Peace" is a common theme in the Scriptures. People long for peace. People work for it. But wicked people cannot have lasting peace (Is 48:22). If sinners are to enjoy peace, it must come from God.

Wicked people do not want the peace God provides. Instead we want to establish peace on our own. In order to quiet a condemning conscience, we softpedal our sin, and regard it as less serious than it is. We want to forget that sin separates a righteous God from fallen humanity (Is 59:2). God's prophets often spoke against the false prophets who proclaimed "Peace, peace," when there was no peace (Jr 8:11). Faithful men like Jeremiah pointed out that we may have peace only when God removes our wickedness. In this way Jesus is the Prince of peace (Is 9:6).

Many believed that when the Messiah would come, he would bring an end to earthly wars and thus establish an earthly peace. The Jews who believed thus at this time hoped Jesus would overthrow such enemies as the Romans. Jesus tells his disciples not to subscribe to the common belief (μὴ νομίσητε) that he had come to impose (βαλεῖν) *such* a peace on the earth.

They should expect to see division instead of harmony, hatred instead of friendship. The reason for this is that Jesus also brought a sword upon the earth. This is not a literal sword. To what does it refer? We can think of Ephesians 6:17 where Paul calls God's word "the sword of the Spirit." Wherever the word of God is preached, there believers will be found (Is 55:10,11). This sword, which works mightily within a person (He 4:12), even divides family members when some believe but others do not.

Those who refuse to believe the word of God will hate those who do. There will be enmity (Gn 3:15) between Satan's kingdom and God's people. Because there will never be a general conversion of all people, such enmity will continue to divide people on earth. This sword of the Spirit still divides believers from unbelievers. See Simeon's words to Mary concerning Jesus (Lk 2:34,35).

vv. 37-39 — *"Anyone who loves his father or mother more than me is not worthy of me; anyone who loves his son or daughter more than me is not worthy of me; and anyone who does not take his cross and follow me is not worthy of me. Whoever finds his life will lose it, and whoever loses his life for my sake will find it."*

When it comes to choices, sinfully weak people prefer the path of least resistance. When following Jesus means suffering at the hands of his enemies, his disciples are tempted to compromise. We need the stern rebuke in this section.

Verse 37 recalls the first commandment: "You shall have no others gods before me" (Ex 20:3). Elsewhere God's word tells us, "Love the Lord your God with all your heart and with all your soul and with all your mind" (Mt 22:37). God the Son demands that he receive first place in our lives. He will not share us with any other god.

These are strong words. They convict us all. We must confess, "I am unworthy" (Gn 32:10). In one way or another we have all failed to put God first.

Jesus shows us the great loss we suffer if we prefer family members to him. He does this so that he can place before us the precious life which he gives to us in the gospel. To follow Jesus may mean that family members reject me. It may mean that I lose some of the opportunities to climb the ladder of success at the workplace. This cross comes from following the Savior. Jesus teaches me to rejoice in the greater gift of eternal life (Ac 5:41).

vv. 40-42 — *"He who receives you receives me, and he who receives me receives the one who sent me. Anyone who receives a prophet because he is a prophet will receive a prophet's reward, and anyone who receives a righteous man because he is a righteous man will receive a righteous man's reward. And if anyone gives even a cup of cold water to one of these little ones because he is my disciple, I tell you the truth, he will certainly not lose his reward."*

It is easy to be welcomed — to be friends of many (Lk 6:26). All one must do is speak the message of the false prophets: "Peace, Peace." Just softpedal sin. Just accept any belief so long as people are sincere. But God's spokesmen are to represent the Savior, not popular opinion.

When God's spokesmen speak God's message, people who welcome them welcome Jesus. When Jesus speaks of people welcoming (δεχόμενος) his disciples, this refers to those who are willing to listen to the word of God they bring. The willing listeners will receive them into their homes in order to learn from them. See Matthew 10:14 where welcoming the disciples and listening to the word they bring are mentioned together.

This section then makes special promises to the faithful hearers of God's faithful spokesmen. They will share in the blessing of eternal life and all the rewards of grace God has prepared for those who love him.

Homiletical Suggestions

The Lord's words at the opening of our text may at first seem to contradict the message the angels brought to the shepherds when Jesus was born. God does indeed bring peace through his Son. This peace comes to all who believe in his saving name.

Many people resist this peace and persecute those who possess it. Jesus presents us with a realistic view of what it means to follow him.

Accept the Sword which the Peace of Jesus Brings

1. Expect that some will reject you for following Jesus (vv. 34-39a)
2. Trust that God will accept you through the merits of Jesus (vv. 39b-42)

Focusing on verse 39 we can divide the text thus:

Find Life in Christ

1. Renounce worldly peace (vv. 34-39a)
2. Receive eternal rewards (vv. 39b-42)

SEVENTH SUNDAY AFTER PENTECOST

The Scriptures

Old Testament — *Zechariah 9:9-12*
Epistle — *Romans 7:15-25a*
Gospel — *Matthew 11:25-30*

The Text – Matthew 11:25-30

vv. 25,26 — *At that time Jesus said, "I praise you, Father, Lord of heaven and earth, because you have hidden these things from the wise and learned, and revealed them to little children. Yes, Father, for this was your good pleasure."*

Matthew wrote "at that time" and "these things." The Holy Spirit considers the historical context important. We need to understand what time and what things.

Starting at Matthew 11:1 we discover when Jesus spoke these words. After instructing and sending out the Twelve, he continued to teach in Galilee. He had taught there for some time and performed many amazing miracles. After answering a question from John the Baptist's disciples Jesus challenged the Galileans to carefully consider their personal response to his ministry and even that of John. "At that time," even after noting the authority of Jesus' teaching (Mt 7:29) and after witnessing countless miraculous signs, most Galileans treated Jesus like a circus come to town, rather than "the one who was to come" (Mt 11:3) from God, the Messiah.

After all that, most messengers of God would be tempted to quit. If after all of that so few believe, what hope is there that any sizable number of people will ever believe God's word? But Jesus didn't grow weary. Instead he seized the opportunity to praise the Father that his good pleasure has devised a way to overcome man's natural rejection and enlighten even one sinner.

Jesus praises the Father with a simple statement of fact, using three aorists (ἔκρυψας, ἀπεκάλυψας, ἐγένετο). That's the way it is, because it pleases the good Lord to work that way. That's why people throughout time don't embrace Jesus for what he so obviously is. Their "wisdom" and "intelligence" prevent them from seeing what God reveals. Those who pride themselves on their objectivity and boast that they are not among the gullible masses of the simple and uneducated (Jn 7:47-52; 9:34) find this teaching of Jesus to be both startling and insulting. "What, are we blind too?" (Jn 9:40) There's the proof that "these things" (v. 25) remain hidden.

What are "these things" that remain hidden to some but are revealed to others? Jesus listed them for us in verses 4-6. The significance and meaning of Jesus' miracles and ministry will always remain a mystery to those who do not combine them with faith (He 4:2).

Jesus assures the well educated that these things can be revealed to them as well. This assurance is found in the absence of the article with σοφῶν, συνετῶν and νηπιόις, which stresses these as qualities, not as specific classes of people. Νήπιος refers to the young milk-drinking child (1 Cor 3:1; He 5:13), but is used here to refer to the same quality Jesus refers to with παιδίον in Mark 10:15. It is the quality of childlike trust which accepts, marvels, delights in and clings to God's revealed truth.

All this is God's *good* pleasure. The "infants" to whom it is revealed see and taste how good God is. Jesus publicly celebrates God's goodness, acknowledging it before all the world in praise. He is very emphatic, speaking with authority and with amen-like conviction: "Yes, indeed that's the way God is." Thrill to this pure gospel! God's children don't have to pass an IQ test. It pleases the Lord of heaven and earth to reveal his great and awesome mysteries even to infants. God's good pleasure (not our good IQ or any other factor) is the cause and source of our salvation. So don't be discouraged by the lack of believers. Drive out the discouraging thoughts. Join Jesus in praising the Father that *any* believe — yes, even yourself.

v. 27 — *"All things have been committed to me by my Father. No one knows the Son except the Father, and no one knows the Father except the Son and those to whom the Son chooses to reveal him."*

Jesus anticipates our eagerness to discover where the Father reveals these things. *All* things are revealed through Jesus. Jesus holds the exclusive rights to reveal and distribute the truth about the one true God. You want to know what God thinks, wills, says, plans, feels, does or promises? You must go to Jesus or to those he authorizes to reveal what he has already revealed. Jesus speaks through the pens of the prophets and apostles in the Holy Scriptures. He has authorized and commanded every Christian to introduce people to the Father by proclaiming his written revealed truth.

Can't you hear the crowd? "What do you mean no one knows you?! I knew you when you grew up. I heard you preach many times. I observed you perform miracles." Yes, they knew *about* him, but they didn't really know Jesus. Matthew seems to emphasize this by using ἐπιγινώσκω instead of γινώσκω as Luke does when he records this event in Luke 10:22. The NIV translators seem to have concluded that they should be translated identically, since they are parallel passages. This is possible since Koine Greek often used the preposition prefix without adding the emphasis or intensity of classical Greek. On the other hand Matthew might be reflecting a vivid recollection of hearing Jesus emphasize this point. Or Jesus may have said this twice, once after the return of the Twelve, and again, with less emphasis, after the return of the seventy.

Don't overlook the significance of γινώσκω. It speaks of knowing by experience, the kind of experience that comes with and belongs to a relationship. Jesus declares his own intimate fellowship with the Father and declares that he has the authority to introduce those he "chooses" to the Father, that they too may really know the Father, that they too may have an intimate Father-child relationship with the Lord of heaven and earth. This relationship is much more than feelings. It is a relationship based on the objective facts of who God is, what he has done and what he promises to do. We can not discover these facts by our own search or speculation. Jesus is the exclusive purveyor of divine reality and the resulting relationship. Now, to whom does he offer his unique gift?

vv. 28-30 — *"Come to me, all you who are weary and burdened, and I will give you rest. Take my yoke upon you and learn from me, for I am gentle and humble in heart, and you will find rest for your souls. For my yoke is easy and my burden is light."*

Here the Son's "choice" (v. 27) and the Father's "good pleasure" (v. 26) are revealed! It's their will that *all* the weary and burdened come into fellowship with the Father through the Son. They want *all* people, for "*all* have sinned" (Ro 3:23) and "*everyone* who sins is a slave to sin" (Jo 8:34).

Of course only the heart that recognizes its burden and longs for relief will find Jesus' invitation truly inviting. Therefore, preacher, be sensitive to your audience. Are they burdened, bruised reeds (Mt 12:20) or lukewarm with self-satisfaction (Re 3:15f)? Such sensitivity is necessary to correctly handle the word of truth (2 Ti 2:15) as heralds of this awesome promise. Like Jesus, prepare the people to see the need for his offer.

Spend some time carefully considering what Jesus' invitation promises. Why, no one but God himself can make and fulfill this claim! "Come to me. *I myself* will give you rest for your soul. Accept my word and unending relief is yours. I personally guarantee peace with God." Does Jesus have the credentials to back up this claim? Later, led as the Lamb of God to the slaughter, he proved he has a gentle and humble heart sympathetic to the plight of the weary and burdened. Rising from the dead verifies that he is the Lord God who has earned the right to give peace and rest to his people. He removes your sin and restores your fellowship with God. Yes, Jesus has the credentials. He is the Son of God.

Jesus uses intriguing imagery to contrast the before and after condition of those who come to him. Who ever heard of a yoke that's easy and a burden that's light? What a contrast to the wearisome burden that was placed on them and remained on them (perfect passive) until they came to Jesus!

Unlike the agrarian people Jesus addressed, few if any of us have seen a draft animal labor all day under a yoke. How many of us have carted water all day with two pails balanced on a wooden yoke resting on our shoulders? In our automated society, this imagery might require a brief explanation.

However, more attention should be given to the Bible's use of "yoke" to speak of slavery (Lv 26:13, 1 Tm 6:1), of the burden of sin's guilt (Lm 1:14) and of the oppressive burden of the law on sinners (Ac 15:10, Ga 5:1). The Galileans were familiar with this yoke imagery. The Lord even promised (Is 9:1-4) that when the Lord's great light appeared in Galilee, he would shatter "the yoke that burdens them."

Ylvisaker notes (*The Gospels*, footnote p. 439) that the rabbis often spoke of the Law as "the yoke of the kingdom." The Law of Moses was a daily burden. It was also their covenant with God. Here Jesus invites them to come under a new covenant. Verse 29 spells out a covenant relationship with God through Jesus' loving-kindness. The imagery of the yoke includes more than the burden. It also implies a binding commitment to an intimate relationship as in 2 Corinthians 6:14. The gospel imperative, "Come to me . . . Take my yoke upon you and learn from me . . . " is the same as "Come follow me" (Mt 4:19) as Jesus defines it in Luke 9:23f. This is not conversion by human decision and dedication! It's gospel that creates the new man and empowers him to do what God commands. Declare it as the good news it is.

The burden of Jesus' yoke is the necessity "to deny yourself" and follow the lead of Jesus' word no matter where it takes you. In other words, let God be your God. Obviously the rest Jesus offers is *not* a do-nothing vacation. It's better! Jesus' yoke is an easy and light burden because he does *all* the work. We love because *he* first loved us. We are committed to him because *he* was first committed to us. *He* paid for all our sins and set us free. *He* fights all our battles (Rv 19:13,14) for us. He equips us with *his* mighty power (Ep 6:10f), the full armor of God. *He* provides our escape from temptation so we can stand (1 Co 10:13).

Jesus is our relief, our rescue, our rest at every turn. Our rest does not rest on us at all. It rests only on Jesus, who broke the yoke of slavery and removed its burden on the cross, who daily lifts us up and carries us on eagles' wings (Ex 19:4).

Homiletical Suggestions

The ILCW readings beautifully reflect the unity of Scripture as they speak to battle-fatigued soldiers of the cross who feel more like prisoners of war than part of the invincible church of Christ. Any Christian who doesn't instantly identify with Paul and say, "Why, that's exactly how I feel!" better wake up. He's been sleeping on duty. Those who share Paul's weary frustration delight to see how Paul deals with it. Paul rejoices in the good news. He partakes of the spiritual medicine God prescribed to disheartened prisoners in Zechariah 9. Rejoice in your King who comes to you with a gentle bedside manner to decisively destroy your enemies. He proclaims a peace that heals the battle-burdened weary warrior. How sweet to hear him proclaim his peace! "Come to me, all you who are weary and burdened." And look! Even our King Brother, the Son of God, praises the Father's good pleasure to overcome the temptation to grow weary in the face of rejection. The Old Testament and Epistle lessons prepare the way for the sermon and offer a wealth of simple vivid examples of the weary and burdened whom Jesus addresses in our text.

Our text consists of three distinct subjects. The first addresses the mind-boggling unbelief in Galilee. In the second Jesus makes it clear that their rejection of him is really rejection of the Lord God of Israel. Finally, Jesus invites the spiritually weary and burdened Galileans to come to him for the real Sabbath rest which God promised to give them. Where do we turn for a theme? One can be found in the yoke of Jesus. It doesn't fit over the pride-swollen heads of unbelievers. Jesus is the only one who offers it. Come try it on. To communicate this consider this outline.

A Yoke Just for You

1. Designed for small children (vv. 25,26)
2. Distributed solely by Jesus (v. 27)
3. Delightful to wear (vv. 28-30)

To the weary this invitation might sound like a sick joke. Jesus uses a play on words to get the people's attention and make his invitation memorable. You might change the above theme to **The Yoke's on You**. Unbelievers think it's a joke. We know better. It's a delightful yoke.

Noting the context of these words, the sending out of the Twelve and the lack of direct fruit from Jesus' witnessing, this text speaks powerfully to weary witnesses of the gospel.

Real Relief for Weary Witnesses of the Lord Jesus

1. Discover why many don't believe in Jesus (vv. 25,27,28)
2. Find your own relief under your Lord's yoke (vv. 25-30)

The above outlines cover the entire text. The imagery and content of verses 28-30 are so precious the preacher might elect to concentrate his efforts there. Since this text comes up at a time when many of your people will be eagerly looking forward to restful vacations, consider this theme and parts.

Jesus Offers the Perfect Never-Ending Vacation

1. His outstretched arms invite *you* to come (v. 28)
2. Take his hand and go with him (vv. 29,30)

Consider using one of the many popular pictures that illustrate Jesus' invitation "Come to me." Most of them express his invitation with his hands and arms. Even on the cross his open arms invite every individual (Jn 12:32,33) to "Come to me."His open arms challenge all of us to admit our burden of sin and our weary helpless need for what he offers.

Jesus' gospel imperative to "take my yoke . . . and learn from me" invites us to abandon our journey on the broad path to destruction (Mt 7:13) and travel side by side with him forever. The English idiom "walk hand in hand" expresses the same close committed relationship to which Jesus refers with the "yoke."

EIGHTH SUNDAY AFTER PENTECOST

The Scriptures

Old Testament — *Isaiah 55:10,11*
Epistle — *Romans 8:18-25*
Gospel — *Matthew 13:1-9,(18-23)*

The Text — Matthew 13:1-9

Although our text begins a new chapter, it is tied to the preceding chapter by the words "that same day." Jesus has had a typically active day of healing (Mt 12:22) and teaching people (Mt 12:46). He has had an emotionally stressful day. He has had to defend himself against the cruel accusation of doing his work by Beelzebub (Mt 12:24). He has had to deal with his mother and brothers who thought he was out of his mind and had come to take charge of him (Mk 3:21). Faced with a similarly difficult day, we might be ready to "call it a day" and quit early, but not Jesus! He's not through yet. The hard-working Messiah once put it this way: "As long as it is day, we must do the work of him who sent me. Night is coming, when no one can work" (Jn 9:4)

The primary God-given work of Christ was to live a perfect life of love and then head to the cross as the sinner's sin-bearing substitute. His secondary work was to teach and preach the good news of his redemptive work. The Savior understood perfectly the piercing questions the Apostle Paul would ask in his epistle to the Romans: "How can they believe in the one whom they have not heard? And how can they hear without someone preaching to them?" (10:14) Jesus did not want to waste a single opportunity to spread the word of God! He himself is the sower in the parable he is about to tell.

vv. 1,2 — *That same day Jesus went out of the house and sat by the lake. Such large crowds gathered around him that he got into a boat and sat in it, while all the people stood on the shore.*

Jesus chose a fishing boat as his classroom lectern. From his position out in the water he would have good visual contact with his listeners, and the water, taking the place of a speaker system, would help to carry his voice to such a large number. The teacher carefully chose and arranged his classroom because what he had to say was so important.

v. 3a — *Then he told them many things in parables, saying:*

The parable was Christ's foremost figure of speech and teaching tool. Our "parable" is merely a transliteration of the Greek word παραβολή, a placing of two things side by side for the sake of comparison. It is helpful in the interpretation of the Lord's parables to actually place the corresponding components side by side. It is extra helpful when Jesus himself explains the parable (as he does here in verses 18-23).

vv. 3b,4 — *"A farmer went out to sow his seed. As he was scattering the seed, some fell along the path, and the birds came and ate it up."*

Jesus' initial hearers would at once picture this agricultural scene. The farmer broadcast the seed over the prepared ground.

In spite of the sower's best skill and efforts, not all the seed would end up in a prime spot. Some would fall on the trampled-down soil of the path. There it would sit on the surface and before long become food for the birds.

Here is Jesus' own explanation of this part of the parable: "When anyone hears the message about the kingdom and does not understand it, the evil one comes and snatches away what was sown in his heart" (13:19). Some of the listeners before Jesus would fall into this category of hard-hearted hearers. "Though seeing, they do not see; though hearing, they do not hear or understand" (13:13). They've seen Jesus' miracles, but don't see anything behind these displays of power. They hear his words of authorirty, but don't want to hear with their hearts. They reject the words, refuse to believe and excuse themselves by accusing Jesus of doing his work by Beelzebub. The prince of demons is at work in their hearts, quickly snatching away the gospel seed. Satan knows the gospel's power and doesn't want to give it a chance to work.

A hard-hearted reception of the gospel is not common only to out-and-out unbelievers and scoffers, however. Even the converted still have remnants of a rock-hard heart. Recall the time Jesus questioned the believing Twelve because they had missed the spiritual intent of his teaching. He asked them, "Why are you talking about having no bread? Do you still not see or understand? Are your hearts hardened? Do you have eyes but fail to see and hearts but fail to hear?" (Mk 8:17,18) And what did Jesus say in rebuke of the Emmaus disciples? "How foolish you are, and how slow of heart to believe all that the prophets have spoken!" (Lk 24:25)

Slowness and hardness of heart are terrible spiritual "soil conditions." And believers aren't above the problem. Sin, doubts and unbelief itself trample our hearts and threaten to prevent the plant of faith from growing inside. That's the point! Let this be our prayer, "Lord, I do believe, help me overcome my unbelief!" (Mk 9:24)

vv. 5,6 — *"Some fell on rocky places, where it did not have much soil. It sprang up quickly, because the soil was shallow. But when the sun came up, the plants were scorched, and they withered because they had no root."*

In certain places in the farmer's field a layer of rock lies close to the surface. Topsoil covers the rock and offers a fertile and warm bed for the seed to quickly generate and sprout. But what will happen? The growing plant cannot sink deep roots into the soil; it is doomed to destruction when the sun blazes down on it. We can picture this easily, but what is the counterpart in the spiritual realm?

Jesus explains, "The seed that fell on rocky places is the man who hears the word and at once receives it with joy. But since he has no root, he lasts only a short time. When trouble or persecution comes because of the word, he quickly falls away" (13:20,21). How sad! But how true to life!

Haven't we seen it happen just as Jesus describes? An adult in the instruction class doesn't miss an opportunity to attend; he is so excited, joyful and enthusiastic! But it doesn't last. When the instruction period comes to an end, the persecution period is just beginning, and he can't take the heat — the heat of ridicule, peer pressure, disappointment or disillusionment. He isn't rooted deep enough in God's word and God's love to draw on their strength and in a matter of months stops hearing the word and falls away from his Savior.

Jesus' warning is clear. Plants of faith lacking roots will not survive. A shallow, short-lived reception of the word will not do in the long run.

Again, all believers have a tendency to listen in a shallow sort of way and need the encouragement, "Grow in the grace and knowledge of our Lord and Savior Jesus Christ" (2 Pe 3:18). We need to pray for our people as did Paul in Ephesians 3:17,18. Such plants of faith will stand up and thrive even in the heat of persecution!

v. 7 — *Other seed fell among thorns, which grew up and choked the plants.*

Any farmer or gardener understands this picture. It's a constant battle to get out and keep out the weeds! Weeds drain strength from the good plants and can actually choke them out.

What are the weeds in the hearts of those listening to God's word? They are "the worries of this life and the deceitfulness of wealth" (13:22). These evil "weeds," according to Jesus' explanation, make the plant of faith unfruitful. No fruits of faith (Ga 5:22,23) will be produced. The worries of this life and the deceitfulness of wealth can stem these wonderful fruits and blessings in the bud.

Paul writes about Judas and others like him when he points out, "Some people, eager for money, have wandered from the faith and pierced themselves with many griefs" (1 Tm 6:10). In this regard, the Lord Jesus himself asks two penetrating questions, "What good is it for a man to gain the whole world, yet forfeit his soul? Or what can a man give in exchange for his soul?" (Mk 8:36,37).

Then let's not forget the thriving, fast-spreading "worry thorn." Like the deceitfulness of wealth, it too robs the plant of faith of the vital nutrients of God's word. Consider Martha (Lk 10:38-42). The typical believer — yes, even the pastor — can be reading his Bible, yet have his mind more on an ailing parent or a financial dilemma or a multitude of other worries; you name it! Such "worry thorns" are in every heart. Only God's promises in the word will root them out! Let's find and use these precious promises personally and for our people.

v. 8 — *Still other seed fell on good soil, where it produced a crop — a hundred, sixty or thirty times what was sown.*

At last we come to the "good news" part of the parable. The farmer's field has good soil in it, and there the seed finds the right conditions to grow and accomplish its God-ordained purpose — to produce a crop.

Jesus compares the good soil to "the man who hears the word and understands it" (13:23). Let it be noted, however, that no one can take credit for making his heart receptive to the message of God's word. "No one can say, 'Jesus is Lord,' except by the Holy Spirit" (1 Cor 12:3). Even the strongest, most fruitful believer was, to begin with, dead in transgressions and sins (Eph 2:1). On the other hand, the unconverted "are darkened in their understanding and separated from the life of God because of the ignorance that is in them due to the hardening of their hearts" (Eph 4:18).

Only a miracle of God can make the heart good soil for the gospel seed. In fact, it is the very gospel seed which performs the miracle. The Law of God gets things ready, crushing the rocks of pride. " 'Is not my word like fire,' declares the Lord, 'and like a hammer that breaks a rock in pieces?' " (Jer 23:29). Then the gospel seed, packed with the power of God for salvation, tells of a love so great it's hard to imagine. God loved the world of sinners to the point that he would send and sacrifice the Son he loved so dearly! Jesus loved us so much that he willingly took our punishment on himself. That saving love penetrates our hearts and gives birth to faith and trust. There is a hidden, miraculous power in the seed of the word — the power of love and life!

A healthy plant of faith will grow from the gospel seed and will produce a crop. The crop is the fruit of the Spirit (Gal 5:22,23). Or, looking at it another way, the crop is more gospel seed. Just as one kernel of seed corn produces a cob full of seed corn, the believer has more and more gospel seeds to sow back into his own heart and into the hearts of family members, friends, fellow church members and acquaintances.

The size of the crop varies from believer to believer and from year to year. The stronger the plant of faith, the bigger the crop. And the greater the God-given abilities and talents, the greater is the potential for effectively spreading the seed to more and more souls. In all of this there is no room for pride if we remember Christ's words, "From everyone who has been given much, much will be demanded; and from the one who has been entrusted with much, much more will be asked" (Lk 12:48). To Jesus the Savior be the glory for all he has done for us and given us!

v. 9 — *He who has ears, let him hear.*

Jesus uses this or a similar proverbial statement several times in the Gospels and at the close of each letter to the seven churches in the book of Revelation. What statement is he making thereby? It's not hard to determine whether I have ears that work or not. And if I do, Jesus is telling me, "Use them! Hear and take to heart what I'm teaching you!" And the point he would drive home through this parable is: "Listen to the word of God with care and prayer."

Homiletical Suggestions

What a valuable passage from the word! What a wide and wealthy field of ideas and insights this parable produces!

That can lead to a problem, however. How does the preacher pack everything into a twenty-minute sermon? How does he say it all without exhausting his listeners? He shouldn't try!

The average hearer in our churches has heard this parable numerous times. Give enough background information to clarify the points of comparison, but be sure to leave plenty of time for spiritual appropriation and application. Let's not spend 15 precious minutes teaching our people all about farming in the olden days. Let's get to the point more quickly!

And let's make sure we have defined and sharpened the point we want to get across. That means choosing a clear and pointed theme and then sticking with it in the writing and delivering of the sermon. The following are some suggested themes.

Recognizing our hearts' natural condition, we will lead our people in the prayer:

Lord, Make Our Hearts Good Soil for Your Gospel Seed!

1. So that we grow in faith (vv. 3b-8a)
2. And sow in love (vv. 8b, 1-3a)

In part one the wise preacher will want to make himself and his people more aware of the threats to a good healthy plant of faith and of the power of the gospel to soften rock-hard hearts, root out thorns, and grant strength and endurance in the heat of persecution and trouble.

In the second section of the sermon, faith's crop will be the focal point. The fruitful hearer becomes a loving sower of the word in the hearts and homes of others.

A more pointed evangelism thrust is certainly possible. The shepherd of God's people may encourage,

You Can Be a Sower of the Word

1. A careful listener has seed to sow (vv. 1-9)
2. Your powerful God will make some seed grow (v. 8)

Or we can view this entire parable from the listening angle. The more we listen to God's word, the more that word will have a chance to work in our hearts. Keying off Jesus' statement, "He who has ears, let him hear" we could exclaim,

Let's Use Our Ears! (v. 9)

1. To listen prayerfully, asking for understanding (vv. 4,8,19,23)
2. To listen persistently, seeking depth of knowledge and conviction (vv. 5,6,8,20,21,23)
3. To listen attentively, blocking out earthly cares and concerns (vv. 7,8,22,23)

NINTH SUNDAY AFTER PENTECOST

The Scriptures

Old Testament — *Isaiah 44:6-8*
Epistle — *Romans 8:26,27*
Gospel — *Matthew 13:24-30,(36-43)*

The Text — Matthew 13:24-30,(36-43)

This chapter of Matthew's Gospel contains a series of seven parables all dealing with the kingdom of heaven. The first four parables (sower, weeds, mustard seed, yeast) Jesus spoke from a boat while the people listened from the shore. The last three parables (hidden treasure, pearl, net) Jesus told to his disciples in a house. Although the parable of the weeds in the wheat field (vv. 24-30) was spoken from the boat, Jesus' explanation (vv. 36-43) was spoken within the house. Three of these seven parables describe the growth of the kingdom of heaven in the heart of individuals (sower, hidden treasure, pearl); four describe the growth of the kingdom of heaven in the world (weeds, mustard seeds, yeast, net).

The parable of the weeds in the wheat field is told by Jesus in verses 24-30. Jesus himself explains what this parable means in verses 36-43. Whether verses 36-43 are read as part of the text or not, the preacher will certainly want to pay close attention to the Lord's explanation and perhaps draw these words into the exposition of the text. That plan will be followed here.

v. 24 — *Jesus told them another parable: "The kingdom of heaven is like a man who sowed good seed in his field."*

Having finished his explanation of why he spoke in parables and of what the parable of the sower meant, Jesus continued to feed the people with the word. The kingdom of heaven is God's gracious rule in human hearts and lives — not a place so much as an activity. Through the gospel promises of God's word and sacraments, Jesus gives us the sure hope of heaven. To explain one aspect of the kingdom of heaven, Jesus points us to the familiar world of farming. This farmer owned his own field and therefore made extra sure that the seed he planted was good seed. He wanted good seed that would germinate and produce wheat, not weeds.

"The one who sowed the good seed is the Son of Man" (v. 37). Jesus himself is meant by the man who sowed good seed in his field.

"The field is the world" (v. 38). The field that is the world is his field, Jesus' field. The world belongs to the Son of man and the Son of God who made it, Psalm 24:1. And since Jesus is given "all authority in heaven and on earth" (Mt 28:18), to him belongs the right of planting the seed that he calls good, the seed that will produce the fruit he is seeking.

"And the good seed stands for the sons of the kingdom" (v. 38). Jesus identifies "the good seed" with "the sons of the kingdom." The sons of the kingdom are those, throughout the world, who are heirs of heaven, because Jesus planted them and the Holy Spirit makes them grow.

v. 25 — *"But while everyone was sleeping, his enemy came and sowed weeds among the wheat, and went away."*

Ζιζάνιον is a weed that closely resembles wheat, and cannot easily be distinguished from the wheat until the heads form. The grains of zizanium are black and harbor a fungus that is poisonous.

"The weeds are the sons of the evil one, and the enemy who sows them is the devil" (vv. 38,39). That there is a personal devil, the enemy of God, is clear from Jesus' words. Because the devil hates God, he takes pleasure in hindering and destroying God's work whenever he can. The kingdom of Jesus Christ is a thorn in his eye, and he works hard to destroy that kingdom. Wherever Jesus is sowing good seed there also the devil is busy. The devil sows his own seeds: "the sons of the evil one," unbelievers. These "plants" may be outwardly righteous, appearing like the wheat, but they are really "the sons of the evil one," about whom Jesus said, "You belong to your father, the devil, and you want to carry out your father's desire" (Jn 8:44).

The farmer has an enemy, perhaps a neighbor, who simply and terribly frustrates the farmer's work. He chooses night to do his evil deed, hoping that the darkness will conceal his sin. The devil carries on his work while everyone sleeps, when it is dark. His deeds of darkness cannot stand the light of day, the light of God's word, for then his lies would be clearly seen for what they are.

In the world, there are both Christ's kingdom, and the devil's kingdom of sin and darkness. The sons of the kingdom and the sons of the evil one live side by side in this world, and may look very much alike. They work at the same jobs, they have the same customs, they seek the same political goals. And yet they are entirely different. True Christians are wheat and produce fruit for eternal life. Unbelievers are weeds and produce poisonous fruit.

vv. 26,27 — *"When the wheat sprouted and formed heads, then the weeds also appeared. The owner's servants came to him and said, 'Sir, didn't you sow good seed in your field? Where then did the weeds come from?' "*

It was not easy to tell the wheat and the weeds apart. It took most of the growing season for the servants to recognize that not all that appeared to be wheat was really wheat. Not until they saw the fruit could they be sure that there were weeds among the wheat. Astonished, they went to the owner, who had expended so much care in sowing good seed, to find out where the weeds had come from.

Since our Lord did not give a particular exposition of these verses, we conclude that these verses are not the main point of the parable, but serve mainly to carry along the story. The servants are the sons of the kingdom, the believers, who are often astonished at the spread of wickedness. Why is it that even where the gospel has been clearly proclaimed for many years, wickedness still abounds? Like the servants, we can take all these matters that our reason cannot comprehend to the Savior.

v. 28a — *" 'An enemy did this,' he replied."*

God's enemy, the devil, is the source of the weed seeds planted among the wheat. That is our Lord's clear explanation of the spread of wickedness. God created a perfect world, but the devil stepped in and caused the fall into sin. Even though Satan carries on his work in secret, still the Lord knows all about it; before the devil ever carries out his mischief, the Lord already knows how he will use the evil for our good (Ro 8:28). The prime example of this is the devil's scheming at the death of Christ; already before creation God planned to use this for our eternal salvation.

v. 28b — *"The servants asked him, 'Do you want us to go and pull them up?' "*

These servants are faithful servants, willing to take on this difficult task in the service of their master. But they don't immediately go out and begin the work as soon as they realize that their master doesn't want weeds in his field. First they ask the master what he would have them do. Our Lord also wants servants who are zealous to do his work, but who first find out from Scripture exactly what their Lord wants them to do to spread his kingdom and to counter the attacks of Satan. There is also a zeal for God that is "not based on knowledge" (Ro 10:2).

The servants thought it best if they would pull all the weeds out of their master's field. Jesus also had to deal with those, even among his own disciples, who would cleanse the world by ridding it of all unbelievers (Lk 9:52-55). And this makes sense to our human reason. Just as the weeds hinder the growth of the wheat, so also the unbelieving world hinders the growth and flowering of the Christian church. Jesus calls the weeds "everything that causes sin and all who do evil" (v. 41). The world tempts the Christians, and some fall, to be replaced by weeds. It makes sense that the weeds should be uprooted. But our Lord does not concur with this plan.

v. 29 — *" 'No,' he answered, 'because while you are pulling the weeds, you may root up the wheat with them.' "*

The Lord's answer to the servants is an unmistakable NO. He will not have the weeds uprooted before the harvest. Jesus is not here speaking of church discipline in contradiction to what he says Matthew 18:15-18. Jesus is not speaking here of unbelievers in the church, but in the world, for he says, "the field is the world" (v. 38). Rather, the Lord wants the church to carry on church discipline out of love for the straying. But the Lord would not have his church engaged in physically ridding the world of weeds. The church has only one weapon, and that is "the sword of the Spirit, which is the word of God" (Eph 6:17). Those who cannot be won with the word of God will not be won by the sword either.

The reason the owner forbids them to pull up the weeds is because of the wheat. They thought they could help the wheat by uprooting the weeds; but the owner maintained that they would also uproot the wheat when they uprooted the weeds. Certainly now that the heads had formed they could tell the wheat and the weeds apart, but what about the intertwining roots? And who today can properly distinguish between unbelievers who will remain unbelievers and unbelievers who will one day believe the word and become wheat? Out of love for the wheat, Jesus forbids us to cut short anyone's time of grace.

v. 30 — *"Let both grow together until the harvest. At that time I will tell the harvesters: First collect the weeds and tie them in bundles to be burned; then gather the wheat and bring it into my barn."*

The will of our Savior is that both weeds and wheat remain in the world until the harvest. This his Christians will have to suffer and endure, and the Lord will give them patience to do so. But the Lord also uses this for good. The fact that his church grows and flourishes in the midst of the wicked world shows the great glory and power of our God. The daily temptations from the world serve to test our faith and make it strong. The wickedness of the world makes us long all the more for "the glorious appearing of our great God and Savior, Jesus Christ" (Tt 2:13).

By saying, "Let both grow together," the Lord would by no means minimize the differences between wheat and weeds. The church has no business forcefully uprooting unbelievers from the world, but it remains very much the business of the church to testify to the truth and to be wheat: to produce fruit for the Savior. "Have nothing to do with the fruitless deeds of darkness, but rather expose them" (Eph 5:11). "You must no longer live as the Gentiles do" (Eph 4:17). We are always to remember that we are "a planting of the Lord for the display of his splendor" (Is 61:3).

"The harvest is the end of the age" (v. 39), in other words, Judgment Day. As long as this present world stands, there will be both believers and unbelievers growing together in the world. But this situation will not continue forever; the harvest is coming. For our comfort, the Lord points us ahead to the harvest, when believers and unbelievers will be separated. We wait patiently for that day to come. Now it seems that the wicked are prospering and "flourishing like a green tree in its native soil" (Ps 37:25); but we have Jesus' promise that the harvest is coming.

The harvesters are angels (v. 39). This is just as Jesus later said: "The Son of Man comes in his glory, and all the angels with him" (Mt 25:31). "As the weeds are pulled up and burned in the fire, so it will be at the end of the age. The Son of Man will send out his angels, and they will weed out of his kingdom everything that causes sin and all who do evil. They will throw them into the fiery furnace, where there will be weeping and gnashing of teeth" (Mt 13:40-42). The temptations presented by unbelievers have plagued the Christians, but they will no more. Christ will put a permanent end to all temptations from the devil and the world. Not only are the weeds separated from the wheat, but they are burned, cast into the fires of hell forever.

Not only are the believers separated from the unbelievers, but they are gathered and brought into the Lord's barn, into heaven. "Then the righteous will shine like the sun in the kingdom of their Father. He who has ears, let him hear" (Mt 13:43). The righteousness that has been credited to their account for Jesus' sake is now theirs in the sight of all. Jesus "will transform our lowly bodies so that they will be like his glorious body" (Ph 3:21). All temptation from our sinful flesh is put to an end. All believers will then be in the kingdom of their Father forever, as his dear children. This message is for us to hear and believe now; later we will see it with our own eyes.

Homiletical Suggestions

This parable has been interpreted in two different ways to answer two perplexing questions: "Why are there hypocrites in the church?" and, "Why are there unbelievers in the world?" Especially on the basis of our Lord's explanation, "The field is the world," the interpretation that Jesus is referring to hypocrites in the church specifically is rejected. Rather, the point Jesus is making has to do with the relationship between believers and unbelievers in the world.

A succinct and catchy treatment of this text, which does not explicitly suggest the application is:

Weeds among the Wheat

1. The sowing (vv. 24,25)
2. The growing (v. 26)
3. The mowing (vv. 27-30)

A more personal and practical outline would be:

What Shall We Do About the Weeds?

1. Recognize their source (vv. 24,25)
2. Accept their presence (vv. 26-29)
3. Be sure of their destiny (v. 30)

TENTH SUNDAY AFTER PENTECOST

The Scriptures

Old Testament — *1 Kings 3:5-12*
Epistle — *Romans 8:28-30*
Gospel — *Matthew 13:44-52*

The Text — Matthew 13:44-52

Our text is a series of parables intended to give new insight into the kingdom of heaven. A parable is a figure of speech, an extended simile. It is a teaching device intended to illustrate one point of doctrine or convey one important truth. To understand a parable we need to look for the point of comparison. The details of the parable help us to understand the picture the parable paints, but they will not necessarily have counterparts in the interpretation of the parable.

The "kingdom of heaven" is not to be understood as a millennial reign of Christ here on earth, for Christ's kingdom is not a political kingdom (Lk 17:20,21; Jn 18:36; Col 1:12-14; Ro 14:17). Nor is the kingdom of heaven to be strictly identified with the invisible church, for the invisible church is limited to believers. Verses 47-50 of our text indicate that the kingdom spoken of here includes both the righteous and the wicked, both believers and unbelievers (hypocrites). In our text the kingdom of heaven is the sphere of gospel activity or proclamation of the gospel. It means God's activity during this time of grace in which he calls sinners to faith and salvation through the means of grace, the gospel in word and sacrament.

The thirteenth chapter of Matthew's Gospel also contains other parables about the kingdom of heaven, including the parables of the sower, of the weeds, of the mustard seed, and of the yeast. The preacher will want to read the entire chapter before he begins his work on this text.

vv. 44,45 — *"The kingdom of heaven is like treasure hidden in a field. When a man found it, he hid it again, and then in his joy went and sold all he had and bought that field. Again, the kingdom of heaven is like a merchant looking for fine pearls. When he found one of great value, he went away and sold everything he had and bought it."*

The first two parables of our text are relatively easy for us to grasp and understand. Both speak of the value of the gospel and the effect it has in the lives of believers.

The man who found a treasure hidden in a field was so impressed with its value that he was willing to give up everything he had in order to buy that field and secure the treasure. He recognized what it was worth and was willing to give up everything to obtain it. The point of the parable is not the question of the morality of his not letting the owner of the field know what a valuable treasure lay hidden in his field. The point of the parable is that the man was so impressed with the treasure that he was willing to give up everything for it.

The gospel's message of salvation is like such a treasure. Nothing is more precious to a person with a burdened conscience than the good news, "Your sins are forgiven." When a human being truly comes to grips with his sins and guilt and comes to realize that even though he deserves to be punished in hell forever, God offers him eternal life instead, he has to be affected. That message of forgiveness of sins, life and salvation will become the most important thing in his life. The knowledge of salvation will dominate and control his life (Ps 51; Lk 19:1-8; 7:36-47).

The second parable is similar to the first. A merchant (ἔμπορος, a wholesaler) is looking for fine pearls. Finally, he finds one which is more exquisite than all the rest. Recognizing how precious and unique it is, he gives up his search and sells everything he owns to purchase it.

Since the fall into sin there has been an emptiness in the lives of people. Because human beings are separated from God by sin from the point of conception (Ps 51:5), there is something lacking in their very existence. The natural knowledge of the law and man's conscience cause a spiritual restlessness, a searching for what is missing (Ac 17:27).

That's why virtually every people of every age of every corner of this planet have had a god or gods whom they have worshiped (Ro 1:18-25; 2:14,15). When many of the mainline Christian denominations in our country became spiritually bankrupt through their rejection of the Bible as the totally inspired and inerrant Word of God, cults with claims of divine authority sprang up to fill the void. People are searching for something to fill the emptiness in their lives.

But the work-righteous systems of the religions of this world and the cults of our country can't bring true happiness or lasting peace. That can come only through the knowledge of sins forgiven and heaven regained by the blood of our Savior Jesus Christ.

When a person discovers that truth (or more accurately — when God reveals that truth to a person through the Holy Scriptures), his life is complete. There is no need to look further. For the gospel offers people something they can't find anywhere else. It offers them eternal life and peace with God as a free gift. There is nothing they have to do or can do to earn it. The message of forgiveness of sins, life and salvation makes every other message pale by comparison. It is the "pearl of great value," the only message that can guarantee heaven. Finding that pearl is life-changing. It becomes the most valuable thing in life. The knowledge of salvation puts everything else in our lives into proper perspective.

vv. 47-50 — *"Once again, the kingdom of heaven is like a net that was let down into the lake and caught all kinds of fish. When it was full, the fishermen pulled it up on shore. Then they sat down and collected the good fish in baskets, but threw the bad fish away. This is how it will be at the end of the age. The angels will come and separate the wicked from the righteous and throw them into the fiery furnace, where there will be weeping and gnashing of teeth."*

This parable of the net was vivid to people living around the Sea of Galilee. Some, like a few of Christ's disciples, were undoubtedly fishermen. All were familiar with the important fishing industry of that region. Jesus spoke of a dragnet (σαγήνη) gathering in all kinds of fish. Fishermen would stretch out the ends of a dragnet over a wide expanse of water and then draw them together. The net would enclose and entrap all the fish in the area encompassed by the net. Since the net covered a large area it gathered in not only the species they were fishing for, but others as well. On the shore they had to separate the good fish from the bad, the edible from the inedible, those which could be sold from the worthless and valueless fish.

When the gospel is proclaimed, it draws many people. But not everyone who comes to hear the gospel really believes it. Not everyone in a visible Christian congregation or assembly is really a Christian. In Christian congregations and assemblies there will also be hypocrites.

That's still true today. Some people go through all the outward motions of worship or congregational membership, but their hearts are somewhere else (Mt 15:7,8). Some are Sunday morning Christians. They give a show of piety for one hour a week, and then live the rest of the time as if they had never heard of their Savior's forgiveness or his will for their lives. Some like to be associated with "good" Christian people. It makes them look good. It's good for their reputations and good for business. Others give the impression of being servants of Christ, but secretly remain slaves to sin and Satan. Their pet sins rule in their hearts and dominate their lives. Their repentance is hollow. Their Christianity is a sham.

We cannot always recognize who the hypocrites are in this life. But on Judgment Day every hypocrite will be exposed. The angels will separate them from believers, just as fishermen separate bad fish from good. The hypocrites (unbelievers) will be thrown into hell where they will be punished and tormented eternally (Mt 13:24-30, 36-43).

Though many today try to deny the fact, hell is a reality. God will punish unbelievers forever (Jn 3:16-18,36; 2 Th 1:8-10; Mk 9:43-48). This parable therefore contains the warning to make use of the time of grace that God has given us (2 Cor 6:1,2). When God calls us with the gospel he wants us to believe (He 3:7-19). Those who spurn the gospel's call may not have another chance.

vv. 51,52 — *"Have you understood all these things?" Jesus asked. "Yes," they replied. He said to them, "Therefore every teacher of the law who has been instructed about the kingdom of heaven is like the owner of a house who brings out of his storeroom new treasures as well as old."*

Jesus asked his disciples a vital question. "Do you understand all these things?" The purpose of his parables was to enlighten his followers and to confuse his enemies (Mt 13:10-15). If his disciples hadn't understood the parables, his purpose would not have been met. But they did understand what Jesus was teaching them. They grasped these new insights into the kingdom of heaven.

In response to their affirmative answer Jesus told them another parable. He told them that since they understood these things they were like an owner of a house who was able to bring out of his storeroom new things as well as old. They were like a master of a house whose storeroom was so well stocked that he was equipped to meet every situation. They were therefore in a position to dispense God's treasures to others.

The religious leaders of the Jews of Jesus' day were not so well equipped. They had become stale in their religious life. They had fallen into dead formalism. They were more concerned with rabbinical tradition than with the vital truths of Scripture. They were more concerned with what the rabbis had said than with what God had said. In their blind zeal they were no longer able to see or understand the real message and purpose of the Bible. Instead of seeing God's message of grace and forgiveness in the Old Testament they could only see rules and regulations for earning their own salvation.

Jesus was training his disciples not only by explaining the message of the Old Testament to them, but also by revealing new truths.

These new truths rested on the foundation of the old. The disicples were living in the age of fulfillment and they had the Son of God himself as their teacher. They were hearing and seeing things not heard or seen before. As Jesus told them, "I tell you the truth, many prophets and righteous men longed to see what you see but did not see it, and to hear what you hear but did not hear it" (Mt 13:17).

Our Savior was training them for the commission he was going to give them. He was preparing them for their lives as his ambassadors. He was teaching them so that they might be able to teach others. He was equipping them to bring the message of salvation to all mankind.

Through his holy word Jesus trains us, too. That training equips us for Christian living (2 Tm 3:16,17), Christian witness (1 Pe 3:15,16; Mt 28:20) and Christian service (Eph 4:11-13). A disciple of Jesus will therefore be eager to learn more and more and to gain an ever deeper understanding of God's truth so that he too will be able to bring out of his storeroom new treasures as well as old. He will want to learn more so that he will be prepared for every opportunity that his Savior lays before him. Christian training does not stagnate, but prepares us to share the precious message of the gospel with others.

Homiletical Suggestions

Our text consists of parables instructing us about the kingdom of heaven. The kingdom of heaven means God's activity of calling sinners to salvation through the gospel. The first two parables speak of how precious that message of salvation is. They tell us that it brings joy and dominates the believer's life. It changes him. It becomes more important to him than anything else.

The parable of the net contains a warning about hypocrisy. It tells us that being a Christian involves more than externals. Being a Christian involves the heart. God isn't looking for outward motions, but for inner repentance.

The final parable teaches us about the purpose and effect of training in God's truth. We are trained so that we can teach others. The more we learn of God's truth, the better prepared we will be to carry out the task he has assigned to every Christian, the privilege of sharing the message of salvation with all mankind. Using the gospel's call as our theme, we can develop the other thoughts of the text under it in this way:

Listen to the Gospel's Call!

1. In true repentance (vv. 47-50)
2. With true appreciation (vv. 44-46)
3. For true service (vv. 51,52)

We might also use the warning against hypocrisy in the parable of the net as our theme and approach the text in this way:

Beware of Hypocrisy!

1. Treasure the gospel (vv. 44-50)
2. Share it with others (vv. 47-52)

Since this text contains so much material, the preacher may wish to use only a portion of the text. The first two parables suggest this outline:

The Gospel Is Your Greatest Possession

1. Recognize its value (vv. 44a,45,46a)
2. Treasure its worth (vv. 44b,46b)

As stated above, the parable of the net contains a warning against hypocrisy and offering mere lip service. That warning needs to be sounded from time to time because so many today deny the reality of hell and eternal punishment. It also needs to be sounded lest, because of the hustle and bustle of modern society, our people lose sight of their calling as Christians and the temporary nature of this life. For none of us know when we will die nor when the last day will be. Our time of grace will not go on forever. God's verdict on Judgment Day will be final. We can issue that warning in this way:

Make Use of Your Time of Grace!

1. Judgment Day is coming (vv. 47-49a)
2. Unbelievers will be punished (vv. 49,50)

Since the text is basically a warning, the preacher will also want to stress the certainty of salvation for all who believe.

Verse 52 of our text reminds us that our Savior instructs us not only for our own sake, but so that we might also instruct others. The word "instructed" in the first part of the verse assumes that instruction has been given. For many of our people their formal religious training really ends when they are confirmed. They need to be encouraged to search ever deeper into the truths of the Holy Scriptures.

Others are content with knowing that they are saved through faith in Jesus, but don't always remember to share that precious message with others. We will want to encourage them, too. We offer this outline:

Dispense God's Treasures!

1. Be prepared to share (vv. 52a)
2. Be willing to share (vv. 52b)

ELEVENTH SUNDAY AFTER PENTECOST

The Scriptures

Old Testament — *Isaiah 55:1-5*
Epistle — *Romans 8:35-39*
Gospel — *Matthew 14:13-21*

The Text — Matthew 14:13-21

Jesus' great miracle of feeding the five thousand is recorded not only in Matthew, but also in the other three Gospels (Mk 6:30-44; Lk 9:10-17; Jn 6:1-14). The details in each account provide us with a very complete picture of the setting for this miracle. According to John's inspired account the Jewish Passover Feast was near, which would mean that the miracle took place about a year before our Lord's death. John the Baptist had been beheaded by King Herod. Jesus had just received this sad report from John's disciples. He had sent out the Twelve in groups of two on an evangelism program. They had now returned, no doubt anxious to tell their Master all that they had done in his name.

This great miracle marks a new period in Jesus' public ministry. He would still meet the crowds to teach and to heal, but now more and more he would withdraw to remote places with his disciples and gradually prepare them for the climax of his mission in this world —his death on a cross to redeem sinful mankind! The main purpose of every one of the Savior's miracles was to prove that he was indeed the Son of God, and yet each miracle is unique. This great miracle once again displays the great love of Jesus Christ — great love that provides food which meets the needs of both soul and body.

> v. 13 — *When Jesus heard what had happened, he withdrew by boat privately to a solitary place. Hearing of this, the crowds followed him on foot from the towns.*

After everything that has happened Jesus wants to spend quiet time alone with his disciples. No doubt, this was quiet time to rest, but it was also time for private teaching and instruction. How important it is for all of us in our lives as Christians to spend time alone with our Lord Jesus for quiet reflection and private meditation upon his word. The solitary place to which Jesus and his little group withdrew was probably in the neighborhood of Bethsaida located on the northeastern shore of the Sea of Galilee.

People from all the little towns and villages along the more populated western shore of the Sea of Galilee walked around the northern shore of the lake just to be with Jesus. Perhaps it was just because most of them were impressed with his miracles that they were willing to brave any obstacles to be in his company. Yet there is a lesson for us in their zeal to be with Jesus. We so often can find all kinds of reasons and excuses not to be in the company of our Savior.

v. 14 — *When Jesus landed and saw a large crowd, he had compassion on them and healed their sick.*

Jesus was in this solitary place for rest and quiet time with his disciples. Yet when he sees this large crowd with men, women and children in it, as well as many who were sick, he cannot send them away. He will not tell them to come and see him another time. It says here that when Jesus saw this large crowd, "he had compassion on them." Another excellent translation of the Greek word ἐσπλαγχνίσθη might be "he was filled with tenderness" or "his heart went out to them." It was this compassion and tenderness of Christ that took him to Calvary. In that word we have yet another beautiful picture of Jesus Christ. The way he looks at human beings is so much different from that of any other person. His feelings for sinful mankind are so much more than just sympathy for sick and hungry people.

It says in Mark's account that our Lord had compassion upon this crowd "because they were like sheep without a shepherd" (Mk 6:34). In spite of his need for rest and in spite of the crowd's mostly materialistic motivation for coming to him, Jesus does not turn his back on them. That's because Jesus sees their great spiritual need for him. Not only does he heal their sick (ἀρρώστους = strengthless ones), but it also tells us in Luke that "he welcomed them and spoke to them about the kingdom of God" (Lk 9:11). What an all-sufficient Savior our Jesus is! What an example this is to us as individual Christians and as Christian congregations. Touched by the Savior's love, our hearts must also go out to all those sheep without the Good Shepherd. Here again is a reminder of that great purpose and mission of the Christian's life — to bring that Good Shepherd to every shepherdless sheep.

vv. 15-19 — *As evening approached, the disciples came to him and said, "This is a remote place, and it's already getting late. Send the crowds away, so they can go to the villages and buy themselves some food."*

Jesus replied, "They do not need to go away. You give them something to eat."

"We have here only five loaves of bread and two fish," they answered.

"Bring them here to me," he said.

In John's account of this event we're told that before Jesus began to teach the crowd and to heal their sick loved ones, he presented a question to disciple Philip as to how they would feed such a large crowd. Of course, Jesus already knew what he was going to do. His question was a test of faith not just for Philip, but for all his disciples (Jn 6:5-7). No doubt this question had been carried by Philip to the others. They had talked about it. They had thought it over. Their advice to Jesus was that even though the time was probably already passed when food could be purchased, if Jesus dismissed everyone right now, some might be able to still get to the villages and towns along the more populated region of the lake and buy food for themselves.

Jesus' answer is most striking. He uses the imperative along with the personal pronoun for emphasis: "You give them something to eat." With that answer Jesus seems to have had a couple things in mind. Sad to say, "Don't bother the Master and us" was an all too familiar attitude displayed by the Twelve. Think of the Syrophoenician woman (Mt 15:23) and those parents who brought their little ones to Jesus (Mk 10:13). Jesus was indeed trying to teach the Twelve that this was not God's way of doing things. Christians don't try to get rid of people who are in need — be it spiritually needy people or physically needy people. Jesus also wanted his disciples to come to him for help, to ask, seek, and knock, to claim God's promises for themselves.

Here the disciples disappoint their Master. They seem to have forgotten about all those miracles they had seen their Lord perform, especially the first one in Cana. If Jesus could supply wine for that wedding, could he not also supply food for all these people?

Their answer to Jesus shows a lack of faith: "We have here only five loaves and two fish." That's not only a lack of faith, it's an answer of near despair. What we see here is a reflection of ourselves, isn't it? So many times in our lives we, too, fail to trust the Lord and his promises to help us in all situations. "You give them . . . We have only five loaves and two fish . . . Bring them here to me." The Savior is going to strengthen weak faith by an unforgettable miracle!

vv. 19-21 — *And he directed the people to sit down on the grass. Taking the five loaves and the two fish and looking up to heaven, he gave thanks and broke the loaves. Then he gave them to his disciples, and the disciples gave them to the people. They all ate and were satisfied, and the disciples picked up twelve basketfuls of broken pieces that were left over. The number of those who ate was about five thousand men, besides women and children.*

The greatness and beauty of this miracle is related to us with very simple words. Jesus issues a command for all the people to sit down on the grass. According to Mark 6:40, the people sat down in groups of hundreds and fifties. Jesus says grace. The aorist ἔδωκεν says it all: "He gave"! The disciples were the waiters who served this great feast provided by the Lord.

"They all ate and were satisfied" — all the men, women and children who were there. There was not one who would not eat. There was not one who was not satisfied. The verb ἐχορτάσθησαν originally was used to describe feeding and fattening up animals. That verb emphasizes that after not eating all day these people must have been extremely hungry. That verb also emphasizes the greatness of Jesus' miracle in that everyone's hunger was satisfied. Again the greatness of Jesus' miracle is emphasized by the fact that more food was left over than was there to begin with! Jesus does not want any of his gifts to be wasted and so he has his disciples gather up the leftovers which fill twelve baskets! The tally of those fed also emphasizes the greatness of Jesus' miracle. No less than 5000 had been fed and that was not counting the women and children who were there!

Homiletical Suggestions

Whenever we preach on one of our Lord's miracles, we always find this basic truth: Jesus Christ is not just some wonderful man or some great teacher; Jesus Christ is the one, the only, the true, and the almighty Lord God. That's a truth we want to proclaim to our people over and over again. Each one of Jesus' miracles proves that beyond a shadow of a doubt.

We also look for something special about Jesus in each of his miracles that we can apply to our own lives and to the lives of our hearers. Each miracle in a special way reveals Jesus' feelings for us. Each miracle in a special way is intended to strengthen our faith in him. The feeding of the five thousand does that in a number of ways. It shows Jesus to be our all-sufficient Savior who loves us dearly and who will care for all our needs. Like those disciples, we sometimes forget that. So often we can see all of our problems, but we don't always see that compassionate and all-powerful Savior there, too, who can help us. Many times we forget that he always has and will provide the best solution to what we might view as an insurmountable problem.

This miracle reminds us to "cast all your anxiety on him because he cares for you" (1 Pe 5:7). This miracle also verifies what St. Paul so triumpantly says: "If God is for us, who can be against us? He who did not spare his own Son, but gave him up for us all — how will he not also, along with him, graciously give us all things?" (Ro 8:31,32) This miracle reminds us, too, of what our most important need is and how Christ meets that need. He feeds the souls of this crowd first and then he feeds their bodies. That simple thought of this text emphasizes what Jesus said in his Sermon on the Mount: "Seek first his kingdom and his righteousness, and all these things will be given to you as well" (Mt 6:33). This is the lesson Jesus sought to teach the crowd on that day when he first nourished their souls and then sent them home with happy souls and full stomachs.

That multitude apparently didn't learn that lesson. Later on they wanted to make Jesus their "bread king." Sometimes we don't always learn that lesson, either. Do we always give our soul's welfare priority over everything else in life? So often we can be more concerned about the grocery bills, the rent, and all the other bills than we are with nourishing our souls on the word, growing in our faith, and advancing the kingdom of God.

The one who fed this great crowd with a meager supply of food is the one who still says to us: "I am the bread of life. He who comes to me will never go hungry, and he who believes in me will never be thirsty" (Jn 6:35).

The following outlines are several ways of sharing the beautiful truths of this part of God's word with his redeemed people:

Depend on Jesus to Meet Your Needs!

1. He knows what those needs are (vv. 13-17)
2. He provides for those needs (vv. 18-21)

First Things First

1. Seek the Savior who takes care of spiritual needs (vv. 13,14)
2. Trust the Savior who takes care of physical needs (vv. 15-21)

Christ Is Our Great Provider

1. With a tender heart he has compassion on us (vv. 13-17)
2. With almighty power he meets all of our needs (vv. 18-21)

TWELFTH SUNDAY AFTER PENTECOST

The Scriptures

Old Testament — *1 Kings 19:9-18*
Epistle — *Romans 9:1-5*
Gospel — *Matthew 14:22-33*

The Text — Matthew 14:22-33

Matthew, Mark and John all record this story of Jesus walking on the water, and each of them places it immediately after the feeding of the 5000. Had the disciples understood all that the miracles of the loaves involved, neither his walking on the water nor his calming of the storm, would have startled them so. But as Mark says, "They were completely amazed, for they had not understood about the loaves; their hearts were hardened" (Mk 6:51,52).

John reports the calming of the storm between the feeding of the 5000 and Jesus' sermon on the bread of life. Considering Mark's comment, it is a fitting bridge between the two events.

The 5000 who had been miraculously fed drew the conclusion, "Surely this is the Prophet who is to come into the world" (Jn 6:14). See Deuteronomy 18:15-18 and Psalm 118:26. Although they were right, they were also wrong. Their dreams of a political messiah prompted them to make plans to force Jesus to become another king among the kings of this world. As this groundswell of support for the movement to make him a bread-king gathered momentum, Jesus took swift and decisive action to thwart it.

v. 22 — *Immediately Jesus made his disciples get into the boat and go on ahead of him to the other side, while he dismissed the crowd.*

He refused to become king on the crowd's terms. He knew that this unholy political pressure constituted a real temptation to his disciples. He decided to divide and conquer. "Jesus *made* his disciples get into the boat."

Having separated the disciples from the multitude, he proceeded to disperse the crowd. Divide and conquer once again. Not only was it in the best interest of the people that they be dismissed before they took hasty and drastic action, their intention was also a real temptation to Jesus. It was almost the same as when Satan offered all the kingdoms of this world to him if only Jesus would bow down and worship the Tempter.

The Lord knew that there was more danger to the disciples in the favor of the crowd than in the fury of the storm. In their disappointment that he would not let the crowd press a crown upon his head, they needed to learn that he was already King — only in a far higher sense than they had imagined.

A final reason why Jesus made his disciples get into the boat and why he sent the multitude away was that he wanted to be alone.

v. 23 — *After he had dismissed them, he went up on a mountainside by himself to pray. When evening came, he was there alone*

The Savior sought the solitude of the mountainside in order to calm his own heart and to view the clamor for his kingship in its proper perspective. He had vanquished Satan when that temptation had arisen earlier, but the devil doesn't give up so easily. Jesus had to overcome temptation again and again. Satan knew that he had to defeat him only once. That was the devil's hope and that was Jesus' burden.

But it is not in accord with all we know about Jesus to imagine that he prayed only for himself. His disciples were in danger on the sea. And another storm was churning in their hearts as they pondered the "missed opportunity" of that day.

Very likely Jesus also prayed for those thousands of people who had been more impressed by the miracle of the loaves than by the message he had spoken to them before the meal.

v. 24 — *but the boat was already a considerable distance from land, buffeted by the waves because the wind was against it.*

The Sea of Galilee lies 680 feet below the level of the Mediterranean, surrounded by hills which are especially precipitous on the east side. When the cool wind rushes down from Mt. Hermon (9200 feet) through the narrow passages between the hills and then collides with the warm air rising off the lake, violent tempests result.

The disciples had previously encountered such a storm (Mt 8:23-27) but that had been in broad daylight and Jesus had been with them in the boat. Now the darkness and his absence compounded their fear.

Matthew, who no doubt had vivid memories of being in that boat, says the vessel was "buffeted." The Greek word is a present passive participle, indicating the constant battering the boat had to endure.

vv. 25,26 — *During the fourth watch of the night Jesus went out to them, walking on the lake. When the disciples saw him walking on the lake, they were terrified. "It's a ghost," they said, and cried out in fear.*

Ylvisaker supposes that when Jesus had finished his prayers he began to walk around the sea to meet his disciples on the other side. "The disciples obviously have remained as near to the coast as possible, and Jesus was presumably at this time on the road, not far from the shore line." So it would not have been a great distance for him either to see them or to walk out to them.

Perhaps it seems like "more of a miracle" to imagine Jesus gazing out across the sea from his retreat on the mountainside and then walking some three or four miles on the sea in the wake of the boat. But is the supernatural element diminished if the distance he walked upon the waves was "only" a hundred yards?

Matthew and Mark both mention that Jesus came walking on the water during the fourth watch of the night. If we take the reference to "evening" in verse 23 to mean the beginning of the first watch (6:00 P.M.), the disciples would have been rowing for at least nine hours by the time Jesus came to join them. The fourth watch extended from 3:00 to 6:00 P.M.

Only the basic fact of Jesus' miracle is recorded for us. There is none of the detailed embellishment that is characteristic of mythology. There is no basis in the text for Lenski's vivid description, for example.

The darkness, the late hour, the imminent danger of drowning, the physical exhaustion all combined to arouse a superstitious fear in the disciples' minds when they saw the Lord. They thought they were seeing a ghost.

v. 27 — *But Jesus immediately said to them: "Take courage! It is I. Don't be afraid."*

With only one exception, every time the word θαρσεῖτε occurs in the New Testament Jesus is the speaker. It is one of those beautiful gospel imperatives, an efficacious word that conveys the power needed to obey. When Jesus says θαρσεῖτε his strong word bestows the courage and good cheer it commands.

Perhaps this is a point of contact with the Old Testament reading. When Elijah was feeling frustrated and depressed, God did not come to him in the wind or the earthquake or the fire, but in a still small voice. That gentle whisper encouraged and energized him for the work he still had to do. So also it was not so much the calming of the wind or the rapid transit to shore that revived the disciple's courage, but the word spoken by their Lord. And we today do well to look to the same source for comfort and strength. A spectacular miracle is not to be desired above the simple words of our God (Lk 16:31).

It is difficult to catch the force of the Greek ἐγώ εἴμι in English. The God of Moses' burning bush had come in the person of Jesus of Nazareth to rescue his own.

Fear began when Adam's guilty conscience was vexed by the approaching footsteps of his Creator in the Eden. And ever since, when sinners are suddenly confronted by holiness (be it God himself or one of his angels) fear springs automatically and uncontrollably in the sinner's heart.

Thus our Lord speaks another of his blessed gospel imperatives: "Don't be afraid." It is a present imperative, meaning that they should stop what they were already doing.

v. 28 — *"Lord, if it's you," Peter replied, "tell me to come to you on the water."*

It seems unlikely that we are to read any lingering doubts into the protasis, "Lord, if it's you. . . . " The conditional clause expresses a condition of reality. If Peter had any question in his mind, why would he step overboard?

What motivated Peter? If he was moved by pride or an inflated ego, why would Jesus not only invite him to come but also enable him to walk on the water without sinking? As Hendriksen says, "The very thought, 'If Jesus can walk on the water, so, with strength imparted by him, can I,' is admirable."

v. 29 — *"Come," he said. Then Peter got down out of the boat, walked on the water and came toward Jesus.*

Let us not fail to take note of the fact that Peter did it. However briefly, Peter kept his eyes on Christ and did as Christ was doing. The same Christ encourages us to take up our crosses and follow in his footsteps. It is certain that without him we can do nothing, but with him all things are possible.

Let us also notice that Peter first asked Jesus' permission, and did receive an explicit personal invitation from the Lord before he got out of the boat. This was not the same thing as when the devil tempted Jesus to jump from the pinnacle of the temple.

How did he do it? The Almighty Creator of the water and of the laws of gravity demonstrated his authority over them. To say more would be speculative and fanciful.

vv. 30,31 — *But when he saw the wind, he was afraid and, beginning to sink, cried out, "Lord save me!" Immediately Jesus reached out his hand and caught him. "You of little faith," he said, "why did you doubt?"*

Peter's abrupt shift from fear to faith was just as suddenly reversed once again. "He saw the wind." And how often don't we falter in our faith because the tempests through which we must pass distract us from Jesus and his word?

Since Jesus had invited him to come, it didn't even occur to Peter that he would have to save himself: "Lord, save me!"

Spurgeon's application of this incident bears repeating: "Short prayers are long enough. There were but three words in the petition which Peter gasped out, but they were sufficient for his purpose. . . . Verbiage is to devotion as chaff to the wheat. Precious things lie in small compass, and all that is real prayer in many a long address might have been uttered in a petition as short as that of Peter."

For the third time in this brief pericope Matthew uses the word "immediately." In comparison to the endless hours of rowing that preceded all this action, it must have seemed that once Jesus arrived on the scene everything happened very quickly.

Hendriksen observes, "Strictly speaking it would not have been necessary for Jesus to reach out his hand to rescue Peter. A simple command would have sufficed. But was not the method which the Lord actually used reassuring? Jesus wanted Peter to feel his love as well as to experience his power."

The Scriptures abound with passages that extol the warm and tender touch of our Savior God. See, for instance, Psalm 37:23,24; 91:11,12; Isaiah 40:11; 41:13; 49:16; John 10:27-30.

Jesus gently chides Peter for his "little faith." When we consider that faith as small as a grain of mustard seed will be sufficient to move mountains, we may be inclined to wag an accusing finger at Peter. Pause and ask yourself, "Have I ever walked on water, even briefly?"

Jesus' question was not, "Why did you come?" It was, "Why did you doubt?" Notice that Peter's doubt was only for a moment. As quickly as Jesus' hand restored him, his faith revived. "Why *did* you doubt?" was Jesus' question. With benefit of hindsight it is obvious that there is no good answer to Jesus' question. Why do we doubt him when the winds gust around us? Another name for doubt is worry. Let us meditate on Matthew 6:25-34 and then confidently pray the Fourth Petition

vv. 32,33 — *And when they climbed into the boat, the wind died down. Then those who were in the boat worshiped him, saying, "Truly you are the Son of God."*

They worshiped him by acknowledging him as the Son of God. These and all of his demonstrations of power and grace elicit the same response from us.

Homiletical Suggestions

Practical application of this text are numerous, but we might summarize in this way: since his ascension Jesus has been separated from his church, but he is interceding for us as we go off to face the storms of life and he will come again in power to rescue us before the waves can overwhelm us. Therefore let us be of good cheer and take courage in the knowledge that I AM is with us always. Let us stop fearing the dangers of this world, real as they are, and worship him who alone is worthy to be called the Son of the Most High God.

Since good gospel preaching focuses on Jesus, we suggest the theme:

Jesus Won't Let Go of Your Hand

1. He upholds you in prayer (vv. 22,23)
2. He saves you from death (vv. 24-33)

The point to emphasize is that Jesus' holding on to your hand is what will save you, not your holding on to Jesus' hand. It ought to be a relatively simple matter then to draw parallels between the way he saved the disciples from the storm and the way he guards and protects us from all danger. Then, proceeding from the general to the specific, the story shifts its focus from the Twelve to Peter. Emphasize that Jesus has saved and does care for each of us individually.

Another possibility is to take Peter's prayer as the theme:

Lord, Save Me!

1. Send me away from temptation (v. 22)
2. Pray for me (v. 23)
3. Rescue me from danger (vv. 24-33)

THIRTEENTH SUNDAY AFTER PENTECOST

The Scriptures

Old Testament — *Isaiah 56:1,6-8*
Epistle — *Romans 11:13-15,29-32*
Gospel — *Matthew 15:21-28*

The Old Testament and Epistle readings for the day emphasize that God's plan of salvation includes Gentiles as well as Jews. His saving grace embraces not only the "chosen nation" but also people of all nations. The text from Matthew presents us with evidence from our Lord's ministry that Gentile sinners also have a place at the table — by faith in Christ Jesus.

The Text — Matthew 15:21-28

v. 21 — *Leaving that place, Jesus withdrew to the region of Tyre and Sidon.*

Jesus withdrew from Capernaum for a time. Recent events (the beheading of John, the attempt to make Jesus a king, the growing opposition of the Pharisees) prompted him to seek some quiet time with his disciples. They went to the northwest, to the borders of Galilee and Syrian Phoenicia, where Jesus hoped for some privacy (Mk 7:24, "He entered a house and did not want anyone to know it"). His presence could not be kept secret, however, and the news went out that the miracle-worker from Galilee was there.

v. 22 — *A Canaanite woman from that vicinity came to him, crying out, "Lord, Son of David, have mercy on me! My daughter is suffering terribly from demon-possession"*

A Gentile woman, a native of Phoenicia, came to find Jesus. She waited outside the house, perhaps, and then followed when he went out with some of his disciples. Her petition was a humble cry for mercy, a plea for her daughter's deliverance from the power of an evil spirit. The woman addressed the plea to Jesus as "Lord, Son of David." Whatever she understood of Israel's hopes, whatever she knew of the promised Savior, one thing is clear: she believed that Jesus was he. She believed that he could and would help her.

v. 23 — *Jesus did not answer a word. So his disciples came to him and urged him, "Send her away, for she keeps crying out after us."*

It certainly didn't look like he would help, though; he just kept on walking. She followed, crying out from behind (ὄπισθεν) the group. That bothered the disciples. Maybe they were embarrassed or maybe they wanted to preserve Jesus' privacy. In any case, they urged him to dismiss (ἀπόλυσον) her.

v. 24 — *He answered, "I was sent only to the lost sheep of Israel."*

Finally he spoke, but did not answer either request, hers or the disciples'. He affirmed simply that his personal ministry was to the Jews; he had been sent to seek and save the lost sheep of Israel. Jesus' divine commission called for his work to be carried out in Israel, then carried to all the world through the preaching of the gospel to the Gentiles.

v. 25 — *The woman came and knelt before him. "Lord, help me!" she said.*

Why didn't she give up and go away? Did she sense that Jesus' words were not an absolute refusal to help her? Were her need too great and her faith too strong for her to give up now? She persisted, even throwing herself at Jesus' feet, and pleaded for help from the Lord.

v. 26 — *He replied, "It is not right to take the children's bread and toss it to their dogs."*

On the surface this reply, too, was anything but encouraging. Of course it is not proper or fitting (καλόν, excellent) to take food meant for the children of the household and give it instead to their pet dogs. (Note that the Lord did not use the derogatory term for "dogs" as the Jews did when referring to Gentiles.) It would not be proper, then, to give Israel's blessings to those who do not belong to Israel. Dogs, even pets, have no right to be treated as children. Children sit at the table; dogs sit under it.

v. 27 — *"Yes, Lord," she said, "but even the dogs eat the crumbs that fall from their master's table."*

She reminds us of Jacob, doesn't she? He wrestled with God and said, "I will not let you go unless you bless me." This Gentile woman's faith was strong, and saw the "Yes" that was hidden under the apparent "No." She completely understood and agreed with Jesus' words. Her place was under the table, she admitted, but that did not prevent her from getting the "crumbs," the blessings that Jesus could give her without depriving "the children" of anything. The Lord could answer her prayer without taking any blessing from the Jews.

v. 28 — *Then Jesus answered, "Woman, you have great faith! Your request is granted." And her daughter was healed from that very hour.*

Her under-the-table prayer was answered; her daughter was healed immediately. And Jesus praised her faith as great. It certainly was! She believed in him as the Lord, the promised Son of David. She trusted in his mercy. She admitted her unworthiness. She accepted his word. She believed that he would not refuse her, though she was a Gentile. And this woman of great faith serves as another preview of the harvest from all nations, Gentiles who are children of God by faith in Christ Jesus.

Homiletical Suggestions

This text does not merely teach us about a faith that won't give up, that persists when the apparent answer is "No." The larger meaning of the pericope matches the other readings for the day. It assures us that the Savior who came to the lost sheep of Israel also has other sheep to bring to eternal life. He died for all because God loved the *whole* world, not just part of it. No race or nation or people, nor any individual sinner is excluded. By faith in Christ Jesus sinners are lost sheep no more, but children of God who sit at the table and enjoy the feast of salvation with all its blessings, including the answers to their prayers. The following outline attempts to bring this out:

By Faith in Christ Jesus

1. Gentiles have a place at the table
2. Believers have their prayers answered

If the preacher wished to focus on the great faith displayed by the woman an outline such as this might work:

This Is a Great Faith

1. It humbly comes to Jesus for help (vv. 21-23)
2. It perseveres in seeking a blessing (vv. 24-28)

There also is a mission flavor to the text (thinking of the woman as one who "didn't belong" or who wasn't "one of us") which could be emphasized this way:

There's Bread Enough for All

1. For those who "don't belong" (vv. 21-25)
2. Through faith in Christ Jesus (vv. 26-28)

FOURTEENTH SUNDAY AFTER PENTECOST

The Scriptures

Old Testament — *Exodus 6:2-8*
Epistle — *Romans 11:33-36*
Gospel — *Matthew 16:13-20*

The Text — Matthew 16:13-20

The text records a pivotal point in Jesus' ministry. The dialog reveals a certain level of understanding on the disciples' part. It heralds the moment when Jesus began his patient instruction concerning the mysteries of his suffering and death.

The text's importance is underscored by its being a point of controversy among Christians. The Roman church has used it for centuries to give a scriptural patina to its claims of papal supremacy. In reality this text is a glorious testimony against any reliance on office, form or organization. The blessed happiness and strength of individual believer and corporate church rests on the Father's revelation of his Son. Nothing more, nothing less, nothing else.

v. 13 — *When Jesus came to the region of Caesarea Philippi, he asked his disciples, "Who do people say the Son of Man is?"*

Jesus entered a strongly Gentile region, its main city beautified in Herodian style. This was a setting of royal wealth and power. It was the backdrop for the question concerning messianic hopes of wealth and power.

Jesus' disciples were to answer for "people." They were to give the general opinion concerning "the Son of Man."

With "Son of Man" Jesus was using his favorite self-designation. It put him at one with his followers. He is our brother, born of a woman. It highlighted humble work and service. At the same time, it pointed back to the wondrous prophecy of Daniel and ahead to Jesus' calm affirmation before Caiaphas.

Jesus already knew people's thoughts and ideas about him. His question to the disciples was pedagogical, asked in loving consideration of their need to grow. They would have an opportunity to compare and contrast what they believed about him with what others believed about him. With his question Jesus highlighted the real issue of life. A person's judgment concerning Jesus is eternally important.

v. 14 — *They replied, "Some say John the Baptist and others say Elijah; and still others Jeremiah or one of the prophets."*

Jesus' work had had great success. Everyone was not only speaking well of him but speaking very highly of him. The names show the high regard in which people held him. Two of those names, Elijah and John the Baptist, had messianic connections. All three echoed aspects of Jesus' work. Jesus' disciples baptized as John had, and he himself called people to repentance. Like a modern day Elijah, Jesus was a man of prayer and a great miracle worker. He took issue with the false religions of his day. Already the authorities had turned against him and he had no place to lay his head. He was another suffering prophet like Jeremiah.

All very complimentary ideas, they all fell short of the mark. These opinions indicate that there was no reliable following of Jesus outside the circle of the disciples. Jesus the prophet, rabbi, religious leader. Even in our day few people have anything bad to say about our Jesus. Sadly, they never want to say quite enough.

v. 15 — *"But what about you?" he asked. "Who do you say I am?"*

A short verse but a very vivid one. In this setting of Gentile splendor, Jesus heard about the prevailing religious opinion. He now asked his disciples very directly about their convictions. There was no opportunity for them to hide behind the opinions of others.

vv. 16,17 — *Simon Peter answered, "You are the Christ the Son of the living God." Jesus replied, "Blessed are you, Simon, son of Jonah, for this was not revealed to you by man, but by my Father in heaven."*

Simon was the spokesman. Here he is already identified as Peter, "the rock." The Gospels show that he was anything but rock-like. His emotions often overwhelmed him and his actions often belied his nickname. It was the blessing of the Father that would turn him into a pillar of the church.

His confession of Jesus as Christ is intensified by "Son of the living God." Not only did Peter identify Jesus with a religious title that went beyond the prevailing views, he showed that he now perceived it in a deeper way. The disciples would still have problems with the political idea of Messiah, but they had learned to see that Jesus was much more than that.

The title Christ incorporates the three principal public offices of Israel: priest, prophet and king. The Christ would indeed be the "Anointed One," anointed with the Spirit and with power. The title held before the Jewish hearer the promise of the great hero of redemption. God would work through the Christ to free his people.

Peter goes on: "the Son of the living God." Not simply Son of Man but also Son of God in a wondrous sense. God is active and living in his Son. How fully the disciples understood the incarnation at this time we cannot say. The exaltation of the Lord and the full revelation of Pentecost had not yet occurred.

Jesus' reaction to this confession is very pointed. You are blessed, happy in a specifically spiritual sense. Jesus is expressing satisfaction with the quality of Simon's faith. Simon has been given a right conception of the title "Messiah."

Simon has been blessed by revelation. Flesh and blood did not inform him of Jesus' identity. Peter did not reason it out for himself. This knowledge was revealed by God. Simon's happiness is a gift from God.

The phrase "my Father in heaven" points both to Jesus' unique identity and to the source of Peter's information.

v. 18 — *"And I tell you that you are Peter, and on this rock I will build my church, and the gates of Hades will not overcome it."*

Here is a ringing promise to Peter and to the church. Much has been written about πέτρος, a rock, and πετρά, the larger boulder or ledge. To bring out the sense the verse might be freely translated: "And I say to you, you are called 'sturdy,' and on this 'strength' I will build my church and it will overcome all the powers of hell." It is impossible to separate Peter and his confession.

It is this confession that is the strength of the ἐκκλησία. The word was used several times in the Septuagint to denote the people of Israel (1 Kgs 8:65; Dt 31:30, et al). Christ's church, the true Israel, will be built on Peter's confession and built by him whom Peter confessed.

Nothing will overcome it. It has the strength of God himself to overcome the gates of Hades. "Gates" is a picture of all the power, durability and dignity of a kingdom. Hades is the realm of death. It does not always mean "hell" but here, where it connotes opposition to the church of Christ, it has that meaning. Hell will not win the final victory over the church. Jesus doesn't say that there will not be sorrow, danger and pain for the church. He does say that the final victory will go to "the called out," those who have been blessed by the Father to see Jesus as their life and hope.

v. 19 — *"I will give you the keys of the kingdom of heaven; whatever you bind on earth will be bound in heaven, and whatever you loose on earth will be loosed in heaven."*

It should be noted immediately that this is the same privilege granted to all of the disciples in Matthew 18:18 and John 20:21,22. The office of the keys is the use of the law and the gospel. The binding key is the harsh preaching of the law to sinners. The loosing key is the gospel in word and sacrament. These are the keys to the kingdom of heaven, that is, to God's gracious rule in our hearts and lives.

There is no higher freedom than to be a forgiven sinner. There is no harsher prison than to be bound under guilt and condemnation. The use of the keys affects a person's eternal destiny. Tremendous power and privilege has been given to men. What human being could ever hope to wield these keys without the blessing of God?

v. 20 — *Then he warned his disciples not to tell anyone that he was the Christ.*

Jesus now warns his disciples, all of them and not only Peter. This certainly implies that Peter's confession was the confession of all. Surprisingly the warning is not to repeat that beautiful confession. They are not to say that Jesus is the Christ. There were to be no hasty new recruits drawn by their own false hopes and ideas concerning the Messiah.

The disciples are not told to avoid the truth. They are told not to use that specific expression of the truth. Satan had warped this truth that Jesus is the Christ. It meant something far different to those who had not been blessed by the Father. Its use could only lead them further down the road of religious error to their eternal harm. It was Jesus' constant loving concern for souls that led to this prohibition.

Later, after the agony of the cross had washed away misconceptions of the word, they would hail him again as Christ. The church would be called "Christian," for it is built on Jesus who is the Christ.

Homiletical Suggestions

The Old Testament reading sandwiches a ringing proclamation of the saving work of God between repetitions of his name, "the LORD." The Epistle reminds us that our God does not work according to the thoughts and ideas of men. These are two key points stressed by the Gospel.

Our text brings us several crucial doctrines. It deals with our knowledge and convictions concerning Jesus. Not every good opinion concerning Jesus is valid or of saving significance.

The text presents the real authority of the church. It is the Father's revelation in men's hearts through the word.

The text also looks at the work and goal of the church. What are we to be doing for people in our congregations and in the world? The work of forgiving and retaining sins is rarely eye-catching or impressive. Yet it is just this work that is crucial to the beginning and the strengthening of people's faith.

These three concepts make this a joyously Lutheran text. The centrality of Christ, the authority of the word and the true work of the church all remind us of those teachings which not only set us apart from other Christians but are also the source of such great comfort and joy. Each of these relate to the others. Each may suggest a useful theme.

Stressing our need of accurate knowledge about Jesus and our responsibility to confess him:

Let Us Confess Christ Clearly

1. The content of our confession (vv. 13-16,20)
2. The source of our confession (v. 17)
3. The result of our confession (vv. 18,19)

Looking at the activity and work of an individual Christian and of the church:

The Church's Power to Do Its Work

1. It lies in the confession of Christ (vv. 13-17)
2. It lies in the authority of the keys (vv. 18-20)

Finally, dealing with the historic point of controversy over this text:

The Church's Authority Comes from the Word

1. It confesses Christ (vv. 13-17,20)
2. It uses the keys (v. 19)
3. It will never be overcome (v. 18)

FIFTEENTH SUNDAY AFTER PENTECOST

The Scriptures

Old Testament — *Jeremiah 15:15-21*
Epistle — *Romans 12:1-8*
Gospel — *Matthew 16:21-26*

The Text — Matthew 16:21-26

Verses 21-28 of Matthew 16 build on the foundation of verses 13-20. Peter has just confessed Jesus as "the Christ, the Son of the living God" (16:16). Jesus now explores the implications of that confession by setting forth his job description as Messiah. He thereby aims to correct the misconceptions the disciples have about the Messiah, as well as to inform them of the true nature of discipleship. Taken as a whole, 16:13-28 provides a vivid summary of the nature of the kingdom of God.

v. 21 — *From that time on Jesus began to explain to his disciples that he must go to Jerusalem and suffer many things at the hands of the elders, chief priests and teachers of the law, and that he must be killed and on the third day be raised to life.*

The words "Jesus began" signal a shift in the scope of his ministry and in the knowledge imparted to the disciples. From now on the cross would loom larger and larger on the horizon and his disciples needed to know that. Jesus had made several veiled references to his death and resurrection before this (9:15; 12:39; 16:4), but this is the first time he spells it out in unmistakable language.

Verse 21 continues a discussion concerning Jesus' identity. The Father had just revealed to Peter that Jesus was the Messiah. Now the Lord continued the revelation by explaining to the disciples the Father's will regarding the Messiah. That they all needed to hear these words is shown by the rest of the story.

Jesus must travel to Jerusalem to suffer, die and rise again. Although he is not specific about the exact nature of his death, verse 24 certainly implies death by crucifixion.

He must (δεῖ) go. There were no other options. Jesus had come for the express purpose of carrying out his Father's will (Jn 4:34), so to Jerusalem he must go to die. His disciples needed to understand that behind the historical events which were to unfold, there stood a plan, unrecognizable to human eyes, but divinely inspired nonetheless. It mattered not to Jesus that everyone else, including his disciples, had completely different expectations about the Messiah; it was what his Father wanted that mattered.

It was also necessary for Jesus to go that he might fulfill the prophecies of the Scriptures concerning the Messiah. The events of Jesus' passion bring to mind the words of Isaiah 53. At Jesus' baptism the Father identified Jesus as the Servant foretold by Isaiah (cp. Mt 3:17 and Is 42:1). Now Jesus must fulfill all the prophecies spoken of the Servant.

v. 22 — *Peter took him aside and began to rebuke him. "Never, Lord!" he said. "This shall never happen to you!"*

Peter took the initiative in reacting to Jesus' passion prediction just as he was the first to answer Jesus' question, "Who do you say I am?" It appears as if Peter thought Jesus' previous words (vv. 18,19) conferred a special privilege upon him. He shows great familiarity with Jesus. As if by a right of his own, Peter leads Jesus aside to set him straight on the agenda for the Messiah.

The "never, Lord!" of the NIV translates the Greek ἵλεώς σοι, κύριε: "May God have mercy on you, Lord." In this exclamation Peter called upon God to shield Jesus from this awful fate. Then in the strongest negation possible, Peter emphasized that this horrible prediction of Jesus simply cannot be true. The word ἐπιτιμάω indicates that Peter took it upon himself to teach and admonish Jesus. Both his attitude and his words indicated that Peter had stepped way out of line.

No doubt Peter's (as well as the rest of the disciples') thoughts on the Messiah were conditioned by the popular misconceptions of the day. See Acts 1:6, for example. Peter did not grasp at all the implication of Isaiah 53 for the Messiah's program of ministry. It was inconceivable that the Messiah's career should end in this fashion. The passion was simply to be ruled out.

The disciples' beliefs at this time would fit very nicely into what Luther called a theology of glory. Such a theology insists that if we are obedient, God will bless us with career advancement, financial success and air-conditioned dog houses. This kind of thinking longs for human triumph and revolts at the cross. Peter's apparent thinking was: "Surely God does not want you to sacrifice your life. What good are you to him then? Follow the Lord, but at all costs, save your life."

We should note that Peter was acting on good intentions. He obviously loved his Lord. But his love was misguided and very much in need of correction.

v. 23 — *Jesus turned and said to Peter, "Get behind me, Satan! You are a stumbling block to me; you do not have in mind the things of God, but the things of men."*

Jesus recognizes the devilish trap set by Satan and deals decisively with it. The Lord's manner of handling temptation serves as a great model for us. He does not dilly-dally with sin. The most effective way to handle temptation is to immediately get it out of your sight, put it behind you, so you do not see or think about it any more. The longer we entertain the temptation in our minds, or keep it before our eyes, the greater the danger of caving in. The stronger the temptation, the more severely we need to treat it (5:29,30).

If it was the Father's will that Jesus go to the cross, then the devil would try his hardest to prevent that. To entrap (σκάνδαλον) Jesus in sin would cause his mission to fall.

Jesus would have none of it. He answers in a way reminiscent of the earlier temptation (4:10). In his words Jesus sets the things of God in opposition to the things of men. This places the things of men very much in the realm of the demonic. Peter was merely expressing the popular views of his day. But the source of such thinking originates in sinful human nature, a powerful ally of Satan. Satan prompts the sin-infected human mind into producing ideas that may look innocent enough, and even good at first glance, but in reality are diametrically opposed to the will of God.

The treacherous aspect of this temptation lay in the fact that it came from a dear friend. To oppose the Father's will made Peter an agent of Satan. Peter may have been an unwitting pawn of the devil, but that just made him all the more dangerous.

Very often the toughest temptations come from our friends, not our enemies. They care about us and so attempt to deflect perils which may be placed in our path by the will of God. Friends hate to see loved ones suffer. They may suggest the easier road, the one free of hardship and pain. Their motive is similar to Peter's: A love more concerned for our comfort than our character.

Jesus' answer illustrates the absolute necessity of placing God above all else, including the closest human relationship. That principle holds true even if a relationship unravels at the seams. For Jesus there was only the will of God to perform. Note that Jesus does not justify the ways of God to man. He simply affirms his Father's will and his intention to do it.

With these words Jesus puts Peter back in his place as a disciple. Before Peter spoke words inspired from heaven; now his thoughts were inspired by hell. A few moments ago, Peter was fit for leadership in the church; now he is out of line and must drop back to the rear. Before he was a building block in the foundation of the kingdom; now he is a stumbling block in Christ's way. Peter was to be part of the foundation, not part of the cornerstone.

Ignorance of the Messiah also meant ignorance of the true nature of discipleship. Jesus now goes on to open his disciples' eyes on that matter.

vv. 24-26 — *Then Jesus said to his disciples, "If anyone would come after me, he must deny himself and take up his cross and follow me. For whoever wants to save his life will lose it, but whoever loses his life for me will find it. What good will it be for a man if he gains the whole world, yet forfeits his soul? Or what can a man give in exchange for his soul?"*

Although faith can only come from above, and not from flesh and blood (v. 17), discipleship involves a lot of effort on our part. θέλω indicates an act of the will — we want to do it. Once the Father has worked faith in Jesus' sacrificial life and death, his Spirit empowers us to pattern our lives after Jesus. God will not force us to follow him; warmed by his love, we want to do it.

The aorist tenses of the verbs ἀπαρνέω and αἴρω indicate the decisive nature of discipleship. Once and for all you say good-bye to yourself. Once you pick up your cross you never put it down. And (note the present) you keep on following Jesus. Discipleship is not an on-again-off-again affair, something you do in a burst of enthusiasm or only when you feel like it. It means following Jesus with dogged endurance, maintaining your loyalty to the end.

Following Jesus means to completely lose sight of self and your own interests and to focus your attention entirely on him. There can be no detachment in being one of Jesus' disciples. To depend solely on the Lord for salvation also means to follow him exclusively, up to and including the cross.

The cross which Jesus speaks of surely implies his crucifixion. Commitment is put in terms of a death march. People often speak of any kind of affliction as a cross. Here Jesus clearly uses the term to refer to the persecutions, troubles, distresses and shame that come our way precisely because we are following him in doing the will of God. If necessary, we too will follow him to the cross. Peter was to live to see these words fulfilled in his own death.

Jesus goes on to say that losing your life is an absolute prerequisite of discipleship. You cannot have one without the other.

Jesus pictures a scene before an earthly court where a person must make a decision about Jesus. To deny him to save your physical life results in the loss of true life within the kingdom. When you give no thought to your earthly life by confessing Jesus and risking the death that follows, you find life within the kingdom.

The choice may not always be so drastic, but the principle remains the same. In verse 25 Jesus contrasts life lived on earth with life in the kingdom. If we play for safety in this life by conserving nad enhancing physical life at all costs, we lose real life in God's kingdom. If we give no heed to the safety and security of this life, giving ourselves in total abandon to the will of God, we shall find real life in Jesus within his kingdom. Temporal loss for eternal gain is a law of Christian existence. Moreover, he is happiest, not who possesses the most, but who is possessed by Christ.

In verse 26 Jesus transfers a proverbial expression about the supreme value of natural life to eternal life. If, as the current understanding went, the loss of human life cannot be compensated for by the whole world, how much more is that true of real life, eternal life. The condition Jesus sets forth is an imaginary one. Let's suppose you could gain the whole world (as the devil once offered to Jesus), and in the process bartered away your soul as payment. Have you not suffered infinite loss rather than gain?

"What can a man give in exchange for his soul?" (v. 26) Jesus' death on the cross is the only acceptable ransom or exchange for our souls (20:28). If we will not receive Jesus' ransom on the cross and the cross bearing way of life that goes with it, there is nothing else we can give in exchange for the salvation of our souls. By his death on the cross, Jesus laid claim to the souls of all humanity. There is nothing we can give in exchange for our souls other than surrendering them to Jesus in faith and discipleship.

The Gospel lesson is complemented very nicely by the thoughts expressed in the Old Testament lesson and the Epistle. Jeremiah, in a parallel to Peter, objects to his "cross," the humiliation, the pain, the loneliness he was enduring because he was following God's will. The Lord in effect says, "Jeremiah, there is no other way." In the beginning verses of Romans 12:1-8, Paul speaks of cross bearing in terms of offering ourselves as living sacrifices to God. This means rejecting the world (the things of men) so that God can transform us to follow his will (the things of God).

Homiletical Suggestions

Peter did not understand God's will concerning the work the Messiah was to accomplish. The same held true of his conception of discipleship. The same holds true for very many today. Since job descriptions are a popular way for defining the scope of a person's duties, this could provide the framework for a sermon.

The Divine Job Description

1. For Christ: Dying while on a cross (vv. 21-23)
2. For Christians: Dying while carrying a cross (vv. 24-26)

"No pain, no gain," is often heard in training for various athletic competitions. There is the pain of injuries, the strain of all out exertion, the grueling regimen of honing muscles to the peak of perfection. Those who prefer the creature comforts of life will never make it. These same truths apply to us as Christians. No less effort is required.

No Pain, No Gain

1. The things of men: No pain is gain (vv. 21-23)
2. The things of God: Gain only through pain (vv. 24-26)

People are often looking for practical pointers for dealing with temptation. There is no better example than that of Jesus in these verses. This sermon could also develop the thought of Satan using friends as tools to tempt us. A possible theme here could be:

Keep The Devil Out Of Your Life

1. Watch warily for Satan (he can use your closest friend) (vv. 21-23)
2. Deal decisively with temptation (no dilly-dallying allowed) (v. 23)
3. Follow faithfully after Jesus (that is the remedy for keeping Satan out!) (vv. 24-26)

A popular game for children is that of "Follow the Leader." A leader is chosen and the rest of the children imitate his actions. The unquestioned leader for the Christian is Jesus. We need to follow him even when the will of God seems strange or alien to our natural way of thinking.

Follow the Leader

1. In accepting the will of God (vv. 21-23)
2. In giving your life to God (vv. 24-26)

SIXTEENTH SUNDAY AFTER PENTECOST

The Scriptures

Old Testament — *Ezekiel 33:7-9*
Epistle — *Romans 13:1-10*
Gospel — *Matthew 18:15-20*

The Text — Matthew 18:15-20

The Good Shepherd loves and cares for all — the sheep who are in his flocks (Jo 10:14), the sheep who are not yet of his flock (Jo 10:16), and the sheep who are wandering from his flock (Mt 18:12-14). As the Good Shepherd loves and cares for all, so he bids us love and care for all. In this text he tells us what we are to do, and how we are to do it, in order to restore the wandering sheep. He also gives us gracious promises of his blessing, so that we will not neglect this work but gladly obey his commands and minister in Christlike love to those who have sinned.

v. 15 — *"If your brother sins against you, go and show him his fault, just between the two of you. If he listens to you, you have won your brother over."*

Who is the object of Jesus' concern in this text? Not the unbeliever, but the "brother" — i.e., a brother in the Lord, a fellow member of the church.

Under what circumstance are we to go to our brother? When he has sinned. Jesus' concern is not that we reform a brother's irritating habits or change his quirks of personality. His concern is that we go to him when he has sinned. This is sin which is open and unrepented. Ylvisaker calls it an "actual, evident, notorious sin against a certain word of God."

Since Jesus tells us to go to the brother privately, the sin is probably not a matter of public knowledge. Public sin can and should be dealt with publicly (see 1 Cor 15:1-5; Ga 2:11-14). However, even in the case of public sin there is ample opportunity for private administration of law and gospel.

The words εἰς σὲ are textually uncertain. Their presence or absence does not affect substantively the meaning of the verse. Every sin is a sin against the Lord, and ultimately every sin against the Lord is also a sin against the Lord's people. With respect to my Christian responsibility, it matters not whether the brother has robbed my house or my neighbor's. His sin is damaging — to himself, to the name of Christ, and to all who bear the name of Christ. In either case, I must go to him.

῞Υπαγε means that we are not to ignore the sin. Don't expect it to go away by itself. Don't say you'd rather not get involved. Don't wait for the brother to come to you. Jesus says: "Go." And we will go, if we take seriously our Lord's command, and if we acknowledge the soul-destroying nature of sin. Later in the verse Jesus speaks of winning the brother over. His word κερδαίνω is used also in 1 Corinthians 9:19-22 and 1 Peter 3:1, in regard to those who were spiritually lost. The Apostle James teaches that to turn a sinner from the error of his way is to save him from death (5:19,20).

How often we are to go Jesus does not say. Go until we have won the brother, or until our private efforts prove to be ineffective and the assistance of others is needed.

Nor are we to talk about this sin with others. Christian love demands that we keep the matter private and speak with the brother privately.

And what is our purpose in going? ῎Ελεγξον means to rebuke and convict. See John 8:46, where it is translated "prove me guilty." See also 1 Corinthians 14:24. Lead him to confess his sin and repent! Our sole purpose is to regain the erring brother — to restore a wandering sheep.

With the future condition ("If he listens to you . . . ") Jesus indicates that there is good probability that the brother will listen. Brothers and sisters in the Lord are sinners who sin against one another. But we should have positive expectation that a loving rebuke will lead to confession and repentance.

> v. 16 — *"But if he will not listen, take one or two others along, so that 'every matter may be established by the testimony of two or three witnesses.' "*

It may be that the brother will not listen and repent. But we should not give up. Recall the Lord's words in Matthew 23:37 and Luke 13:8. Rather, says Jesus, we should bolster our admonition with the testimony of one or two others.

These may be helpful in several ways. First, for various reasons the erring brother may be unwilling to listen to me but willing to listen to others. Second, their presence and consent adds weight to the testimony that the brother has sinned and must repent. Third, should it become necessary to bring the matter before the entire congregation these companions will be able to testify concerning the erring brother's obstinacy.

v. 17 — *"If he refuses to listen to them, tell it to the church; and if he refuses to listen even to the church, treat him as you would a pagan or a tax collector."*

By "the church" Jesus means the gathering of believers of which all the parties are members. There is no higher earthly court of appeal; the church is the "court of last resort" (Ylvisaker). The assembly of believers will hear the case and plead with the sinner. Although he did not listen to the one or two or three, in the end he may be brought to repentance by the united testimony of his fellow church members. This is the result which God and God's people desire.

He may, however, refuse to listen even to the church. If the church's ministry is rejected, the church (σοι = first the accuser, but then also the entire church) must treat the sinner as a pagan or a tax collector — that is, as one outside the kingdom of God, as an unbeliever. Excommunication is and must be an act of love. It is the strongest possible preaching of the law, done with holy intent to lead the sinner to recognize and repent of his sin, so that "his spirit [may be] saved on the day of the Lord" (1 Cor 5:5).

Note also: To treat the sinner as a pagan or tax collector is not to treat him rudely or scorn him. We should do as Jesus did. He loved pagans and tax collectors even as he loved his disciples. In love he preached to them and in love he prayed for them. The excommunicated sinner needs the love of Christ's people now more than ever!

v. 18 — *"I tell you the truth, whatever you bind on earth will be bound in heaven, and whatever you loose on earth will be loosed in heaven."*

The Lord will not have anyone regard lightly the actions of his church. He therefore solemnly affirms this truth (Ἀμὴν λέγω ὑμῖν), that the church's actions on earth are fully backed by the Father in heaven. Ὅσα, a neuter plural, refers to the sinful words or actions: these are bound to the impenitent sinner, but graciously released from the penitent sinner. Δήσητε and λύσητε are second person plural: whether binding or loosing, the members of the church act together and in unity.

Ἔσται δεδεμένα and ἔσται λελυμένα are periphrastic future perfects. The normal force of the perfect should be observed. Heaven's action is not subsequent to the church's action. All sins which the church through its ministry of the keys either retains or forgives "will have been bound" and "will have been loosed." Through the ministry of law and gospel Christ's church withholds forgiveness from the impenitent and grants forgiveness to the penitent; and what the church does on earth is in perfect harmony with heaven and indeed has already been accomplished in heaven.

v. 19 — *"Again, I tell you that if two of you on earth agree about anything you ask for, it will be done for you by my Father in heaven."*

Perhaps too frequently in our ministry to sinners the essential element of prayer is lacking. To guard against this failure Jesus adds another word of instruction (πάλιν, in the sense of "furthermore"). We are to go and rebuke; we are to take others along; we are to tell the congregation: and all this we are to do imploring the blessing of the Father, who even more than we desires the sinner's salvation. As brothers and sisters in Christ, we are to pray together with united mind and spirit (συμφωνήσωσιν). Pray that the Father will enable us to minister in Christian love. Pray that he will give us appropriate words. Pray that the Holy Spirit will work through our words to touch the sinner's heart. And pray with real confidence that the Father hears our prayer and will graciously grant the blessings we seek.

v. 20 — *"For where two or three come together in my name, there am I with them."*

Συνηγμένοι εἰς τὸ ἐμὸν ὄνομα refers not just to believers gathered in a church meeting or worship service. Ultimately the words are descriptive of a relationship, the relationship of branches and Vine, members and Head. They are a simple, eloquent picture of Christ's church: people, whether few or many, united by faith in the saving name of Jesus and by commitment to honor his name in all things. And to complete the picture we see, according to Christ's promise, the Lord himself with and among his people.

So this last verse provides a fitting conclusion to the entire text. Already at the time of the sin (v. 15) Jesus was there (and his honor was at stake). All through the process of seeking after the brother who had sinned (vv. 16-18), Jesus was there and was also seeking. Jesus was there to hear the prayers of his people and grant his blessings of guidance and strength (v. 19). Yes, Jesus is with those who are united in his name and for the sake of his name: and the one who finally rejects the ministry of the church thereby rejects Jesus himself; but the repentant sinner who receives the forgiveness of the church receives the forgiveness of Jesus himself.

Homiletical Suggestions

The Lord's instructions in this text are clear, but all too often the Lord's people fail to obey them. Perhaps our members think of these words as dealing only with official actions of the church. If so, the preacher will emphasize that Jesus is speaking also — indeed, first of all! — about personal ministry. He will point out both the opportunity and the need for Christian brothers to practice an ongoing, daily ministry of law and gospel one to another. He will also seek to provide some strong motivation, so the Lord's people will respond to Jesus' words with willing obedience.

Remember, then, that Jesus' word about going to a sinning brother is a divinely authoritative command. Disciples are not to be in the business of judging our Master's commands: this one he means, and this one he doesn't. The appropriate response is a simple response of faith: "Because you say so, I will do it." (Remember also the example Jesus himself provides. When Peter sinned against him, Jesus didn't fail to act. In love for the sinner, Jesus went to Peter to restore him.)

Many feel that their sins disqualify them from speaking with a brother about his sin. But it was to sinful disciples that Jesus first issued the command "Go." It was as a sinner — a forgiven sinner —that David instructed sinners (Ps 51:13). Awareness of our sin does not disqualify us. Rather, it will prompt us to go in humility. If someone is caught in a sin, Paul says, "restore him gently" (Ga 6:1).

A big obstacle to the practice of brotherly discipline is the fact that many are altogether casual about sin: "So what if my brother is doing such and such? It's no big deal." The urgency of Christ's command stems from the deadly nature of sin. Sin caused Jesus to die, and unrepented and unforgiven sin will cause the brother to die as well. Recall, for example, Galatians 5:19-21; 1 John 1:6; 3:7-10. Will I casually sit by and watch as a brother partakes of spiritual poison?

And there are those who insist: "It's none of my business." Or: "I just don't want to get involved." But the fact is that God has involved us. The Old Testament lesson declares the grim consequences of sin for the sinner, and more: it declares that God will hold accountable the one who fails to warn a sinning brother. If love for our brothers means anything, it means concern for their eternal condition; and that should spur us to prompt action. The Lord is telling us: Yes, you are your brother's keeper.

But the heart of our text is the gospel. Let the gospel be the heart of the sermon, and it will provide positive and powerful incentives to comply with Jesus' instructions. We see the church as the family of the forgiven, people of God with whom the Lord dwells. Once upon a time Jesus died for sinners, and still today as living Lord he ardently desires their salvation. So do not fail to solicit his blessing! Pray for the one who has sinned. Trust that Jesus will hear our prayers and grant wisdom, guidance and strength for our ministry to the sinner.

Further, our text encourages us by holding forth the positive expectation that when we do as Christ commands desired results will occur. Brothers will listen: they will acknowledge their sin and repent (v. 15). Most often church discipline will not reach the stage of formal church action, but will begin and end with brotherly admonition.

And of course: all warning would be wasted effort were it not for the fact that with the Lord there is forgiveness. The joy of this text is that it discloses the deadly nature of sin and at the same time displays the healing balm of forgiveness in Christ. What a grand privilege it is for the people of God to be ministers of the gospel of forgiveness! What a joyous privilege to be representatives of Jesus, who in his place and by his command give his forgiveness to those who had been caught in the deadly trap of sin. The people of God share in his happiness over every sinner who repents.

When brotherly admonition is neglected, the church becomes a haven for impenitent sinners. When brotherly admonition is practiced, the church becomes, as it should be, a hospital for sinners. Through mutual and Spirit-filled ministry the people of God are loosed from the crippling bonds of sin and find healing and restoration in the Savior. Through mutual and Spirit-filled ministry the family of the forgiven becomes a family of the righteous, where the Lord dwells and where the Lord is greatly glorified.

Suggested sermon outlines:

Admonish One Who Has Sinned!

1. Because unrepented sin is soul-destroying (v. 18)
2. Because Jesus desires his salvation (vv. 12-17)
3. Because Jesus will bless our ministry (vv. 19,20)
4. Because Jesus has given us the Keys (v. 18)

Tough and Tender Love for Sinners

1. It will not fail to uphold the law of God (vv. 15-17)
2. It will not fail to offer the fogiveness of God (vv. 18-20)

Our Ministry to One Who Has Sinned

1. The Manner of our Ministry
   A. Minister with due regard for the deadly nature of unrepented sin
   B. Minister in Christlike love for the sinner
   C. Minister with confident prayer for Jesus' blessing
2. The Method of our Ministry
   A. First go alone
   B. If need be, get the help of one or two others
   C. Finally make use of the testimony of the church
3. The Means of our Ministry
   A. Clearly proclaim the law of the Lord
   B. Freely offer the forgiveness of the Lord

SEVENTEENTH SUNDAY AFTER PENTECOST

The Scriptures

Old Testament — *Genesis 50:15-21*
Epistle — *Romans 14:5-9*
Gospel — *Matthew 18:21-35*

The Text – Matthew 18:21-35

Jesus told the familiar parable of the unmerciful servant in response to a specific question from Peter: "How often must I forgive someone who sins against me?" This question did not simply come to Peter out of the blue. It flowed logically and naturally in the discourse between Jesus and his disciples that began at the beginning of chapter 18. Since this text is a part of a larger unit, the preacher will want to be aware of the preceding discussion and how the conversation arrived at the point of Peter's question.

The discussion begins at the start of chapter 18 with another question from the disciples: "Who is the greatest in the kingdom of heaven?" The Savior instantly perceived an underlying misconception about the forgiven sinner's relationship to God and to other believers. Jesus took this opportunity to correct their thinking by discussing a number of related issues, such as forgiveness from God, humility, trust, concern for souls and forgiveness for others. He directed them away from any desire to attain power, position or glory through their relationship with God. He told them clearly in verse 3 that greatness in God's kingdom was to be found in only one way: "Unless you change," he said to them, "and become like little children, you will never enter the kingdom of heaven." True greatness in God's eyes and in God's kingdom is achieved only when a sinner humbly admits his unworthiness and then trusts in God's forgiving power and love in Christ. God measures greatness with a different yardstick than man does.

Jesus then builds on his reference to children to make another related point. Not only will forgiven sinners abandon any hopes for attaining greatness in man's eyes; forgiven sinners will also direct their efforts to helping others attain greatness in God's eyes. Their own gift of forgiveness from God will move them to want others to share — and never to lose — that most precious gift. They will show this desire in two ways. Negatively, they will not want to do anything which will cause another child of God to be harmed in his faith

(18:5-9). Positively, they will want to display the same kind of searching love for sinners that God himself has, as portrayed in Jesus' touching example of the shepherd who goes out to search for one lost sheep (18:10-14).

From here the discussion continues its natural flow. Jesus gives a practical answer to the implied question, "How can we practice that searching love for sinners?" The familiar words of Matthew 18:15-18 follow. Believers who are filled with love for fellow sinners will make repeated and energetic efforts to bring back those who have strayed. Motivated by love for souls and a desire to restore the lost, they will go again and again to admonish and correct. They will even be willing to join with other believers in carrying out the final act of loving discipline known as excommunication. All of this they do in love, all to bring the sinner back to God.

The disciples were absorbing the impact of these words of Jesus when Peter posed another question. The text begins at this point.

v. 21 — *Then Peter came to Jesus and asked, "Lord, how many times shall I forgive my brother when he sins against me? Up to seven times?"*

Peter's question is direct and to the point. How often should he be willing to forgive someone who sins against him repeatedly — perhaps with the very same sin? Is there a point, he wondered, at which he would be justified in refusing to forgive?

Peter is often criticized for his question. The charge is made that he is displaying a legalistic view of forgiveness; that he is too eager to find that point at which his obligation to forgive ceases; that he is taking pride in his magnanimous offer to forgive all the way up to seven times.

It may well be that Peter had some of these thoughts and that his views of forgiveness were off the mark. But a more charitable view of Peter is also open to us. Jesus had just encouraged the disciples to have a searching love for sinners and to be ready to make repeated attempts to bring sinners to repentance. It may well have occurred to Peter that this practice, if faithfully carried out by believers, could easily be abused. A sinner brought to repentance and assured of his forgiveness could easily turn around and sin again — and again. Peter may have been concerned that people could take advantage of God's forgiveness and the forgiveness offered by the brothers they have offended. His question could well have been natural and innocent: "Is there a limit to God's forgiveness? Is there a limit to the times that I should forgive others? At what point am I to say, 'That's enough; I can forgive you no more!'?"

Peter's dilemma is one that all of us have faced. Relationships between sinful people are often marred by sinful words and actions — some recurring over and over again. In every marriage, in every family, in every friendship, Christians will be faced with the situation in which forgiveness is requested of them — again. We, too, may wonder with Peter whether our forgiveness toward others has limits. Our own nature leads us to want to limit forgiveness; other people may encourage us not to let someone take advantage of our willingness to forgive. Since we may find ourselves standing in Peter's shoes, Jesus' answer to Peter is an answer to us and to our hearers.

v. 22 — *Jesus answered, "I tell you, not seven times, but seventy-seven times."*

The Greek words ἑβδομηκοντάκις ἑπτά are translated in the text of the NIV "seventy-seven times." The alternate translation, "seventy times seven," is offered in the footnote. The choice of translation makes no difference; Jesus' point is clear. Forgiveness is not a numbers game; it has nothing to do with keeping score. A *continuing and constant* obligation of love is to be ready to forgive and to forgive again — *with no limits at all.* Jesus then tells a parable to illustrate his point.

vv. 23-25 — *"Therefore, the kingdom of heaven is like a king who wanted to settle accounts with his servants. As he began the settlement, a man who owed him ten thousand talents was brought to him. Since he was not able to pay, the master ordered that he and his wife and his children and all that he had be sold to repay the debt."*

A parable is an extended simile. Jesus often used stories and examples drawn from everyday life to illustrate an important spiritual truth. Keep in mind that most parables have only one major point of comparison. Some minor lessons can sometimes be drawn from the details of the story, but it is usually best not to proceed too far afield from the main point.

In the parable, the king decides that it is time to settle accounts with his servants. The huge sum of money involved (millions of dollars) seems to indicate that this servant was not a slave or a household steward. More likely he was a government official who was subject to the king. His debt was most likely an amount of tribute that he, as a vassal, was obligated to pay his royal superior. For some unexplained reason, the servant was not able to meet his obligation. The king did what he had every right to do: he gave orders for the man, his family and all his possessions to be sold, as partial compensation for the debt.

vv. 26,27 — *"The servant fell on his knees before him. 'Be patient with me,' he begged, 'and I will pay back everything.' The servant's master took pity on him, canceled the debt, and let him go."*

The servant had no other options. He threw himself on the mercy of the king. He promised to repay the debt in full, but the king knew well that it was a debt that could never be repaid. For no other reason than his own kindness and mercy, the king had pity on the servant and canceled the debt. Σπλαγχνίζομαι is a verb that is filled with emotion; it is a feeling of deep, heartfelt compassion and sympathy for a person in trouble. The same word is often used in Scripture to describe the mercy and compassion of God for sinners.

Already it is becoming clear that the story is a picture of God's relationship to the sinner. The preacher is certainly justified in drawing the parallels between the actions of the king and the way that God deals with sinners. The preacher can point to the *enormity* of our debt of sin and guilt before God. He can describe *our inability to repay* such a debt. He can lead his hearers to marvel at the *grace and mercy of God*, who cancels our debt of sin for no other reason than his grace in Christ. And he can point to the *completeness* of the forgiveness which God offers to sinners.

vv. 28-30 — *"But when that servant went out, he found one of his fellow servants who owed him a hundred denarii. He grabbed him and began to choke him. 'Pay back what you owe me!' he demanded.*

"His fellow servant fell to his knees and begged him, 'Be patient with me, and I will pay you back.'

"But he refused. Instead, he went off and had the man thrown into prison until he could pay the debt."

The first servant had received mercy from the master; now he had an opportunity to show the same kind of mercy to a fellow servant. His joy in his own canceled debt should have been boundless. It should have been natural for him to want to show the same kind of love to someone else, especially since the debt owed to him was minuscule compared to what his own debt had been. But the one who had been forgiven much could not find it in his heart to forgive even a little. He demanded payment, and when it was not forthcoming, he exacted the punishment.

vv. 31-35 — *"When the other servants saw what had happened, they were greatly distressed and went and told their master everything that had happened. Then the master called the servant in. 'You wicked servant,' he said, 'I canceled all the debt of yours because you begged me to. Shouldn't you have had mercy on your fellow servant just as I had on you?' In anger his master turned him over to the jailers to be tortured, until he should pay back all he owed.*

"This is how my heavenly Father will treat each of you unless you forgive your brother from your heart."

The injustice and thanklessness of the unmerciful servant was so apparent and so horrifying to the fellow servants that they immediately informed their master. The master was understandably outraged. The servant had every legal right to do what he did. But his action showed an absolute lack of appreciation for what for his own forgiveness. So the master dealt with him according to the servant's own standards. The punishment was severe. But it was fair, and it was deserved.

In a very pointed application to the parable, Jesus says, "This is how my heavenly Father will treat each of you unless you forgive your brother from your heart." God is gracious and merciful. His forgiveness is free and full. This is the positive lesson of thc parable. Those who appreciate God's gift of forgiveness will be more than ready to turn around and forgive those who sin against them. But there is a negative lesson as well. If a forgiven sinner has an unwillingness to forgive, a desire to withhold mercy from others, or a need to seek revenge, it can only mean that God's forgiveness means little to him. In wanting to exact punishment from others, he places himself under the judgment and justice of a holy God.

Homiletical Suggestions

Since this entire section of God's word comprises Jesus' answer to Peter's question, "How often should I forgive my brother when he sins against me?" the theme of the sermon will naturally focus on some aspect of our continuing obligation to forgive others. In general, the parts in the outlines below will all deal essentially with three thoughts: our response to God's full and free forgiveness to us is a willingness to forgive others — thankfully, unconditionally and repeatedly.

The Forgiven Forgive

1. They recognize God's love for them (vv. 21-27)
2. They reflect that love by forgiving others (vv. 28-35)

When Your Brother Sins Against You . . .

1. Forgive thankfully
2. Forgive unconditionally
3. Forgive repeatedly

Forgiveness Has Its Limits

1. Forgive only with the love God has for you
2. Forgive only as often as God forgives you
3. Forgive only as completely as God forgives you

How Can I Ever Forgive You?

1. I will remember the way God forgives me (vv. 21-27)
2. I will respond by forgiving you (vv. 28-35)

EIGHTEENTH SUNDAY AFTER PENTECOST

The Scriptures

Old Testament — *Isaiah 55:6-9*
Epistle — *Philippians 1:1-5,19-27*
Gospel — *Matthew 20:1-16*

The Text — Matthew 20:1-16

The Old Testament reading includes the familiar words, " 'My thoughts are not your thoughts, neither are your ways my ways,' declares the LORD" (Is 55:9). Jesus' parable illustrates that message powerfully: human thinking — "you don't get something for nothing" — is contrasted with the gracious mind and heart of God. Just before Jesus told this parable Peter had unwittingly revealed that his understanding of God's gracious way of dealing with people was still a bit fuzzy, and that he was still thinking in a very human way: "We have left everything to follow you! What then will there be for us?" (19:27) Jesus' reply was that there would, in a sense, be rewards for his disciples. But then he warned that there would be some expectations that would be turned completely upside-down: "But many who are first will be last, and many who are last will be first" (19:30). Then Jesus told this parable to explain how God's thinking and actions produce results that are bitterly disappointing to anyone who is stuck in a purely human mindset, but that are overwhelmingly gratifying to anyone who simply receives God's grace.

vv. 1,2 — *"For the kingdom of heaven is like a landowner who went out early in the morning to hire men to work in his vineyard. He agreed to pay them a denarius for the day and sent them into his vineyard."*

This was a familiar scene in first century Palestine, as it still is in parts of the American southwest: freelance laborers assemble early in the morning at a commonly known location in hope of being hired on for the day, particularly during harvest time. A denarius was a fairly generous although not unusual wage for a day's unskilled labor.

vv. 3-7 — *"About the third hour he went out and saw others standing in the marketplace doing nothing. He told them, 'You also go and work in my vineyard, and I will pay you whatever is right.' So they went. He went out again about the sixth hour and the ninth hour and did the same thing. About the eleventh hour he went out and found still others standing around. He asked them, 'Why have you been standing here all day long doing nothing?' 'Because no one has hired us,' they answered. He said to them, 'You also go and work in my vineyard.' "*

The vineyard owner needed more workers than he had found at dawn, so he went back to look for more at "the third hour . . . the sixth hour and the ninth hour and . . . the eleventh hour," i.e. 9:00 A.M., 12:00 P.M., 3:00 P.M., and 5:00 P.M. Here we start to get a hint of this vineyard owner's unique approach to dealing with his help. There are no recriminations, no questions asked.

"Doing nothing" makes it sound as though they were idlers. Ἀργός really contains the idea of "without work, deprived of work." After the enlarging of the temple under Herod the Great had been completed, many laborers in Jerusalem were left without work. In fact, a relief project employed as many as 18,000 men.

Note that the initiative in the hiring lay with the landowner. This reminds us that the Lord took the initiative in calling Peter and his fellow disciples, just as he took the initiative in calling us.

vv. 8-10 — *"When evening came, the owner of the vineyard said to his foreman, 'Call the workers and pay them their wages, beginning with the last ones hired and going on to the first.' The workers who were hired about the eleventh hour came and each received a denarius. So when those came who were hired first, they expected to receive more. But each one of them also received a denarius."*

Now it becomes clear that this vineyard owner doesn't operate in the usual way — "you do so much for me and I'll do so much for you." What a person deserves is beside the point for him; it's his generous heart that determines what a person gets. In the spiritual realm, in the kingdom of heaven, that fact doesn't go down too well with someone who hasn't had the Holy Spirit work a miracle in his heart, so that he is in agreement with God's heart.

The law (Lv 19:13) required that payment be made for the day's work at sunset. For the last to be paid first is a necessary detail of the story. It allows for the first hired to observe how the last hired were paid. It provides them with the "basis" for their grumbling (vv. 11,12).

vv. 11,12 — *"When they received it, they began to grumble against the landowner. 'These men who were hired last worked only one hour,' they said, 'and you have made them equal to us who have borne the burden of the work and the heat of the day.' "*

As with every parable of Jesus, you don't want to try to assign a specific meaning to every detail of the story; instead, you have to concentrate on the point of comparison. In the case of this parable, it's easy to get sidetracked on the matter of what exactly to say the denarius is. The same denarius is given to those who grumble and those who don't. If we were supposed to understand the denarius to mean salvation, then that would mean that these grumblers are genuine disciples of Jesus and heirs of eternal life. Can you imagine a disciple of Jesus grousing because, say, the thief on the cross receives a place in heaven right alongside a lifelong, hardworking church member?

A Christian is by definition someone whose heart has been changed to accept and rejoice in God's way of dealing with sinful human beings, and therefore someone who is delighted whenever anyone receives God's promise of eternal life, no matter how many years that person gets to live as part of the church militant or how much he accomplishes during that time.

Here is precisely the point that this parable is addressed to: is your heart in tune with the workings of God's heart? Do you expect to receive wages from God for living right, or do you look at yourself as a recipient of God's grace? Rather than representing a specific blessing, such as everlasting life in heaven or the benefits of church membership on earth, the denarius simply represents whatever a person expects to receive from God, whether that be the results of his own efforts, or the results of Jesus' efforts.

Peter's question, "What then will there be for us?" (19:27), revealed that he still had a lot of inclination to think in terms of his own merit when he thought of what he would receive from the Lord. Jesus' reply in 19:28,29 indicated that there are, in a sense, some rewards for believers who struggle to carry out the will of their Lord: there will be degrees of glory (NOT degrees of happiness!) in heaven (v. 28), and there are joys of fellowship with other disciples here on earth (v. 29). And in the next verses of the parable he also points out that there are even, in a sense, rewards for the nominal Christian as a result of his work-righteous efforts — rewards which, however, will turn to ashes in the mouth of the superificial churchgoer.

vv. 13-15 — *"But he answered one of them, 'Friend, I am not being unfair to you. Didn't you agree to work for a denarius? Take your pay and go. I want to give the man who was hired last the same as I gave you. Don't I have the right to do what I want with my own money? Or are you envious because I am generous?' "*

The vineyard owner's statement begins on a somewhat ominous note: he addresses the griper as ἑταῖρε. This word can have either of two opposite connotations, depending on context, like "buddy" or "pal." Normally those words, like ἑταῖρος, indicate special closeness. But they can also be used to indicate the opposite, as in, "Smile when you say that, pal." In 22:12 ("Friend, how did you get in here without wedding clothes?") and 26:50 (Jesus to Judas: "Friend, do what you came for") the word is used with this same kind of ambivalence.

To this griping "friend" the vineyard owner says, "Take your pay (τὸ σόν — what is yours) and go" (ὕπαγε — go away, get out of here). Compare this with what Jesus said about the people who make a public production of praying, fasting and charitable giving (6:2,5,16): "I tell you the truth, they have received their reward in full." The gripers had set their sights fatally low. What they thought they wanted was justice, and in verse 13 the vineyard owner tells them that justice is all they'll get from him: οὐκ ἀδικῶ σε — "I am not being unfair to you." He tells them to take τὸ σόν and get away from him, just as Jesus will say on the last day to those on his left, "Depart from me" (25:41). Compare οὐκ ἀδικῶ σε (v. 13), when the vineyard owner talks about his dealing with the gripers, with ἐγὼ ἀγαθός εἰμι (v. 15) when the vineyard owner talks about his dealing with the latecomers. Those who set their sights merely on receiving justice will, tragically, receive it. Those who don't demand that God give them what's coming to them but instead wait on his goodness will —praise God! — receive it.

In verse 14 θέλω is placed prominently at the beginning of the sentence: no one forces the Lord to administer any blessing because good behavior obligates him to be good the person who behaves himself; the Lord gives his blessings without obligation, as he wishes. If anyone has a problem with the way God carries out his goodness, the problem lies with the eye of the beholder: his eye is πονηρός, evil. The expression "evil eye" is still used in connection with envy and covetousness in Mediterranean lands. A person should not expect God's goodness to conform to our ideas of what is good and fair. Rather, everyone needs to learn about God's grace.

v. 16 — *"So the last will be first, and the first will be last."*

This is a closing warning about how serious a matter it is to be conformed to God's way of thinking. Reject God's way of thinking and, no matter how good your life might look, even if you look like one of the πρῶτοι in terms of how much you've done for the Lord, you'll still end up as one of the ἔσχατοι — in this case, "last" as in, "You lose."

Homiletical Suggestions

The two foci of attention in the parable are the mind of the grumbling laborers and the mind of the vineyard owner. A two part outline based on the vineyard owner's promise would be:

God Says, "I Will Give You What Is Right"

1. What we may think is right (vv. 1,2,10-12)
2. What God considers to be right (vv. 3-9,13-16)

The parable has a warning for everyone whose life is filled with kingdom activities, that we don't start doing everything for its own sake, rather than doing it as an act of submission to the lordship of Jesus. An outline that would cover that warning might be:

As You Do God's Work, Think God's Way!

1. We may think we're earning God's blessings (vv. 1,2,10-12)
2. But God wants to give us what we haven't earned (vv. 3-9,13-16)

Since this parable contrasts natural religion — "I have to earn God's favor" — with the true religion revealed in the Bible, it could lend itself to an evangelism sermon, taking its cue from the wording of 19:30 and 20:16.

Help a Loser Finish First!

1. People who think they're ahead of the game may be coming in dead last (vv. 1,2,10-12)
2. They can become winners if they find out about the mind of God (vv. 3-9,13-16)

NINETEENTH SUNDAY AFTER PENTECOST

The Scriptures

Old Testament — *Ezekiel 18:1-4,25-32*
Epistle — *Philippians 2:1-5(6-11)*
Gospel — *Matthew 21:28-32*

The Text — Matthew 21:28-32

The parable of the two sons and Jesus' explanatory words were spoken on Tuesday of Holy Week. He was addressing the high priests and elders in the temple courtyard after they had questioned him about where his authority came from. Through this parable, Jesus not only shows the Jewish leaders their spiritual shortcomings, but he also shows them that the Father desires their repentance. For we have a God who is not "wanting anyone to perish, but everyone to come to repentance" (2 Pe 3:9).

vv. 28-30 — *"What do you think? There was a man who had two sons. He went to the first and said, 'Son, go and work today in the vineyard.' 'I will not,' he answered, but later he changed his mind and went. Then the father went to the other son and said the same thing. He answered, 'I will, sir,' but he did not go."*

The Lord begins this parable with a standard question, τί ὑμίν δοκεῖ, "What do you think?" It is directed to the Jewish leaders and expects an opinon from them concerning what he is about to say. The manner of asking is not hostile. Jesus had used the same method in discussing matters with his disciples, such as the question of the temple tax in Matthew 17:25.

What follows is a brief parable. A man has two sons. He has a request, an invitation really, for both of them. The invitation is stated in the same way to both young men. And it is preceded with a loving form of address. Τέκνον is the word for "child." It is an affectionate word, much softer than υἱός. The context makes it clear that a male child is being addressed. The father tenderly asks his sons to work in his vineyard that day.

Although the sons are addressed in the same loving way, their responses are poles apart. The first son replies with a flat-out "No." He will not go and work. Later on, he changes his mind and goes to work in the vineyard. Μεταμέλομαι is not quite as forceful a word as μετανοέω, but the meaning is virtually the same. In this verse it means "change one's mind." Later on (v. 32), Jesus will use it again. Then it has the spiritual meaning of "repent."

The second son responds in the opposite way. To his father's request he says, 'Εγῶ, κύριε. Two things can be noted. The ἐγῶ with the absence of θέλω puts the emphasis on the "I." Personally, the son is ready to go. Secondly, he answers by addressing his father as κύριε, sign of respect. The son respects his father's word and is willing to carry it out. Only, he doesn't. Jesus tells us he never got to the vineyard.

vv. 31,32 — *"Which of the two did what his father wanted?" "The first," they answered. Jesus said to them, "I tell you the truth, the tax collectors and prostitutes are entering the kingdom of God ahead of you. For John came to you to show you the way of righteousness, and you did not believe him, but the tax collectors and prostitutes did. And even after you saw this, you did not repent and believe him."*

Once the parable was spoken, it was time for Jesus to make sure the Jewish leaders understood the application. Instead of repeating his question, "What do you think?" and so giving them the opportunity to state opinions, Jesus asks a pointed question. Literally, the question is, "Which of the two did the will of the father?" In essence, this is the larger question Jesus wants to get at. "Who is doing the will of the heavenly Father?" The leaders naturally point to the first son as the one who did what his father wanted.

Immediately Jesus brings the truth home to these leaders. He shows them that they are not the first son, but the second, and that they are not doing the will of the heavenly Father. Jesus says,' Αμὴν λέγω, "Truly I say to you," or as the NIV translates, "I tell you the truth." Jesus used that formula to introduce a solemn declaration. What follows is a truth intended to make these leaders pause and take a good, honest look at their relationship to the true God.

The truth is, "the tax collectors and prostitutes are entering the kingdom of God ahead of you." Tax collectors and prostitutes were generally despised in Judea. They were considered to be the lowest social class, the "sinners." Religiously, they were not considered worthy of being ministered to. They were treated as a lost cause.

What a shock it must have been for these leaders to hear that the despised ones were preceding them into God's kingdom. Βασιλείαν τοῦ θεοῦ refers to God's kingdom of grace, the family of believers. Note that Jesus does not use the strongest language here. He doesn't say, "The tax collectors and prostitutes are in the kingdom of God and you aren't." He could have, but his desire is for the salvation of these leaders. So he uses the verb προάγω. The "sinners" were going in *before* these leaders. The "sinners" had an edge in faith. But the kingdom was still open. There still was room for repentance on the part of the Jewish leaders.

The next verse reminds them that they haven't repented. John the Baptist is used as a reference. It was John who had called the people to repentance and told them "Produce fruit in keeping with repentance" (Mt 3:8). Some of the tax collectors and prostitutes had done exactly that. Few of the chief priests and elders had.

John came to the people of Judea ἐν ὁδῷ δικαιοσύνης, "in the way of righteousness." Is Jesus referring to the way John lived, an upright life, or is he referring to what John preached, the way to heaven through the righteous life and work of the Messiah? The reference can be to both truths. The life John led according to the Law should have made an impression on all, especially the Pharisees who held such a life in high regard. Most important, however, is the message. NIV's "show you the way of righteousness" puts the emphasis on the message of forgiveness in Christ, the Lamb of God (Jn 1:29). John was primarily a preacher. The leaders did not heed him when they were shown the way of righteousness. The tax collectors and prostitutes did.

Like the rebellious first son, the tax collectors and prostitutes were saying "No" to God's gracious invitation. But when John preached sin and grace to them, they repented and went to work in the Lord's vineyard. Like the agreeable and respectful second son, the Jewish leaders appeared to be doing what was right in God's eyes. But appearances can be deceiving. The leaders never got around to doing the work of the Father. As Jesus said, "The work of God is this: to believe in the one he has sent" (Jn 6:29). The leaders didn't repent at John's preaching. They didn't repent even when they saw the repentance of the "sinner." Πιστεῦσαι is an infinitive of result. The repentance of the "sinners" should have resulted in the repentance of the leaders. At this point it hadn't. This parable was one more effort to bring those Jewish leaders to repentance and faith in the Savior.

Homiletical Suggestions

Jesus spoke this parable to the chief priests and elders. The people we preach to will not be like those leaders. Chiefly, they will be members of the kingdom of grace. However, at times, they may exhibit some of the same tendencies of the Jewish leaders: self-righteousness, holier-than-thou attitudes, and a lack of desire to get to work in God's kingdom. For these reasons, the text offers ample opportunity to warn against such tendencies. A sermon on this text can invite the hearer to examine times when he has acted like the second son, talking well, but not following through on his Christian commitment.

At the same time, it is doubtful that we will find many like the tax collectors and prostitutes among our hearers. Yet our people need to hear that rebellious sinners are loved by their Lord. One can invite the hearers to see in themselves the first son. At times, we have said "No" to our God by doing things we know are wrong. But God's grace has not been turned aside from us. The Lord has called, the Holy Spirit has worked faith in us, and, like the first son, we have gone to work in the vineyard.

Some other thoughts are present. There is the recognition of God's will, that all repent and be saved. There is the need for us to accept all who do repent, regardless of their previous lifestyle. There is the reminder of the power of law and gospel as evidenced in the ministry of John the Baptist. And there is the need to learn from the faithful example of others, something which the Jewish leaders failed to do (v. 32).

The most direct approach to the text is to use the two sons as a point of comparison. Since our people will fall somewhere between these two extremes, it would be wise to add a concluding paragraph encouraging our people to be a third son, one who says "Yes" and readily goes to work. Such an approach could be treated as follows:

Which of the Sons Are You?

1. The one with the empty words? (vv. 30,32)
2. The one with the repentant action? (vv. 29,31,32)

Somewhat similar is the following outline which keys off Jesus' second question (v. 31).

Who Is Doing the Will of the Father?

1. Good appearances don't count (vv. 30,31,32)
2. Faithful responses do (vv. 28,29,31,32)

Rather than using the parable as a starting point, one could use the two examples of faithful action in the text, the preaching of John the Baptist and the repentance of the "sinners." This would produce an outline as follows:

We Have Reason to Do the Father's Will

1. We have heard the saving truth (vv. 28,32)
2. We have seen its saving effect (vv. 29,31,32)

TWENTIETH SUNDAY AFTER PENTECOST

The Scriptures

Old Testament — *Isaiah 5:1-7*
Epistle — *Philippians 3:12-21*
Gospel — *Matthew 21:33-43*

The Text – Matthew 21:33-43

In considering this text as a whole there are a number of things we need to consider. First is the fact that it is a parable. But it is different from most of Jesus' parables in some points. It is only briefly explained. Jesus has the people supply an ending, which he then accepts. There is an application which uses a picture other than that of the parable.

The context also bears noting. This parable was spoken apparently on the last "great" Tuesday of Jesus' life. So it is appropriate that it should point ahead to his suffering and death, and that it should be placed at the "end-times" of the church year.

vv. 33,34 — *"Listen to another parable: There was a landowner who planted a vineyard. He put a wall around it, dug a winepress in it, and built a watchtower. Then he rented the vineyard to some farmers and went away on a journey. When the harvest time approached, he sent his servants to the tenants to collect his fruit."*

Who is the landowner in this parable? Who or what does the vineyard represent? Are there any other comparisons that might be made here?

Though Jesus doesn't give a direct answer to the first question, he does imply that the landowner is God, at the end of the parable, by adducing and applying the passage from Psalm 118. Also, the Old Testament reading, Isaiah 5:1-7, indicates the same conclusion. See also Isaiah 27:1-7.

As to who or what the vineyard represents, that, too, is answered by the passages in Isaiah where the vineyard is specifically called "Israel": the people God has chosen as his own and for whom he did so many things. There are some who think it might represent people in general, but then various parts of the parable don't make sense. Note the list of things the landowner did. He planted, built a wall, dug a winepress, built a watchtower. This is a general description of God's loving care and concern for his people. He provided for them, protected them, showed his love, with no expenses spared.

Who are the tenants, then? We note that in the verses right after our text (vv. 45,46), the Pharisees realize that the parable was aimed at them. They, the religious leaders, were responsible for tending the Lord's vineyard and returning a harvest to him. They were to take care and watch out for the spiritual welfare of God's people.

The servants, as often in Scripture, represent "my servants, the prophets." God's spokesmen came telling of the Savior, encouraging the people in faithful works, warning against unfaithfulness, in many ways and over a long period of time. What are the fruits God expects to be produced? In spiritual terms, they are all the fruits that faith produces, or even better, "fruits of the Spirit." God looks for these whenever his word is preached.

vv. 35-39 — *"The tenants seized his servants; they beat one, killed another, and stoned a third. Then he sent other servants to them, more than the first time, and the tenants treated them the same way. Last of all he sent his son to them. 'They will respect my son,' he said. But when the tenants saw the son, they said to each other, 'This is the heir, Come, let's kill him and take his inheritance.' So they took him and threw him out of the vineyard and killed him."*

How were God's prophets mistreated by the people in general and by the leaders of the people? Consider the lives of Jeremiah, Elijah and others. Often they were mistreated, some were killed, many rejected, many held in contempt. See also the comment the writer to the Hebrews makes about this (11:35-38).

The son of the parable is obviously Jesus, the Son of God, the one God sent "in due time." Here the parable actually switches to future events, since what happened to Jesus is being predicted here. Actually, the leaders of the people had already decided to get rid of Jesus (Jn 11:49; Mk 11:18; Lk 19:49). It was mainly a matter of "How?" and "When?" They recognized that he claimed to be the Son of God, but they refused to accept him as such, or as the Savior. They wanted the inheritance themselves. But they forget the consequences as spelled out in the following verses.

vv. 40,41 — *"Therefore, when the owner of the vineyard comes, what will he do to those tenants?" "He will bring those wretches to a wretched end," they replied, "And he will rent the vineyard to other tenants who will give him his share of the crop at the harvest time."*

This concludes the parable. It is a unique ending in which Jesus asks his listeners to supply the conclusion. His words in verse 43 confirm the correctness of their answer.

Here we learn that the owner, God, will return. Though many don't expect it, also among religious leaders, it will happen one day — and then what will happen to those unprepared, especially those who have misled the people in spiritual matters?

Will God be pleased with the many religious leaders, those who have come "as wolves in sheep's clothing"? What about those who accidently or purposefully have misled believers and kept people from believing the truth? This is certainly a text that plainly applies to religious leaders. Christian pastors, and believers in general, especially need to ask themselves, "Am I among those who have persecuted God's servants, his spokesmen? Have I neglected to hear God's plain word, or rejected it, loved other things more than him? Have I lived according to his word?" How the First Commandment, and also the Second and Third apply here!

Who supplied the conclusion to the parable (v. 41) we are not told. In verse 45 we read that the chief priests and Pharisees recognized that the parable was spoken against them — and they looked for a way to arrest him right then.

vv. 42,43 — *Jesus said to them, "Have you not read the Scriptures: 'The stone the builders rejected has become the capstone; the Lord has done this and it is marvelous in our eyes?' Therefore I tell you that the kingdom of God will be taken away from you and given to a people who will produce its fruit."*

Jesus uses the quotation from Psalm 118:22,23 as a comment on the parable he just told. The psalm specifically refers to Jesus, whom many of the people and especially the leaders rejected. He has become the capstone or cornerstone, the foundation of God's Building, the church. Those in the Old Testament times and the people of Jesus' day, who were trying to build an earthly kingdom of God, rejected him as the only means of getting to heaven. But he is the one who holds the whole building together.

In verse 43 Jesus goes back to the parable briefly, commenting that the reply was correct and confirming that the "vineyard" is the kingdom of God. That kingdom was taken away from the people of Israel. God's chosen people today are all those from every nation whom God has chosen to believe in him and be saved. The fruits they produce are all the many and varied fruits of faith. In all their variety, they are produced only by faith in Jesus as one's Savior.

Homiletical Suggestions

There are a number of different outlines that suggest themselves, though application can be rather difficult unless we first apply it to ourselves. It is a good time to refer to the need for daily repentance, for examining ourselves. The sermon can offer encouragement to produce fruits of faith, to let the Savior's light shine in our lives.

Although the parable speaks quite a bit about the past history of the people of Israel, it also refers to Jesus himself, and to his return. An appropriate end-times sermon treatment might be the following. It calls on the hearer to do what the tenants of the parable and Israel in history did not do?

Be Ready for God's Harvest Day

1. Respect his messengers (vv. 33-36,42)
2. Receive his Son (vv. 37-39,42)
3. Remember his judgment (vv. 40-43)

Any treatment of the text must take verse 42 into consideration. It is part of Jesus' interpretation of the parable. Also, it is in Christ that God has extended his grace to all and through Christ that God will judge all. An outline which keys on verse 42 but treats the rest of the discourse is:

Jesus Rules in God's Kingdom

1. God has appointed him (vv. 37,42)
2. His messengers represent him (vv. 33,34,42)
3. Some people reject him (vv. 35-39,42)
4. What will you do with him? (vv. 41-43)

The warning of verse 43 receives the emphasis in the theme of this outline:

Let Us Not Forfeit God's Grace

1. He has called us to faithful service (vv. 33,34,42)
2. He will punish faithless rebellion (vv. 35-43)

TWENTY-FIRST SUNDAY AFTER PENTECOST

The Scriptures

Old Testament — *Isaiah 25:6-9*
Epistle — *Philippians 4:4-13*
Gospel — *Matthew 22:1-10*

The Text — Matthew 22:1-10

Jesus' parable of the wedding banquet is similar to the parable of the great banquet in Luke 14:15-24. There are significant differences, however. The parable in Luke is spoken at the house of a prominent Pharisee, and puts more emphasis on individual excuses offered for refusing the invitation. Luke does not emphasize judgment or the reason for that judgment, as the parable in Matthew does. Other individual differences in emphasis could also be noted.

Context accounts for the difference. The Matthew parable is spoken by our Lord on Tuesday of Holy Week, a day of intense teaching and confrontation, and of straight talk about unbelief. Jesus, in the face of open hostility, explains that hostility, its history, and its tragic results. This parable is a part of his extended response to Matthew 21:23, where the chief priests and elders asked: "By what authority are you doing these things. . . ? And who gave you this authority?"

He responds with authority, as he always did. This parable must not be considered apart from the context of its setting and time, Tuesday of Holy Week at the temple courts; its hearers, the chief priests and elders; or the parable of the two sons (21:28-32) and the parable of the tenants (21:33-46) which precede it. The parable of the tenants also in many ways resembles the wedding banquet parable. But while the former focused on the Old Testament prophets and Jesus himself, the parable of the wedding banquet carries the illustration further, includes the entire populace, and gives further explanation of judgment.

vv. 1,2 — *Jesus spoke to them again in parables, saying: "The kingdom of heaven is like a king who prepared a wedding banquet for his son."*

Jesus replied again (ἀποκριθεὶς ὁ Ιησοῦς πάλιν) to the chief priests and elders, but this time he is undoubtedly responding to their thoughts. The previous parables had made their impact on them (21:45,46), and they were anxious to arrest him. He responds with an explanation of their actions and God's respondent judgment. He speaks "in parables," plural, indicating the customary way in which Jesus taught spiritual lessons. While they did not spiritually apprehend or accept his parables (see Mt 13:10-17), they certainly understood that he was referring to them (21:45).

῾Ωμοιώθη, passive, is historical aorist with the force of a present, expressing present reality: "The kingdom of heaven *is like*." The parable is not limited to past history or to the Jews of Jesus' day. This is a parable about sinful history from the Fall to Judgment Day. Wedding feast or banquet is frequently used to depict the joys of the messianic kingdom.

v. 3 — *"He sent his servants to those who had been invited to the banquet to tell them to come, but they refused to come."*

Who are the δοῦλοι, the slaves who are sent by the king? Are they the Old Testament prophets who paved the way for the coming of Christ? Are they John the Baptist and the disciples, who were present at the dawn of the New Testament era? Are they the later apostles and missionaries who proclaim the victorious feast of Christ? Arguments can be advanced for and against each. It is not the point on which the parable turns, and is therefore perhaps best understood as God's servants of all time who proclaim the invitation of the gospel to attend the feast. But with the reference to "son" in verse two, it would be most unnatural and strained to include Jesus as one of the δοῦλοι here.

In the gracious good will of the king, "those who had been invited" are now specially summoned by the servants. "But they refused to come." Θέλω is a strong expression of the will, and the imperfect indicates not only that they were unwilling, but they continued in the state of unwillingness. Call to mind the words of the hymnist: "Delay not, delay not! The Spirit of grace, long grieved and resisted, may take his sad flight" (TLH 278:3).

v. 4 — *"Then he sent some more servants and said, 'Tell those who have been invited that I have prepared my dinner: My oxen and fattened cattle have been butchered, and everything is ready. Come to the wedding banquet.' "*

In light of the continuous unwillingness displayed, the king's grace is even more astounding. Those who see only God's justice and a tyranny of hatred for sin should read the words of this parable. Other (ἄλλους) servants are now sent with the message. Nothing needs to be done; the king has prepared everything. The exhortation to come is again extended.

vv. 5,6 — *"But they paid no attention and went off — one to his field, another to his business. The rest seized his servants, mistreated them and killed them."*

Verses five and six give two different reactions to the invitation. The farmer and the businessman are each immersed in their own earthly pursuits. These are people who prefer sight to faith, the material to the spiritual, who say "A bird in the hand is worth two in the bush."

But the gospel also arouses enmity in prideful men, and verse six gives this reaction. The hatred and abuse of the Jews toward the Old Testament prophets and Christ himself has already been treated in the parable of the tenants (21:33-44). But the Jews were not the only people who reacted viciously to the message of law and gospel. So have unbelievers of every race and time. In these verses Jesus points out two different, but common, forms of rejection that were being demonstrated by the Jewish populace and are still being demonstrated today: indifference and enmity.

v. 7 — *"The king was enraged. He sent his army and destroyed those murderers and burned their city."*

The king's wrath has been stirred by the persistent refusal and willful sin of those invited. C.S. Lewis wrote that there are only two kinds of people in the world: Those who say "Thy will be done" and those to whom God says "*thy* will be done." "It is a dreadful thing to fall into the hands of the living God" (He 10:31). Verse seven is a reminder of God's perfect justice. For those who refuse his grace in Christ Jesus, there remains only a day of reckoning. They are "murderers," murderers of the prophets and apostles, and murderers of the Savior, because their unbelief leaves the blood-guilt on their hands.

Certainly the destruction of Jerusalem in A.D. 70 is a direct fulfillment of this verse. But just as the destruction of Jerusalem was a partial fulfillment of the final judgment in Jesus' discourse (Mt 24), so here it is a partial picture of the wrath of God which can fall at any time on those who persistently and repeatedly refuse his gracious invitation.

vv. 8,9 — *"Then he said to his servants, 'The wedding banquet is ready, but those I invited did not deserve to come. Go to the street corners and invite to the banquet anyone you find.' "*

The king's glorious grace shines forth! Those invited were not worthy. His gracious invitation had declared them worthy, but their refusal had returned them to their state of guilt. Yet the king will celebrate with guests! Three specifics of verse nine call attention to God's gracious will to save. "Go" (πορεύεσθε), durative present, might be translated "keep going." It is our ongoing responsibility to "go and make disciples of all nations . . . " (Mt 28:19). The NIV translation of διεξόδους, "street corners," appears weak. More accurately it would be the place where a street cuts through (δία) the city boundary and goes out (ἐξ) into the open country. Thayer suggests that "the phrase figuratively represents the territory of heathen nations, into which the apostles were about to go forth." This best fits the evangelistic context here. Ὅσους ἐάν furthers the sweep of this calling. The servants are to call everyone, whomever they find. All are to be invited to the wedding banquet.

v. 10 — *"So the servants went out into the streets and gathered all the people they could find, both good and bad, and the wedding hall was filled with guests."*

The servants are not, as Lenksi suggests, the very ones who had been sent to the Jews. They had been murdered. It is, instead, the new servants of verse eight, among whom we must include all Christians. The servants faithfully call everyone with whom they come into contact, "both good and bad." The distinction is in outward appearance only, as Jesus pointed out in the parable of the two sons (21:28-32). The feast is filled with guests. The king's gracious good will has been fulfilled.

Homiletical Suggestions

The Old Testament reading also focuses on the glorious feast which God has prepared for his people. It is the wonderful privilege of the preacher to remember that his hearers are Christians who rejoice to hear about the banquet which Jesus has provided both now and in perfect fulfillment eternally.

But it would be dangerous to assume that the warnings of this text are historical facts which need not be applied today. The Christian cannot help rejoicing at the beautiful illustrations of grace in this text, but sinful human beings must also be reminded of the dangers of neglecting or rejecting the gospel invitation. God's grace and man's rebellion provide the sharp counterpoints on which the outline may be developed.

A simple progression which follows the text and offers two sections of gospel comfort surrounding the stern law message of the middle would be:

The Wedding Hall Will Be Full!

1. We've been invited to a beautiful banquet (vv. 1-4)
2. Many people refuse this invitation (vv. 5-8)
3. The king still calls us (vv. 9,10)

A very simply outline which could apply Jesus' strong warnings in the bulk of this text without missing the ever-present gospel invitation would be:

Amazing Grace!

1. Grace extended (vv. 1-3a,4)
2. Grace rejected (vv. 3b,5-7)
3. Grace sustained (vv. 8-10)

TWENTY-SECOND SUNDAY AFTER PENTECOST

The Scriptures

Old Testament — *Isaiah 45:1-7*
Epistle — *1 Thessalonians 1:1-5a*
Gospel — *Matthew 22:15-21*

The Text — Matthew 22:15-21

The familiarity of this text, as with many other texts from the historic Gospel series, may lead us to pass over it in favor of something richer or deeper. We then stand the chance of losing an opportunity to review some basic teachings.

The incident recorded in our text takes place during Holy Week. Jesus had entered Jerusalem in triumph, which didn't sit too well with the scribes and Pharisees. His enemies had been continually trying to trap Jesus, but he always showed his superiority over them. He would not allow himself to fall into his enemies' hands until all the Scriptures had been fulfilled.

In the preceding chapter the chief priests and elders had questioned Jesus' authority, looking for a way to discredit him. He would not give them an answer since his previous actions (i.e. his many miracles) should have made it clear that his authority was from God. These people were simply unwilling to believe the truth.

Even though his enemies were constantly trying to bring about his death, Jesus continued to show his love for sinners by speaking many parables of warning. In the opening verses of chapter 22 it is the parable of the wedding banquet which he used to direct the attention of the people to the truth that he is the only way to salvation. Even though there were only a few days left before his own death, Jesus did not spend the time in fretting and worrying, but in actively proclaiming the words of truth. If only his enemies had listened, they too could have enjoyed the gift of eternal life.

v. 15 — *Then the Parisees went out and laid plans to trap him in his words.*

All Jesus' efforts to warn the Pharisees and all his enemies had fallen on deaf ears. It's interesting that the Pharisees were going to try to trap him in his words. It was the very words of Jesus which could set them free from sin, death and the power of the devil. But they were going to try to use his words for their own sinful purpose, to destroy him. With the authority which Jesus had shown in the past, it should have been obvious that their tactics would not work.

We need to remember that the word of God can both save and destroy. Men often try to abuse God's word and use it for their own sinful purposes, as was the case here with the Pharisees. But in the end it is God alone who determines what will happen when his word is taught in all its truth and purity. In this case the Pharisees would feel God's full wrath because they had once again remained unmoved by the words and actions of Jesus.

vv. 16,17 — *They sent their disciples to him along with the Herodians. "Teacher," they said, "we know you are a man of integrity and that you teach the way of God in accordance with the truth. You aren't swayed by men, because you pay no attention to who they are. Tell us then, what is your opinion? Is it right to pay taxes to Caesar or not?"*

Evidently the Pharisees did not want to confront Jesus face to face again, especially after he had decribed them in the parable of the tenants (Mt 21:33-46). So they sent their disciples. But they also enlisted the help of another group, the Herodians. This was a somewhat strange alliance since normally the Herodians and Pharisees represented two different political ideas. The Pharisees pushed for the supremacy of the Jewish nation whereas the Herodians were ready to follow the family of Herod in collaborating with Rome. Despite their differences, however, they were united in their hatred of Jesus.

Such an alliance of evil is very typical. Many times enemies will unite in order to defeat a common enemy. Both the Herodians and Pharisees here were afraid that if Christ's kingdom was really the messianic kingdom, their influence over the people would be at an end. The Pharisees would lose their spiritual leadership over the people and the Herodians were afraid that the dynasty of Herod would fall.

The plan of these men was to get Jesus to speak out against the Roman government. Even though neither the Pharisees nor the Herodians really cared for the Romans, they could use the government to their advantage. If Jesus would speak out against the government they would have reason to turn him in. Then it would be the Romans who would take care of him permanently. The enemies of Jesus were eager to accuse him of treason, since this crime was punishable by death.

Luke unmasks their pretense. He says, "They hoped to catch Jesus in something he said so that they might hand him over to the power and authority of the governor" (Lk 20:20). Then it would make no difference how popular he was with the common people.

Both the Pharisees and Herodians seemed certain that Jesus would have to speak against the Romans. After all, he had just received praise as the Son of David when he came into Jerusalem. And if he were establishing a new kingdom as the promised Messiah, there would be no room for him to speak kindly of the Romans. And if and when he spoke against the Romans, the Pharisees and Herodians as "good citizens" would have to turn him in.

In the event, however, that Jesus told the Jews, God's chosen people, that they owed taxes to the Romans, a heathen nation, he would lose his credibility among the Jews. After all, the Romans were pagan unbelievers. The Jews thought that they should never be forced to serve the Romans who they thought were unworthy of any respect. Now if Jesus said the Jews owed money to the Romans, the Jews would no longer believe anything he said and they would never proclaim him as their king or the Messiah. Then the Herodians and Pharisees would continue to hold their influence over the Jews in spiritual as well as temporal matters. The Herodians and Pharisees would be able to continue manipulating the Jews.

Once again this looked like a fool-proof plot against Jesus. His enemies finally seemed to have succeeded in trapping him. They thought there was no way for him to escape this time.

Of course the enemies were not going to reveal their hand too soon. They came with the pretense of friendship, but brought their trick question hoping to trap Jesus.

It's interesting that they speak of Jesus as being truthful (v. 16). If only they would have been as truthful in their dealings with him as he was in all things. The enemies also stated that Jesus wasn't swayed by men because he did not pay attention to who they were. Perhaps they understood more about him than they realized. Οὐ μέλει σοι περὶ οὐδενός means "you care for no man," "you court no man's favor." Thus the translation in the NIV, "you aren't swayed by men."

Whenever Jesus spoke he spoke freely and truthfully, not worrying what anyone else would say, not even Caesar, the head of the Roman government. This is true in regard to all people. In God's eyes there is no difference between people. The only thing that really counts is whether a person has faith in the true God or not. Of course these enemies of Jesus weren't really concerned with faith in the true God. They were simply ready to say anything that might cause him to be caught off guard and fall into their trap.

v. 18 — *But Jesus, knowing their evil intent, said, "You hypocrites, why are you trying to trap me?"*

Jesus once again showed his omniscience. He knew what his enemies were trying to do to him. But since he is almighty God, there was no way that they would be able to succeed in trapping him in his words.

Evil intentions and trickery are nothing new. They go all the way back to the Garden of Eden where we recall that "the serpent was more crafty than any of the wild animals the Lord God had made" (Gn 3:1). Deceit was used to cause Adam and Eve to fall into sin, and through the years countless souls have been deceived and led into eternal destruction. Sadly enough, souls, even those of faithful Christians, will continue to be deceived as time goes along by the trick questions used by Satan and his followers. And the only way to escape from such deceit is through our trust in the Lord Jesus. We need to cling tightly to the cross of Christ and God's word so that we are not confused or led astray.

The word "hypocrites" properly describes the enemies of Jesus. They pretend to have an important question for him, but their purpose is to trap him. It's this disguise that only Jesus can unmask. There are plenty of hypocrites who through close scrutiny will be revealed for what they really are.

vv. 19-21 — *"Show me the coin used for paying the tax." They brought him a denarius, and he asked them, "Whose portrait is this? And whose inscription?" "Caesar's," they replied. Then he said to them, "Give to Casesar what is Caesar's and to God what is God's."*

Jesus' enemies had spent plenty of time devising their question, but Jesus disposed of it in rather short order. Since he was a man of truth this deceit did not catch him off guard.

It was clear even to the Jews that the Roman money was the currency in the land. Using this money didn't necessarily mean that you agreed with everything the Roman government was doing. The Romans were the rulers in the land and the Jews were obligated to serve the government. Perhaps it was somewhat degrading for God's chosen people to be the subjects of the unbelieving Romans, but they themselves were responsible for their problem. The Jews had continually rebelled against the Lord and as punishment for their disobedience they had to "give to Caesear what is Caesar's."

At the same time, however, they had to realize that they also owed obedience to the Lord. And that's the lesson Jesus wanted to teach them. The Jews were obligated to obey the secular government when it came to secular matters. They were obligated to obey God when it came to spiritual matters.

'Απόδοτε (v. 21) is an aorist imperative used constatively. In other words, Jesus tells them to continue to pay to Caesar what is due to him and to God what is due to him.

Homiletical Suggestions

The most obvious point which this text brings to mind is the fact that we live under God and under the authority of the ruling government. No matter whether we approve or disapprove of the government in our land we have to remember that "there is no authority except that which God has established" (Ro 13:1). God is the one who has given those in government the authority over us. Yet that authority only extends over secular matters. When it comes to spiritual matters we must obey God rather than men. With that in mind we suggest:

God Is Our Ruling Authority

1. Give yourself to God
2. Pay taxes to his representative

Along these same lines, the text, especially verse 21, seems to divide itself into two parts with this as the obvious outline:

Jesus Teaches About Church and State

1. They are separate and distinct
2. Both deserve our loyalty

A slightly different idea which can be drawn from this text has to do with our Christian stewardship. God has richly blessed us with numerous gifts, but we dare not keep these things selfishly only for ourselves. Our first obligation, of course, is to the Lord to use our time, talents and treasures for his glory and the work of his kingdom. But the Lord has also given us a government which provides us with protection and the freedom to worship our God in the way we want. For that reason we will also have a Christian desire to respect the governing authorities and support them with our treasures. We do it willingly, knowing that the government has received its power from the Lord. Thus we suggest:

Our Willing Service to God

1. In supporting the state (vv. 17,19-21a)
2. In supporting the church (vv. 18,21b)

TWENTY-THIRD SUNDAY AFTER PENTECOST

The Scriptures

Old Testament — *Leviticus 19:1,2,15-18*
Epistle — *1 Thessalonians 1:5b-10*
Gospel — *Matthew 22:34-40(41-46)*

The Text — Matthew 22:34-40

The final week of Jesus' ministry culminated in Jerusalem. It was a hectic week to say the least. The devil stepped up his assaults on Jesus through his assistants, the Pharisees and Sadducees. But in spite of the crucifixion looming before him, in spite of the nagging thought that his little flock would soon be scattered, Jesus spoke out with boldness and authority as never before. The people marveled all the more and the enemies gritted their teeth in hatred at Jesus' words.

This war of words was waged in the temple courts. Jesus soundly defeated the Pharisees in round one. He unmasked their hypocrisy and deceit when he instructed them, "Give to Caesar what is Caesar's, and to God what is God's" (Mt 22:21)

Jesus squared off against the Sadducees in round two that day. They did not believe in life after death or in angels. Their question about marriage at the resurrection was another hypocritical trap to make Jesus look bad and discredit him among the people. They lost face, too. Jesus emphatically stated that there will be no marriage at the resurrection and that God is the God of the living not the dead (Mt 22:32).

vv. 34-36 — *Hearing that Jesus had silenced the Sadducees, the Pharisees got together. One of them, an expert in the law, tested him with this question: "Teacher, which is the greatest commandment in the Law?"*

It is the time for round three. Again it is the Pharisees, looking to make up for the earlier incident. Who are these Φαρισαῖοι? They were the "Separatists" who prided themselves on the "right" exegesis of the Scriptures in life and teaching. Their following included some of the best legal minds of the day. They majored in minors. They were more concerned with the letter of the Law than the spirit of the Law. This legalistic approach to Scripture excluded any thought of a spiritual Messiah.

The Pharisees were Jesus' most embittered opponents. In their self-righteous pride they denied God's grace and salvation in Jesus. This denial, combined with their jealousy over Jesus' popularity with the people, ignited their hatred and culminated in his murder.

The Σαδδουκαῖοι, on the other hand, were the theological liberals. The Pentateuch was about as far as their adherence to Scripture went for they were stung by the message of the Prophets. They were spear-headed by the high-priestly family. Rich and self-indulgent, they wanted to get Jesus out of the way so that they could continue business as usual within the temple courts. They had not forgotten Jesus' purging of his Father's house.

We can picture the Pharisees huddling in the corner with their hands to their mouths covering the smirks when the news came to them about Jesus' "muzzling" of their political adversaries. It was their chance again.

This round had to be won. They couldn't afford to lose face with the people any longer. They would send their most skilled debater into the fray. Notice the polite flattery in an attempt to catch Jesus off guard: "*Teacher*, which is the greatest commandment in the Law?" On the surface the question looks harmless. But there is a seductive element in this question that needs to be brought into sharp focus. Ylvisaker, in the Gospels, points out that "the rabbins had found in the Law — 'Torah' — 613 commandments which they divided into 248 positive precepts, in accordance with the number of parts in the human body, and 365 negative ordinances, corresponding to the days of the year; and they listed numerous rules for the graduated import of the various commandments."

Keil states that the question was a part of their preparatory theology and was regarded as one of the greatest problems of the day. The question was loaded. The Pharisees planned to have it explode in Jesus' face. They reasoned that they could get him to speak disparagingly about certain elements of the law by elevating others.

The problem with the Pharisees' thinking is that they had become so steeped in the letter of the law that they viewed the commandments inversely to God's perspective. They ranked the commandments from the perspective of being broken instead of being obeyed. Problems arise immediately when trying to decide how one violation of the law ought to be ranked in the order of seriousness over against the rest. Does adultery deserve more punishment than theft, or murder more than slander? Here is the evidence of the extent to which these people spent their time majoring in minors, splitting hairs. Their question runs along the line of asking how many angels can stand on the head of a pin.

Jesus' answer to the Pharisees' question reveals how God intends his holy will to be viewed and obeyed. God gave us his word as a recipe for the beautiful life with him.

vv. 37,38 — *Jesus replied: "Love the Lord your God with all your heart and with all your soul and with all your mind.' This is the first and greatest commandment."*

Jesus goes to the Scriptures for his answer. He quotes from Deuteronomy 6:5, as the first and foremost commandment that the Lord wills. Ἀγαπήσεις is the future tense of ἀγαπάω and means: to love, to value, esteem, feel or manifest generous concern for, be faithful towards, to delight in, to treasure up. Robertson reminds us that the future tense is used in legal phraseology as a substitute for the imperative. The future is volitive and expresses the Lawgiver's will.

Who is to be the object of this love? Κύριον τὸν θεόν σου "the Lord your God" is to be the object of all human affections first. This is God's unchanging will and command. This is man's purpose and function that God originally planned. This commandment reflects the Lord's original blueprint for the crown of his creation. Moses by inspiration placed this commandment at the head of the list in his recapitulation of the Decalogue. That is why Jesus regards it as the first and greatest commandment in keeping with the law written by the inspired pen of Moses.

Why does the Lord, Yahweh, deserve such adoration? The answer lies in this precious name. This great and awesome name is the epitome of the gospel. Yahweh is the covenant God, the "I am that I am." He is the never-changing God who drew mankind back into a covenant relationship with himself through his Son, Jesus Christ. In John 20:29 Thomas made the good confession regarding Jesus —"my Lord and my God." Jesus is Lord. Jesus is God. As the incarnate Word, Jesus is love in action. His unquenchable, unconditional love drove him to willingly sacrifice his holy and precious life-blood for the sin-payment of the entire world (1 Cor 5:21).

Θεόν σοῦ is the Greek equivalent of the Hebrew *Elohéka.* This word tells us that the Lord is the God of power and might and that he employs this power in our behalf, for our good. Both titles, and especially when they are combined, denote divine love and grace toward us. By these names God proclaims the gospel to all as the supreme motive for us to return his love. In Christ, his person and work, these words take on real meaning and give life to those in the darkness of sin and unbelief. "We love because he first loved us" (1 Jn 4:19). God commands us to love him and in Christ alone man finds the power, the motive, and the will to do exactly that. Jesus kept this commandment perfectly for us and God credits his righteousness and holiness to our account. After the torch of the law has been applied to the sinful heart, it is the name of Jesus that brings the healing comfort of forgiveness and is the miraculous medicine that brings our will into harmony with the Creator's.

To what extent are we to love God? Jesus says emphatically: ὅλῃ καρδίᾳ, ψυχῇ, διανοίᾳ. Three times he uses the word "whole." He allows no divisions or substractions when it comes to God's full entitlement to our affections (Mt 6:24). The point that Jesus makes is that God's whole-hearted love is to be reciprocated in the response of man's entire being.

From the biblical perspective the καρδιά is the center or hub of man's being and personality (Pr 4:23). The ψυχή, life or soul, has a variety of meanings. Here it probably refers to the seat of man's emotions. The διανοία is the mind, understanding, intelligence — the organ where thoughts begin and develop. According to the will of the mind the heart or personality acts. In the Hebrew original and LXX of Deuteronomy 6:5 the reading is: "heart, soul and might." Mark 12:30 has "heart, soul, mind and strength." There is no essential difference in these versions. Jesus is emphasizing the point that man should love God with all the "powers" or "faculties" with which God has endowed him. That is the proper and God-pleasing use of our life.

> vv. 39,40 — *"And the second is like it: 'Love your neighbor as yourself.' All the Law and the Prophets hang on these two commandments."*

This second mandate is quoted from Leviticus 19:18. This commandment is like the first one in that love is the focal action. Love for God will project itself into the lives of fellow human beings. 1 John 4:20 is an excellent commentary on this commandment: "If anyone says, 'I love God,' yet hates his brother, he is a liar. For anyone who does not love his brother, whom he has seen, cannot love God, whom he has not seen."

God has given us one another on whom to practice and imitate his love. This is not optional for mankind. God wants us to love our neighbor. The words here seem to indicate two commandments, but love unites them in one. True love for God finds its fulfillment in focusing one's attention on the full gamut of needs that our neighbor has. What love does is beautifully detailed in Matthew 25:31-40 and 1 Corinthians 13:4-7.

The whole Law and Prophets hangs on these two commandments. Figuratively, these two commandments are the steel peg from which all the Scriptures hang suspended. Pull out the peg and the other words fall into a heap of disorder and disarray.

The answer that Jesus gave to this lawyer was so complete, so rich and satisfying, so precise and illuminating in every way that the man had to give his full consent (Mk 12:32,33). This incident finally stopped all questioning by his adversaries. They realized that they were no match for this man. Action would be the only way permanently to squelch the words of Jesus.

Homiletical Suggestions

The close of the church year fixes our hearts on the closing of our own lives and finally the closing of this life as man knows it. Jesus warns us about the end-times in Matthew 24 and 25. One of his warnings reads: "Because of the increase of wickedness, the love of most will grow cold, but he who stands firm to the end will be saved" (Mt 24:12,13). Agape-love will grow cold and wane as evil and wickedness multiply in the end-times.

This text is God's call to the elect to love as he does. The whole purpose of God calling us out of the loveless darkness of sin and unbelief is to fill us with his unconditional love in Jesus. God had to do the loving before man could even think of the word correctly, much less carry it out. Selfishness, self-centeredness, lovelessness are all sins this text speaks against. Perfect love is what God demands and deserves. We cannot meet such a demand. Our sinful natures are naturally bent in on themselves at the expense of God and our neighbors. Our sinful nature thinks like the devil and wants to be its own god.

These commandments point out our urgent need for God's perfect and unconditional love in Jesus Christ. God lavishes his love on mankind through the preaching of the word and the adminstration of the sacraments. Through the love of Jesus Christ and in a personal relationship with the living Lord Jesus, God guides, empowers and inspires us to imitate his love, always relying on Christ's perfect life of love.

Jesus' answer to the lawyer is the blueprint for the beautiful life of love that God has called us to live. In Jesus this life becomes reality.

Live the Life Beautiful!

1. In Christ's love for God (vv. 34-38)
2. In Christ's love for man (vv. 39,40)

As God's children we easily forget that Jesus is the power source for the life of love. The parts of this theme would be similar to the first.

Power to Love

1. In Jesus' obedience to his Father (vv. 34-38)
2. In Jesus' commitment to man (vv. 39,40)

One could approach the text from the angle of what love does.

Love in Action

1. Drives away fear of punishment (vv. 34-38)
2. Derails selfishness (v. 39b)
3. Desires the best for others (v. 39a)

Another idea might be to speak about the effects of God's love for us in Christ. Something happened to us at our baptism, something good and powerful.

Moved by His Love!

1. To love the Lord (v. 37)
2. To love oneself (v. 39b)
3. To love one's neighbor (v. 39a)

TWENTY-FOURTH SUNDAY AFTER PENTECOST

The Scriptures

Old Testament — *Amos 5:18-24*
Epistle — *1 Thessalonians 4:13,14(15-18)*
Gospel — *Matthew 25:1-13*

The Text — Matthew 25:1-13

This text is taken from a discourse of Jesus about the end of the world. This discourse covers two chapters in which Jesus tells us the signs of the second coming (24:4-31), uses the illustration of the fig tree (32-35), tells us that the last days will be like those at the time of Noah (37-44), relates the parable of the talents (25:14-30) and ends his discussion with a picture of Judgment Day, when all people will be separated as a shepherd divides the sheep from the goats (31-46).

In the middle of these lessons about the end of the world, Jesus speaks the words of the text appointed for Pentecost 24. To understand this text we will need to find his purpose in using this parable as part of this long discussion about the end of the world.

v. 1 — *"At that time the kingdom of heaven will be like ten virgins who took their lamps and went out to meet the bridegroom."*

"The kingdom of heaven", βασιλεία τῶν οὐρανῶν, is a term that is used often. We immediately think of the kingdom which God has in heaven, the everlasting kingdom of glory. And it is true that this phrase is used to refer to the kingdom of glory in the world to come. But it is also commonly used to mean God's kingdom on earth. This is true especially in the case of parables. The kingdom of heaven on earth is God's gracious activity of calling people to faith and ruling in their lives.

The parable is based on the Jewish marriage customs of Jesus' day. There was a religious ceremony of betrothal which legally bound the couple together as man and wife. Weeks or months later the bridegroom went to the house of the bride in order to bring her to his home. The bride's attendants, the virgins, went out to meet the groom and escort him to the bride. They took their lamps to light the way and to provide festive lights for the happy occasion.

vv. 2-4 — *"Five of them were foolish and five were wise. The foolish ones took their lamps but did not take any oil with them. The wise, however, took oil in jars along with their lamps."*

It is easy to see why the five were foolish; they didn't take any fuel along with them for their lamps. The other five were wise in taking oil with them. Outwardly — carrying their lamps — they all looked the same.

In this parable the Lord speaks about those who profess to be Christians and look forward to his return. Like the ten virgins, church members also look much the same. But even the world knows that not all church members are true Christians. Jesus points this out when he says that out of these ten virgins five were foolish.

The Lord is not just referring to hypocrites here. He is speaking about those who really do expect the Lord's return. The foolish are those who think they are prepared for the Lord but are not. Some of them are perhaps like those in the parable of the sower and the seed, who believe for a while but in time of temptation fall away. Perhaps some of them are the lukewarm Christians who attend church only out of habit. Among the foolish are those who don't make diligent use of the means of grace. They neglect Bible reading, their attendance at worship and their reception of the Lord's Supper. In short, their supply of faith is not maintained and replenished by the means of grace.

vv. 5-7 — *"The bridegroom was a long time in coming, and they all became drowsy and fell asleep. At midnight the cry rang out: 'Here's the bridegroom! Come out to meet him!' Then all the virgins woke up and trimmed their lamps."*

The bridegroom did come. Deep into the night the ten virgins sleep but are awakened by the call "Here's the bridegroom!" Suddenly he is there. There is no longer any time to prepare. The Lord will return in the same way. The Lord will return "in the twinkling of an eye" (1 Cor 15:52). He will appear "with the voice of the archangel and with the trumpet call of God" (1 Th 4:16). All will wake up.

It is only now that the five foolish virgins begin to realize that they are not prepared. Before the bridegroom came the virgins seemed much alike. When the midnight cry was heard the difference began to appear. That is how it will be on Judgment Day, when the Lord reveals the condition of all.

vv. 8,9 — *"The foolish ones said to the wise, 'Give us some of your oil; our lamps are going out.' 'No,' they replied, 'there may not be enough for both us and you. Instead, go to those who sell oil and buy some for yourselves.' "*

When the five foolish virgins find out that they are not as prepared as they thought they were, they become afraid and want the oil of the wise virgins. But the wise virgins cannot share their oil. Each person must believe for himself. A wife cannot give her faith to her husband nor parents to their children. If we are going to help them, we must help them now before the Bridegroom comes.

vv. 10-12 — *"But while they were on their way to buy oil, the bridegroom arrived. The virgins who were ready went in with him to the wedding banquet. And the door was shut. Later the others also came. 'Sir! Sir!' they said. 'Open the door for us!' But he replied, 'I tell you the truth, I don't know you.' "*

The five foolish virgins go to buy oil while the five wise virgins go with the bridegroom into "the wedding banquet." The five wise virgins are with their beloved bridegroom and they spend their time in joyful celebration. This is what will happen to us believers on the last day. Peter says that we "will receive a rich welcome into the eternal kingdom of our Lord and Savior Jesus Christ" (2 Pe 1:11).

To be known by God is a great comfort. "Fear not, for I have redeemed you; I have called you by name; you are mine" (Is 43:1). When you are known by God you belong to him and he gives you everything that is his. But God says to the foolish virgins, "I don't know you." The folly of the five foolish virgins does not merely lead to embarrassment, but to terrible doom. The doors of heaven are shut to them. They were not admitted to the marriage feast of the Lamb. The Lord does not consider their outward religious profession. The Lord says he doesn't know them and they are closed out of heaven forever.

If we have no other claim than that we lived like Christians, if the outer shell of Christianity is not filled by true faith in Jesus, we will be excluded from the wedding banquet.

v. 13 — *"Therefore keep watch, because you do not know the day or the hour."*

Γρηγορεῖτε is a present imperative: "keep on watching."

Just knowing that the Bridegroom is coming is not enough. The Bridegroom is coming. That he hasn't come yet means that the Lord is still giving us time to be prepared. The writer to the Hebrews says, "Therefore make every effort to enter that rest" (He 4:11). In our text we are simply told to watch. We do not know when the Bridegroom will return. The sooner we are prepared the better. If we knew the day of the Lord's return we wouldn't need to watch. We want to watch and make sure we belong with the wise and not the foolish virgins.

Homiletical Suggestions

The ILCW-A Old Testament reading (Amos 5:18-24) for this Sunday, Pentecost 24, asks the question, "Why do you long for the day of the Lord?" In this reading the Israelites were told, "That day will be darkness and not light." They were looking forward to the Lord's coming but it would be bad for them. God wanted them to examine themselves and to understand that they were not acceptable to God.

Jesus' words in the Gospel text for this day urge us to do the same thing. Just because you know Jesus is going to return does not mean you are prepared to meet him. Jesus wants us to be prepared for his coming, prepared with the oil of faith which trusts him alone for salvation.

Our purpose in this sermon will be to direct our hearers to examine themselves to see whether their Christianity is an outward shell or a real living condition of their hearts. Here are some suggested themes with that goal in mind:

Before and After the Lord Returns

1. Before that day many will think they are prepared (vv. 1-5)
2. After that day it will be too late to prepare (vv. 6-13)

The Bridegroom Is Coming

1. His coming is sure (vv. 6,10-13)
2. Is your preparation sure? (vv. 1-5,7-9)

Make sure you are ready for the Lord's return!

1. Many who think they are ready are not (vv. 1,2,5-9,11-12)
2. You can be sure you are ready (vv. 3,4)
3. You can look forward with joy (v. 10)
4. Keep watching (v. 13)

TWENTY-FIFTH SUNDAY AFTER PENTECOST

The Scriptures

Old Testament — *Hosea 11:1-4,8,9*
Epistle — *1 Thessalonians 5:1-11*
Gospel — *Matthew 25:14-30*

The Text — Matthew 25:14-30

Our Savior's words are part of his response to the question of his disciples. They came to him privately and asked, "Tell us, when will this happen, and what will be the sign of your coming and of the end of the age?" (Mt 24:3) Jesus proceeded to answer the question at length. He told this parable to teach what his followers are to do until he returns.

Even though there have been efforts by some commentators to make this parable and that recorded in Luke 19:11-27 the same, they are not! The Parable of the Ten Minas was told by Jesus as he drew closer to Jerusalem before Palm Sunday. The Parable of the Ten Talents was told on the Mount of Olives after he had made his triumphal entry of Palm Sunday. The former was spoken to the multitudes; the latter to his disciples in private. In the first the lord gave the same amount to each servant; in the second the master blesses with greater and lesser gifts. The Parable of the Ten Minas shows that, as there are differing responses to the good news of salvation, so shall the eventual rewards of grace differ. That of the Talents shows that, according as we have been blessed by God, so shall it be required of us.

vv. 14,15 — *"Again, it will be like a man going on a journey, who called his servants and entrusted his property to them. To one he gave five talents of money, to another two talents, and to another one talent, each according to his ability. Then he went on his journey."*

The "man going on a journey" pictures Jesus, who is soon to leave his disciples to enter the glory of heaven, to be gone for an indefinite time, and then at last to return. This man called his servants to inform them of his plans and of the honorable way he intended to use them while he was gone. Each talent represented the wages of nineteen years work by a day laborer. To turn all this wealth over to people who were only servants implied that he was honoring them with a great trust. Their responsibility was to show themselves worthy of such trust.

The point stressed in this parable is that each servant was blessed according to his own ability. What did the lord want these three servants to do with their talents? Put them to work! When would he come back? They didn't know. Would he be sure to come back? Absolutely.

vv. 16-18 — *"The man who had received the five talents went at once and put his money to work and gained five more. So also, the one with the two talents gained two more. But the man who had received the one talent went off, dug a hole in the ground and hid his master's money."*

Here the Savior pictures those who bear his name. Some are faithful and get results. Others are unfaithful, and the results are obvious. The 100% gains represent what the Lord requires of us: that we return to him according to what we have received from him. Equal faithfulness will produce unequal results, five or two talents. The point is that we are to put gifts to work for the Lord.

In the case of the unfaithful servant Jesus didn't intend to teach that those with the fewest gifts are bound to prove unfaithful. On the contrary, this servant had no more than he could handle. It was not the amount of the trust that made him unfaithful. If he had been burdened with more talents than he could handle he would have had an excuse. Nor could he claim that if he had had more talents he would have proved faithful. His unfaithfulness would only have been greater.

Jesus sketches this servant's guilt. The talent his lord gave him was buried and left to lie idle and unproductive. What a terrible waste! It is the very nature of our gifts from God that they would be productive! The master's trust aroused no response in this servant's heart. He kept it in a manner which clearly revealed what his real attitude toward the gift and the giver was: he buried it. In this he is a picture of all who carry the name Christian but refuse to use their gifts in service to the Savior.

vv. 19-23 — *"After a long time the master of those servants returned and settled accounts with them. The man who had received the five talents brought the other five. 'Master,' he said, 'you entrusted me with five talents. See, I have gained five more.' His master replied, 'Well done, good and faithful servant! You have been faithful with a few things; I will put you in charge of many things. Come and share your master's happiness!' The man with two talents also came. 'Master,' he said, 'you entrusted me with two talents; see, I have gained two more.' His master replied, 'Well done, good and faithful servant! You have been faithful with a few things; I will put you in charge of many things. Come and share your master's happiness!' "*

The first and second servants heard the same commendation. But please note that their reward for work well done was not an early retirement or a vacation trip. Their faithfulness led to even greater usefulness.

"Well done, good and faithful servant!" No higher commendation can come to any believer from the lips of Jesus. It outranks any flattery or honor the world may try to give. And the Savior holds up this commendation before us that it may be used by the Spirit of God to motivate us toward the same kind of faithfulness.

Now the master could easily have stopped with his words of praise as many masters would have. Or, he could have given each faithful servant a small sum from the profit which those talents had earned. But not this master! He said, "You have been faithful with a few things; I will put you in charge of many things. Come and share your master's happiness." Those "few things" were just enough to try us out to see what kind of servants we would be.

In giving those "many things" our Lord and Savior shows himself to be a God whose one thought is our elevation and joy. What better happiness is there than the heavenly joy of being with Christ himself?

The parable applies to our whole lives as Christians. But let us apply it to the part we have in carrying out the Great Commission. It takes different kinds of people with different abilities so that the good news of a Savior from sin can be preached to all of creation. It takes people with administrative ability, people with financial gifts, people with the gift to learn languages, people with the gift to witness to others, people with the gift to pray, people with the gift to comfort, people with the gift to teach Sunday school lessons to little children, people with the gift to babysit for parents who would like to attend a Bible Class. It even takes people with the gift of being available: sometimes our greatest ability is our availability.

vv. 24,25 — *"Then the man who had received the one talent came. 'Master,' he said, 'I knew that you are a hard man, harvesting where you have not sown and gathering where you have not scattered seed. So I was afraid and went out and hid your talent in the ground. See, here is what belongs to you.' "*

Too bad this servant could not give the master a glowing report as the other two had done. Was this servant lazy? The master said he was (v. 26). Was he stupid? Undoubtedly. Was he ungrateful? Absolutely. The master had entrusted a talent to his care, a huge sum of money.

The servant's excuse for responding in such an unproductive way was that his master was a "hard" man, strict, exacting, no nonsense.

But does the master sound like such a hard man? If a person gives you some cash to invest, his cash, and he expects a profit on it, is he really being "hard"?

The servant spoke a half truth. Yes, we are servants of Jesus Christ, and that may sound as if he profits by our labor. But think of what it cost him to elevate us to the position of being his slaves. Nothing short of his own blood. We could never repay him for that. Secondly, all our gifts are his, graciously entrusted to us that we might use them to honor him. Finally, this ungrateful servant only saw the gain that was to be turned over to the lord. He never saw what his lord had in mind for his beloved servants.

vv. 26,27 — *"His master replied, 'You wicked, lazy servant! So you knew that I harvest what I have not sown and gather where I have not scattered seed? Well then, you should have put my money on deposit with the bankers, so that when I returned I would have received it back with interest.' "*

Now, instead of trying to defend himself against this servant's slanders, the master convicts him out of his own mouth. He shows the servant that he is lying. To be entrusted with this talent and to do nothing at all with it was not simply lazy or stupid, or even ungrateful. The master calls it "wicked." If this servant really thought that his master was that hard and grasping, the very least this servant should have felt compelled to do is to deposit that talent with the bankers so that it would have earned something for the master. That's why it was given in the first place. There would have been no risk in that. There would have been less labor in that than in digging a hole and hiding it. Obviously, the master was displeased. Obviously, he had a right to be disappointed.

vv. 28-30 — *" 'Take the talent from him and give it to the one who has the ten talents. For everyone who has will be given more, and he will have in abundance. Whoever does not have, even what he has will be taken from him. And throw that worthless servant outside, into the darkness, where there will be weeping and gnashing of teeth.' "*

The tragedy of the third servant was that he did nothing. He didn't misplace his talent. He didn't waste it on wild living. He didn't do bad business with it. He did nothing. He buried it. And, because he didn't use it, he lost it altogether.

The command to give this one talent to the servant who already had ten might come as surprise to us. Yet, it shouldn't. Of the three servants he was best able to take on the additional responsibility.

Yes, in God's kingdom of grace the rich get richer and the poor lose what they had.

Most tragically, those who are worthless to the Lord will not remain in his kingdom of grace. They will never enter his kingdom of glory. They are sent outside, to perdition. To spare us that destiny the Lord takes us into his confidence, fits us out with his great and gracious gifts, and gives us opportunity to demonstrate our faith in him and our love for him.

Homiletical Suggestions

As citizens of God's kingdom, we are responsible to him for how we use the gifts and abilities he has given us. One of the most glaring faults of our day is that of irresponsibility. The Bible's strongest antidote for this poison of irresponsibility is before us in this parable.

Because of Jesus' use of the word in our text, talent has acquired the meaning of gift, aptitude or ability in serving God. The parable calls on each of us to consider whether our talents are being used.

That's why a good illustration to use in introducing this text would be an audit, to bring out the idea that a day of accounting will come.

Did You Know that Your Talents Will Be Audited?

1. God gives each of us talents (vv. 14,15)
2. God provides each of us with opportunities to use our talents (vv. 16-18)
3. God will require an accounting of those talents (vv. 19-30)

Another way to preach this text would be to emphasize the finite time which remains to put our gifts to good use. While he is away, here's what he wants us to do:

Do Business with Your Gifts Till I Come Back!

1. I'm pleased when you show a profit with them (vv. 14-17,19-23)
2. I'll be disappointed if you try to bury them (vv. 18,24-30)

Another outline:

Either Use Them or Lose Them

1. What happens when you use your gifts from God
2. What happens when you don't use those gifts

TWENTY-SIXTH SUNDAY AFTER PENTECOST

The Scriptures

Old Testament — *Malachi 2:1,2,4-10*
Epistle — *1 Thessalonians 2:8-13*
Gospel — *Matthew 13:1-12*

The Text – Matthew 13:1-12

These tough words from the lips of our Lord introduce "The Discourse of the Seven Woes," which is peculiar to Matthew's Gospel. The time is Passion Week. The place is the temple court.

vv. 1-3a — *Then Jesus said to the crowds and to his disciples: "The teachers of the law and the Pharisees sit in Moses' seat. So you must obey them and do everything they tell you."*

If ever there was a statement from Jesus to silence the critics who wanted to portray him as an irreverent revolutionary or a blasphemous antinomian, this is it. Far from denying the teaching authority of the scribes and Pharisees, Jesus readily acknowledges them. That they "sit in Moses' seat" means that they have the teaching authority to expound God's word.

Jesus enjoins the crowd, even his own disciples, to "obey them and do everything they tell you." "Obey" has the sense of "perform in detail." "Do" has the sense of "observe habitually."

Their obedience was not optional. It was a moral necessity. Far from being a rebel, an anarchist, a lawbreaker or a revolutionary, Jesus makes clear to friend and foe alike that he has come ". . . not to abolish the Law or the Prophets . . . but to fulfill them" (Mt 5:17). Indeed, affirms Jesus, "I tell you the truth, until heaven and earth disappear, not the smallest letter, not the least stroke of a pen, will by any means disappear from the Law until everything is accomplished" (Mt 5:18). Furthermore, "I tell you that unless your righteousness surpasses that of the Pharisees and the teachers of the law, you will certainly not enter the kingdom of heaven" (Mt 5:20).

A more forceful endorsement of the law could scarcely be conceived. In the sect of the Pharisees we find an elite group of Israelites who prided themselves on striving for complete moral perfection before God and man. They made it their single goal in life to keep the law of Moses and the traditions which the elders had devised to preserve it, interpret it and apply it to everyday life. By their efforts, they claimed, they were representing the pure Jewish community, the true people of God preparing itself for the coming of the Messiah.

v. 3b — *"But do not do what they do, for they do not practice what they preach."*

Do as they say but do not do what they do. What they do does not agree with nor follow from what they say. Preoccupation with the external moral requirements of the law, apart from its spirit, left pharisaism ensnared in narrow and rigid formalism, a dead orthodoxy.

v. 4 — *"They tie up heavy loads and put them on men's shoulders, but they themselves are not willing to lift a finger to move them."*

The Pharisees ostensibly were concerned about the judgment of God, forgiveness, justice, etc. However, their attitude was the negative one of pride, separation and the fine details of law rather than love. In their view performance of the law and its provisions merited God's forgiveness and assured eternal salvation. They knew nothing of the faith which works by love.

Therefore they were not concerned about how their rules and regulations affected God's people and created hardships for them. Nor would they make an effort to help others keep them.

vv. 5-7 — *"Everything they do is done for men to see. They make their phylacteries wide and the tassels on their garments long; they love the place of honor at banquets and the most important seats in the synagogues; they love to be greeted in the marketplaces and to have men call them 'Rabbi.' "*

The phylacteries were little boxes attached to the forehead and on the left arm near the heart. They contained pieces of parchment with texts written on them, figurative injunctions to keep in memory God's law and dealings (Ex 13:1-16; Dt 6:4-10;11:13-22). The size of the phylacteries indexed the measure of one's zeal, but did not result in or guarantee actual obedience.

In formal compliance with Numbers 15:37-40 they also attached tassels to their garments to remind them of the commandments of the Lord. The conspicuous length of these tassels advertised the Pharisees' exceptional zeal for the law of God.

They loved it when people deferred to them in public places and greeted them with respect.

vv. 8-10 — *"But you are not to be called 'Rabbi,' for you have only one Master and you are all brothers. And do not call anyone on earth 'father,' for you have one Father, and he is in heaven. Nor are you to be called 'teacher,' for you have one Teacher, the Christ."*

Among Jesus' followers, in their relation to one another, there are no superiors or inferiors. Only brothers and sisters in Christ. Among fellow Christians there is to be no distinction of rank, no one-upmanship, no religious "grandstanding." For Christ alone holds rank, to the glory of the heavenly Father. Thus Jesus' strong prohibition, μὴ κληθῆτε, literally, "Do not *seek* to be called. . . . "

Titles in the church can never be more than polite addresses of courtesy, recognizing a person's call to responsibility and service. They are not accorded by divine right. Thus Jesus himself concludes:

vv. 11,12 — *"The greatest among you will be your servant. For whoever exalts himself will be humbled, and whoever humbles himself will be exalted."*

In contrast to the Pharisee who sought to be great by exalting himself and his exaggerated external piety, Jesus holds up the true measure of greatness in the kingdom of God. It is humble service to him and his sheep. Whoever, then, in simplicity and sincerity of heart, renders such self-sacrificing service, flowing from true faith in Christ, is accounted great in the sight of the divine Master. The verdicts and judgments of men do not count.

He who seeks rank or position in Christ's church, who strives for honor and praise before men, will be placed by Jesus in the lowest position. His inordinate ambition may even rob him of his faith in the Savior and lead him to the lowest place of all. That is, it may lead to an eternal habitation with the father and teacher of pride, the devil.

The truly humble, however, he who has only loving service to the Lord in mind, will be exalted by the Lord in due season and praised by him (1 Pe 5:6). The best example of this is Jesus himself.

Homiletical Suggestions

It is easy in a sermon on this text to get so bogged down in denouncing the Pharisees and the teachers of the law that we fail to do what we have been called to do: preach the gospel.

Therefore, as we strive to paint the Pharisee and his life before God as the hideous thing it is, let us take care also to present Jesus and his humble life of obedience, love, mercy, compassion and self-sacrifice.

If we are to heed the warnings of our text, and to avoid the unspiritual pride of the Pharisees and teachers of the law, it is to him we must continually look for guidance, forgiveness, approval and praise.

Two possible outlines:

Give Glory to Your Master

1. Avoid loveless self-seeking (vv. 1-7)
2. Learn the greatness of service (vv. 8-12)

The Way to True Greatness

1. Not in loveless hypocrisy (vv. 1-4)
2. Not in vain ambition (vv. 5-7)
3. But in humble service (vv. 8-12)

TWENTY-SEVENTH SUNDAY AFTER PENTECOST

The Scriptures

Old Testament — *Jeremiah 26:1-6*
Epistle — *1 Thessalonians 3:7-13*
Gospel — *Matthew 24:1-14*

The Text — Matthew 24:1-14

vv. 1,2 — *Jesus left the temple and was walking away when his disciples came up to him to call attention to its buildings. "Do you see all these things?" he asked. "I tell you the truth, not one stone here will be left on another; every one will be thrown down."*

This episode took place late in the afternoon of Tuesday, during holy week. Jesus had finished his warnings and "woes" on the Pharisees and Sadducees in the temple courts and was making his way out of the colonnaded complex when the disciples called his attention to the magnificent edifice. Their comment was perhaps generated by his stinging denunciation of the hypocritical religious leaders of the Jews, "Look, your house is left to you desolate" (23:38). They wondered how this impressive structure, nearly 50 years in the building by King Herod's skilled engineers, could be laid waste. The Master's reply indicates that they should have known that nothing man-made, no matter how grandiose, will last. "Do you see (literally, "don't you see," ὀυ βλέπετε) all these things?" The comprehensive statement, "not one stone here will be left on another," obviously refers to the destruction of Jerusalem by the Roman legions in A.D. 70, which included a thorough demolition of the temple buildings. Although a few subterranean layers of retaining wall blocks were not "thrown down," the devastation of this stronghold of the Jewish heritage was total.

v. 3 — *As Jesus was sitting on the Mount of Olives, the disciples came to him privately. "Tell us," they said, "when will this happen, and what will be the sign of your coming and of the end of the age?"*

Across the Kidron Valley east of the temple mount rises the Mount of Olives, so named for its abundant olive orchards. Perhaps resting near the summit of this high hill which overlooked the massive wall around the temple area, Jesus was approached by several of his disciples (Peter, James, John and Andrew, according to Mark's Gospel). In private they asked two questions about the timing of these awesome events: the destruction of the temple and Christ's "coming" at "the end of the age." Apparently they already knew something about the Lord's παρουσία and the συντελείας τοῦ αἰῶνος, terms rich in eschatological significance, from previous discourses. His words in 23:39, "You will not see me again until you say, 'Blessed is he who comes in the name of the Lord,' " may have piqued their curiosity once more. Signs, of course, were important to the Jews of that time (cf. Mk 8:11; 1 Cor 1:22), since they were always looking for evidence of God's intervention.

vv. 4-8 — *Jesus answered: "Watch out that no one deceives you. For many will come in my name, claiming, 'I am the Christ,' and will deceive many. You will hear of wars and rumors of wars, but see to it that you are not alarmed. Such things must happen, but the end is still to come. Nation will rise against nation, and kingdom against kingdom. There will be famines and earthquakes in various places. All these are the beginning of birth pains."*

Jesus indicated that looking for visual signals of his coming in glory may be slippery business. "Watch out" is a warning directed at sign-seekers lest they be misled. This, we know, has happened several times in our own century. Many have attempted to win a following by imitating or impersonating Christ, from Simon Magus (Ac 8:9-24) in apostolic times to Sun Myung Moon in present times. They come in his "name" (ὀνόματι), claiming divine authority for what they say and do.

Instead of specific signs to announce the end, Jesus describes general conditions which will continue until he comes again. "Wars and rumors of wars" have certainly persisted throughout the New Testament era around the world. Ethnic groups and governmental regimes (ἔθνος and βασιλεία) have clashed constantly. These do not "alarm" Christians because "such things must happen" in a world full of sinful men with whom God is graciously being patient (2 Pe 3:9). Natural disasters caused by climatic changes or seismic shifts ("famines and earthquakes") also will occur with regularity on a dying planet which groans for its own liberation (Ro 8:19-22). But these phenomena do not necessarily forecast an imminent end; they are the early contractions of a "birth" process which leads to a definite result. A new heaven and a new earth will be created (2 Pe 3:13).

vv. 9-11 — *"Then you will be handed over to be persecuted and put to death, and you will be hated by all nations because of me.*

At that time many will turn away from the faith and will betray and hate each other, and many false prophets will appear and deceive many people."

"Then" simply means simultaneous activity, not sequential. At the same time the world is experiencing turmoil, the church will also suffer tribulation. Disciples will be persecuted and executed. They will be hated by the enemies of Christ in every country because of what he stands for (διὰ τὸ ὄνομά μου).

Again, this animosity toward Christians has persisted from the first generation to the current generation of believers. Clearly Jesus understood that his message would gain converts in "all nations" and that his church would exist down through the ages even though fierce opponents from without and false prophets from within would seek to destroy it — whether overtly or subtly (cp. Mt 16:18). Unfortunately, these agents of the devil will succeed in causing many to "turn away from the faith" (literally, "be offended," or "be tripped up" σκανδαλισθήσονται). Former brothers will even "betray and hate each other" under these treacherous circumstances.

vv. 12-14 — *"Because of the increase of wickedness, the love of most will grow cold, but he who stands firm to the end will be saved. And this gospel of the kingdom will be preached in the whole world as a testimony to all nations, and then the end will come."*

Things will get worse as the end approaches. "Wickedness" (literally, "lawlessness" ἀνομίαν) will "increase." The deteriorating state of affairs will have a debilitating effect on Christians, too. NIV and many modern translations render ἀγάπη τῶν πολλῶν as "the love of most" or "most people." This is the Greek idiom, though KJV's "many" is not an impossibility. On this "cooling" recall the church in Laodicea (Re 3:14-16). Enthusiasm for God's word and work will decline. Empathy for other people's problems will dissipate.

Nonetheless, those who endure "will be saved." Built on the rock of Christ's words, Christians will be rescued from this evil world and preserved in eternal glory (Mt 7:24).

And "this gospel of the kingdom," the good news of God's redemptive ruling in our hearts through Christ, will be proclaimed "in the whole world." Our Lord's witnesses will share this "testimony" wherever they go in fulfillment of the Great Commission (Mt 28:18-20; Mk 16:15; Lk 24:47,48; Jn 17:20; Ac 1:8).

"Then the end will come." The answer to the disciples' questions was couched in general terms but definite information was given. Despite difficult times, there will be enough time for the gospel to be spread around the world before the end of time. Of this Jesus assures his disciples in all ages.

Homiletical Suggestions

An overlapping of themes seems to affect the ILCW selection of readings for the end of the church year and the beginning of the ecclesiastical calendar. The preacher will want to be aware that the gospel lessons for the second last Sunday of the church year and the first Sunday in Advent are taken from the same sections of the Lord's eschatalogical discourse, although different evangelists will be quoted from year to year. The concepts of end-times and second coming are inevitably intertwined to some extent, and variations are offered to avoid repetition. Nevertheless, one should plan which points will be emphasized if he is preaching on the gospel lessons for consecutive Sundays.

The distinction in this text appears to be the warning signs of the end as compared to the admonition to constant vigilance later in this chapter because "no one knows about that day and hour" (v. 36). Although the two subjects are related, it may be best to keep them separate in serial sermons.

The original inquiry prompting this lecture by Jesus — "When will the temple be destroyed?" — is not addressed in these verses. It is treated rather in verses 15ff which again act as a springboard to the more important issue of Christ's return at the end of time (vv. 26ff). Therefore, mention of the destruction of Jerusalem would only supply historical background for this sermon, even though the Old Testament lesson for the day predicts it.

Focusing on Jesus' statements in these passages a sermon will concentrate on the signs of the end times. This makes for attention-arresting preaching. Everyone must wonder when "the end of the age" will arrive. The signs that our Lord reveals will surely find application in modern settings. Who can resist the identification of the false Christs and false prophets who abound today? Who can overlook the persecution of Christians or their love growing cold in the twentieth century church? Who can remain oblivious to the increase of wickedness in American society?

The picture drawn by Jesus accurately fits our age as it has fit every age. A comment on the endless contradictions and mistakes of millennialism at this point would not be out of order. There is no room for a glorious kingdom of Christ on earth in this text. Things will get worse, not better before the end. The whole post-ascension epoch has been and will continue to be about the Lord's reigning over the hearts of men through the preaching of his word. That is the "gospel of the kingdom."

This sets the stage for the positive thrust of these verses for the hearers. Steadfastness will be rewarded (v. 13). Mission work will enjoy worldwide success (v. 14). Here we can find immediate encouragement for our congregations. The signs of the end should sustain our faith and spur us on to sharing it as we see the inevitable day of the Lord drawing ever nearer.

Contemporary illustrative material will be available, we believe, as long as this sermon book is in circulation. Just read the newspaper for the latest futurist sensation. However, the historical context in verses 1-3 should not be ignored.

Suggested basic outlines follow:

The End Is Coming!

1. So notice the signs of the times (vv. 1-12)
2. And stand firm in the faith (vv. 13,14)

The Future Is Now

1. Jesus foretells what it will be like at all times (vv. 1-12)
2. So that we will keep the faith for all times (vv. 13,14)

LAST SUNDAY AFTER PENTECOST

The Scriptures

Old Testament — *Ezekiel 34:11-16,23,24*
Epistle — *1 Corinthians 15:20-28*
Gospel — *Matthew 25:31-46*

The Text — Matthew 25:31-46

Jesus' words are the conclusion of his long answer to the disciples' question, asked in private: "When will this happen, and what will be the sign of your coming and of the end of the age?" (24:3) Now Jesus is ready to lay out for our expectant eyes the sequence of events and conversations that will occur when he finally does come.

vv. 31-33 — *"When the Son of Man comes in his glory, and all the holy angels with him, he will sit on his throne in heavenly glory. All the nations will be gathered before him, and he will separate the people one from another as a shepherd separates the sheep from the goats. He will put the sheep on his right and the goats on his left."*

Jesus, the Son of Man — the name which he uses most often to describe himself — came once in grace; in a stable of Bethlehem, on a donkey into Jerusalem, to a hill with a cross. Today he graciously comes in word and sacrament (Is 55:11). But there will be that day —unknown to all but God the Father — when he will come again. Jesus Christ will come as the one divinely appointed Judge (Ac 10:42; 17:31), the Son of Man come to judge the sons and daughters of man with the perfect justice and mercy of God.

When he comes he will come in glory bringing all the glorified angels, those spirit beings who do his bidding (Ps 103:20), with him. His ultimate glory is established with his sitting on the throne of glory. We understand this throne as the exercise of holiness, power, will, redemption and regency. There Jesus sits at rest, in control, in the place of honor. Matthew here gives us a vivid and comprehensible image of Jesus on the Last Day, more than any other portion of Holy Writ.

While this vision may be more than mortal mind can presently imagine, on that day it will be seen by "all nations." This is the same "all nations" which Matthew records in the Great Commission (Mt 28:19) but here it has absolutely no limits. We remember how Jesus spoke of the resurrection of the dead — of all the dead; some to life and some to condemnation (Jn 5:28,29). They shall join the living and appear before his throne. We marvel at the power of God which shall effect such a massive resurrection. We magnify the truthfulness of God which arranges such a public forum. We are mystified at how a globe of people shall all see him. Yet we trust it will be as he said: all the nations will be gathered before him.

But do not consider this an indiscriminate assembly of chaos and disorder. There is a very definite pattern here, one which the Son of Man shall establish. For this vision of the Son of Man, Judge of all, is tempered by another tender reference to the ways of the Good Shepherd (Jn 10). The sheep will be gathered on his right hand, the goats on his left. Whether the angels shall do this gathering under the authority of the Son of Man (Mt 13:41 indicates this) or whether it is Jesus as the Good Shepherd separating his flock at the end of the day, is not explained here. The important note is that he is the active agent. No person will be saying, "I'm on the left" or, "I'm on the right." For the Christian the former would be a presumption excluded on the basis of Ephesians 2:9, where salvation is purely of God's grace, so that no one can boast. And no one would willingly profess preference for the left side. This gathering of the sheep and the separation of the goats is the ultimate, final act of the Lord's grace in action as he guarantees that not one of those whom the Father has chosen to receive eternal life shall be lost (Jn 10:29). Jesus makes sure of that. He does the gathering.

And so they are placed on the right and on the left. When the left and right are made opposites, the right denotes honor, the left dishonor. This is a Greek idiom here applied to the relationship between God and people. The right denotes those who, of God's grace, believed in the Jesus who himself is now sitting at the right hand of God. The left is reserved for those who rejected this Son of Man.

vv. 35,36 — *"Then the King will say to those on his right, 'Come, you who are blessed by my Father; take your inheritance, the kingdom prepared for you since the creation of the world. For I was hungry and you gave me something to eat, I was thirsty and you gave me something to drink, I was a stranger and you invited me in, I needed clothes and you clothed me, I was sick and you looked after me, I was in prison and you came to visit me."*

In the kindest possible words of pure grace the King addresses the sheep on his right. This grace is recorded in the blessed position in which they stand with God. They are the children of God who know God as Father. They are heirs reigning with Christ, now to come into the kingdom and receive their inheritance. They will be the kingdom of priests and kings who serve God day and night in his temple (Re 1:6).

Since this is a public judgment, evidence must be presented. This evidence must be understood by all and it must support the verdict. Jesus mentions feeding the hungry, giving drink to the thirsty, caring for the stranger, clothing those who need clothes, looking after the sick and visiting the imprisoned. These six works are concrete samples; by no means is it an exhaustive list of the works of the righteous. All the good works described in the Scriptures and performed by the righteous will be recited on Judgment Day.

The righteous will live by faith apart from observing the law (Ro 3:28). However, these works affirm the presence of living faith (Ja 2:17).

It is significant that those on the right — Jesus calls them the righteous — do not have one single sin mentioned against them. They have been justified freely by his grace through the redemption that came by Christ Jesus (Ro 3:24). This redemption is so perfect and complete that God is reconciled with the sinner, no longer counting a man's sins against him (2 Co 5:19). Only the good works of the righteous are mentioned — the works for which they were created in Christ Jesus, those good works which God prepared in advance for them to do (Ep 2:10). These good works follow the righteous to heaven (Re 14:13), but are by no means a way to get them to heaven. Heaven is their "inheritance" — God's free gift to them, his children by faith in Jesus.

> vv. 37-40 — *"Then the righteous will answer him, 'Lord, when did we see you hungry and feed you, or thirsty and give you something to drink? When did we see you a stranger and invite you in, or needing clothes and clothe you? When did we see you sick or in prison and go to visit you?' The King will reply, 'I tell you the truth, whatever you did for one of the least of these brothers of mine, you did for me.' "*

We are struck at the humility and selflessness of the righteous. It is from humility that they declare themselves unworthy of any praise for their good deeds. This response bears much the same spirit as that of the servants who said, "We are unworthy . . . we have only done what you told us to do" (Lk 17:10).

The righteous may or may not remember the good works they performed during their life, but they are surprised that Jesus took note of them and recognized that they were done "for him." That is not to say that Jesus was the farthest thing from their minds in performing these deeds, but rather they did these good works because the deed needed to be done. They were not done to win Jesus' favor. The righteous know they have that already! These works show as much.

Nevertheless, Jesus puts his great seal of truth and authority on the righteous and all their good works by replying, "I tell you the truth, whatever you did for one of the least of these brothers of mine, you did for me." As evidence that this judgment is not based on merit but on motive, Jesus says, "you did for me."

vv. 41-46 — *"Then he will say to those on his left, 'Depart from me, you who are cursed, into the eternal fire prepared for the devil and his angels. For I was hungry and you gave me nothing to eat, I was thirsty and you gave me nothing to drink, I was a stranger and you did not invite me in, I needed clothes and you did not clothe me, I was sick and in prison and you did not look after me.' "*

There is considerable similarity in the words which Jesus speaks to those on his left and those he spoke to the righteous. He talks about the same works, but these they did not do. Notice that it is only the sins of omission which Jesus chooses to rehearse. Again, this is not an exhaustive list but a concrete sample of those works which he told them to do. They, unbelieving, did not do them in spite of the basic humanitarian nature of the works, to say nothing of the divine mercy. No doubt space and time would not permit such a list of all the sins of commission which the unbeliever exposed during his life and of which he remains guilty to this very last day.

The judgment against those on his left could not be sterner than it is. Jesus said "Be departing. . . . " That is utter and total separation from God. "Be departing into the hell prepared for the devil and his angels." Yes, Jesus knew there was a hell, he believed in hell. Well did he know, though, that God never created hell for people; he never intended it to be a place of torment for man and woman. It was originally prepared as the place of eternal punishment for the devil and his angels who sinned (2 Pe 2:4). For people there was the rescue provided through faith in Jesus Christ (Jn 3:16). But for those who reject Christ, there is hell. And they bring this punishment upon themselves. The judge's verdict is based on evidence of such rejection.

vv. 44,45 — *"They also will answer, 'Lord, when did we see you hungry or thirsty or a stranger or needing clothes or sick or in prison, and did not help you?' He will reply, 'I tell you the truth, whatever you did not do for one of the least of these, you did not do for me.' "*

On that day everyone will admit Jesus is Lord (Ph 2:11), even these on the left. But it is too late and the spirit of unbelief still flows in their response. There are no tears of remorse, contrition, repentance or sorrow. Nor is there even pity on those who were hungry, thirsty, needing clothes, the strangers, the prisoners. No plea for mercy or forgiveness comes from their lips, only bitterness and argument over the perfect judgment of a righteous king.

In fact, considering the flow of conversation even in this judgment they have little time for the word of the King. Notice how the righteous repeat Jesus' listing of their deeds verbatim — albeit in astonishment. The response of those on the left is considerably abridged. Notably they leave out all but one reference to the personal pronoun just as they have tried to excuse themselves from personal responsibility by mentioning only once that they did not help.

There is likewise a spirit of self-righteousness evident in their reply which is as if to say, "Had we only known that you wanted us to do this, we would have done it." Still they do not believe that apart from Jesus we can do nothing (Jn 15:5).

But the king will have none of it. Again he establishes the truth and authority of his judgment with the statement, "I tell you the truth, whatever you did not do for one of the least of these, you did not do for me." With these words of Jesus still ringing in their ears, words of accusing truth, they will depart, cursed, into the eternal punishment.

v. 46 — *"Then they will go away to eternal punishment, but the righteous to eternal life."*

Quite naturally our hearts fear such a holy judgment. We quake at the words of Jesus. We may feel inadequate as Christians to perform any of the good works God has prepared for us to do. Yet Jesus ends this discourse on the happy, blessed promise again that the "righteous will enter eternal life." This is the eternal promise of the gospel of Jesus Christ. May our work be produced by such faith, our labor be prompted by such love and our endurance be inspired by this hope in our Lord Jesus Christ!

Homiletical Suggestions

The Old Testament lesson from Ezekiel 34, the Good Shepherd chapter of the Old Testament, pictures the King coming as the Good Shepherd who provides, protects and preserves God's fold. The Epistle, from 1 Corinthians, provides compelling reason why Jesus Christ will be the Judge, since he is the firstfruit of those who sleep and the one whom God has put over all things until all things are subject to Christ. At the Last Judgment Christ brings all things under his feet in reality.

This day may seem far removed from us as Christians and as preachers. But the Lord has included it in his word and tells us always to be ready. Therefore it is worth sharing and proclaiming to the joy and edifying of Christ's holy people. It is even more necessary and appropriate to consider this text when today there is much interest and publicity concerning reincarnation, new age spirituality and the evolution of man in body and soul.

A theme fitting our present video age would be

The Final VCR
(Vision of the Christ's Return)

1. Jesus gives us a vision of the events of the Last Day (vv. 31-33)
2. Jesus gives us an audio of the words of the Last Day (vv. 34-45)
3. Jesus gives us the promise to keep us until the Last Day (v. 46)

A theme based on the Lord's Prayer would be

Your Kingdom Come

1. With the King on the throne — then and now (vv. 31-33)
2. With the kingdom works — then and now (vv. 35,36)
3. With the King's judgments (vv. 34,40,41,45,46)

This outline from R. C. H. Lenski, in *The Gospel Selections of the Ancient Church* (Lutheran Book Concern, 1936, p. 969) is worth preserving:

The Last Day Is the Disciples' Happiest Day

1. Then the Lord will again appear in his glory
2. Then the Lord will separate his disciples from all enemies
3. Then the Lord will pronounce the most gracious verdict
4. Then the Lord will take all his disciples to reign with him

A theme based on the Apostle's Creed would be

"He Shall Come to Judge the Living and the Dead"

1. Judge Jesus will come in glory for final judgment (vv. 31-33)
2. Judge Jesus will give the final judgment based on faithful evidence (vv. 34-36)

REFORMATION DAY

The Scriptures

Old Testament — *Jeremiah 31:31-34*
Epistle — *Romans 3:19-28*
Gospel — *John 8:31-36*

The Text — John 8:31-36

John's primary purpose in writing his Gospel was to identify Jesus Christ as true God, the eternal Son of the Father. This theme is presented at the outset (1:1,14) and is carried through the rest of the book. From this main trunk John branches out to present a host of other Christian truths, all of which have their foundation in the deity of Christ. Many of these interrelated themes are stated in the opening verses of the first chapter. There are many but a few key ones should be noted for they have a direct bearing upon this text for Reformation Day.

One cannot speak of God the Father or the Son of God without also talking about man's relationship to them. So John quickly addresses this subject and presents man's response to the Son's entrance into the world. There are those who believe in him and there are those who will not believe (1:11,12). From this point on, John's Gospel is an accounting of instances of each.

Much of the time incidents of believer or unbeliever approaching Christ are presented separately, but often both groups of people are thrown together. It seems John delights in presenting the sharp contrasts which are thus made evident in each group. In this way their contrasting natures and attitudes, their opposing reactions and emotions, their different levels of growth in knowledge and spiritual insight and their critical responses to sure blessings from Christ are made evident for all to see. John presents us with the challenge, "Which group do you want to be a part of: the lost or the found, the believer or the unbeliever, the understanding or the ignorant, the light or the darkness" and as drawn from the text itself, "the slave or the free?"

Therefore these supplementary themes are stated at the outset: (1) Through faith in Christ, the Son of God, man receives the gift of eternal life (1:4,12). (2) In Christ man is brought out of the darkness of sin and ignorance and into the light of knowledge and truth (1:9,17). (3) Through faith in Christ we become the adopted children of God (1:12). (4) Through unbelief man remains in the darkness of sin and ignorance (1:5,10). (5) Through unbelief man does not receive Christ and forfeits the blessing of sonship (1:11,12). What is amazing is that each of these themes is developed in the six short verses of this text for Reformation Day. This provides a wealth of material for the Reformation preacher.

v. 31 — *To the Jews who had believed him, Jesus said, "If you hold to my teaching, you are really my disciples."*

It is difficult and even unnecessary to determine which particular group of people Jesus is addressing, true believers or one-time believers who had fallen away. In all likelihood both groups are being addressed. The immediate context and the greater context in which these verses are found would indicate that this is the case (cf. 6:66; 7:43; 8:30). This is one place where believers and unbelievers are found approaching Christ together. It is a statement intended for all to hear.

Through the use of the present general condition Jesus offers a general statement of fact which will always hold true in the life of every true believer. Those who are followers (μαθηταί) of Christ enter his school of instruction. They prove themselves to be true (ἀληθῶς) disciples if they continue (μείνητε — aorist subjunctive) in Christ's (ἐμῷ) teaching (λόγῳ). This is the essence of discipleship and the rule Christ sets before us. Just claiming the name Christian for oneself is not enough. One must adhere to Christ's gospel teaching and no other, abide by it from beginning to end, grow up into it, dwell in it, conform oneself to it, study it and neither add anything to it nor take anything away from it.

v. 32 — *"Then you will know the truth, and the truth will set you free."*

Three basic concepts can be drawn from this verse. The first touches upon the nature of Christ's λόγος mentioned in v. 31. He identifies it as truth (ἀλήθειαν). God did not come to this world to lie to men. God does not act as man so often does that he should lie (Numbers 23:19). When God in Christ speaks to man through his word he teaches man that which is real, certain and sure (17:17). It was for this purpose that he came into the world (1:9,14). This understanding alone will motivate the disciple to continue in Christ's teaching.

Secondly, when the true disciple abides in Christ's word he is enlightened by God with the knowledge of truth. The Greek word γνώσεσθε (future middle indicative) not only includes the intellectual comprehension of certain facts but also the knowledge which comes from experiencing the power of Christ's word of truth in our lives. It brings us spiritual peace and rest for our souls, a change in living and a dedication to the Christian mission which once was not there.

Thirdly, when the true disciple abides in Christ's word the power of the truth liberates (ἐλευθερώσει) him from all that has enslaved him. This too then becomes a motivating factor to faithful discipleship. It is this concept which Jesus expands upon in the remaining verses.

v. 33 — *They answered him, "We are Abraham's descendants and have never been slaves of anyone. How can you say that we shall be set free?"*

The objection is raised not by those who believe but obviously by those who will not receive the truth (1:11). Jesus' words implied that they were living in bondage as slaves. To this they vehemently object. From one standpoint it is amazing that they should do so. The Jews had repeatedly fallen under the all-controlling power of foreign nations and kings. From Egypt to their bondage under Rome they had often been living as slaves

However, they may not be rejecting the idea that they are in political bondage. Yet, if they reject the judgment that they are religious slaves their objection is just as remarkable, if not more so.

These people resent Christ's remark because it places them in the same standing as the Gentiles who were enslaved to the idols of their false religions. They are convinced of their religious liberty because of their physical attachment to Abraham. They had forfeited sonship by their unbelief, but in their pride they could not recognize this (1:5). They should have known, for the whole reason they had so often fallen under political bondage was that they had disobeyed God's law. Their claim to sonship and freedom based upon physical descent is a deception and is much the same as when people today are convinced that their relationship with God is right just because they hold membership in a church.

Note the emphatic positon of σύ. "Who are YOU to say this," they derogatorily remark. They will not accept the authority or the nature of the one who is speaking (1:10,11).

v. 34 — *Jesus replied, "I tell you the truth, everyone who sins is a slave to sin."*

Here the dreadful consequence of disobedience to God's law comes to the fore. The double ἀμὴν introduces a solemn statement of truth which cannot be altered.

Jesus has no particular class or group of people in mind with these words. He says, "Everyone who sins. . . . " Just as verses 31 and 32 apply to all, so does this verse. Any man, woman or child, descended from Abraham or not, who misses the mark of God's law (ἁμαρτίαν) whether it be in thought, word or deed is obeying the dictates of his sinful nature (ἁμαρτίας) to which we are all enslaved from the moment of conception. Jesus is affirming the reality of original sin in much the same way as he did in his conversation with Nicodemus (3:6). Sin is not just a doing of wrong deeds but a wrong condition of the heart. Man disobeys God because he possesses a propensity toward evil that enslaves him. By nature he can do no other. The more he rebels the more this universal statement is shown to be true.

In this verse the law comes from the lips of our Savior to condemn us all, so that our hearts might be made ready to acknowledge our sin and gladly receive the gospel truth that in him we are set free from sin.

v. 35 — *"Now a slave has no permanent place in the family, but a son belongs to it forever."*

These Jews were basing their certainty of sonship on physical descent from Abraham (v. 33). But their sin had made them slaves in God's house even though they were God's chosen people waiting for the consolation of Israel. They were not true children of God and so they really had no permanent place in God's family. To Nicodemus Jesus had said, "Unless a man is born again, he cannot see the kingdom of God" (3:3). To these Jews Jesus says, "Unless you are set free from your slavery to sin you have no lasting place in the household of God."

This verse also identifies Jesus' unique *position* among them. He came to them not as a slave in God's house but as God's one and only Son (1:14) with permanent, eternal standing in his household. It identifies also a unique *characteristic* of Christ which makes him stand out from the rest of mankind. He is Son not only because he is one in essence with the Father (1:1) but also because he is without sin (8:46). This characteristic of Christ and this position which he holds in his Father's household makes him able to win something for us that we desperately need.

v. 36 — *"So if the Son sets you free, you will be free indeed."*

Jesus is the Son *par excellence*. In his unique *standing* as God and because of his unique *position* as Son he has the *authority* and *power* to lead men into the household of God to be children and permanent residents by setting them free from their spiritual bondage. Furthermore, this is his *purpose* in coming into the world (1:12). This is the Father's great desire for fallen man (3:16).

The more vivid future condition with ἐλευθερώσῃ (aorist subjunctive) in the protasis and ἔσεσθε (future indicative) in the apodosis expresses more than mere probability. Christ can bring to pass that which is definite, certain, real (ὄντως). Only Christ can set man free. Note the emphatic position of ὁ υἱός. No other man in heaven or on earth can do this, no other angelic spirit, no other organization but only Jesus, the Son. He declares man free from sin on the basis of his perfect life and substitutionary death. All those who look to him as his disciples know this truth (vv. 31,32), receive this declaration and are released from their prison. This is justification and on this point, the hallmark of Lutheran teaching, the Reformation preacher rests his case.

Homiletical Suggestions

The text seems to lend itself best to the development of thoughts that center upon God's word as truth or the freedom from slavery to sin which Christ has won for us. In either case there is plenty of room for drawing in the historical realities of the Reformation and its blessings in our daily lives.

Martin Luther's efforts to restore the truth and authority of God's word to its proper place in the church are a reflection of Christ's work in first bringing the gospel to men. We see how Christ struggled to lead those lost in the darkness of sin and ignorance into the light of truth. Luther had to struggle as well to bring the truth of God's word to light. As Christ was victorious, Luther too, by God's grace, was victorious. As Christ was unwilling to compromise the truth, so Luther was unwilling to compromise. As we have benefited eternally from Christ's work, so we also have become rich heirs of Luther's reforms. Luther should represent to us the kind of disciple spoken of in our text, one who holds steadfast to the teaching of Christ. We will strive to be like him.

The concepts of freedom from sin in Christ and slavery to sin are concepts easily taken for granted and perhaps not always understood. Luther's personal struggle with sin and the personal torment it brought to him should serve as a useful illustration of its enslaving power. Spiritual slavery is like a strong prison chain that binds us. The first link is sin itself and then down the line follows death, both physical and spiritual; then spiritual ignorance, unbelief, enmity toward God, guilt, impenitence, the inability to please God; and the links of the chain go on and on. Christ breaks the chain, frees us and lifts us from our gloom to new heights through the truth of the gospel which brings forgiveness, life, peace with God, understanding, faith, love for God, joy, repentance and the desire along with the ability to live our lives to the glory of God.

On Reformation Day it is quite natural to reflect upon the condition of the church in Luther's day; what he faced then and what we face all over again. The Reformation preacher will not shrink from addressing these issues. Yet, he will not lose sight of those blessings which endure to this day. Christ's word is still being taught in its truth and purity, and through its proclamation the slaves are being set free. We are among those who have been so blessed.

On the concept of God's word as truth:

Hold Firm the Truth

1. The truth that comes from Christ (v. 31)
2. The truth that sets men free (vv. 32-34)
3. The truth that leads to sonship (vv. 35,36)

On the concept of freedom from slavery to sin:

The Reformation Cry For Freedom

1. A cry that came forth from bondage (vv. 33-35a)
2. A freedom attainable in Christ. (vv. 31,32,35b,36)

A homily following the path of history could first highlight the text (Christ's activity and teaching), then apply the words of the text to Luther's times, and finally stress our work in view of Reformation blessings:

Setting the Sinner Free

1. Christ's delivering work and word
2. Luther's reforms
3. Our assignment

FESTIVAL OF HARVEST

The Scriptures

Old Testament — *Deuteronomy 26:1-11*
Epistle — *2 Corinthians 9:6-15*
Gospel — *Matthew 13:24-30*

The Text — Matthew 13:24-30

In this chapter of Matthew Jesus spoke seven parables on the kingdom of heaven. In every case the kingdom of heaven is that gracious reign of God in which he rules and protects the hearts of people through faith.

Jesus used events familiar to his listeners to make known the unfamiliar, to reveal a mystery to them about the kingdom of heaven, Matthew 13:10,11. By means of illustrations he enlightened them to grand truths concerning the kingdom of heaven, as his explanation of this parable in Matthew 13:36-43 shows.

The use of this text for Harvest Festival must be in keeping with Jesus' purpose for teaching the parable. Obviously it was not his intention to teach about the mechanics of a harvest, the blessings of a harvest, what to do with a harvest or even where a harvest comes from. The parable turns our thoughts from the lesser harvest of our fields on earth to God's greater harvest. The sermon must do the same.

v. 24 — *Jesus told them another parable: "The kingdom of heaven is like a man who sowed good seed in his field."*

It is significant that in Jesus' introduction to this parable he uses the constative aorist, ὡμοιώθη. This parable has a great deal to teach about the prevaililng situation in the kingdom of heaven, past, present and future.

The description of the farmer shows his good intentions. He sowed good (καλὸν) seed, seed that met the standards of the purpose for which it was intended.

The farmer is Jesus. He it is who builds the kingdom of heaven in this world. It is his gracious will to save all through faith in him (cf. vv. 37,38a).

v. 25 — *"But while everyone was sleeping, his enemy came and sowed weeds among the wheat, and went away."*

The field belonged to the farmer, but another came to despoil the results of his good intentions. Under the cover of darkness he peppered his wheat with weeds to ruin the harvest.

God does not rule and protect in the kingdom of heaven as he does in his kingdom of power. He does not rule and protect by his omnipotence, which cannot be successfully resisted or thwarted.

God rules and protects by his grace. This can be resisted. This has an implacable and persistent enemy in Satan, the prince of darkness (cf. vv. 38b,39a).

So where God plants the kingdom of heaven in this world, Satan attempts to plant the kingdom of sin and unbelief — with an amazing success rate!

The sleeping of the farmer and his servants in the parable has no didactic value. It does not correspond to inattention to mission work, for it is the one who sowed the seed, the Son of Man, who sleeps. Jesus included this detail to explain in the story how an enemy could attempt to despoil a field.

v. 26 — *"When the wheat sprouted and formed heads, then the weeds also appeared."*

The weeds, ζιζάνια, are usually understood to be darnel or cheat. This type of grass looks like wheat until it forms heads.

Sons of the evil one, followers of Satan's lies, like darnel, infect the church. They look as though they belong. Disguised as believers, they often go undetected for a long time. Some are never found out in this life.

But their effect is felt. Their self-righteousness, neglect of word and sacrament, failure to practice good stewardship, inattention in worship, downplaying of the Great Commission, and a myriad of other symptoms smoothly couched in a hypocritical demeanor all combine to weaken the faith of others and to hinder growth in knowledge and love. Dealing with their neglect, cross-purposes and objections saps the resources of time, talent and treasure of the wheat they grow next to.

v. 27 — *"The owner's servants came to him and said, 'Sir, didn't you sow good seed in your field? Where then did the weeds come from?' "*

The servants' question voices the surprise that a good farmer and good seed on a field could produce a mixed crop.

Christians are often perplexed when wickedness appears in a setting they assumed was immune to the devil's attacks.

v. 28 — *" 'An enemy did this,' he replied. The servants asked him, 'Do you want us to go and pull them up?' "*

Jesus, the master teacher, gains the attention and confidence of his audience. With a wry sense of humor, he has the servants ask a question only foolish farmhands would even consider.

His listeners shake their heads and smile as they imagine dunderheaded servants stomping through a tender wheatfield, trying to pull up weeds without harming the wheat.

What fools we all can be! Anger, disappointment, disgust — even misguided devotion to God, his word, his law and gospel — all can lead to cries to "clean house" in the church. The unveiling of hypocrisy can foment witch hunts that seek to expunge every trace of impurity and fruitlessness that attaches itself in any way to the church.

v. 29 — " *'No,' he answered, 'because while you are pulling the weeds, you may root up the wheat with them.'* "

To the owner belongs the voice of reason. Due to the hypocritical growth of the darnel, by the time it was seen the wheat had matured too much to be disturbed. Its roots, interlaced with the weeds, did not permit their uprooting with its destruction.

Jesus teaches an essential truth about the church. The kingdom of heaven is his kingdom, ruled and protected by the power of his grace. He does not permit even the well-intentioned efforts of his servants to cleanse the church in a way that will harm the church.

Jesus does not oppose evangelical discipline or separation. But he warns against false ideas about the kingdom of heaven in this world. There is no "pure" church here. He forbids the use of any means to remove anyone from the company of the church save that which brings anyone into the church — the power of his word.

v. 30 — " *'Let both grow together until the harvest. At that time I will tell the harvesters: First collect the weeds and tie them in bundles to be burned; then gather the wheat and bring it into my barn.'* "

The enemy damaged the crop. The weeds weakened the wheat. The farmer's field did not yield as much per hectare as it would have otherwise.

But his plan has failed. The crop remained and was gathered in. The weeds were destroyed.

Jesus gives hope by pointing to the harvest (cf. v. 39b). The problem of hypocrisy he resolves by the ultimate display of his power on the Last Day (cf. vv. 40-42). The purity of the church as an article of faith becomes the glory of the church as a matter of experience (cf. v. 43).

Homiletical Suggestions

As was noted, this parable dare not be used as a pre-text for a sermon on the harvest of the fields or the Lord's role in it. Jesus' parable teaches us mysteries about the kingdom of heaven.

That does not mean that those two thoughts are mutually exclusive. This parable can be preached in a way that the harvest of the fields and the mystery of the kingdom of heaven can both be dealt with effectively. This is possible with either of two approaches.

First, the parable can be explained (not interpreted) and the application made to our harvests (planting, frustration, hard work, patience, reaping — all under the gracious hand of God). In the second part of the sermon the parable can be interpreted (cf. Matthew 13:36-43) and the application made to the church (synod, local congregation, visible church in general).

A Two-Harvest Year!

1. The harvest of the fields
2. The harvest of the field

The second approach is probably better. Break the parable down into two or three parts. Each part can be explained, interpreted and applied. The specific thoughts associated with a harvest festival will then be found in the application, e.g. the use of the harvest from God to enlarge the harvest for God.

Bring in the Lord's Harvest!

1. The harvest planted by the Lord (vv. 24-26)
2. The harvest protected by the Lord (vv. 27-29)
3. The harvest delivered to the Lord (v. 30)

Wait Patiently for the Harvest

1. Patiently take the bad with the good (vv. 24-29)
2. Wait for God to take the bad from the good (v. 30)

Ingredients of a Happy Harvest

1. Good seed (vv. 24-26)
2. Patient work (vv. 27-29)
3. Full barns (v. 30)

MISSION FESTIVAL

The Scriptures

Old Testament — *Isaiah 62:1-7*
Epistle — *Romans 10:11-17*
Gospel — *Luke 24:44-53*

The Text — Luke 24:44-53

Luke closes his gospel and opens the book of Acts in similar fashion: he speaks of Jesus' ascension and his directive and encouragement to witness to him. The ascension marks the end of all that Jesus did while he was present here on earth in bodily form. It also marks the beginning of his reign at the right hand of God for the benefit of his church on earth.

vv. 44-47 — *He said to them, "This is what I told you while I was still with you: Everything must be fulfilled that is written about me in the Law of Moses, the Prophets and the Psalms." Then he opened their minds so they could understand the Scriptures. He told them, "This is what is written: The Christ will suffer and rise from the dead on the third day, and repentance and forgiveness of sins will be preached in his name to all nations, beginning at Jerusalem."*

Throughout his life on earth Jesus was concerned that the Scriptures be fulfilled. That's not too surprising, for if they had not been fulfilled in him we would have no forgiveness. Yet Jesus was not satisfied with just fulfilling the Scriptures. He also strove to share the depth of his understanding of the Father's will with his disciples. Throughout the years of his earthly ministry he had sought to accomplish that, but the disciples did not understand. They still didn't understand, so Jesus opened their minds.

We recognize that Jesus was not teaching anything new as he opened the disciples' understanding of the Scriptures. He was teaching them those things that needed to be told them to help them understand the purpose of his life, his death, his resurrection and their purpose in life. With what Jesus spoke at this time — and he was speaking also of the Father's promise to send the Holy Spirit —he was doing all that needed to be done to help us understand God's plan of salvation. It is this understanding that is gained from the Scriptures which is able to make us wise for salvation.

God's plan for salvation includes repentance on the part of the sinner. Repentance is a total change of heart and mind, a one-hundred-eighty-degree turn from the thoughts of the Old Adam regarding this life, to thoughts of God and an eternal life of serving Jesus out of grateful love for him.

God's plan also includes proclaiming the forgiveness of sins which is the news that the sins of which we are guilty are not held against us, not because we did not do them, but because they had been canceled, wiped out, forgotten. What wondrous news! What a joyous proclamation! What a gracious plan to accomplish for us what we could never hope to accomplish for ourselves.

This joyous proclamation was to resound first from Jerusalem. What an impression those words must have made upon the disciples who for fear of the Jews might well have been minded to go elsewhere. What a thought-provoking statement to a group of self-willed men who out of disgust for the people who had so brutally treated the Savior might have determined to turn their backs on the Jews. Jesus was telling them that the Jews would receive another opportunity to see him as their Savior. How the love of Jesus for all people must have been impressed upon the disciples as they heard this instruction. What an impression this makes on us. We who are witnesses of these things might be tempted to feel that witnessing is for people far away whom we will never meet or people who strike us as being "our kind of people." The love of Jesus is much different: the news of forgiveness and salvation is for all.

v. 48 — *"You are witnesses of these things."*

The word witnesses, μάρτυρες, includes two thoughts. The first is that they had witnessed all that Jesus had said and done. Secondly, they were to share what they had seen and heard and believed. While the disciples could share what they believed about Jesus based upon firsthand knowledge, they are not the only qualified witnesses of the things Jesus said and did. With the eyes of faith we see the life and work of Jesus as we read the Scriptures. In this way we are witnesses of everything he has done to save us and we are to bear witness to that.

Since the Greek has no verb here we must supply one from context. Jesus speaks of the disciples as witnesses who will bear witness. Acts 1:8 sheds light on this passage. The future ἔσεσθε suggests that we understand a continuing action. No time is untouched by Jesus words, "You are witnesses of these things." May the Holy Spirit impress this message on our hearts so that we may be Jesus' witnesses in our every word and action and thus be used by the Spirit as he works the gift of faith in the hearts of others.

v. 49 — *"I am going to send you what my Father has promised; but stay in the city until you have been clothed with power from on high."*

The disciples had not yet been turned into confident and powerful witnesses by the Holy Spirit. What a change came over them when they received the Father's promised outpouring of the Holy Spirit on Pentecost. Suddenly they were not only able to speak in unknown languages, but they were able to speak with understanding of all the things that Jesus had done and said during his life on earth.

This verse is a powerful reminder for us that without God we can do nothing. It is our gracious God who clothes the witnesses of Jesus with power, even as it is our gracious God who clothes his children with the robe of Christ's righteousness so that we may live with him forever. What a powerful reminder that with our Lord by our side we can be his witnesses, for with God nothing is impossible.

vv. 50-53 — *When he had led them out to the vicinity of Bethany, he lifted up his hands and blessed them. While he was blessing them, he left them and was taken up into heaven. Then they worshiped him and returned to Jerusalem with great joy. And they stayed continually at the temple, praising God.*

Jesus' ascension is a comfort for us at all times, but it especially meets our needs when it comes to witnessing. By ourselves we could never hope to bear witness to Jesus, but with his abiding presence to give us the help we need, witnessing is something that we not only can do, but we can do well. It was Jesus' desire to give his church this comfort and assurance that led to the manner of his ascension. As he leaves for the last times, he does so in such a way as to impress upon his followers the truth that he has ascended to the right hand of the Father. Thus he can rule over all things for the best interest of the church and be with all of his witnesses in a new and better way at one and the same time. As he left, Jesus was in the process of blessing his disciples. That work has not ceased. He is at work at the right hand of God blessing us right now.

Homiletical Suggestions

The Old Testament reading, Isaiah 62:1-7, speaks of the Lord's determination not to rest until his people receive needed spiritual rest in the announcement of forgiveness and salvation. In order to accomplish this blessed goal, God will post watchmen on the walls of Jerusalem to warn those who delight in their Savior of all dangers to their faith. In pastors and teachers, in beloved brothers and sisters in Christ, God has kept his promise to us.

The Epistle reading, Romans 10:11-17, comforts us with the knowledge that no one who trusts the Lord will ever be put to shame. We are also reminded that we will want to hear the message of Christ in order to remain in the faith, for it is the only means our Lord has given us to receive and retain the precious gift of grace.

The Gospel, Luke 24:44-53, ties the other two readings together. Jesus reminds us on what basis one speaks to others about him, from where the strength to do so is received, of his knowledge, of what we need to be his witnesses, and of his work to meet our needs.

Notice that as the disciples returned to Jerusalem they were filled with great joy rather than sadness at Jesus' departure. They were already at work praising God instead of regretting that Jesus had given them such a difficult assignment. God's word and the assurance that Jesus is at the right hand of God to give us everything we need as we strive to serve him can do for us what it did for the first disciples. It gives us that joyous faith which desires to be God's instrument of service.

In the outline below, we are reminded that Jesus does not ask only foreign missionaries to serve as his witnesses. He asks each of us to do so.

Jesus Makes Us Missionaries

1. He commissioned us (v. 48)
2. He instructs us (vv. 44-47)
3. He enables us (v. 49)
4. He blesses us (vv. 50-53)

The next outline shows that before any witnessing can be done, God's word must be known and believed. Then the Holy Spirit uses God's people to speak what they know and believe. Finally, Jesus works from God's right hand to grant what is needed to do his work at every moment.

Jesus Blesses His Church so His Work May Be Done

1. He blesses it with his Word (vv. 44-48)
2. He blesses it with his Spirit (v. 49)
3. He blesses it with his eternal presence (vv. 50-53)

The final approach to the text addresses the joy of being Jesus' witness.

Privileged to Be Jesus' Witnesses

1. Jesus is the fulfillment of Scripture (vv. 44-46)
2. Jesus has given us power to bear witness (vv. 47-49)
3. Jesus meets our needs and helps us bear witness (vv. 50-53)

THANKSGIVING DAY

The Scriptures

Old Testament — *Deuteronomy 8:1-10*
Epistle — *1 Timothy 2:1-4*
Gospel — *Luke 17:11-19*

The Text — Luke 17:11-19

Ten were blessed with healing; one returned to give thanks. The final days of Jesus' ministry on earth were sad ones. The crowds no longer followed him. His teachings were too demanding (Jn 6:60). Yet there were a few like Lazarus, Zacchaeus and this Samaritan who understood the Messiah and his work. They were the ones who returned.

vv. 11-13 — *Now on his way to Jerusalem, Jesus traveled along the border between Samaria and Galilee. As he was going into a village, ten men who had leprosy met him. They stood at a distance and called out in a loud voice, "Jesus, Master, have pity on us!"*

Jesus was on his way to Jerusalem to die. He would cross the Jordan River in Galilee, go south, cross again at Jericho and head toward Jerusalem along with other Jewish Passover worshipers. He traveled between Samaria and Galilee on his way toward the Jordan River. This was the customary path for Jews because of the hostility that existed between Samaritans and Jews.

The term "leprosy" covers a number of related diseases. The tuberculoid type causes numbness, paralysis and then atrophy. Another causes ulceration, loss of tissue and deformity. In biblical usage the term probably included a larger number of skin diseases.

Leviticus 13:1-46 charged the priests to make quarantine decisions for ancient Israel. Once a skin disease was diagnosed, "the person ... must wear torn clothes, let his hair be unkempt, cover the lower part of his face and cry out, 'Unclean! Unclean!' As long as he has the infection he remains unclean. He must live alone; he must live outside the camp" (Lv 13:45,46).

The leper's whole appearance and conduct was to identify him as a bearer of contagion and therefore an outcast from society. He was as good as dead, hopelessly marked, cut off from priests and people, from temple and sacrifice, spiritually excluded. We see why leprosy was regarded as a picture of sin. The removal of that horrible separation, rescue from death, a return to the religious life of Israel would be reasons for thanksgiving.

The ten men asked for mercy from the Master. They depended on him for healing and salvation. They trusted him, and so it is difficult to call the nine who did not return unbelievers, despite the ingratitude they demonstrated.

v. 14 — *When he saw them, he said, "Go, show yourselves to the priests." And as they went, they were cleaned.*

Jesus came to fulfill the law and that is evidenced here. God had given the levitical law of cleansings and designed the sacrifices. Jesus obeyed the law and taught his disciples to do the same. He expected the ten lepers to fulfill the law's requirements.

The ten left on their journey to the priests without waiting for a miracle. Spirit-engendered faith led to Spirit-guided obedience. The miracle took place on the way. As we preach on this account, we must be careful not to deprecate their trust and obedience. Their real failing was the lack of thanksgiving which should have followed naturally from their faith and obedience.

vv. 15,16 — *One of them, when he saw he was healed, came back praising God in a loud voice. He threw himself at Jesus' feet and thanked him — and he was a Samaritan.*

The Samaritan recognized that Jesus had healed him. So Jesus deserved his thanks and his unending devotion. Help your Thanksgiving worshipers trace their blessings back to the Source. Who guides the eye and hand of the surgeon and blesses the ministrations of the nurse? Who creates the love of parents? Who brings the rain and the heat at the right time? Who stops natural disasters from continuing their destruction? The more we recognize the Source of our blessings, the easier it is to see the connection between the gifts we receive, the thanks we give and the obedience we render to Jesus, committing ourselves to all that he commands.

vv. 17-19 — *Jesus asked, "Were not all ten cleansed? Where are the other nine? Was no one found to return and give praise to God except this foreigner?" Then he said to him, "Rise and go; your faith has made you well."*

With the statement, "Your faith has made you well," Jesus seems to open the door to the abuses of the faith-healers. They shake their heads over the unhealed and say, "Your faith was not strong enough." But let's look again at what has happened in the text. The nine believed Jesus and his word enough to go to the priests. They had faith. Their confidence in Jesus saved them because he whom they trusted is able and willing to help in time of need.

Faith always saves in this way. The Samaritan was no more healed than the others, but his faith continued to work as it led him to receive this blessing with thanksgiving. Recall Luther's explanation to the Fourth Petition.

So it is never the size or quantity of faith which saves. It is always the One on whom faith depends. Jesus saves. Perhaps we do not rejoice enough in the work which God can accomplish through a faith the size of a grain of mustard seed. Maybe it's a good thing we can't see our faith and how small it really is. If there is something for thanksgiving here, then it must be that even small faith receives the Savior's blessing. A bigger faith, however, also returns to say, "Thank you, Jesus."

Perhaps the thanks-givers feel that their lives have been less than pleasing, less than perfect. These words of Jesus form a perfect absolution to the wearied and burdened sinner. For all of us who cry out, "Have mercy on us!" Jesus announces, "Your faith has made you well."

Turn to those who have come to give thanks on this day and say, "Rise and go; your faith has made you well." The Samaritan had begun to put his faith into practice by returning to give thanks. Jesus tells him, "Keep it up. You're on the right track. This is a good beginning. The faith that is at work in you now will continue to work the good works for which you have been created anew in me" (Eph 2:10).

Save the question, "Where are the others?" for those who did not come to give thanks on this day. In the sermon for Thanksgiving Day you are addressing those who did return to praise God. Out in those pews you may find some surprises. What a joy fills our hearts to see members whom God has healed, foreigners and strangers whom God has made members of the family of believers. Don't miss those new members, visitors, the straying who have returned. Their faith has made them well, because their faith rests in the Healer.

Homiletical Suggestions

It is possible to devastate tender consciences with this text. Jesus condemns the nine thankless ones, but does his condemnation apply to your hearers? Thankfully prepare a sermon for the believers who will join you in thanksgiving. Assume that they have come to give thanks. Commend them for returning to give thanks. Empower them so that they are able to continue thanksgiving through obedience. Jesus does.

The worshipers may well be imagining a large table filled with food, surrounded by friends and family. There may also be some who on this day face empty plates, empty houses, empty lives. A gentle pastoral message is necessary to lift both groups from a shallow vision of thanksgiving toward a more profound view of God's grace, toward contentment in all circumstances.

Jesus uses this thankgiving as an example and an encouragement for his people to continue giving thanks. We need to hear our Savior's commendation and use it as a motive for continuing to live as thankful Christians.

Thank You for Giving Thanks

1. Spoken by a giving Savior (vv. 14,17,18)
2. Heard by a healed people (vv. 13,15)
3. Lived by a grateful church (v. 19)

In situations where a reason for thanksgiving is not so apparent to us earth-bound people, Jesus still offers the hope and promise of blessings. Even if we cannot see them, there is reason for giving thanks.

Our Reasons for Giving Thanks

1. Jesus shows pity (vv. 11-14a)
2. Jesus shows power (v. 14b)
3. Jesus gives praise (vv. 17-19)

O Give Thanks To Jesus

1. He pities the hurting (v. 13)
2. He guides the healing (v. 14)
3. He heals the trusting (v. 14b)
4. He praises the grateful (vv. 17-19)